AF823182

THE PUBLICATIONS

OF THE

Selden Society

περὶ παντὸς τὴν ἐλευθερίαν

VOLUME CXXVI

FOR THE YEAR 2009

Selden Society

FOUNDED 1887

To Encourage the Study and Advance the Knowledge of the History of English Law

2009

Patron

HIS ROYAL HIGHNESS THE PRINCE PHILLIP, DUKE OF EDINBURGH, K.G.

President

THE RIGHT HONOURABLE LORD JUDGE, C.J.

Vice-Presidents

DR PAUL BRAND, F.B.A.

THE RIGHT HONOURABLE BEVERLEY MCLACHLIN, C.J.

THE HONOURABLE DR B.H. MCPHERSON, C.B.E.

Council

Mr David Ainger
The Hon. Morris S. Arnold
Mr Richard Bagley
The late Professor Thomas G. Barnes
Professor Joseph Biancalana
Professor C.W. Brooks
Mrs Marjorie Chibnall, F.B.A.
Professor M.T. Clanchy, F.B.A.
Professor W.R. Cornish, Q.C., F.B.A.
Dr David Crook
Professor Charles Donahue, Jr.
Sir Matthew Farrer, G.C.V.O.
Professor Richard H. Helmholz, F.B.A.
Professor Sir James Holt, F.B.A.
Mr John Howell, Q.C.
Professor J.G. Hudson
The late Dr R.F. Hunnisett
Professor D.J. Ibbetson, F.B.A.
The Revd Professor A.D.E. Lewis
Professor Janet Loengard
Dr Michael Macnair
Dr John Maddicott, F.B.A.
His Honour E.F. Monier-Williams
The Rt Hon. Lord Mustill, F.B.A.
Mr M.J. Prichard
The Rt Hon. Lord Rodger of Earlsferry, F.B.A.
Professor A.W.B. Simpson, F.B.A.
Professor P.G. Stein, Q.C., F.B.A.
Mr A.C. Taussig
Professor Dr R.C. Baron van Caenegem, F.B.A.
The Revd Professor T.G. Watkin
Mr D.E.C. Yale, Q.C., F.B.A.

Literary Director

Professor Sir John Baker, Q.C., F.B.A.

Assistant Literary Director

Dr N.G. Jones

Honorary Treasurer

Mr Christopher Wright, (Rooks Rider, 19 Clerkenwell Close, London EC1R 0RR)

Secretary

Mr Victor Tunkel, (School of Law, Queen Mary, Mile End Road, London E1 4NS)

Trustees

Professor M.T. Clanchy, F.B.A. — Mr P.W.E. Taylor, Q.C.

Mr Christopher Wright

Honorary Secretaries and Treasurers Overseas

Australia: Mr Aladin Rahemtula, Supreme Court Library, Brisbane, Queensland 4000

Canada: Professor DeLloyd J. Guth (Treasurer), Professor Margaret McGlynn (Secretary), Faculty of Law, University of Manitoba, Winnipeg R3T 2N2

New Zealand: Mr Francis Dawson, Dawson Harford & Partners, 48 Courthouse Lane, Auckland

United States: Professor Charles Donahue Jr (Treasurer), Mr David Warrington (Secretary), Harvard Law School, Langdell Hall, Cambridge MA 02138

SELECT ECCLESIASTICAL CASES FROM THE KING'S COURTS 1272–1307

EDITED FOR
THE SELDEN SOCIETY
BY

DAVID MILLON

J. B. Stombock Professor of Law
Washington and Lee University
Lexington, Virginia

LONDON
SELDEN SOCIETY
2009

© Selden Society 2009

Printed on acid-free paper

ISBN 978 0 85423 127 0

Printed in the UK by Henry Ling Ltd, at the Dorset Press, Dorchester, DT1 1HD

PREFACE

This book originated many years ago as my Ph.D. dissertation submitted to Cornell University. Professor Brian Tierney, my supervisor, provided advice when needed and, through the history department, saw to it that I had funds to do the archival research necessary to collect the cases printed here. He also made it possible for me to spend a second year in London when a personal crisis slowed my progress. For his faith in me and for his support I will always be grateful. I am very pleased finally to have the opportunity to thank him publicly. Thanks also are long overdue to the other members of my doctoral committee, Professors Clive Holmes and Mary Beth Norton, whose many useful suggestions made the dissertation much better than it would have been.

For nearly a quarter century my academic home has been Washington and Lee University's School of Law. I came here knowing little about the university or this part of the world and uncertain about my future. It turns out that I have had the immense good fortune to find myself part of a community of teachers, students, and staff that has nourished my professional life beyond anything I could have hoped for. This project has benefited greatly from countless conversations with colleagues and students, especially my late friend and fellow legal historian Professor Roger Groot. I have also been the beneficiary of generous financial support from several deans and the Frances Lewis Law Center.

Professor Robert Palmer's monumental undertaking to digitize the medieval and early modern plea rolls and make them publicly available via the internet has been invaluable. All the previously unpublished cases printed in this volume or cited in the notes were found through my searches of the plea rolls, initially in the Round Room of the Public Record Office in Chancery Lane, more recently at the magnificent National Archives building in Kew. Nevertheless, the ability to review citations and check transcriptions for accuracy from the comfort and convenience of my study greatly facilitated completion of this project.

I owe a huge debt to Professor Paul Brand, who painstakingly read the entire manuscript and corrected many errors in the transcriptions and translations. He deserves a large measure of credit for any merit this volume might possess. Errors that remain are, of course, solely my responsibility. Thanks are also due to Professor Sir John Baker, who has provided unfailing encouragement as well as extraordinary patience throughout this project's lengthy gestation.

I will always be grateful to Joan for her support, inspirational courage, and cheerful willingness to endure the challenges of graduate school, law practice, and a move to an unfamiliar new home. More recently, Robin's patience and steadfast partnership made it possible for me to endure a nightmare that would otherwise have been unendurable. I would never have finished this book without her.

Finally, I dedicate this book to my children, Miles, Claire, and Emma. Through life's ups and downs they have been a constant source of joy and pride. I hope this gives them some sense of how much they mean to me.

D. M.

CONTENTS

ABBREVIATIONS AND SHORT-FORM CITATIONS

Unedited documents

CP 40	Plea Rolls, Court of Common Pleas (PRO)
JUST 1	Eyre Rolls, Assize Rolls, etc. (PRO)
KB 26	Curia Regis Rolls, Court of King's Bench (PRO)
KB 27	Coram Rege Rolls, Court of King's Bench (PRO)

Edited cases and other documents

Borough Customs	*Borough Customs*, ed. M. Bateson (Selden Soc. vols. 18 and 21)
BNB	*Bracton's Note Book*, ed. F. W. Maitland (3 vols., London, 1887)
Bracton	*Bracton: On the Laws and Customs of England*, ed. G. E. Woodbine, rev. and transl. S. E. Thorne (4 vols., Cambridge, Mass., 1968–76)
Brevia Placitata	*Brevia Placitata*, ed. G. J. Turner (Selden Soc. vol. 66)
Britton	*Britton*, ed. F. M. Nichols (2 vols., Oxford, 1865)
C.—, q.—, c. –	Causa –, quaestio –, canon –, *Decretum magistri Gratiani*, in *Corpus Juris Canonici*, vol. 1, ed. A. Friedberg (Leipzig, 1879; repr. Graz, 1959)
CRR	*Curia Regis Rolls* (20 vols., London, 1923–2006)
CPR	*Calendar of Patent Rolls* (72 vols., London, 1891–1986)
Canterbury Cases	*Select Cases from the Ecclesiastical Courts of the Province of Canterbury, c. 1200–1301*, ed. N. Adams and C. Donahue Jr. (Selden Soc. vol. 95)
Casus Placitorum	*The Casus Placitorum and Reports of Cases in the King's Courts, 1272–1278*, ed. W. H. Dunham Jr. (Selden Soc. vol. 69)
Councils & Synods	*Councils & Synods: With Other Documents Relating to the English Church II, A.D. 1205–1313*, ed. F. M. Powicke and C. R. Cheney (Oxford, 1964)
Defamation Cases	*Select Cases on Defamation to 1600*, ed. R. H. Helmholz (Selden Soc. vol. 101)
Drogheda, *Summa Aurea*	*Die Summa Aurea des Wilhelmus de Drokeda*, in *Quellen zur Geschichte des Römisch-Kanonischen Processes im Mittelalter*, ed. L. Warhmund (2 vols., Innsbruck, 1914)
Earliest Law Reports	*Earliest English Law Reports*, ed. P. A. Brand (Selden Soc. vols. 111, 112, 122, 123)
Early Registers	*Early Registers of Writs*, ed. E. de Haas and G. D. G. Hall (Selden Soc. vol. 87)

Grosseteste, *Epistolae*	*Roberti Grosseteste Episcopi Quondam Lincolniensis Epistolae*, ed. H. R. Louard (Rolls Series vol. 25)
Glanvill	*Tractatus de Legibus et Counsuetudinibus Regni Anglie qui Glanvilla Vocatur*, ed. G. D. G. Hall (London, 1965)
King's Bench Cases	*Select Cases in the Court of King's Bench under Edward I*, ed. G. O. Sayles (Selden Soc. vols., 55, 57, 58)
King's Bench, Trinity 1297	*Placita Coram Domino Rege Apud Westmonasterium De Termino Sancte Trinitatis Anno Regni Regis Edwardi, Filii Regis Henrici, Vicesimo Quinto; The Pleas of the Court of King's Bench. Trinity Term, 1297*, ed. W. P. W. Phillimore (London, 1898)
King's Council Cases	*Select Cases before the King's Council 1243–1482*, ed. I. S. Leadam and J. F. Baldwin (Selden Soc. vol. 35)
Mansi, *Conciliorum*	G. D. Mansi, *Sacrorum Conciliorum Nova et Amplissima Collectio* (58 vols., Florence, 1759–98)
New Natura Brevium	A. Fitzherbert, *The New Natura Brevium of the Most Reverend Judge, Mr. Anthony Fitz-Herbert* (6th ed., 1718)
Parl. Rolls	*The Parliament Rolls of Medieval England 1275–1505, vol. I (Edward I, 1275–1294)*, ed. P. A. Brand (London, 2005)
Plac. Abbr.	*Placitorum in Domo Capitulari Westmonasteriensi Asservatorum Abbreviatio: Temporibus Regum Ric. I, Johann., Henr. III, Edw. I, Edw. II*, ed. W. Illingworth (London, 1811)
PRO	Public Record Office, Kew (administered by The National Archives)
Prynne, *Records*	W. Prynne, *An Exact Chronological Vindication and Historical Demonstration of the Supreme Ecclesiastical Jurisdiction of our British, Roman, Saxon, Danish, Norman, English Kings* (London, 1668)
Register of Writs	*Registrum Omnium Breuium Tam Originalium Quam Iudicialium* (London, 1634)
Reg. Pontissara	*Registrum Johannis de Pontissara, Episcopi Wyntoniensis*, ed. C. Deedes (Canterbury and York Society vols. 19 and 30)
Rot. Parl.	*Rotuli Parliamentorum* (6 vols., London,1783)
Select Charters	*Select Charters and Other Illustrations of English Constitutional History*, ed. W. Stubbs, rev. H. W. C. Davis (9th ed., Oxford, 1921)
Sext. (followed by book, title, chapter numbers)	*Liber Sextus Decretalium*, in *Corpus Juris Canonici*, vol. 2, ed. A. Friedberg (Leipzig, 1879; repr. Graz, 1959)
SR	*Statutes of the Realm* (11 vols., Record Commission, London,1810–28)
X (followed by book, title, chapter numbers)	*Decretales Gregorii Noni*, in *Corpus Juris Canonici*, vol. 2, ed. A. Friedberg (Leipzig, 1879; repr. Graz, 1959)

YB 21 & 22 Edw. I	*Year Books of the Reign of Edward the First, 21 & 22 Edward I*, ed. A. J. Horwood (Rolls Series, London, 1873)
YB 30 & 31 Edw. I	*Year Books of the Reign of Edward the First, 30 & 31 Edward I*, ed. A. J. Horwood (Rolls Series, London, 1863)
YB 32 & 33 Edw. I	*Year Books of the Reign of Edward the First, 32 & 33 Edward I*, ed. A. J. Horwood (Rolls Series, London, 1864)
YB 2 & 3 Edw. II	*Year Books of 2 and 3 Edward II (1308–1309 and 1309–1310)*, ed. F. W. Maitland (Selden Soc. vol. 19)
YB 3 & 4 Edw. II	*Year Books of 3 and 4 Edward II (1310)*, ed. F. W. Maitland and G. J. Turner (Selden Soc. vol. 22)
YB 4 Edw. II	*Year Books of 4 Edward II (1310–1311)*, ed. G. J. Turner (Selden Soc. vol. 26)
YB 5 Edw. II	*Year Books of 5 Edward II (1312)*, ed. W. C. Bolland (Selden Soc. vol. 33)
YB 8 Edw. II	*Year Books of 8 Edward II (1314–1315)*, ed. W. C. Bolland (Selden Soc. vol. 41)
YB Eyre of London 1321	*The Eyre of London, 14 Edw. II (1321)*, ed. H. M. Cam (Selden Soc. vols. 85 and 86)

Books and Articles

Adams, 'Prohibition'	N. Adams, 'The Writ of Prohibition to Court Christian', *Minnesota Law Review* 20 (1936), 272–293
Adams, 'Tithes'	N. Adams, 'The Judicial Conflict over Tithes', *English Historical Review* 52 (1937), 1–22
Ault, 'Village Church'	W. O. Ault, 'The Village Church and the Village Community in Mediaeval England', *Speculum* 45 (1970), 197–215
Baker, *Legal History*	J. H. Baker, *An Introduction to English Legal History* (4th ed. 2002)
Baker, *Order of Serjeants*	J. H. Baker, *The Order of Serjeants at Law: A Chronicle of Creations, with Related Texts* (London, 1984)
Barraclough, *Papal Provisions*	G. Barraclough, *Papal Provisions: Aspects of Church History, Constitutional, Legal and Administrative in the Later Middle Ages* (Oxford, 1935)
Beckerman, 'Forty-Shilling Limit'	J. S. Beckerman, 'The Forty-Shilling Jurisdictional Limit in Medieval Personal Actions', in *Legal History Studies 1972*, ed. Daffyd Jenkins (Cardiff, 1975), 110–117
Blackstone, *Commentaries*	W. Blackstone, *Commentaries on the Laws of England* (4 vols., Oxford, 1765–69, repr. Chicago, 1979)
Brand, *Making of the Common Law*	P. Brand, *The Making of the Common Law* (London, 2003)
Brundage, *Canon Law*	J. A. Brundage, *Medieval Canon Law* (London, 1995)
Burt, 'Demise of the General Eyre'	C. Burt, 'The Demise of the General Eyre in the Reign of Edward I', *English Historical Review*, 120 (2005), 1–14

Cheyette, 'Statute of Provisors'	F. Cheyette, 'Kings, Courts, Cures and Sinecures: The Statute of Provisors and the Common Law', *Traditio* 19 (1963), 295–349
Churchill, *Canterbury Administration*	I. J. Churchill, *Canterbury Administration: The Administrative Machinery of the Archbishopric of Canterbury, Illustrated from Original Records* (2 vols., London, 1933)
Coke, *Institutes*	E. Coke, *The Second Part of the Institutes of the Laws of England* (5th ed., London, 1671)
Constable, *Monastic Tithes*	G. Constable, *Monastic Tithes: From their Origins to the Twelfth Century* (Cambridge, 1964)
Crook, 'Later Eyres'	D. Crook, 'The Later Eyres', *English Historical Review*, 97 (1982), 241–268
DDC	*Dictionnaire de Droit Canonique*, ed. R. Naz (7 vols., Paris, 1935–65)
de Zulueta, 'Drogheda'	F. de Zulueta, 'William of Drogheda', in 2 *Mélanges de Droit Romain Dédiés à Georges Cornil, vol. 2* (Ghent, 1926), 641–657
Deeley, 'Papal Provision'	A. Deeley, 'Papal Provision and Royal Rights of Patronage in the Early Fourteenth Century', *English Historical Review* 43 (1928), 497–527
Denton, *Winchelsey*	J. H. Denton, *Robert Winchelsey and the Crown 1294–1313: A Study in the Defence of Ecclesiastical Liberty* (Cambridge, 1980)
Donahue, 'Roman Canon Law'	C. Donahue Jr., 'Roman Canon Law in the Medieval English Church: Stubbs vs. Maitland Re-examined after 75 Years in the Light of Some Records from the Church Courts', *Michigan Law Review* 72 (1974), 647–716
Douglas, 'Frankalmoin and Immunity'	A. W. Douglas, 'Frankalmoin and Jurisdictional Immunity: Maitland Revisited', *Speculum* 53 (1978), 26–48
Douie, *Pecham*	D. L. Douie, *Archbishop Pecham* (Oxford, 1952)
Duggan, 'Becket Dispute'	C. Duggan, 'The Becket Dispute and the Criminous Clerks', *Bulletin of the Institute of Historical Research* 35 (1962), 1–28
Esmein, 'Serment Promissoire'	A. Esmein, 'Le Serment Promissoire dans le Droit Canonique', *Nouvelle Revue Historique de Droit Français et Étranger* 12 (1888), 248–277, 311–352
Flahiff, 'Prohibition I'	G. B. Flahiff, 'The Writ of Prohibition to Court Christian in the Thirteenth Century [Part I]', *Mediaeval Studies* 6 (1944), 261–313
Flahiff, 'Prohibition II'	G. B. Flahiff, 'The Writ of Prohibition to Court Christian in the Thirteenth Century [Part II]', *Mediaeval Studies* 7 (1945), 229–290

Flahiff, 'Use of Prohibitions by Clerics'	G. B. Flahiff, 'The Use of Prohibitions by Clerics against Ecclesiastical Courts in England', *Mediaeval Studies* 3 (1941), 101–116
Fraher, 'Becket Dispute'	R. M. Fraher, 'The Becket Dispute and Two Decretist Traditions: The Bolognese Masters Revisited and Some New Anglo-Norman Texts', *Journal of Medieval History* 4 (1978), 347–368
Gabel, *Benefit of Clergy*	L. C. Gabel, *Benefit of Clergy in England in the Later Middle Ages* (Northamptom, Mass., 1928)
Genestal, *Privilegium Fori*	R. Genestal, *Le Privilegium Fori en France, du Décret de Gratien à la Fin du XIVe Siècle* (2 vols., Paris, 1921–24)
Graves, '*Circumspecte Agatis*'	E. B. Graves, 'Circumspecte Agatis', *English Historical Review* 43 (1928), 1–20
Gray, '*Ius Praesentandi*'	J. W. Gray, 'The Ius Praesentandi in England from the Constitutions of Clarendon to Bracton', *English Historical Review* 67 (1952), 481–509
Harben, *Dictionary of London*	H. A. Harben, *A Dictionary of London* (London, 1918)
Harding, 'Plaints and Bills'	A. Harding, 'Plaints and Bills in the History of English Law, Mainly in the Period 1250–1350', in *Legal History Studies 1972*, ed. D. Jenkins (Cardiff, 1975), 65–86
Hartridge, *Vicarages*	R. A. R. Hartridge, *A History of Vicarages in the Middle Ages* (Cambridge, 1930)
Helmholz, *Canon Law*	R. H. Helmholz, *Canon Law and the Law of England* (London, 1987)
Helmholz, *History*	R. H. Helmholz, *The Canon Law and Ecclesiastical Jurisdiction from 597 to the 1640s* (Oxford History of the Laws of England, vol. I, Oxford, 2004)
Helmholz, *Marriage Litigation*	R. H. Helmholz, *Marriage Litigation in Medieval England* (Cambridge, 1974)
Hemmeon, 'Burgage Tenure'	M. de W. Hemmeon, 'Burgage Tenure in Medieval England', *Law Quarterly Review* 26 (1910), 215–230, 331–348; 27 (1911), 43–59
Hemmeon, *Burgage Tenure*	M. de W. Hemmeon, *Burgage Tenure in Mediaeval England* (Cambridge, Mass., 1914)
Holdsworth, *HEL*	W. S. Holdsworth, *A History of English Law* (16 vols., London, 1903–66)
Howell, *Regalian Right*	M. Howell, *Regalian Right in Medieval England* (London, 1962)
Hyams, 'Norwich Inquiry'	P. R. Hyams, 'Deans and their Doings: The Norwich Inquiry of 1286', in *Proceedings of the Sixth International Congress of Medieval Canon Law*, ed. S. Kuttner and K. Pennington (Vatican City, 1985), 619–646

Jones, '*Gravamina*'	W. R. Jones, 'Bishops, Politics, and the Two Laws: The *Gravamina* of the English Clergy, 1237–1399', *Speculum* 41 (1966), 209–245
Jones, 'Relations'	W. R. Jones, 'Relations of the Two Jurisdictions: Conflict and Cooperation in England during the Thirteenth and Fourteenth Centuries', *Studies in Medieval and Renaissance History* 7 (1970), 77–210
Lawrence, 'Thirteenth Century'	C. H. Lawrence, 'The Thirteenth Century', in *The English Church & the Papacy in the Middle Ages*, ed. C. H. Lawrence (New York, 1965), 119–156
Logan, *Excommunication*	F. D. Logan, *Excommunication and the Secular Arm in Medieval England: A Study in Legal Procedure from the Thirteenth to the Sixteenth Century* (Toronto, 1968)
Lyon, *Constitutional and Legal History*	B. Lyon, *A Constitutional and Legal History of Medieval England* (New York, 1960)
Maitland, *Roman Canon Law*	F. W. Maitland, *Roman Canon Law in the Church of England* (London, 1898)
Makower, *Constitutional History of English Church*	F. Makower, *The Constitutional History and Constitution of the Church of England* (London, 1895)
McKisack, *Fourteenth Century*	M. McKisack, *The Fourteenth Century, 1307–1399* (Oxford, 1959)
Millon, *Common Law and Canon Law*	D. Millon, *Canon Law and Common Law During the Reign of Edward I* (unpublished Ph.D. dissertation, Cornell University, 1982)
Millon, '*Circumspecte Agatis*'	D. Millon, '*Circumspecte Agatis* Revisited', *Law and History Review*, 2 (1984), 105–127
Millon, 'Ecclesiastical Jurisdiction'	D. Millon, 'Ecclesiastical Jurisdiction in Medieval England', *University of Illinois Law Review* (1984), 621–638
Millon, 'Historiography'	D. Millon, 'Positivism in the Historiography of the Common Law,' *Wisconsin Law Review* (1989), 669–714
Milsom, *Historical Foundations*	S. F. C. Milsom, *Historical Foundations of the Common Law* (2d ed., London, 1981)
Milsom, *Studies*	S. F. C. Milsom, *Studies in the History of the Common Law* (London, 1985)
Moorman, *Church Life*	J. R. H. Moorman, *Church Life in England in the Thirteenth Century* (Cambridge, 1945)
Morris, 'Consistory Court'	C. Morris, 'A Consistory Court in the Middle Ages', *Journal of Ecclesiastical History* 14 (1963), 150–159
Morris, 'William I'	C. Morris, 'William I and the Church Courts', *English Historical Review* 82 (1967), 449–463
Owen, 'Ecclesiastical Jurisdiction'	D. Owen, 'Ecclesiastical Jurisdiction in England 1300 to 1500: The Records and their Interpretation', in *The Materials, Sources and Methods of Ecclesiastical History*, ed. D. Baker (Oxford, 1975), 199–221

Pantin, *English Church*	W. A. Pantin, *The English Church in the Fourteenth Century* (Cambridge, 1955)
Phillimore, *Ecclesiastical Law*	R. Phillimore, *The Ecclesiastical Law of the Church of England* (2 vols., 2d ed., London, 1895)
Plucknett, *Concise History*	T. F. T. Plucknett, *A Concise History of the Common Law* (5th ed., Boston, 1956)
Plucknett, *Edward I and Criminal Law*	T. F. T. Plucknett, *Edward I and Criminal Law* (Cambridge, 1959)
Pollock & Maitland	F. Pollock and F. W. Maitland, *The History of English Law before the Time of Edward I* (2 vols., 2d ed., repr. Cambridge, 1968)
Powicke, *Thirteenth Century*	F. M. Powicke, *The Thirteenth Century, 1216–1307* (2d ed., Oxford, 1962)
Richardson & Sayles, 'Early Records'	H. G. Richardson and G. O. Sayles, 'The Early Records of the English Parliaments', *Bulletin of the Institute of Historical Research* 6 (1929), 129–155
Richardson & Sayles, 'Easter Parliament'	H. G. Richardson and G. O. Sayles, 'The Clergy in the Easter Parliament, 1285', *English Historical Review*, 52 (1937), 220–234
Rodes, *Ecclesiastical Administration*	R. E. Rodes Jr., *Ecclesiastical Administration in Medieval England: The Anglo-Saxons to the Reformation* (Notre Dame, Ind., 1977)
Sheehan, *Will*	M. M. Sheehan, *The Will in Medieval England: From the Conversion of the Anglo-Saxons to End of the Thirteenth Century* (Toronto, 1963)
Stubbs, *History*	W. Stubbs, *The Constitutional History of England in its Origins and Development* (3 vols., 3d ed., Oxford, 1880)
Sutherland, 'Mesne Process'	D. W. Sutherland, 'Mesne Process upon Personal Actions in the Early Common Law', 82 (1966) *Law Quarterly Review* 482–496
Sutherland, *Quo Warranto*	D. W. Sutherland, *Quo Warranto Proceedings in the Reign of Edward I, 1278–94* (Oxford, 1963)
Thompson, *English Clergy*	A. H. Thompson, *The English Clergy and their Organization in the Later Middle Ages* (Oxford, 1947)
Tierney, '*Per venerabilem*'	B. Tierney, '"*Tria quippe distinguit iudicia . . .*" A Note on Innocent III's Decretal *Per venerabilem*', *Speculum* 37 (1962), 48–59
VCH Worcester	*The Victoria History of the County of Worcester*, ed. H. A. Doubleday, W. Page and J. W. Willis-Bund (4 vols., London, 1901–24)
VCH York	*The Victoria History of the County of York*, ed. W. Page (3 vols., London, 1907–13)
Waugh, 'Pecham and Pluralities'	W. T. Waugh, 'Archbishop Pecham and Pluralities', 28 *English Historical Review* 28 (1913), 625–635

Woodcock, *Canterbury Courts*	B. Woodcock, *Medieval Ecclesiastical Courts in the Diocese of Canterbury* (Oxford, 1952)

Superscript abbreviations in the text

d	marked for deletion
i	interlineation

INTRODUCTION

1

EDWARD I AND THE CHURCH COURTS

Both church and state in England had by the later thirteenth century developed their own legal systems: hierarchies of courts staffed by professional judges and lawyers administering substantive rules according to carefully regulated procedures. Broadly speaking the two jurisdictions operated independently of each other, each concerned with a range of legal matters peculiarly its own. The primary responsibility of the ecclesiastical courts was to enforce the canon law as it directed the spiritual welfare of all Christians. This was a matter both of prosecuting sinners and adjudicating disputes between individuals in which some sacramental matter was at issue, such as a marriage agreement or testamentary bequest. The royal courts on the other hand concerned themselves mainly with more worldly causes: the land law, crime, and the developing law of contractual obligations and civil wrongs.

While in theory the church's jurisdiction was spiritual and the crown's secular, in practice the two fora were not independent of each other either in respect to the classes of persons subject to each or the subject matters justiciable in each. This was probably unavoidable because the church was not independent from secular life. Clerks lived in civil society, and were as capable as laymen of contracting obligations or committing tortious or criminal offences. The religious houses bought and sold real estate like lay landholders. And every lay person, king or villein,[1] was subject like every clerk to the church's penitential jurisdiction. Accordingly, in England personal status—religious or lay—did not determine whether one was subject to one forum or the other. Except for the clergy's exemption from the king's law for major crimes, every individual was liable to suit before an ecclesiastical or secular judge according to the nature of the cause of action.[2]

Yet the principle of jurisdiction according to subject matter rather than personal status also resisted neat categorical distinctions. Some pleas heard by the king's courts had an at least arguably spiritual aspect, while certain ecclesiastical suits might for one reason or another involve a matter considered by the crown to be outside the church's jurisdiction. A claim for land based on disturbance of possession was justiciable at common law by a writ of novel disseisin, but if the land in question was the property of a church an unjustified taking might amount to sacrilege according to canon law. The common law provided remedies for breach of contractual obligations, but such claims could also fall within the church's jurisdiction because of its responsibility to enforce the sanctity of oaths. Canon law normally settled rival claims for tithes between two rectors, but a church court ruling could diminish the value of the patron's right to present a clerk to a benefice—a right protected by common law—if the ruling resulted in the loss of substantial revenue. The primary concern of this volume is jurisdictional disputes such as these. The aim is to explain where and in what manner the boundaries were drawn.

William I ordained that bishops should administer canon law (*episcopales leges*) in church courts constituted for that purpose rather than in local secular courts as previously.[3]

[1] Excepting only members of the small Jewish community, who were expelled in 1290.

[2] See Helmholz, *History*, 315.

[3] *Select Charters*, 99–100. See Morris, 'William I'.

Only a century later, however, does one find a clear statement by the crown of the respective competence of the ecclesiastical and royal courts. Henry II, his reign so important in this as in other areas of the common law's development, issued the Constitutions of Clarendon in 1164.[4] Here he laid down specific definitions of the judicial authority of church and state over certain controversial matters. Though it was necessary later to renounce two clauses—the claims to try criminous clerks and to restrict appeals to Rome—in the wake of Becket's murder, those concerned with jurisdiction over ecclesiastical patronage, real property, and pleas of debt remained to serve as the basis for relations between the two fora during the rest of the middle ages. The crown made further changes in matters of detail and procedure and the clergy complained often during the thirteenth and fourteenth centuries, but Henry II succeeded in defining the common law's limits on church court activity in England.[5]

Soon after the Constitutions of Clarendon, as a necessary complement to the jurisdictional pronouncements, the crown made available writs of prohibition for individuals sued in ecclesiastical courts concerning matters that did not belong there. These writs commanded judges and suitors in the king's name to cease prosecution of the plea in question. Writs of attachment, issued separately from the writs of prohibition themselves, compelled those who ignored writs of prohibition to answer for their contempt in a royal court. Here, if those who had disobeyed the prohibition claimed that the church did in fact possess authority to adjudicate the suit, the king's justices settled the jurisdictional question.

The focus of this volume on the reign of Edward I (1272–1307) may require some explanation. Historians have long appreciated its importance in the evolution of English government generally and of the common law in particular. A period of significant constitutional developments as well as legislative and judicial initiatives in the growth of a national legal system, it seems natural to question the impact of these events on the church courts. Edward's reign is also noteworthy because it occasioned several clashes between church and state. John Pecham and Robert Winchelsey, archbishops of Canterbury from 1279 to 1292 and 1294 to 1313 respectively, were both especially zealous guardians of the church's liberties,[6] not hesitating to confront the crown in their defence.[7] Edward outlawed the clergy when it refused his demand for a subsidy.[8] Conflicts were not limited to disputes between monarchy and national church. Pope Boniface VIII's opposition to Edward's attempt to tax the English clergy provoked a well-known political crisis.[9] The

[4] *Select Charters*, 163–167.

[5] For a useful survey of the English church courts' institutional structure and subject matter jurisdiction, see Helmholz, *History*, 206–234. Common-law jurisdictional rules notwithstanding, it will be seen below that the church in fact heard many cases that were supposed to be off limits.

[6] See Douie, *Pecham*; Denton, *Winchelsey*; Powicke, *Thirteenth Century*, 672–680.

[7] In 1279 Pecham, presiding over the provincial council at Reading, issued general sentences of excommunication against those who infringed upon the church's liberties—especially those who interfered with legitimate church court actions by means of writs of prohibition. He was forced by King Edward to withdraw the sentences later that year. Pecham reiterated them in 1281, but only with respect to causes customarily recognized as ecclesiastical. See Douie, *Pecham*, ch. 3; Powicke, *Thirteenth Century*, 472–480.

[8] Denton, *Winchelsey*, 107–135.

[9] Pope Boniface VIII published the famous bull *Clericis laicos* in 1296, which denied lay authority to tax the clergy without papal assent. The following year he recognized secular power to tax during periods of emergency, as defined by the local rulers. See Lawrence, 'Thirteenth Century', 133–137.

extent to which the jurisdictional relations of the two fora reflected these dramatic events seems an appropriate question.

It has typically been thought that Edward mounted a campaign aimed at restricting the scope of the church courts' authority. For example, Jones stated that during the thirteenth and fourteenth centuries the crown applied 'steady pressure' on the church courts, Edward I instigating a particularly radical effort to limit their activity.[10] According to Flahiff, during the few decades prior to the issue of the writ *Circumspecte agatis* in 1286, 'the temporal power had seemed in practice to be attempting to limit appreciably the cases considered as spiritual'.[11] Denton writes of 'a distinct increase in the aggression of royal government towards ecclesiastical jurisdiction early in the 1290's.[12]

Views such as these[13] seem to have been based primarily on *Circumspecte agatis* and on the several sets of clerical complaints concerning the crown's alleged intrusions into the church's judicial territory presented during Edward's reign.[14] The writ has been seen as a grant to the clergy, signalling the crown's retreat from its policy of hostility.[15] Scholars have also concentrated attention on the clergy's grievances as evidence of royal policy, for example suggesting that the frequency of these protests against the use of prohibitions suggests that the crown was imposing severe restrictions on the church courts.[16] Flahiff cited a statement from 1283 as evidence of 'an unusually strong offensive against the jurisdiction of the ecclesiastical courts'.[17]

A second theme, often complementary to the 'steady pressure' or 'assault' theories, is present in much of the literature. According to this the actual boundaries between the two jurisdictions were uncertain and ill-defined before Edward's reign. *Circumspecte agatis* again plays a key role in the discussion. According to Sayles it 'mapped out more boldly the frontier lines' in what had previously been a 'vague no-man's land'.[18] Earlier writers suggested continuous efforts by the church courts to expand their jurisdiction,[19] while a student of the registers of the archbishops of Canterbury found evidence of encroachments by both church and state.[20] All this suggests a fluid situation, marked by more or less constant competition between the two fora, at least until 1286.

In order to resolve these questions, the present volume is based on a comprehensive examination of common law records from Edward I's reign. The cases make it possible to determine the manner in which the king's courts resolved jurisdictional controversies.

[10] 'The reign of Edward I was a time of trial for the church courts. The attitude and conduct of the crown and its courts show that the secular power was making a serious effort to restrict the church courts to matrimonial and testamentary matters where the laity and their chattels were concerned'.: Jones, 'Relations', 94. See also ibid. 80, 101–102, 204.

[11] Flahiff, 'Prohibition I', 309.

[12] Denton, *Winchelsey*, 3.

[13] E.g., Stubbs, *History*, 2:119; Lyon, *Constitutional and Legal History*, 455.

[14] These gravamina, which are printed in *Councils & Synods*, continued a tradition begun earlier in the thirteenth century and maintained during the fourteenth. See Jones, '*Gravamina*'. The significance of the grievances from Edward I's reign is discussed in Millon, *Canon Law and Common Law*, 220–226.

[15] E.g., Jones, '*Gravamina*', 225; Adams, 'Prohibition', 232; Makower, *Constitutional History of English Church*, 394.

[16] E.g., Jones, 'Relations', 168.

[17] 'Prohibition I', 305.

[18] *King's Bench Cases*, 2:lii. See also Stubbs, *History*, 2:114; Makower, *Constitutional History of English Church*, 32.

[19] Stubbs, *History*, 2:118–119; Makower, *Constitutional History of English Church*, 392–393.

[20] Churchill, *Canterbury Administration*, 1:529.

Most prohibition pleas came before the court of Common Pleas, so the rolls of that court have been searched thoroughly, membrane by membrane, for every term of the reign from 1272 to 1307.[21] This has yielded 324 prohibition pleas in which both parties appeared in court, pleadings were exchanged, and an issue framed for proof. The King's Bench plea rolls have also been searched completely, revealing that that tribunal heard only occasional prohibition pleas.[22] Besides these two permanent courts, the crown commissioned justices itinerant to visit the counties at various intervals during Edward's reign as previously. These courts were fully competent in civil and criminal matters, but also heard few prohibition pleas.[23] The inquest into the activities of the church courts in Norwich diocese, conducted in connection with the Norfolk eyre of 1286, is exceptional and proves to be very enlightening.

This research is the basis for this volume's analysis of law and procedure during the reign of Edward I. For comparison with earlier practice, the *Bracton* treatise, left uncompleted some time before mid-century, is especially valuable, as is the large collection of cases extracted from the plea rolls of the 1220's and 1230's known as *Bracton's Note Book*. In addition, Flahiff conducted extensive research in the plea rolls and discussed and published a great deal of this material in his articles on the writ of prohibition. It is thus possible to draw definite conclusions concerning the content and administration of the law during Edward's reign and the extent to which these were a departure from practice during previous reigns.

Sections 2 and 3 of this Introduction examine first the procedural and then the substantive law of the writ of prohibition. Prohibition was the direct means of limiting the scope of the church's jurisdiction. The crown also possessed another, indirect, means to this end. Certain common law actions were concerned with matters at least arguably 'ecclesiastical'. These remedies thus drew cases into the king's courts that might otherwise have been adjudicated by the church. Section 4 considers several important legal topics from this point of view, focusing on ecclesiastical patronage, annual rents, tithes, and benefit of clergy. Section 5 offers a new perspective on the significance of *Circumspecte agatis* and its relation to the larger question of Edward I's policy toward the church courts.

There has been a tendency in the literature to stress the discordant nature of the jurisdictional relationship between church and state. The focus of this volume is largely on areas that were contested or were potential sources of controversy. The story is not entirely one of conflict, however. Neither church nor state exerted steady pressure on the other, and the occasional jurisdictional skirmishes never reached true crisis proportions. Edward I did not mount a campaign against the church courts and the clergy made no serious effort to extend the scope of their judicial authority beyond the frontiers established by the crown earlier in the thirteenth century. It turns out that writs of prohibition only occasionally interfered with the activities of the ecclesiastical courts during the middle ages, but church court judges and suitors rarely stepped across the jurisdictional lines mapped out for them.

[21] For those terms for which more than one roll survives the most extensive record (generally the chief justice's roll) was used. No rolls are extant for the following terms: Michaelmas 1273, Hilary, Easter, and Trinity 1274, and Trinity 1278.

[22] King's Bench rolls survive for virtually every term from 1273 onwards.

[23] The class number is JUST 1, formerly JI. The rolls have been searched for eyres conducted in the following counties during Edward's reign: Devon, Kent, Lincolnshire, Middlesex, Oxfordshire, Norfolk, Suffolk, and Yorkshire.

The one major exception was debt and contract, but here the common law's unattractive remedies had the effect of leaving the field to its competitors, despite the jurisdictional rules embodied in the prohibition *de catallis et debitis*. There was also significant cooperation between the two fora. Questions relating to marriage or ecclesiastical patronage were routinely referred to the bishops when they came up in the course of common law litigation. The bishops in turn relied on the secular machinery of the writ *de excommunicato capiendo* to enforce spiritual sanctions.

By relying on the initiative of private individuals, the prohibition process reveals a certain 'hands-off' policy on the part of the crown toward the church. Individuals, lay or ecclesiastic, had a large say in determining where the jurisdictional boundaries really were located. Each prospective litigant, just as he or she might be subjected to one forum or the other depending on the matter at issue, no doubt looked at the two legal systems in terms of their respective functions and remedies. This was a matter of convenience, not ideology or royal policy. Probably the suitor seeking a remedy would not have understood the modern tendency to see church and state as competitors rather than as two parts of an integrated whole.

2

PROHIBITION: PROCEDURE

The writ of prohibition was the means by which defendants in church courts challenged the authority of those courts to hear the suits brought against them. The writ was a command from the king ordering the judge or suitor to proceed no further with the case because the matter at issue belonged to the king's jurisdiction. Because church court judges and suitors seem often to have disregarded writs of prohibition and proceeded despite them, the common law offered a remedy for those wronged by disobedience of prohibitions. This took the form of an action requiring that the church court judge or suitor (or both) justify his or her disobedience in a royal court. As defendants in these actions church court judges or suitors could vindicate their non-compliance by establishing that the original cause had indeed been a legitimate matter for ecclesiastical jurisdiction.[24]

Flahiff based his excellent and comprehensive study of the writ of prohibition primarily on a careful study of common law court records extending up to the reign of Edward I.[25] This was fully sufficient for him to achieve his aim, a detailed history of the writ from its origins through the first hundred or so years of its use. The concern of the present volume is with the reign of Edward I, for the reasons presented above. For this period Flahiff searched systematically only records for the years 1275, 1280, and 1285. His work therefore did not purport to offer a complete description of prohibition procedure during the last quarter of the century or of how, if at all, it differed from earlier practice.

A thorough study of the plea rolls from Edward I's reign now makes it possible to correct a few factual misconceptions of Flahiff and others concerning that period. In addition, it raises some difficult questions that have not previously received satisfactory analysis. For example, it turns out that Flahiff's conclusion that jury trial replaced wager of law as the usual mode of proof in common law cases concerning writs of prohibition during the reign of Edward I was unwarranted.[26] This factual misconception raises an important question of interpretation. Wager of law required only that the defendant find eleven other people—friends or even relatives were apparently acceptable—to swear oaths attesting to his or her credibility. Not surprisingly, virtually every case decided by this method ended in the defendant's acquittal. It is therefore necessary to explain why church court defendants continued to use writs of prohibition even though judges or suitors who ignored them could so readily escape punishment at common law. Previous scholarship has not been helpful in answering this question.

Several historians have incorrectly regarded the Statute of Consultation of 1290 as confirmation of a procedure already available to ecclesiastical judges for overruling writs of prohibition obtained under false pretenses. This procedure allowed the church court judge to seek guidance from a royal justice about whether he might legitimately proceed with the case before him. However, the plea rolls contain several cases in which the procedure was employed, but the prohibitions decidedly were not overruled: instead, the church court

[24] The substantive rules determining what causes were legitimately ecclesiastical is the subject of section 3 below.

[25] See Flahiff, 'Prohibition I & II'. See also Flahiff, 'Use of Prohibitions by Clerics'; Adams, 'Prohibition'; Helmholz, *Canon Law*, 59–99.

[26] 'Prohibition II', 267, 274. See also Helmholz, *Canon Law*, 66.

judges or suitors were required to answer in a royal court for non-compliance with a prohibition just as they would have had to do even without having obtained a consultation. An alternative explanation for the purpose of consultation is needed.

Finally, there is the problem of canonical sanctions. Excommunication was a potential factor in the prohibition process either as the church court's retaliation against a defendant in an ecclesiastical suit for resort to a royal writ of prohibition or simply because the defendant, having obtained a prohibition, refused to answer the court's citations and was excommunicated for contumacy like any other church court defendant who did not appear on the day assigned for trial. Excommunication was a particularly powerful weapon because those who did not seek absolution were liable to imprisonment by royal officers upon application from the ecclesiastical authorities. The imprisonment procedure was virtually automatic, without any secular inquiry into the basis or circumstances of the sentence of excommunication. Was it sufficiently threatening to discourage prospective users of prohibitions? And to what extent could excommunication and caption prevent plaintiffs from prosecuting common law suits alleging disobedience of writs of prohibition? In fact the court records reveal that effective remedies were available to deal with these problems, but historians have generally overlooked their significance.

The writ of prohibition

The purpose of the writ of prohibition during the thirteenth century was to prevent the ecclesiastical courts from hearing causes that were not, according to common law, within the church's jurisdiction.[27] If, however, an ecclesiastical judge ignored a prohibition, believing perhaps that the cause before him was legitimately spiritual or simply refusing to respect the crown's authority to order him not to proceed, the writ of prohibition also provided the point of departure for a series of procedures allowing the question of jurisdiction to be adjudicated by the king's justices. The writ of prohibition together with the common law action for non-compliance thus constituted a remedy for the individual unjustly impleaded in a church court—that is, sued in a cause not spiritual.

The writ commanded in the king's name (*Prohibemus* . . .) that the ecclesiastical judge proceed no further in the cause before him because that plea belonged to the crown's jurisdiction. The prohibition could also issue to the church court plaintiff (the *actor*), forbidding further prosecution of his or her suit. *De cursu* writs—that is, of standard formula, issued as a matter of course—were available for use when the complainant had been sued in church court concerning a lay fee or for goods or money not connected with a testament or a matrimonial agreement.[28] There was also a particular form, called by its incipit

[27] For the use of prohibitions during the sixteenth and seventeenth centuries against Chancery, conciliar jurisdictions, and the admiralty court, see Baker, *Legal History*, 120, 121, 123; Plucknett, *Concise History*, 663.

[28] An example from the *Bracton* treatise (4:252) of a writ of prohibition, with variations, addressed to judges:

> Rex talibus iudicibus salutem. Prohibemus vobis ne teneatis placitum in curia christianitatis inter A. petentem et B. tenentem de tanta terra cum pertinentiis, vel de laico feodo ipsius B. in tali villa. Vel aliter: de debitis vel catallis quae non sunt ex testamento vel matrimonio, et unde praedictus B. quaeritur quod predictus A. iniuste trahit eum in placitum coram vobis, quia placita de laico feodo et de debitis et catallis quae non sunt de testamento vel matrimonio spectant ad coronam et dignitatem nostram.

A similar example addressed to the adversary party begins: 'Rex tali salutem. Prohibemus tibi ne sequaris . . .' (*Bracton*, 4:253). *Bracton* then presents various other forms: *Bracton*, 4:253–259.

Indicavit, for patrons of churches where a rector was being sued for church revenues and the loss of those revenues threatened to diminish the value of the advowson to its owner. *Indicavit* prohibitions were also available to halt the trial in church court of a dispute over the right to present a clerk to an ecclesiastical benefice. By the end of the thirteenth century the *de cursu* prohibitions included also a form for one accused in church court of trespass against the king's peace. Still others to fit exceptional circumstances were available *de precepto*, for special cases as they arose.[29]

Chancery issued writs of prohibition only upon the complaint of a party to the ecclesiastical suit. He or she was ordinarily the defendant (*reus*) against whom the church suitor had brought the allegedly non-spiritual action. The chancery clerks made no attempt to ascertain whether the complainant's jurisdictional allegation was legitimate and there is no evidence that a complainant was required to provide documentary evidence—such as the libel—indicating the nature of the church court action.[30] The many cases in which it emerged that a prohibition had been obtained through misrepresentation show clearly the ease with which they were issued. A good example is a Common Pleas case from 1294, in which the plaintiff claimed that a church court had ignored a prohibition against further proceedings in a suit concerning trespass against the king's peace.[31] A jury verdict revealed, however, that the plaintiff had actually been cited to answer an accusation of adultery. He would not have obtained his prohibition had he described the ecclesiastical suit accurately, since correction of sins such as adultery was obviously a matter for the church courts and therefore not subject to prohibition.[32]

Having obtained the writ of prohibition, the church court defendant or his or her representative delivered it to the judge or plaintiff.[33] Cases in the king's courts alleging disobedience of a prohibition indicate that the writ could be presented either to judge or suitor but church court defendants sometimes obtained writs against both, either a single writ addressed to both[34] or else two separate writs of prohibition.[35] Delivery usually was made while the church court was in session but not necessarily.[36] This was probably done at least before the cause was on the point of judgment, because, as *Bracton* puts it, if the suit had been terminated there was no longer anything to prohibit.[37] But occasionally a prohibition might arrive after final sentence but in time to prevent execution, as occurred in one case according to a church court suitor's statement in Common Pleas: '*per predictam prohibitionem supersedit in executione facienda*'.[38] It seems possible then that church court

[29] The various forms and their earlier history are discussed below in section 3. See generally Flahiff, 'Prohibition I'.

[30] Fitzherbert wrote in 1534 that prohibition issued simply 'upon his surmise, surmising that he is sued in the Spiritual Court for a temporal cause . . .'.: *New Natura Brevium*, 97. It was also necessary to pay the usual fee of one-half or one mark. Adams, 'Prohibition', 277 n. 2; Pollock & Maitland, 1:195.

[31] Case no. 1.19.

[32] The common law did preclude the exaction of pecuniary penance. See below, p. lxv.

[33] One case included an allegation that the writ was delivered to the church court plaintiff's proctor but also noted that the plaintiff herself was notified: Case no. 1.2a.

[34] See Cases nos. 1.8 and 1.18a.

[35] See Cases nos. 1.11, 1.25a, 1.26a, and 1.28. Obtaining more than one writ presumably involved extra expense. It is not clear why church court defendants went to this trouble when one writ seems to have been sufficient.

[36] E.g., Cases nos. 1.7a (delivery made during session of county court) and 1.23d (delivered on the Fleet Bridge in London). See also CP 40/31, m. 90d (1279) (delivered to prohibition plea defendants 'in domo sua apud Grantham').

[37] *Bracton*, 4:269. Hence Adams' remark that 'the remedy was preventative and not remedial': 'Prohibition', 277–278.

[38] CP 40/102, m.174 (1293). See also Case no. 1.7a.

defendants might at times have resorted to prohibitions only after it had become clear that the suitor had won the case. There is nothing in the plea rolls to suggest that this was not allowed.[39]

A special form of prohibition was developed during the 1270's that appeared to issue on the initiative of the king rather than at the request of a private party. Preceding the prohibitory clause was a *cum*-clause declaring that, whereas pleas concerning chattels and debts not testamentary or matrimonial (or concerning lay fee, advowson, etc., as applicable) pertained to the 'king's crown and dignity', the king has learned from several unnamed people (*velut ex relatu plurium accepimus*) that such a plea is taking place in a church court. The writ then prohibited further proceedings against the church court defendant.[40]

Although formally the *ex relatu plurium* writs emphasized the offence against the crown, these prohibitions (and the writs of attachment commanding appearance in a royal court to answer for non-compliance) actually issued only upon the complaint of a party, just as the usual forms did. The difference was that the *ex relatu plurium* writs were available when the complainant was a clerk. A register of writs from around 1300 gave the more usual forms of prohibition, then added: '*Si sit clericus, tunc: Sicut ex relatu plurium*'.[41] Similarly, a fourteenth-century register indicates that the writ issued only if the party seeking it was a clerk, even though it appeared to be '*pro rege*'.[42]

Prior to the development of the *ex relatu plurium* forms clerks and laymen alike obtained prohibitions without distinction as to the form of the writ.[43] From 1277 to 1300, however, the Common Pleas rolls record 33 cases resulting from the new form.[44] In each the actual plaintiff (the king was the nominal plaintiff) was clearly a clerk. And, until late in the reign of Edward I, clerks seeking prohibitions used only the special form.[45]

39 Cf. a statement by the common law justices and barons of the Exchequer made in 1605 that prohibitions might issue at any point, 'as well after judgment and execution, as before': Coke, *Institutes*, 2:602.

40 Rex tali archidiacono et ejus commissario salutem. Cum placita de catallis et debitis in regno nostro, que non sunt de testamento vel matrimonio, ad coronam et dignitatem nostram pertineant, et talis, velut ex relatu plurium jam accepimus, priorem de M. super catallis et debitis hujusmodi trahat in placitum in curia christianitatis, vobis prohibemus ne placitum illud ulterius tenere presumatis in curia christianitatis, presertim cum hujusmodi placita ad nos et non ad alium pertineant in regno nostro. Teste etc. Fiat alia parti ne sequatur sub eadem forma, mutatis mutandis.
Flahiff, 'Use of Prohibitions by Clerics', 113 n. 59. See the same article for the subject of *ex relatu plurium* prohibitions generally.

41 Flahiff, 'Use of Prohibitions by Clerics', 110 n. 47.

42 Flahiff, 'Use of Prohibitions by Clerics', 110 n. 47. The rule was stated in the *Register of Writs*: 'Nota que si ascun clerk, come persone, chapeleyne, ou autre dordre que soit south dascun order, soit emplede en court christien de chose dount lay conysaunce homme avera cest brief que ensuit [i.e., the *ex relatu plurium* form]'. *Register of Writs*, 34. See also *YB 8 Edw. II* 197–198. This form of the writ was not available if the complainant was lay person: e.g., CP 40/121, m. 285 (1297).

43 E.g., Case no. 1.1a, in which the prohibition plea plaintiff was a clerk.

44 The first completed case occurs in the roll for Trinity term 1277. See Case no. 1.4. Because cases such as this did not arise until after the writ of prohibition had been purchased and delivered, the actual writ used in that case probably issued at least a year or two previously. The earliest example of the *ex relatu plurium* form in a register is found in one dated probably 1272–74. Flahiff, 'Use of Prohibitions by Clerics', 113. For additional examples, see Cases nos. 1.21 and 1.29.

45 Toward the end of Edward I's reign clerks begin to reappear as plaintiffs in prohibition pleas in their own right: e.g., CP 40/125, m. 157d (1298); CP 40/129, m. 23 (1299) (one of the defendants was the bishop of Bath and Wells); CP 40/130, m. 170d (1299). Flahiff notes an *ex relatu plurium* writ specifically for lay persons in a 1294 register ('Use of Prohibitions by Clerics', 110 n. 47), but the only examples of such that I have found involved laymen serving as executors of clerks, both in cases prior to that date: CP 40/31, m. 118d (1279); CP 40/89, m. 58 (1291). In other cases, executors of clerks used the more usual form: e.g., CP 40/31, mm. 100, 101 (1279).

The purpose of the *ex relatu plurium* form was the protection from ecclesiastical sanctions of clerks who obtained prohibitions, by naming the king as plaintiff rather than the clerk himself. Earlier in the thirteenth century Bishop Grosseteste had advocated canonical censure of clerks who used royal prohibitions; in his view they should do so under no circumstances.[46] Although the Council of Reading, held under Archbishop Pecham's presidency in 1279, detailed penalties only against clerks who sought prohibitions fraudulently by misrepresenting the actual subject of the ecclesiastical suit,[47] no doubt some church officials continued to disapprove of clerks resorting to prohibitions at any time. The royal inquest of 1286 into the activities of the church courts in Norfolk revealed one judge's attitude toward clerks who brought writs of prohibition into his court. A clerk and a layperson were co-defendants in a suit concerning a 'lay contract'; the latter produced a prohibition, which caused the judge to halt proceedings. Then, however, he cited the clerk for obtaining a prohibition '*cum clericus esset*' and assessed a fine, even though the clerk was prepared to prove his innocence.[48] A rubric in a register of writs explained the aim of the *ex relatu plurium* form in terms of the need to protect clerks from that sort of retaliation: '*Prohibitio [pro] clericis ne videantur convolasse ad vetitum examen*'.[49] It is not clear whether the new form was necessary to counteract increasing pressure from the church authorities or was aimed simply at increasing the freedom of clerks to resort to writs of prohibition.

The prohibition plea

The church court judge or suitor did not necessarily obey the prohibition by promptly halting proceedings. The words of the writ express the intention that the suit, concerning a matter not within the church's jurisdiction, cease at once but in fact the church court judge could proceed if he believed the cause was properly a matter for the church's jurisdiction. Judges also might choose to proceed if they simply were unwilling to defer to the king's authority. The church court defendant, who had brought the prohibition, could then initiate a common law action alleging refusal to obey the writ. This action would require appearance in a royal court to justify the non-compliance. If the king's court found that the judge or suitor had proceeded after receipt of the prohibition unlawfully—that is, according to common law the cause had not been a legitimately spiritual one—the person to whom the prohibition had been addressed was subject to payment of a fine to the royal court and damages to the wronged party. If on the other hand the defendant in the common law suit proved that his or her refusal to yield to the writ of prohibition had been justified, the plaintiff lost the case and was liable to fine for initiating a 'false claim'. The defendant was released without penalty but could not himself or herself claim damages from the plaintiff.[50] The common law suit alleging refusal to obey a prohibition is termed an action of attachment on a prohibition or simply a prohibition plea.

46 Grosseteste, *Epistolae*, 227.
47 *Councils & Synods*, 845–848.
48 Case no. 3.21. For the 1286 inquest, see below section 5.
49 From the register cited above, note 40. Clerical *gravamina* offer further evidence that this was the purpose of the *ex relatu plurium* prohibitions: see *Councils & Synods*, 874, 1139.
50 The clergy complained to the king in 1300 and 1301 that defendants in prohibition pleas who acquitted themselves should be compensated for their expenses and inconvenience. *Councils & Synods*, 1210.

The defendant at common law incurred no liability by the mere fact of having ignored a writ of prohibition. If he or she were able in the course of the prohibition plea to establish that the church court cause was spiritual there was no penalty for disobedience of the writ of prohibition. In other words there was no liability for refusing to obey a prohibition that was in fact illicit. So, although the writ of prohibition appeared to be an unqualified command to halt an ecclesiastical suit, it actually provided the mechanism for initiation of litigation by which the king's justices could decide a dispute over jurisdiction. The availability of this means of adjudicating the validity of prohibitions counteracted the potentially abusive ease with which prohibitions were available. At the same time, the prohibition plea offered a remedy for parties who actually were impleaded unjustly in church courts.

If one whose prohibition had been ignored decided to bring an action at common law on the jurisdictional question, it was that person's responsibility to obtain a writ of attachment, which is not to be confused with the writ of prohibition itself. He or she was under no obligation to do so but unless a church court defendant took the initiative it was not possible to have the benefit of the common law remedy. Although the pleadings in court often referred to contempt of the king or offence to his crown and dignity,[51] there is no evidence that the king's officials ever issued writs of attachment without first having received a complaint from a private party. If the complainant were a clerk, the writ of attachment included the *ex relatu plurium* clause, with the king only nominally the plaintiff.[52] Like the writs of prohibition themselves, attachment proceedings required an aggrieved party to initiate them.

Bracton includes an example of a writ of attachment against a judge and a suitor unwilling to obey a prohibition; it recited the charge against them and assigned a day on which to appear and explain why they had held and sued a plea (*ostensurus quare tenuit/secutus est*) contrary to prohibition.[53] Most often, the writ commanded appearance before the court of Common Pleas, usually sitting at Westminster, less often before the justices itinerant in the counties. Occasionally a prohibition plea was heard in King's Bench. Like the writ of prohibition itself, at the plaintiff's discretion the writ of attachment might issue against the judge or suitor alone or against both.[54]

As with other litigation at common law, securing the appearance of the defendant in a prohibition plea could be a lengthy affair. Prohibition pleas followed the general pattern

[51] E.g., Cases nos. 1.4, 1.11, 1.13, 1.16a , 1.17, 1.18c, 1.20, 1.21, 1.23b, 1.23c, 1.23d, 1.26a, 1.27, and 1.29. One case included the assertion that 'huiusmodi placitum prohibitionis etc. coronam et dignitatem regiam specialiter tangit': Case no. 1.24.

[52] E.g., Cases nos. 1.4, 1.21, and 1.29.

[53] The writ to attach both judge and party, with variations: 'Rex vicecomiti salutem. Si A. fecerit te securum de clamore suo prosequendo, tunc ponas per vadium et salvos plegios B. talem ordinarium, quod sit coram nobis vel iusticiariis nostris apud Westmonasterium vel coram iusticiariis nostris ad primam assisam cum in partes illas venerint, ostensurus quare tenuit placitum in curia christianitatis de laico feodo ipsius A. in tali villa contra prohibitionem nostram, vel de advocatione talis ecclesiae, vel de catallis et debitis quae non sunt de testamento vel matrimonic et huiusmodi. Pone etiam per vadium et salvos plegios C. quod tunc sit ibi ostensurus quare secutus est idem placitum in eadem curia christianitatis contra prohibitionem nostram. Et habeas ibi nomina plegiorum et hoc breve. Teste etcetera' (*Bracton*, 4:272).

[54] Flahiff, 'Prohibition II', 249 n. 13. If an ecclesiastical judge had prosecuted a suit *ex officio* the prohibition plea plaintiff might accuse him of having sued '*Coram seipso*': e.g., CP 40/55, m. 46 (1284). Early in the reign of Edward II church court judges attempted to quash a prohibition plea by denying that they had sued as the plaintiff's writ alleged. Chief Justice Bereford rejected this argument, recognizing that they could 'sue' *ex officio*; furthermore if the writ abated a 'povers home' would be denied justice: *YB 4 Edw. II* 97–98.

of other civil litigation at common law.[55] The writ originating the action was addressed to the sheriff of the county in which the church court case was pending. This writ—the original writ—initiated proceedings, stating the accusation and assigning a time and place for the defendant's appearance in a specified royal court. The sheriff was then required to return the writ to that court endorsed with a statement of the result of action taken to secure the defendant's appearance. Since this initial communication to the sheriff almost never resulted in an appearance and was not expected to, further writs issued judicially—from the court to which the original writ had been returned—at the plaintiff's suit. These judicial writs commanded the sheriff to take gradually more stringent steps to compel the accused to appear at the next term. The series of sequential steps necessary in this as in other civil actions, known as mesne process, followed a fixed format and typically extended over several terms.[56] At its most prolonged it might take two years or even longer. The plea rolls record each step with an entry noting that the plaintiff (usually through an attorney) presented himself or herself on the assigned day against the defendant, who did not appear; therefore another judicial writ, the next one in the regular sequence, has been issued. In this way, the sheriff was ordered to take the next step, increasingly stringent, against the defendant. These entries continue from term to term until either both parties finally meet in court or else the case ends prior to the defendant's appearance. The plea rolls contain many cases—that is, series of sequential process entries between the same parties over several consecutive terms—that stop abruptly with one last process entry and then disappear from the record without a trace.[57] In such cases, there is therefore no pleading, proof, or judgment. Presumably the case either settled or the plaintiff gave up for some reason.

Consultation

Before considering what happened when both parties to a prohibition plea appeared in court it is first necessary to look at the procedure whereby the ecclesiastical court, upon receipt of a prohibition, might seek formal authority to proceed after having referred the jurisdictional question directly to the royal justices. If the justices were satisfied that the church court suit was in fact spiritual, and the prohibition therefore obtained under false pretenses, the suit might then proceed. *Bracton* includes several examples of possible responses to queries from church courts.[58] It is apparent from this discussion of the procedure, which is referred to as consultation (*consultatio*), that it was an informal one. Two of *Bracton*'s examples rehearse in detail the circumstances of the causes in question. In another briefer example the justices simply state that they have considered the judges' letter explaining the nature of the cause and grant permission to the church court to proceed with it, the prohibition notwithstanding.[59] Although *Bracton* refers to the justices' reply as

[55] See generally Baker, *Legal History*, 53–67.

[56] On process generally, see Pollock & Maitland, 2:578–597; Baker, *Legal History*, 64–66; Sutherland, 'Mesne Process'. In prohibition pleas the steps were attachment by pledges, attachment by better pledges, *habeas corpus*, distraint, more severe distraint, still more severe distraint, and finally outlawry. Flahiff, 'Prohibition II', 249–252.

[57] For a suggested explanation of these disappearances, see below, p. lii.

[58] *Bracton*, 4:262–264.

[59] *Bracton*, 4:263.

a '*breve*', the examples did not follow a standard format. There are no examples of 'writs' of consultation in the registers of the mid-thirteenth century. By the end of the middle ages, however, many such writs, in set forms, were available.[60]

Proliferation and formalization were due to the so-called Statute of Consultation of 1290, which has been seen as official recognition of the practice of consultation in use since *Bracton* was written in the earlier thirteenth century.[61] But a close look at the statute,[62] which nowhere used the word '*consultatio*,' reveals that its purpose was subtly though significantly different. *Bracton*'s *consultatio* was an informal procedure employed by an ecclesiastical judge wishing to obtain permission to continue despite a prohibition. The statute, however, was concerned with the special situation of the suitor who found himself or herself without a remedy in either the spiritual or lay forum because the ecclesiastical judge had deferred to a royal prohibition and no alternative action was available for pursuit of the claim at common law. The statute therefore explicitly provided that the church court plaintiff (*ad instanciam querentis*)—not the judge—should apply to the chancellor or chief justice of King's Bench for an order to the judge to proceed with the ecclesiastical suit. The applicant should present the church plaintiff's libel to establish the subject matter of the cause. The order to proceed was to be granted if it were clear that the plaintiff had no common law remedy for the adjudication of the cause because the matter really was one for the church's cognizance.[63] Rather than an opportunity for ecclesiastical judges to obtain permission to proceed, the Statute of Consultation actually provided litigants with assistance when judges were unwilling to do so.[64] This was obviously the purpose of the writs of consultation in the printed *Register*: all are orders to church court judges to proceed, usually because they have deferred to an illicit prohibition.[65] Consultation was thus a sort of 'appeal',[66] but against the ecclesiastical judges themselves rather than against the king's authority to issue a prohibition.

A Common Pleas case clearly raised the issue actually dealt with by the statute. Hugh, a clerk, had tried to recover a pension, allegedly due to him from an ecclesiastical foundation, in an action before justices itinerant in Norfolk in 1286.[67] The justices dismissed his claim as a spiritual matter for the church courts. Hugh therefore initiated an ecclesiastical suit against the same party, Ralph, incumbent of the benefice, but Ralph then obtained a writ of prohibition. The ecclesiastical judge obeyed the prohibition, so Hugh sued at common

[60] *Register of Writs*, 44–58.

[61] E.g., *Canterbury Cases*, 101. See also Adams' earlier statement that the statute 'merely recognized a practice which had been in use for over half a century'. 'Prohibition', 291–292.

[62] *SR*, 1:108, also printed in *Councils & Synods*, 1091. The statute was issued in response to a petition in the Hilary or Easter parliament of 1290. For the petition, see *Rot. Parl.* , 1:47b, also printed in *Councils & Synods*, 1090 n. 3. For its date, see Richardson & Sayles, 'Early Records'.

[63] Sayles' interpretation seems to have been based on a careless reading of the text: 'if a prohibition were directed to an ecclesiastical court, its *presidents* had the right to bring the matter before the chancellor or the chief justice of the king's bench and obtain a decision from them whether or not the action ought to continue in the ecclesiastical court, notwithstanding the prohibition': *King's Bench Cases*, 3:lxxiv–lxxv (emphasis added).

[64] E.g., *Canterbury Cases*, D.7 at 421 (judge having deferred to prohibition, plaintiff obtains consultation warranting further proceedings).

[65] See *Register of Writs*, 44–58. In a few examples the judges themselves, acting as both judges and suitors, complained that their *ex officio* prosecutions had been unjustly halted by prohibitions.

[66] The term is Holdsworth's: *HEL*, 1:229.

[67] Case no. 2.12.

law again, this time in Common Pleas. The jurisdictional question was again raised and Hugh complained of the injustice of his situation[68] in response to Ralph's claim that the cause was purely spiritual. The bench asked Ralph whether he had brought his prohibition against Hugh's suit before or after the ruling of the justices itinerant; he declined to answer, stating that his use of prohibition did not thereby confer jurisdiction over an ecclesiastical matter upon a royal court. At this point the Common Pleas case was adjourned (no conclusion was recorded), probably to consider the propriety of Ralph's use of prohibition. At any rate, it was clear that after the judge had deferred to the prohibition, even though unnecessarily, there was little that Hugh could do. Had this occurred after 1290 he would have sought a consultation. Evidently he initiated his Common Pleas suit instead—an act of desperation, given the earlier ruling against him issued by the king's justices—because the consultation procedure established by the statute was not yet available.[69] One can imagine that Hugh could have had a hand in the petition that resulted in the Statute of Consultation. His grievance certainly posed precisely the problem it sought to address.

The actual focus of the statute, explicit in its language and suggested in the case just discussed, is important because it has been described as 'a victory for the church'[70] or at least a 'grant' to it.[71] In fact the statute was designed not to placate the ecclesiastical judges or the clergy generally, but rather for the benefit of those seeking justice in the church courts. It provided a remedy for the individual suitor, and he or she might as well have been a lay person as a clerk such as Hugh. As an effort to improve a judicial system that comprised both secular and ecclesiastical courts and served both clergy and laity, the statute is not relevant to attempts to see the interests of church and state as mutually exclusive.

Once the statutory consultation procedure had been made available several cases indicate that it was a remedy for a church court suitor where the judge had deferred to a prohibition.[72] In the typical case, the prohibition plea defendant would plead that the church court judge had halted proceedings in response to a prohibition. The church court suitor, now the defendant in the prohibition plea, had then sought a consultation from the chief justice of King's Bench[73] by presenting the libel to him.[74] In an unusual case, a rector who had obtained a judgment in church court only to have execution of the sentence blocked when the judge deferred to a writ of prohibition, sought a consultation from the king's council and came away with an order to the judge to proceed with execution.[75] Typically, though, it was the chief justice of King's Bench who heard the request and, if he determined that the matter alleged in the libel was indeed a spiritual one, he would write to the ecclesiastical judge granting permission to proceed with the case. For example, one consultation informed the

[68] 'nec esset juri consonum quod ipse in utraque curia in casu proposito recederet sine remedio'.

[69] The case was not heard in Common Pleas until Michaelmas term 1293, but it could well have taken three years to get there, especially considering Ralph's intransigence. Or Hugh may have pressed this suit even after consultation was available to him, in order to challenge Ralph's recourse to prohibition contrary to a ruling by a common law court. Or perhaps Hugh hoped that Common Pleas would reverse the previous judgment on the spiritual nature of the pension he was claiming. This jurisdictional issue was questionable at this time. See below, pp. xcvii–xcviii.

[70] Jones, 'Relations', 93.

[71] *King's Bench Cases*, 3:lxxiv.

[72] See Cases nos. 1.20, 1.21, 1.26a, and 2.16. See also CP 40/102, m. 174 (1293).

[73] See Cases nos. 1.20, 1.21, 1.23a, and 1.26a.

[74] E.g., Case no. 1.21.

[75] Case no. 2.16.

judges that they might exercise jurisdiction over rivals' claims to particular tithes as long as the suit did not threaten to deprive the current recipient's church of a quarter of its value.[76] The consultation might be written on the back of the libel.[77] It would then be delivered to the church court judge, who could rely on it as a basis for resumption of the suitor's case.

As important as the purpose of the statute is the question of the actual function of consultation in the prohibition process. An historian has written that the writ of consultation as given 'statutory form' by the 1290 statute 'quashed the prohibition and allowed the church to continue prosecuting the original plea'.[78] This statement misses the more important question, not of whether a consultation 'quashed' a prohibition, but whether it barred a subsequent attachment suit if the judge and party proceeded after obtaining a consultation. The statute said nothing about this, but the rule was that the church court could proceed and the church court defendant could also initiate a prohibition plea, alleging in effect that the ecclesiastical suit was not as represented in the consultation. This issue would require resolution and the consultation itself did not provide the necessary answer.

After 1292, clearly a result of the statute, there are several examples of cases in which defendants in prohibition pleas pleaded consultations as their warrant for proceeding.[79] In each, despite the consultation, the royal court had to determine just as in other prohibition pleas whether the ecclesiastical suit had been legitimately spiritual. An example shows why this was necessary. In a case from 1295 a defendant stated that after receiving a prohibition in a dispute over tithes he went before Gilbert de Thornton (then chief justice of King's Bench), who 'issued a consultation to the [ecclesiastical] judges that they might have cognizance in the ecclesiastical forum of tithes both major and minor as long as the tithes demanded did not extend to a quarter part of the value of the whole church, royal prohibition notwithstanding'.[80] The consultation thus stated the legal rule applicable to this particular jurisdictional question. It did not, however, say anything about the factual question of the actual value of the goods involved in the ecclesiastical suit. Consultation procedure, which relied on the statement of the case presented in the libel, made no provisions for the chief justice to inquire into the truth of its allegations. So, after presenting the consultation to the court hearing the prohibition plea it was still necessary for the defendant to plead that the church court suit had indeed conformed to the justice's authorization. In this example, the prohibition plea defendant pleaded that 'he sued no plea other than in that form'. He then offered to prove his plea by jury, as in most other cases of this kind.[81]

The question of jurisdiction, and hence of the legitimacy of the defendant's ecclesiastical suit, turned on the factual question of whether the tithes exceeded the maximum

[76] Case no. 1.21. For discussion of the one-fourth rule, see below, p. lxxi.

[77] Case no. 1.26a.

[78] Jones, 'Relations', 86.

[79] Cases nos. 1.20, 1.21, and 1.23a. See also JUST 1/375, m. 62d (Kent, 1292); JUST 1/1089, m. 17 (Yorkshire, 1293); CP 40/102, m. 174 (1293); KB 27/146, m. 36d (1295), printed in *King's Bench Cases*, 3:43–44; CP 40/113, m. 58 (1296); KB 27/150, m. 24 (1297); CP 40/121, m. 268d (1297); *YB 30–31 Edw. I*, pp. 440–47 (1302); *YB 32–33 Edw. I*, pp. 408–411 (1304); CP 40/159, m. 5 (1306).

[80] Case no. 1.21. This case illustrates my point particularly well because it turned out that the consultation was not really relevant to the plaintiff's ecclesiastical suit. As warrants for the continuation of proceedings it was therefore necessary that consultations be open to challenge. For discussion of this case, see below, pp. lxxiii–lxxiv.

[81] For proof by wager of law rather than jury, see JUST 1/1089, m.17 (Yorkshire, 1293) and CP 40/159, m. 5 (1306). These cases are exceptional; generally proof would by jury if a prohibition plea defendant pleaded a consultation.

value allowed by common law. The consultation in effect said, 'the church may hear this cause—if the cause if as the plaintiff has said it is'. A much earlier case suggests that this rule was also operative with respect to the consultation procedure described in *Bracton*. A plaintiff lost his prohibition plea because he was unable to show that the church court suit was other than as sanctioned by the consultation.[82]

The prohibition plea plaintiff might also argue that the church court action, described in the libel as a spiritual matter and therefore sanctioned by the consultation, was not in fact spiritual because the claim asserted was invalid. Thus, for example, although a consultation might acknowledge the church's jurisdiction over testamentary legacies or mortuaries, if in fact such claims had no merit—because under the circumstances there was no right to claim property as a legacy or a mortuary—they therefore amounted to claims for lay chattels instead and thus did not involve matters within the church's jurisdiction.[83] It would therefore be for the king's justices to determine the subject matter of the church court case and whether it was in fact spiritual. As discussed below, this was the same issue presented in the typical prohibition plea.

The writ of consultation was not designed to bar a prohibition plea. It did not prevent the complainant's prosecution of an attachment suit, which ended up requiring the church court suitor or judge to prove that the ecclesiastical action was in fact spiritual. Moreover, the defendant in the attachment suit would have been able to plead that the suit had concerned a spiritual matter even without obtaining a consultation. This move was always available to defendants in prohibitions pleas. Instead, the Statute of Consultation ordained a remedy for ecclesiastical suitors unable to prosecute their actions because judges deferred to writs of prohibition in cases where they were not justified in doing so. Not long after the statute's enactment there are cases of ecclesiastical judges themselves seeking consultations in response to writs of prohibition.[84] These cases and also the apparent need for the statute have implications for our understanding of the ways in which ecclesiastical judges reacted to prohibitions, but this will be considered in another context.[85]

While consultation may have been of little help to those summoned to defend themselves in prohibition pleas, on a practical level consultations probably were useful for ecclesiastical suitors in legitimately spiritual causes, not only by encouraging excessively timid judges to proceed despite writs of prohibition, but also by discouraging church court defendants from initiating or persisting in prohibition pleas. The suitor's libel must usually have been an accurate representation of the substance of the claim, even if stated briefly and in conclusory terms.[86] A consultation based on the libel would probably have been sufficient to dissuade the party who had obtained the prohibition from further challenging the church's jurisdiction in many cases. A consultation would not of course have stopped church court defendants who were convinced that the action was not spiritual. It seems unlikely, though, that there would have been many cases in which they could confidently have expected to prove that the ecclesiastical suit did not actually involve the matter described in the libel.

[82] *BNB*, 2:679.
[83] See Cases nos. 1.23a (alleged claim for legacy) and 1.26a (alleged claim for mortuary).
[84] Cases nos. 1.28 and 1.29.
[85] See below, pp. lxxxii–lxxxiii.
[86] Helmholz, *History*, 321.

Pleading and proof

The records of prohibition pleas in which both parties actually appeared in the royal court begin with a brief rehearsal of the plaintiff's writ of attachment, which includes the accusation against the defendant. The plaintiff, usually through an attorney, then elaborated on these allegations in the *narratio* or *counte*. If the claim was that the defendant sued a plea in church court concerning, for example, debts and chattels not related to testament or marriage, the record usually states precisely what those debts or chattels were, perhaps a cow or a measure of grain, perhaps 20 shillings. It also identifies the judge who heard the suit, when and where the prohibition was delivered, and, usually, the witnesses to the delivery. Next follows an assertion that the defendant, having ignored the prohibition (*spreta prohibitione*), proceeded with his or her suit until the plaintiff was suspended from entry to the church and then excommunicated (*suspensus ab ingressu ecclesie et postea excommunicatus*). Finally the plaintiff claimed damages.

Bracton advises that the plaintiff profer the written claim (the libel or *editio*) that initiated the action in the church court,[87] but if this ever happened the prohibition plea records do not mention it. *Bracton* also instructs the plaintiff to produce a suit of witness (*secta*), numbering two or three at least, to support the allegations. The records typically note at the end of the plaintiff's *narratio* that he or she '*inde producit sectam suam*', but there is no plea roll evidence from the reign of Edward I to suggest that the justices interrogated them or that they played a significant role in prohibition pleas.[88]

Faced with the plaintiff's allegations, the defendant's possible answers were limited. Certain details were not traversable, such as the date and place of delivery of the prohibition, the names of the witnesses, and the use of ecclesiastical sanctions against the plaintiff.[89] Instead, the defendant might plead that the suit in church court was actually spiritual, so prohibition did not lie against it. It might have concerned, for example, tithes or some other matter within the church's jurisdiction.[90] Alternatively the

[87] *Bracton*, 4:274–275.

[88] *Britton* (1: 150–151) states (regarding actions of replevin) that unless the plaintiff produces a *secta* the opponent would not be held to a defence. A treatise on pleading from late in the reign of Henry III or early in Edward I states that the plaintiff's *secta* must agree among themselves as to the allegations if the prohibition plea is to proceed: *Brevia Placitata*, 18, 171–172. Moreover the plaintiff loses the suit if he or she offers a *secta* but cannot produce it: id. at 63. It is probable that—earlier in the thirteenth century at least—a plaintiff could offer a *secta* or documentary evidence alternatively. For a case from 1252 showing that one or the other was necessary, see Flahiff, 'Prohibition I', 254 n. 46.

[89] On account of this, strict factual accuracy in the pleadings should not be assumed. For example, in two separate prohibition pleas that clearly resulted from the same suit in church court, the plaintiff once accused the judge of hearing a cause concerning 40 shillings and elsewhere accused the plaintiff of suing for 50 shillings. He mentioned suspension and excommunication in one *counte* but not in the other: CP 40/60, mm. 94d, 121d (1285). See also a case in which the *counte* included no reference to ecclesiastical sanctions but the jury's verdict did. Case no. 1.8.

[90] E.g., 'Et bene cognoscit quod petiit ab ipso quasdam decimas . . . set bene defendit quod nuncquam secuta est predictum placitum de decem marcatis meremii in prefata curia contra prohibitionem predictam': CP 40/15 m. 39d (1276). See also CP 40/34, m. 16d (1280) ('nuncquam secutus fuit aliquod placitum in curia christianitatis de laicis catallis ipsius Willelmi immo de decimis spectantibus ad ecclesiam suam'); CP 40/54, m. 27d (1284) ('ipse aliquo tempore petiit ab ipso quasdam decimas pertinentes ad ecclesiam suam . . . set bene defendit quod nuncquam secutus fuit aliquod placitum exigendo ab eo predictas tres acras bosci nec predictam petiam warenne'); CP 40/81, m. 2d (1290) ('ipse secutus fuit placitum in curia christianitatis de decimis et oblationibus predicte ecclesie sue de Clandon sicut ei bene licuit set bene defendit quod ipse nuncquam secutus fuit placitum de aliquibus laicis catallis ipsius Willelmi contra prohibitionem').

defendant might deny having continued to sue or hear the suit after receipt of the plaintiff's prohibition.[91] A third possibility was a simple denial that a writ of prohibition had been received at all.[92] Because the basis for the attachment plea was the alleged disobedience of a prohibition, a successful denial of ever having received one acquitted the defendant without the question of the actual nature of the ecclesiastical suit arising at all.

Most often the defendant simply pleaded the general issue, thus concealing the actual basis for the denial: the defendant 'denied that he (or she) ever sued (or held) the alleged plea in church court contrary to royal prohibition',[93] occasionally adding the phrase 'as is alleged against him (or her)' (*sicut ei inponit*).[94] The exact implications of these denials are ambiguous; various constructions are possible. They might amount to a denial of having sued a plea contrary to the prohibition: that is, the actual suit was not as described by the prohibition plea plaintiff but in fact concerned a spiritual matter and was therefore licit. In this context the '*sicut ei inponit*' clause would have indicated acknowledgement of having sued a plea in church court but denial that it was as the plaintiff described it. The general denial could also signify that a prohibition was either never received—hence there were no proceedings contrary to it—or that, having received it, the defendant did not proceed any further. Finally, the defendant could simply have been denying having ever sued or heard the plea in question at all.

The ambiguous quality of the general denial was discussed in a case in which the defendants denied generally and the king's attorney objected that the plea had multiple meanings (*predicta responsio sua quam pretenderunt verificare multiplex fuit et plures causas veritatis habere potuit*) and the various possibilities were rehearsed.[95] The defendants then pleaded more specifically that their suit was for tithes that did not amount to a quarter of the value of the adverse party's benefice and cited a consultation authorizing them to proceed. While it might thus appear that the king's justices had decided to steer defendants away from general denials to more specific pleas, in fact general denials continued to be used in prohibition pleas

[91] E.g., 'Et bene defendit quod nuncquam post predictam prohibitionem ei exhibitam secuta fuit idem placitum in curia christianitatis': CP 40/28, m. 16 (1279). See also CP 40/17, m. 116 (1276); CP 40/18, m. 24d (1277); CP 40/19, m. 39d (1277).

[92] E.g., 'Et bene defendit quod predictus Johannes de Crek' nuncquam predictis die anno et loco detulit ei regiam prohibitionem predictam': CP 40/41, m. 43d (1281). See also CP 40/15, m. 30 (1276) (similar); CP 40/31, m. 101d (1279) ('Et bene defendit quod predicti Ricardus et Robertus nuncquam detulerunt ei aliquam prohibitionem de supersedendo de predicto placito'). Occasionally one finds cases in which the defendant denies ever having sued or held the plea in question at all, without mention of prohibition in his denial: e.g., Case no. 1.10. See also CP 40/28, m. 31d (1279) ('Et bene defendit quod numquam secutus fuit idem placitum in predicta curia christianitatis'); CP 40/78, m. 82 (1289) ('Et bene defendit quod predictum placitum non tenuit in curia christianitatis sicut ei inponit').

[93] E.g., 'Et bene defendit quod numquam tenuit predictum placitum contra prohibitionem predictam': CP 40/41, m. 4d (1281); 'Et bene defendit quod nucquam secutus fuit placitum in curia christianitatis de laico feodo ipsius Ricardi contra prohibitionem predictam': CP 40/8, m. 21 (1275); 'Et bene defendit quod nuncquam secutus fuit idem placitum de advocatione predicte quarte partis ecclesie versus predictum priorem in eadem curia christianitatis': CP 40/21, m. 28 (1277).

[94] E.g., 'Et bene defendit quod nuncquam secutus est predictum placitum in prefata curia contra regiam prohibitionem sicut sibi inponit': CP 40/15, m. 102 (1276).

[95] Case no. 1.20.

frequently after this case. Perhaps in this case the defendants decided they wished to rely on the consultation, which might not otherwise have come to the jury's attention.

Pleading brought the parties to some question suitable for submission to proof. If this was to be by jury the plea roll typically states that the defendant 'put himself (or herself) upon the country' (*ponit se super patriam*). The court then ordered the sheriff of the county in which the alleged wrong took place (that is, the refusal to yield to the prohibition) to summon a local jury of 12 to appear before the royal justices to answer under oath the factual question to which the dispute had been reduced. Justices itinerant might take the verdict in the county if they arrived there before the day assigned for the jury's appearance at Westminster or *coram rege*. The verdict would then be returned to the central court for the final judgment. Prohibition pleas could also be decided by wager of law (or compurgation). These cases record the defendant's declaration that he or she was prepared to prove the facts alleged in response to the plaintiff's claim 'as the court should adjudge' (*sicut curia consideraverit*). This standard plea roll phrase is always followed by the court's award of wager of law, usually formulated thus: '*Ideo consideratum est quod vadiat ei legem se duodecima manu*'.[96] That is, the defendant swore that the plea was true and undertook to support this oath by those of 11 oath-helpers or compurgators swearing to the defendant's credibility.[97] As such, the oath-helpers did not purport to validate the facts pleaded by the defendant; their role was simply to attest to the defendant's trustworthiness. The defendant's oath and undertaking were the 'wager'; he or she was obliged to appear in person at a later date with the oath-helpers 'to make (or complete) his or her law' (*perficere legem suam*). Pending the reappearance the defendant produced pledges to guarantee it.[98]

Wager of law was the more usual mode of proof in prohibition pleas during the reign of Edward I. Leaving aside the *ex relatu plurium* cases, in which proof was necessarily by jury because wager of law was not allowed against the king,[99] compurgation was used twice as often as trial by jury. No clear trend is apparent during the last decades of the thirteenth century. Wager of law significantly outnumbered jury trial during the five-year period from 1276 to 1280 and during the 1290's but the numbers are roughly equivalent during the 1280's. Clearly, though, Flahiff's statement that 'it is the jury which in the

[96] On wager of law, see Baker, *Legal History*, 74; Plucknett, *Concise History*, 115–116.

[97] Coke wrote that the defendant 'himselfe must bee sworne de fidelitate, and the eleven de credulitate.': *Institutes*, 1:295. The English translation of *Britton*, to the effect that 12 oath-helpers were required, is not warranted by the French text, which speaks of making one's law 'ove sa duzime mayn': *Britton*, 1:150–151.

[98] The defendant 'was to put in sureties or vadios, that at such a day he will make his law': Blackstone, *Commentaries*, 3:341.

[99] Holdsworth, *HEL*, 1:307. Blackstone gave the reason: 'The king also has his prerogative; for, as all wager of law imports on the plaintiff for dishonesty, therefore there shall be no wager on actions brought by him' (*Commentaries*, 3:347). Protesting in 1280 against the new *ex relatu plurium* prohibitions, the clergy objected particularly to the unavailability of the more usual mode of proof: '. . . nec potest iudex coram iusticiariis uti iure commoni, scilicet de lege facienda cum manu tertia [sic], si neget se contra prohibitionem venisse, sed dicunt iusticiarii: Rex est pars. Et tunc, sive velit sive nolit iudex vel pars, ad inquisitionem procedetur' (*Councils & Synods*, 874; see also id. at 1209–1210). Note, however, Case no. 1.3, in which wager of law was allowed in a case in which the king was nominally the plaintiff on the question of whether the defendant had excommunicated the actual plaintiff for using a writ of prohibition. The separate question of whether the defendant had also excommunicated the king was put to a jury.

latter half of the thirteenth century crowds out wager of law in all pleas of prohibition'[1] is inaccurate. During the 20 Common Pleas terms from 1291 to 1295 inclusive, wager of law decided over three-fourths of the 55 prohibition pleas in which the king was not the nominal plaintiff; from 1296 to 1300 the ratio is three to two.[2] During the final seven years of Edward I's reign, wager of law outnumbered jury trial 30 to six.[3]

Proof by compurgation had definite advantages for the defendant over jury trial, foremost of which was that acquittal was nearly certain. Virtually the only defendants who failed to clear themselves were those who did not appear on the day appointed to make their law.[4] If the defendant came with his or her oath-helpers the plaintiff's case was as good as lost. A few cases graphically suggest the plaintiff's hopeless position: when the court assigned wager of law some simply agreed to dispense with the whole procedure (*remisit ei legem*), allowing the defendant to go free on the spot and leaving themselves liable to fine.[5]

In some cases, the record notes that after waging law the defendant made it immediately (*incontinenti* or *instanter*).[6] In one case, unusual in this respect, a defendant waged his law and was ordered by the court to return to make it the next day.[7] Later in the middle ages professional oath-helpers were available to offer their assistance for a fee; apparently the court porters could be hired for this purpose.[8] The ability of some prohibition plea defendants to make their law immediately or only a day after having waged it might seem to suggest that paid compurgators could be found around Westminster Hall during the reign of

[1] 'Prohibition II', 267. See also id. at 274.

[2] Statistics from Common Pleas cases:

Term & Year	Mode of proof: Wager of Law	Jury	King as plaintiff
Hil.–Mich. 1275	3	0	2
Hil. 1276–Mich. 1280	40	7	8
Hil. 1281–Mich. 1285	18	16	9
Hil. 1286–Mich. 1290	18	17	6
Hil. 1291–Mich. 1295	42	13	6
Hil. 1296–Mich. 1300	24	16	5
Hil. 1301–Mich. 1305	22	4	4
Hil. 1306–Trin. 1307	8	2	4

[3] Helmholz writes that jury trial replaced wager of law during the early decades of the fourteenth century and had largely if not entirely disappeared by 1335: *Canon Law*, 66.

[4] In a total of 175 Common Pleas cases in which proof was by wager of law only six defendants were found liable, each because of default. In several cases, the defendant simply failed to appear on the appointed day to complete the wager: CP 40/19, mm. 39d, 65d (1277); CP 40/27, m. 63 (1278); CP 40/105, m. 100 (1294); CP 40/109, m. 81 (1295). In one case, after wager of law was assigned, the defendant's attorney 'recessit in contemptu curie et non invenit plegios de lege', so the plaintiffs were awarded their damages: CP 40/67, m. 52d (1287). In a King's Bench case from 1299, cited in Coke, *Institutes*, 2:644, the defendant came to make his law and 'incepit jurare et post quartum juratum defecit de lege etc.' ; the plaintiff recovered his damages and the defendant was fined: KB 27/159, m. 28d (1299). Nothing else comparable to this failure has been found in the records of the royal courts. See also Helmholz, *Canon Law*, 65–66 (finding that plaintiffs prevailed in only seven percent of wager of law cases decided between 1285 and 1335).

[5] E.g., CP 40/31, m. 113d (1279); CP 40/41, m. 43d (1281). See also Case no. 1.14, in which the plaintiff ceased to pursue the claim further after assignment of wager of law.

[6] E.g., Cases nos. 1.3, 1.10, and 1.23a. See also CP 40/23, m. 3d (1278); CP 40/55, m. 116 (1284); CP 40/60, mm. 85d, 121d (1285); CP 40/91, m. 59d (1291); CP 40/136, m. 37d (1301); CP 40/149, m. 111 (1304).

[7] Case no. 1.6.

[8] Baker, *Legal History*, 74.

Edward I, but there is no direct prohibition plea evidence to that effect.[9] It is also possible that some defendants brought their oath-helpers with them, confident that wager of law would be assigned in their case.

Once the defendant made his or her law, acquittal followed automatically (*ideo inde sine die*). In one case the church court suitor made his law immediately (*incontinenti*); the church court judge, who had also waged his law on the prohibition plea, was thereby acquitted as well, because he could not have heard the case contrary to prohibition if the church court plaintiff did not sue it.[10] Following acquittal, the plaintiff was then amerced for the 'false claim'.[11] The royal courts did nothing to ensure that those who served as compurgators were honest and knowledgeable about the defendant's credibility. Noting that oath-helpers were admitted more readily than jurors, *Bracton* states that they might be the defendant's friends or members of his or her household and need not share the defendant's social status.[12] Compurgators should be 'trustworthy and of good repute', but *Bracton* makes no mention of any means by which a plaintiff could challenge their honesty. If a litigant believed that a jury had brought a false verdict, the common law action of attaint was available and could be brought against the jurors. Under this procedure, a new jury of 24 ruled on the veracity of the original verdict.[13] No such remedy was available in cases decided by wager of law. There was no action of attaint against defendants who waged their law and made it according to approved form or against their oath-helpers.[14] The court might ask plaintiffs if they were willing to admit defendants with their compurgators to make their law, but plaintiffs lost their suits and subjected themselves to amercement if they actually refused to do so.[15]

Occasional cases reveal especially clearly that the danger of perjury in wager of law was real. For example, in a prohibition plea involving multiple defendants, one denied having sued a plea in Court Christian on the date alleged and waged his law.[16] He made his law

[9] One case identifies the defendant's wager of law pledges as Walter le Cryur and Hamo de la Bare: Case no. 1.6. Walter was probably an usher; he is one of four ushers amerced for contempt by the justices of Common Pleas in 1286. CP 40/62, m. 23. Hamo was an attorney who became a serjeant of Common Pleas by as early as 1275: Baker, *Order of Serjeants*, 499. It cannot be determined whether men like these were also available to serve as oath-helpers. We are indebted to Dr Paul Brand for these references.

[10] CP 40/136, m.37d (1301) ('Et similiter quia predictus Robertus placitum illud tenuisse non potuit nisi ad sectam predicti Alexandri unde idem Alexander per predictam legem se acquietavit etc., consideratum est quod idem Robertus inde sine die etc.'). See also Case no. 1.28.

[11] The records in such cases usually do not state the amount of the fine but where they do sums varied from 40 shillings (CP 40/91, m. 59d (1291)), to 5 marks (CP 40/18, m. 50d (1277)), to as much as 100 shillings. CP 40/64, m. 64d (1286); CP 40/78, m. 82 (1289). Flahiff noted the following sums: 40 shillings (1225), 5 marks (1243), 10 marks (1243). 'Prohibition II' 280. Amercements were sometimes pardoned in cases of hardship ('pardonatur quia pauper'). E.g., Case no. 1.8. See also CP 40/23, m. 20 (1278); CP 40/96, m. 198d (1292).

[12] *Bracton*, 4:275–276.

[13] Convicted jurors were imprisoned, their goods confiscated, their real property destroyed, and their reputations permanently tainted. These penalties were so harsh that attaint juries were evidently reluctant to impose liability. Doctrinal limitations and procedural disadvantages also contributed to attaint's limited practical utility. See Millon, 'Historiography', 686–700.

[14] 'Estre ceo ne gist nule atteinte . . . en defences encountre sutes par ley': *Britton*, 2:227.

[15] In one case the defendant came, 'paratus cum lege sua'. The plaintiff, 'quesitus si vellet predictam legem admittere, dicit quod non'. No reason for the refusal is recorded. The defendant was thereupon released sine die and the plaintiff adjudged to be 'in misericordia pro falso clamore': CP 40/64, m. 64d (1286). See also CP 40/104, m. 131d (1294).

[16] Case no. 1.23a.

immediately and was acquitted. The others—all minors—acknowledged the alleged suit, contradicting the first defendant's denial, but claimed that it was for a legacy and that they desisted upon receipt of a writ of prohibition until they had obtained a consultation. They put this defence to a jury, which said that they had indeed brought suit in Court Christian, their claim based on a will that had been revoked by the testator.

In another case, an ecclesiastical judge was accused of hearing a plea and proclaiming sentence of excommunication against those responsible for a writ of prohibition, including the king himself.[17] The judge denied having issued the sentence against the church court plaintiff and was allowed to wage his law, which he made immediately. The question of whether he had also declared a sentence against the king was treated as separate. As to this, a jury found that he had excommunicated anyone deferring to or otherwise supporting the prohibition, not excepting the king; presumably this sentence also included the church court suitor. If so, here too a jury verdict contradicted a denial proved by wager of law.

Similarly, Edmund, earl of Cornwall brought a prohibition plea against Beatrice, his father's widow.[18] She denied proceeding after receipt of the prohibition and waged her law. Elsewhere on the roll for that term is another suit by Edmund against the judge in the same ecclesiastical cause.[19] The judge also denied disobeying the prohibition but Edmund objected that he should not be allowed to wage his law because there was documentary proof, in the form of the church court records (*acta*) sealed by the defendant himself, that proved he was lying. This suit was adjourned and no ruling on this question was enrolled. It is apparent, however, that either in this case or at some point soon thereafter the justices decided not to allow the use of documentary or other evidence to impugn a prohibition plea defendant's wager of law; no examples of similar efforts to do so are found after this case, suggesting that the king's courts were unwilling to take such evidence into account in wager of law cases. Further, although Edmund's argument in the case against the judge obviously contradicted Beatrix's denial as well, she was allowed to make her law at a later term. The record indicates that the court may have entertained objections against her resort to wager of law because final judgment, which ordinarily would have followed automatically, was postponed and the case was adjourned '*de audiendo judicio super lege ista*'. There is no record of a ruling on this point either, but later cases likewise confirm that a prohibition plea plaintiff could not use evidence produced in one prohibition plea to challenge the right to wager of law of the church court judge or suitor in another prohibition plea based on the same church court case. Proof that a prohibition plea defendant's denial was untrue would not be allowed to block access to wager of law. Nor was there any way for a prohibition plea plaintiff to charge a defendant with perjury after successful compurgation.

It is not entirely clear what factors were involved in determining mode of proof in prohibition pleas but the choice between wager of law and jury trial was probably the defendant's. There is not much in the records or in contemporary treatises that bears directly on this question. *Bracton* does not mention that a prohibition plea could be decided other than by wager of law. The *Casus Placitorum*, a collection of precedents and procedural rules from the reign of Henry III, includes an item indicating that defendants in prohibition

[17] Case no. 1.3.
[18] Case no. 1.2a. Edmund was the offspring of an earlier marriage.
[19] Case no. 1.2b.

pleas could ordinarily wage their law but might in certain cases put themselves upon a jury instead.[20] Many years later Coke wrote that during the later thirteenth century 'and long after' the defendant in a prohibition plea had the right to wage his or her law.[21] There is no evidence to suggest that a jury might be imposed upon the defendant except in those cases in which the king was plaintiff or wager of law was not allowed for some other reason.[22]

In other actions in which either sort of proof was available it was up to the defendant to choose. Thus in actions of debt or covenant in which no sealed document was adduced defendants usually waged their law. Actions of detinue also left the matter of proof to the defendant: if he or she chose to plead to the general issue—a simple '*non detinet*' in response to the allegation of detention of the plaintiff's property—wager of law followed. A special plea either challenging a material fact in the plaintiff's count or admitting it but pleading additional information in defence could put the case before a jury.[23]

One detinue case includes an uncommonly detailed discussion of how a jury might be imposed on a defendant under certain circumstances. The defendant was accused of refusing to return the dowry given him by the father of the bride. Immediately after the wedding he obtained a divorce in the Court of Arches, apparently on account of an earlier agreement to marry someone else still living (*ratione cuiusdam precontractus*). The disappointed bride then claimed that the goods and money should be returned to her. The defendant denied having received the property in question and the standard plea roll phrase indicates that he asked to wage his law. In a typical detinue action—or prohibition plea—the award of compurgation would have followed. But here the record then states specifically that the justices asked how he would prefer to prove his plea and, in response to another request for wager of law (*dicit quod credit quod erit inde ad legem suam*), instead required that he put himself upon a jury. Clearly under normal circumstances the defendant was free to wage his law if he chose to, but here—because known facts seem to have suggested that the denial was fraudulent and therefore 'rendered him suspect'—the

20 *Casus Placitorum*, 1.

21 *Institutes*, 2:644.

22 One could not wage another person's law, so executors could not do so on behalf of a deceased debtor. In such cases, rather than allowing trial by jury the common law denied a remedy to those who did not produce a sealed document evidencing the obligation: Baker, *Legal History*, 326.

23 It has been suggested that a similar distinction was at work in prohibition pleas: juries tried pleas requiring proof of 'some fact connected with the main issue, or some exception about which the main issue will turn' in contrast to the 'flat denial of having proceeded in Court Christian contrary to a prohibition' triable by compurgation. Flahiff, 'Prohibition II', 267. The records, however, reveal that no such distinction was operative. There are many examples of juries trying general denials from the later 1270s onwards: e.g., Case no. 1.8; CP 40/30, m. 35 (1279); CP 40/31, m. 116d (1279); CP 40/41, m. 80d (1281); CP 40/42, m. 82 (1281); CP 40/52, m. 29 (1284). Before then, juries were used only rarely in any prohibition pleas. Yet one also finds numerous cases from the same years in which defendants made precisely the same sorts of denials and were allowed to wage their law: e.g., Case no. 1.10; CP 40/30, m. 54d (1279); CP 40/31, m. 78 (1279); CP 40/36, m. 96 (1280); CP 40/41, m. 4d (1281); CP 40/58, m. 29 (1285). Defendants resorted to either method of proof to prove more precisely focused pleas, such as denials of proceeding after a prohibition was received. Wager of law: Case no. 1.6; CP 40/31, mm. 4d, 114d (1279); jury: CP 40/31, m. 90d (1279); CP 40/33, m. 54 (1280); CP 40/36, m. 66d (1280) . Similarly as to assertions that the suit in church court had actually involved tithes. Wager of law: CP 40/34, m. 16d (1280); CP 40/54, m. 27d (1284); CP 40/81, m. 2d (1290); jury: CP 40/28, m. 29 (1279); CP 40/38, m. 21 (1281); CP 40/53, m. 28 (1284). Clearly it could not have been the degree of specificity of the defendant's plea that determined mode of proof in a case in which three co-defendants all made general denials and two waged their law while the third put himself upon the country: CP 40/111, m. 87d (1296); similar are CP 40/98, m. 66d (1293) and CP 40/145, m. 152 (1303).

court ordered him to request a jury.[24] While it is conceivable that some of the prohibition pleas decided by juries rather than wager of law likewise were cases in with the royal courts imposed juries on defendants whose denials of wrongdoing were particularly suspicious, there is no evidence of the king's justices allowing and then acting on arguments to that effect in prohibition pleas.

If proof in prohibition pleas was generally a matter of the defendant's choice, the obvious question is why anyone would choose a jury if he or she could have wager of law. The ease with which defendants could acquit themselves by compurgation seems readily apparent; of its compelling advantages their can be no doubt. Nevertheless jury trial had attractions of its own. Though it naturally involved a lesser degree of certainty for the defendant (even a man convinced of his own innocence can never be sure a jury will agree with him), the action of attaint offered protection from a perjured verdict. Jury trial may also have had advantages in convenience. Defendants who waged their law were required to reappear in person at a later date to make their law; they were also responsible personally for securing the presence of the oath-helpers. Once defendants put themselves on the country, however, it became the duty of the sheriff to summon the jurors and ensure their appearance. Defendants could also receive the verdict and final judgment vicariously through their attorneys, obviating the need for a return visit to the court in which the case was pending. Moreover there must have been some men—perhaps of exceptionally bad reputation or limited acquaintance—who simply could not find 11 others willing to risk their souls on his behalf. Again, professional perjurers may not have been available. Finally, it will be argued below that jury verdicts may have been useful for confirming that church court suits had actually concerned spiritual matters;[25] this would have been desirable when prohibition plea defendants wished to resume those suits against the plaintiffs after acquittal on the prohibition plea.

The beginning of the use of the jury in typical prohibition pleas coincided with the appearance of the special *ex relatu plurium* action in which the king was nominally the plaintiff and jury trial therefore mandatory. As noted above, this occurred during the 1270's. Contemporaries perhaps saw this new method of deciding a certain class of prohibition pleas as an attractive alternative to the older customary mode of proof. General skepticism about its efficacy as a dispute resolution mechanism seems an unlikely explanation, because wager of law survived through the rest of the middle ages for other forms of action. Nevertheless, for the reasons suggested above, jury trial did offer some advantages and some defendants, wishing to avail themselves of them, might well have pressed for jury trial over wager of law once it was available in the *ex relatu plurium* cases. The royal justices, now trying all *ex relatu plurium* cases by jury, may not have had any strong

[24] CP 40/81, m. 48d (1290): 'Et [Edmundus] bene defendit quod predictus Ricardus pater etc. nunquam dedit eidem Edmundo aliqua bona seu catalla ratione predicti matrimonii nec idem Edmundus aliquid unquam inde recepit. Et hoc paratus est defendere contra eam et sectam suam si quam habeat sicut curia consideraverit. Et Edmundus quesitus quid intendit sibi considerari dicit quod credit quod erit inde ad legem suam etc. Et quia predictus contractus fuit adeo manifestus et predicta catalla adeo manifeste ei liberata fuisse dicuntur et manifeste ducta que potius in verificatione patrie caderet quam per legem ipsius Edmundi qui per predictum divorcium reddidit se suspectum etc., dictum est ei quod aliud dicat etc. Et Edmundus dicit quod predictus Ricardus pater etc. nunquam dedit ei aliqua bona seu catalla ratione predicti matrimonii nec idem Edmundus aliquid de predictis catallis recepit sicut predictum est. Et hoc petit quod inquiratur per patriam'.

[25] See below, p. xli.

objections to allowing defendants to put themselves upon juries in the older sorts of prohibition pleas if they chose to do so. But to have eliminated entirely the option of the traditional mode of proof—if such an innovation were even contemplated—presumably would have been too radical an imposition.

As we have seen, wager of law continued to predominate as the preferred mode of proof in prohibition pleas even after the jury had become generally available. This fact raises a question that must have been of real, practical concern to litigants. The mode of proof could decisively influence a case's outcome. On one level this was a matter of whether the prohibition process functioned as an effective means of identifying and punishing judges and suitors who ignored the crown's orders to halt legal proceedings in ecclesiastical courts that did not belong there. To individual plaintiffs suing prohibition pleas, the claim for damages depended upon a determination that the allegations were true. Yet the availability of compurgation meant that defendants could choose a mode of proof that hardly ever resulted in a judgment in the plaintiff's favour. Wager of law was employed often and apparently at the defendant's discretion and was virtually foolproof. Why did the crown provide actions against ecclesiastical judges and suitors that allowed the defendants to acquit themselves at will? And—even more important—why did anyone use them?

Final prohibitions

Because wager of law decided the majority of prohibition pleas, it must have been clear to prohibition plea plaintiffs that there was almost no chance of winning their cases and collecting damages. Moreover, defeat meant subjection to fine for prosecuting a false claim. Historians have remarked on the ease with which those accused of ignoring prohibitions cleared themselves,[26] but they have failed to explain how a procedure that allowed wager of law could succeed in attaining its apparent objectives of punishing infringements on secular jurisdiction and providing relief to those unjustly impleaded in church courts. If most defendants readily acquitted themselves, the cown could not identify those who had disobeyed prohibitions and therefore could not see to it that wronged parties received compensation.

In fact, while unwilling to abandon wager of law in prohibition pleas, the common law did offer meaningful protection to church court defendants from unjust prosecution. This was accomplished by means of judicial injunctions forbidding ecclesiastical judges and suitors from resuming proceedings in church courts after having been acquitted in prohibition pleas. I refer to these injunctions as 'final prohibitions' to distinguish them from the writs of prohibition that provided the initial basis for the suits at common law challenging the church's jurisdiction. These final prohibitions were backed up by the availability of actions for contempt, and these were triable only by jury; wager of law was unavailable. Thus, although prohibition plea plaintiffs might have lost their common law suits alleging disobedience of a writ of prohibition, the king's courts did seek to guarantee that the ecclesiastical actions brought against them, if not legitimately spiritual, would vex them no

[26] In this vein, Flahiff writes: 'Two things are particularly striking in all these wager of law proceedings: the ease with which the parties succeed in making the law, and the patience with which the authorities continue to allow so inconclusive a mode of proof' ('Prohibition II', 270). See also Adams, 'Prohibition', 285.

further. This protection thus provided church court defendants with what they had sought in the first place and in a sense compensated for the weakness of the prohibition plea process as a means of determining liability. The availability of such protection was therefore of great importance to litigants seeking relief through the prohibition process, though its significance in this regard has been overlooked by modern commentators.

The plea rolls from throughout the thirteenth century show that in many prohibition pleas the justices ordered defendants who had acquitted themselves by compurgation not to pursue their suits any further in ecclesiastical court. In such cases the records note that, after the defendants made their law and were dismissed *sine die*, the justices forbade them (*prohibitum* or *inhibitum est*) to proceed with the church court action that had been the object of the writ of prohibition. The justices' injunction is stated in the record in various ways; no standard formula was employed.[27] There is also clear evidence that such orders were at times issued by the common law courts but not entered on the plea rolls. In two Common Pleas cases, prohibition plea defendants waged their law and were acquitted; the records include no mention of a final prohibition in either case. A few terms later, however, we learn from additional entries that the same defendants were accused of proceeding with their church court suits despited having been ordered to stop after the earlier acquittals.[28] It thus seems that final prohibitions may have issued routinely but were only occasionally recorded on the plea rolls. The absence of a formal record did not bar a later action for contempt.

Final prohibitions were only issued in certain situations. Several followed the defendant's general denial.[29] Others occurred in cases in which defendants asserted that they had halted their pleas in church court upon receipt of a prohibition,[30] or that they had never held or sued the plea in question at all,[31] or else that the suit in church court was not as the plaintiff alleged.[32] The important point is that in none of the cases that ended with final prohibitions had the defendant made a positive assertion of the spiritual nature of the church court action, for example, by pleading that it had actually involved tithes or matrimonial chattels. By issuing final prohibitions against further proceedings in church court, the common law justices treated these defendants as having tacitly admitted that they had

27 E.g., Case no. 1.1a ('Et inhibitum est predicto priori ne teneat predictum placitum etc.'). See also CP 40/23, m. 13 (1278) ('Et iterato prohibitum est per justiciarios quod ulterius non sequatur etc.'); CP 40/31, m. 4d (1279) ('Et prohibitum est ei ex parte domini regis ne decetero trahat ipsum in curia christianitatis etc. in placitum etc.'); CP 40/33, m. 36 (1280) ('Et inhibitum est ei ne amodo sequatur predictum placitum etc.'); JUST 1/485, m. 2 (Lincolnshire, 1280) ('Et prohibitum est predicto magistro Ricardo ne amplius placitum illud in prefata curia sequatur etc.'). For examples from the reign of Henry III, see Flahiff, 'Prohibition II', 258 n. 70.

28 See CP 40/20, m. 13d (1277) (prohibition plea ending in acquittal) and CP 40/24, m. 27 (1278) (contempt action); CP 40/95, m. 43 (1292) (prohibition plea ending in acquittal) and CP 40/98, m. 87 (1293) (contempt action).

29 E.g., JUST 1/485, m. 2 (Lincolnshire, 1280); CP 40/95, m. l0ld (1292); CP 40/98, m. 130 (1293); CP 40/100, m. 53d (1293); CP 40/102, m. 34 (1293); CP 40/103, m. 57 (1294); CP 40/105, m. 80d (1294); CP 40/139, m. 153d (1301).

30 E.g., CP 40/23, m. 13 (1278); CP 40/24, m. 27 (1278) (action for contempt of final prohibition; earlier case upon which the contempt action was based is CP 40/20, m. 13d (1277)); CP 40/57, m. 35d (1285) (earlier case CP 40/31, m. 4d (1279)).

31 E.g., Case no. 1.1a; Case no. 1.9 (earlier case not found). See also JUST 1/367, m. 52 (Kent, 1278); CP 40/98, m. 87 (1293) (earlier case CP 40/95, m. 43 (1292)).

32 E.g., CP 40/98, m. 89d (1293) (denied suing 'de laicis catallis' of the plaintiffs); CP 40/104, m. 133d (1294) ('Et bene defendit quod ipsa nuncquam secuta fuit placitum in curia christianitatis de laicis catallis predicti Roberti que non etc.').

no right to continue prosecuting their ecclesiastical suits. Although these defendants had acquitted themselves by wager of law of the charge of ignoring a prohibition, they thereby forfeited any right to continue to pursue their actions in church court against the plaintiff. The plaintiff lost the prohibition plea but secured an end to the ecclesiastical suit that had prompted resort to the writ of prohibition in the first place.[33]

If the ecclesiastical judge or suitor disobeyed the final prohibition, a special remedy was available to the plaintiff. This action alleged both the personal wrong against the complainant and the public wrong of contempt. The latter element, based on the refusal to respect an order by the king's justices, meant that jury trial was the only mode of proof available to the accused. Contempt suits of this sort were initiated not by original writ but by judicial writs based upon complaints brought directly to the king's officials, usually the court that had previously decided the prohibition plea.[34] It is probably because judicial writs such as these did not find their way into the registers of writs that historians have missed their importance. An example is a case from 1275, in which the complainant alleged that, after an ecclesiastical judge had acquitted himself in a prohibition plea by making his law, he had nonetheless continued to hear a church court suit against the complainant despite having been ordered not to do so. The judge's defence, a denial that he proceeded after the final prohibition, was put to a jury.[35] Similar was a clerk's complaint that an ecclesiastical suit against him—the church court suitor had previously made her law in a prohibition plea and received a final prohibition from the justices—had now devolved to the Court of Arches, '*in contemptum dignitatis et corone regis et lesionem manifestam necnon et dicti Willelmi dampnum et gravamen*'.[36]

If the royal justices issued final prohibitions enforceable by contempt actions to prohibition plea defendants who did not assert that their ecclesiastical causes had been legitimately spiritual, one may ask why any defendant who wanted to maintain a right of action in church court did not simply plead that the cause had concerned some spiritual matter. There is no evidence that the justices issued final prohibitions to defendants who succeeded in proving such pleas, even if by wager of law. And, since compurgation was readily available, proof would not only be fairly easy but false pleas would likely escape detection. Nevertheless, pleas asserting the spiritual nature of ecclesiastical suits were in fact relatively rare. This may have been due to some requirement that evidence, such as

[33] The rolls do not record final prohibitions in all cases in which the defendant did not assert his right to proceed despite the prohibition. However, of the five contempt actions that were brought between 1272 and 1301 upon final prohibitions issued in Common Pleas, two at least cited final prohibitions that had not been enrolled upon determination of the prohibition plea: CP 40/24, m. 27 (1278); CP 40/98, m. 87 (1293). In another contempt suit, Case no. 1.9, the earlier case has not been found, so we do not know whether a final prohibition was recorded. It is possible therefore that a final prohibition was issued. Alternatively, the justices may have omitted to issue formal orders in some cases if the prohibition against further proceedings was implicit in all acquittals in which the defendant did not affirmatively claim a right to proceed further.

[34] In other cases, an aggrieved party could go either to chancery for an original writ or 'directly to the king's justices who might issue a judicial writ to summon the defendant'. Harding, 'Plaints and Bills', 66. The records of contempt cases initiated by judicial writs speak as though the complaint was made directly to the king—e.g., 'Questus fuit domino regi . . .' (CP 40/24, m. 27 (1278)), 'Ostensum fuit domino regi . . .' (CP 40/47, m. 94 (1282))—but in fact the complainant usually petitioned the court that had earlier decided the prohibition plea and issued the final prohibition. But cf. Case no. 1.9, in which a plaintiff brought his complaint (querela) before justices of assize sitting in Devon based on a final prohibition said to have been issued in Common Pleas.

[35] Case no. 1.1b.

[36] CP 40/57, m. 35d (1285). See also Case no. 1.9; CP 40/146, m. 14 (1303).

the libel, be produced before the justices would accept such a plea. *Bracton* recommends that prohibition plea plaintiffs be prepared to offer the suitor's written complaint (*editio*) in support of their claims;[37] a defendant whose church court suit had actually been spiritual would certainly have been willing to do so.[38] Alternatively, a jury's verification of the defendant's plea would have served the same purpose in the absence of documentary evidence. If so this may have been an incentive to choose this mode of proof over wager of law. Similarly, a church court plaintiff, met with a prohibition but determined to proceed in the ecclesiastical forum, could obtain a consultation only upon presenting the libel to a royal justice. Then, should the church court defendant go forward with a prohibition plea anyway (in effect denying the spiritual nature of the cause as presented in the libel), as noted above the church court plaintiff typically would be required to prove by jury an entitlement to proceed in the ecclesiastical forum.

In prohibition pleas not involving consultations that ended in jury verdicts rather than wager of law, final prohibitions did not play a significant role. They seem to have been issued only in unusual circumstances. In one case, the defendant acknowledged the suit in ecclesiastical court, claiming that it was legitimately spiritual, but the jury contradicted his defence.[39] An injunction against further proceedings in church court therefore may have seemed appropriate. In the other case, the prohibition plea plaintiff was acquitted but the circumstances may have rendered that verdict suspect.[40] The prohibition plea plaintiff had alleged delivery of a prohibition to the church court suitor who was said to have thrown it back at him and then trampled upon it (*eam predicto Matheo ejecit et sub pedibus suis conculcavit*). The prohibition plea plaintiff then produced the writ in Common Pleas, with the seal thus damaged (*subpeditatam*), but the jury later said that no prohibition had been delivered so the church court suitor could not have behaved contemptuously toward it as alleged. Judgment therefore was entered for the prohibition plea defendant, but here too a final prohibition may have seemed warranted in light of the apparent evidence that he had in fact ignored a writ of prohibition.[41]

Typically, cases decided by juries did not end with final prohibitions. Final judgment in such cases, based on a jury's factual testimony rather than the ritual of compurgation, seems itself to have provided the guide to whether proceedings might licitly resume in the church court. Jury verdicts of acquittal represented clear statements of the illegitimacy of the prohibition plea plaintiff's claim. Conviction determined the illegitimacy of the ecclesiastical suit; regardless of whether a final prohibition was explicitly ordered, there were to be no further proceedings in the church court. The absence of contempt actions

[37] *Bracton*, 4:274.

[38] For examples, see Flahiff, 'Prohibition II', 266 n. 17. I have found no similar evidence from Edward's reign, but much of what transpired in the royal courts remains hidden behind the formulaic entries. The earlier practice may well have persisted without having been noted on the increasingly formalized court records.

[39] Case no. 1.16a.

[40] CP 40/95, m. 14 (1292).

[41] The court did, however, order the sheriff to produce the prohibition plea plaintiff because of the apparently false representations, 'ad respondendum domino regi quam predictis [prohibition plea defendants] de predictis transgressione et contemptu'. In a third case case involving a final prohibition issued after verdict of acquittal, the prohibition plea defendant made a general denial and a jury verdict affirmed that he had not sued a plea in Court Christian contrary to prohibition: CP 40/145, m. 209d (1303). After a judgment of acquittal the court nevertheless ordered the defendant not to sue further in church court. Nothing in the record suggests why the final prohibition was issued in this case. Perhaps there were special circumstances that were not enrolled.

following jury verdicts—no examples have been found—indicates that the parties to such cases respected their finality.

Most prohibition pleas did not, however, end with jury verdicts, so it is necessary to appreciate the importance of final prohibitions and contempt actions. It should be apparent that the primary accomplishment of the prohibition process was not the identification of offenders or the provision of damages for wronged parties. There were too few convictions for that. Instead, it offered what may have been of greater importance to those who found themselves unjustly impleaded in church courts, namely an effective means of securing the permanent cessation of the suit against him. As the defendant in a legal action, the first thought was not of some abstract jurisdictional question but rather of how to avoid liability. The prohibition process offered a way to do so, if the suit was not a proper matter for ecclesiastical cognizance. Even if the church court judge or plaintiff could not establish that it was, acquittal on the prohibition plea was still easily attained through wager of law, but a final prohibition backed up by the threat of a contempt action—in which trial would be by jury and acquittal therefore would not be so easy—discouraged further proceedings against the church court defendant. The final prohibition was therefore an essential complement to the inadequacy of wager of law in prohibition plea procedure.

Rather than attacking that problem directly by mandating jury trial in all cases, the common law system instead provided a fix that made it possible to retain the traditional form of proof at the defendant's discretion. Even if final prohibitions and contempt actions were effective in halting cases in church courts that did not belong there, it still should be noted that this solution to the problem presented by wager of law came at a cost. A more serious effort to resolve prohibition pleas by determining what had actually happened in church court could have yielded relatively quicker results. One can imagine that church court cases might have continued even after a jury verdict to the effect that the church court judge and suitor had wrongfully disobeyed the writ of prohibition. The fact noted above, however, that there seem to be no contempt cases following jury verdicts for prohibition plea plaintiffs suggests that parties viewed judgments in these cases differently from those decided by wager of law. As we have seen, in those cases it was not uncommon for ecclesiastical proceedings to resume, such that final prohibitions and contempt actions were deemed necessary. Probably because they were viewed by the parties as resolving questions of fact not decided when wager of law was the form of proof, the jury cases seem to have had a measure of finality that wager of law cases did not. If this had been the usual method of proof in prohibition pleas, the more elaborate and therefore lengthier procedure that was more common—prohibition plea decided by wager of law and therefore resulting in acquittal, followed by final prohibition and contempt action triable only by jury—would not have been necessary.

Ecclesiastical sanctions and the prohibition process

It could take quite a while—easily as much as a year or two—for the church court defendant finally to obtain relief in the king's court in the form of the final prohibition. Meanwhile, though canonical procedure was itself often less than expeditious,[42] the church

[42] See Helmholz, *History*, 312; Woodcock, *Canterbury Courts*, 53–54.

court might well have ignored the writ of prohibition and continued to hear the cause even to the point of a definitive sentence. A sentence of excommunication might then provide the basis for a royal writ of caption subjecting the church court defendant to imprisonment pending absolution, which would of course interfere with the ability to prosecute the prohibition plea. Additional common law actions were therefore available to protect church court defendants from ecclesiastical proceedings and canonical sanctions after presentation of a writ. In the eyes of the common law justices such proceedings amounted to contempt, so remedies were available for the users of prohibitions both before and after they had initiated prohibition pleas in royal court.

Where the church court defendant had presented a writ of prohibition to the court and then initiated a prohibition plea, the royal justices could order the prohibition plea defendant to proceed no further in the church court pending resolution of the common law suit. Such injunctions might be issued upon completion of the pleadings and adjournment pending the parties' return to receive the prohibition plea defendant's compurgation or hear the jury's verdict.[43] They might also be issued pending judicial rulings on questions of law before or after completion of the defendant's proof.[44] These orders were not necessarily entered on the record.[45]

If these kinds of injunctions were ignored, the prohibition plea plaintiff could bring a separate action for the contempt.[46] These contempt actions were initiated by plaint rather than original writ.[47] Proof was always by jury.[48]

The specific wrong alleged in these cases was usually the invocation of canonical sanctions against those who had sought writs of prohibition and attachment in order to prevent them from prosecuting common law actions for disobedience of the prohibition.

43 E.g., Case no. 1.2a. See also CP 40/23, m. 2d (1278) ('Prohibitum est etiam predicto Petro sub pena forisfacture quod non ulterius sequatur idem placitum in curia christianitatis etc.'); KB 27/144, m. 15d (1295) ('Et inhibitum est per justiciarios predicto Johanni ne sequatur placitum etc. in curia christianitatis quousque etc.').

44 E.g., CP 40/69, m. 28 (1287) (order issued pending a technical ruling on the pleadings prior to assignment of proof); KB 27/151, m. 8 (1297), printed in *King's Bench, Trinity 1297*, 45–47 (jury verdict taken but final judgment postponed; meanwhile defendant commanded to proceed no further in the church court).

45 See Case no. 1.18a, in which the prohibition plea defendants waged their law and then returned to complete it. No order to halt church court proceedings was enrolled. Later, when the defendants appeared with their compurgators, the prohibition plea plaintiff complained that they had continued the church court case despite having been ordered by the king's justices to proceed no further and that he had filed a bill with the King's Council 'de predicto contemptu'. Common Pleas was nevertheless willing to allow them to complete their law, at which point the prohibition plea plaintiff 'recessit in contemptu domini regis'. Case no. 1.23c refers to a 'breve regis de judicio' ordering a church court judge to proceed no further while a prohibition plea was pending. The record of that plea, Case no. 1.23a, includes no reference to this order.

46 E.g., Case no. 1.2c. See also CP 40/27, m. 98 (1278); KB 27/153, m. 28d (1298), printed in *King's Bench Cases*, 3:60–61 (contempt action based on injunction issued in KB 27/151, m. 8 (1297), printed in *King's Bench, Trinity 1297*, 45–47.

47 E.g., Case no. 1.9. See also Case no. 1.2c; CP 40/21, m. 92 (1277) ('Questus fuit domino regi . . .'); CP 40/115, m. 73d (1296) ('Monstravit domino regi . . . sicut ex gravi querela . . .').

48 In one case involving especially prominent parties—the widow of Edward I's uncle and Edward's first cousin—the complainant offered to prove the defendant's contempt by means of the testimony of a justice of Common Pleas sent to the church court to witness proceedings there in disobedience of an injunction to halt pending completion of wager of law: Case no. 1.2c. He also proffered the church court's own records (acta) attesting to this. Common Pleas evidently accepted the truth of the complainant's evidence when it rejected the defendant's technical objection to the writ and stated that she should respond because she had disobeyed the injunction in contempt of the king. The contempt action nevertheless remained unresolved pending another technical objection to the writ. Whether, given the apparently clear evidence of contempt, the case would still have gone to a jury is unclear.

These common law remedies were necessary because the ecclesiastical judge could apply sanctions—suspension from sacraments and excommunication—against the church court defendant who refused to submit to the church's jurisdiction by ignoring citations to appear before an ecclesiastical tribunal.[49] This would have been the likely course of action for the user of a prohibition. The church court could also proceed to definitive sentence in the defendant's absence, the order for execution of the judgment likewise enforceable by sanctions.[50] In some cases, resort to a writ of prohibition itself was alleged to have resulted in excommunication.[51]

Whatever the psychological or spiritual effects of excommunication, there were important practical and juridical consequences. Excommunicated persons were disabled from suing at common law.[52] However, the prohibition plea *counte* typically alleged excommunication at the suit of the defendant, so it would appear that sentences issued in the course of church court actions that were themselves the subject of prohibition pleas were ignored by the common law courts.[53] As Chief Justice Bereford said in response to a letter of excommunication adduced against a prohibition plea plaintiff in 1312, 'this excommunication is the cause of his plea'; the defendant was then ordered to plead to the main issue.[54] If, however, the prohibition plea plaintiff had been excommunicated for some reason unconnected with the action against him or her in church court, the prohibition plea would be dismissed until absolution had been obtained.[55]

Far more important than the fact of excommunication was the liability of the unabsolved excommunicate to imprisonment. Upon written application from the ordinary, the royal writ *de excommunicato capiendo* issued to the local sheriff, ordering him to arrest and detain one who had not sought absolution within 40 days of the sentence.[56] This procedure worked effectively and more or less automatically. That is, the writ of caption

[49] In England the accused was subject to excommunication if he or she did not appear after three citations. See Drogheda, *Summa Aurea*, 34–35.

[50] Brundage, *Canon Law*, 129–130.

[51] E.g., Cases nos. 1.3 and 1.13. See also CP 40/27, m. 133 (1278). A colourful example is CP 40/149, m. 205 (1304), in which the prohibition plea plaintiff claimed that when he presented a church court judge with a writ of prohibition the latter 'illud fregit et dilasceravit et ad terram projecit et in ipsum Henricum ratione brevis regis sibi prorrecti sentenciam excommunicationis sepius fulmanavit'. For related proceedings involving these parties, see Cases nos. 1.25a and 1.25.b.

[52] *Bracton*, 4:326.

[53] *Bracton*, 4:326–327. For example, a jury stated that a prohibition plea plaintiff, sued in church court for 40 shillings, was suspended from sacraments 'propter suam manifestam contumaciam'. Nevertheless, because the church court suitor in defiance of a writ of prohibition then proceeded to obtain a judgment on his claim and demanded execution of the sentence, Common Pleas held for the prohibition plea plaintiff. Case no. 1.7a. See also Logan, *Excommunication*, 47.

[54] YB 5 Edw. II, 237. But cf. a case from 1295, in which three actions, two by original writ and one by plaint, against the same defendants were combined: a prohibition plea, a trespass suit, and a complaint 'formatum de rotulis ad querelas' alleging excommunication and caption for the purpose of impeding the common law actions. The defendants produced a certificate of excommunication from the bishop of Lincoln stating that the plaintiff 'excommunicatus est . . . propter ipsius contumaciam'. His common law suits were then dismissed 'quousque idem Nicholaus beneficium absolutionis meruerit': CP 40/109, m. 42 (1295). The roll does not record the precise circumstances of the ecclesiastical sentence or reveal whether there was any attempt to argue that the sentence was itself the cause of the plaintiff's action. The outcome of this case seems to have been unique, however, so the plaintiff's excommunication may have been the result of something other than the ecclesiastical suit that was the occasion of his prohibition plea.

[55] E.g., CP 40/141, m. 1 (1302).

[56] See generally Logan, *Excommunication*.

issued *de cursu*, without inquiry into the circumstances or validity of the sentence of excommunication.[57] An action was available against royal officers who failed to carry out its command.[58] Caption thus lent a sharp edge to a weapon that might otherwise have been of limited utility as a means of impeding prohibition pleas.

If arrested and imprisoned on the order of ecclesiastical adversaries, a plaintiff seeking to prosecute a prohibition plea was threatened with loss of the action and amercement by the royal justices for default. Because the caption procedure was so automatic, the common law made available another contempt remedy to protect users of prohibitions from imprisonment designed to impede their access to royal justice. These actions were not based on judicial orders to halt the proceedings in church court issued in the course of prohibition pleas. Rather, the abusive resort to ecclesiastical sanctions and writs of caption was itself sufficient basis for a plaint. So, for example, in 1298 we find a suitor complaining in Common Pleas that the defendants denounced him to the archbishop of Canterbury as excommunicate after they had been summoned to answer for their non-compliance with a prohibition but prior to their appearance before the royal justices.[59] This led to a writ of caption and the complainant's imprisonment for the purpose of impeding his prohibition plea. In other cases, the parties to the prohibition plea appeared and proof by compurgation or jury was assigned but meanwhile the church court case continued resulting in the prohibition plea plaintiff's excommunication and subjection to imprisonment on a writ of caption.[60] Or, writs of caption might be deployed against users of prohibitions before they were even able to initiate a prohibition plea.[61] Here too the purpose was to prevent prosecution and adjudication of the claim that a church court judge or suitor had ignored a writ of prohibition.

These contempt remedies were not innovations of Edward I. *Bracton* includes a writ available to the users of prohibitions excommunicated and imprisoned before they could secure their adversaries' appearance in a royal court in a prohibition plea.[62] There are no examples of its use during Edward's reign until the 1290's; it is common thereafter.[63] Perhaps this was due to some change in church court practices that rendered resort to the already existing remedy necessary. Suitors made use of contempt actions after assignment of proof in prohibition pleas but pending its completion on several occasions throughout the reign,[64] but these remedies too had been available during the reign of Henry III.[65]

[57] See Logan, *Excommunication*, especially pp. 86–87.

[58] E.g., a royal bailiff was summoned to answer why he had ignored a writ de excommunicato capiendo, because 'dominus rex sacrosancte ecclesie in querelis suis deesse non vult': CP 40/130, m. 297 (1299).

[59] Case no. 1.24. See also Cases nos. 1.18b and 1.26b; CP 40/107, m. 61 (1295); CP 40/113, m. 87 (1296); CP 40/116, m. 114 (1297); CP 40/133, m. 94 (1300); CP 40/149, m. 134d (1304); CP 40/152, m. 98 (1304).

[60] E.g., CP 40/21, m. 92 (1277) (contempt suit) and CP 40/19, m. 65d (1277) (earlier prohibition plea between same parties, in which defendant waged his law and day was given for completion but no judicial prohibition enrolled); CP 40/115, m. 73d (1296) (contempt) and CP 40/113, m. 33d (1296) (prohibition plea, in which jury summoned but no injunction); CP 40/163, m. 84 (1307) (contempt) and CP 40/158, m. 231 (1306) (earlier prohibition plea, wager of law assigned).

[61] Case no. 1.19.

[62] *Bracton*, 4:270–271. See also cases cited in Flahiff, 'Prohibition II', 244 nn. 87, 89.

[63] See cases cited above, note 158.

[64] See cases cited above, note 159.

[65] See cases cited in Flahiff, 'Prohibition II', 268 n. 31.

Imprisonment was obviously as much an impediment to prosecution of a contempt action as to a prohibition plea. Accordingly, when a contempt action was filed the royal justices typically ordered the local sheriff to inquire into the true cause of the complainant's detention and, if it were as alleged, release him or her from custody pending resolution of the contempt and prohibition pleas.[66] The justices would not necessarily take the sheriff's response at face value. On one occasion they refused to accept the sheriff's response that the plaintiff was actually imprisoned not on account of his prohibition plea but rather because of a matrimonial offence and unwillingness to submit to penance.[67] According to the court, an unnamed person, acting on behalf of the plaintiff, informed the justices that bailiffs of the archbishop of Canterbury had given this answer to the sheriff's inquiries in order to impede the plaintiff's prohibition plea against two clerks who were in the archbishop's service. Moreover, the court stated, it would also be inconsonant with right and equity and contrary to Magna Carta for the prohibition plea plaintiff to forfeit his claim on account of imprisonment under these circumstances. So, the sheriff was again ordered to release the plaintiff if the circumstances of his detention were illicit. Because of the suspicious circumstances surrounding the plaintiff's imprisonment, Common Pleas eventually granted him safe conduct pending prosecution of his plaint.[68]

As we have seen, the prohibition plea required the defendant to justify having proceeded contrary to a royal writ ordering a halt to the church court case, but there was no liability for the mere fact of having done so if it could be shown that the case was legitimately within the church court's jurisdiction as defined by the common law. Disobedience of a writ of prohibition was a wrong only if the grounds for the prohibition were valid. The availability of contempt actions for continuation of church court suits pending final determination of prohibition pleas seems, however, to contradict this principle; contempt actions were made available upon request, merely upon an assertion that the church court case was continuing despite a writ of prohibition. Were the contempt actions designed to enforce a requirement that all ecclesiastical judges and suitors defer to prohibitions promptly and regardless of their validity until the jurisdictional question was settled in the royal court?

In fact the spiritual nature of the ecclesiastical suit was an acceptable defence in contempt actions just as it was in prohibition pleas; failure to halt church court proceedings while the prohibition plea was pending was not necessarily a wrong. In one series of cases the prohibition plea defendants denied the charges against them and waged their law.[69] Later they returned to complete it, but the plaintiff asserted that he had since been excommunicated by them, despite an order from the bench forbidding further proceedings in the

[66] E.g., 'preceptum fuit vicecomiti quod si sibi constare posset quod predictus Nicholaus occasione predicta et non alia captus et in prisona regis Oxon' detentus sit, tunc ipsum Nicholaum a predicta prisona deliberaverat et ipsum pacem inde habere permitteret, quousque predictum placitum inde inter eos in prefata curia hic motum plenarie terminetur etc.': CP 40/107, m. 61 (1295). See also Case no. 1.24. The sheriff might also be ordered to refrain from executing a writ of caption if the complainant had been excommunicated while a prohibition plea was pending: see Case no. 1.18b.

[67] Case no. 1.24.

[68] In another case, a sheriff returned that a prohibition plea plaintiff was imprisoned for refusal to perform penance after an adultery conviction. It was attested in Common Pleas, however, that he had been arrested and imprisoned at the instigation of the prohibition plea defendants. Process was therefore continued against the defendants and the sheriff was ordered to deliver the complainant from gaol if the cause of his imprisonment was as alleged: CP 40/136, m. 192 (1301).

[69] See Cases nos. 1.18a - 1.18c.

church court. He had on account of this brought a bill of complaint to the king's council and therefore now objected to the defendants being allowed to complete their wagers of law on the prohibition plea. But, rather than treating the contempt charge as evidence of perjury on the part of the defendants, Common Pleas released the defendants and fined the plaintiff for what was construed as his refusal to prosecute his prohibition plea. His contempt action was then considered separately. This finally went to a jury several terms later, which acquitted the same defendants on the ground that the plea in question had been purely spiritual. This was sufficient to justify the ecclesiastical sanctions that had been leveled against the plaintiff pending completion of the prohibition plea.

In another contempt case, it was alleged that the defendants sued a plea characterized as trespass against the king's peace in a church court.[70] Despite a writ of prohibition, they pursued the claim until the complainants were excommunicated. Then they obtained a writ of caption against them. This was done, it was said, in order to prevent a prohibition plea in the king's court. A jury later stated that the ecclesiastical suit had only concerned adultery and was therefore legitimately spiritual. A verdict for the defendant on the contempt action thus excused both defiance of the writ of prohibition and the resort to canonical sanctions.

Problems could arise, however, if a church court judge or suitor successfully defended a prohibition plea by means of wager of law only to have that defence contradicted by a later jury verdict on a contempt action to the effect that the cause in question was in fact not spiritual. This could occur because the contempt action involved the same issue raised in the prohibition plea, that is, whether the church court was justified in ignoring the prohibition. However, a defendant's plea denying proceedings after receipt of a prohibition could be proved by wager of law, while the plaintiff's contempt claim, that sanctions were applied against him or her after delivery of the prohibition, would be decided by a jury. If the defendant's wager of law was in fact dishonest, the contempt action might have provided the occasion for addressing the inadequacy of wager of law in a particular case without eliminating it outright as an option available to prohibition plea defendants. This may have been the motivation behind the several cases beginning during the 1290's in which church court defendants alleged that canonical sanctions had been deployed in order to impede their prohibition pleas.[71]

This problem seems to have been appreciated by the common law justices but it was not resolved during the reign of Edward I. In one series of cases, a church court judge was acquitted on a prohibition plea by wager of law.[72] The following term Common Pleas heard a complaint that the judge had continued to hear the cause in church court while the prohibition plea was pending, resulting in the defendant's excommunication.[73] This was characterized as contempt of the king and a wrong to his crown and dignity. The church court judge responded that he had cleared himself of the charge of proceeding in defiance of a prohibition by means of wager of law. He argued that he therefore should not have to answer the contempt charge because it was merely 'accessory' to the 'principal action',

[70] Case no. 1.19.

[71] See Cases nos. 1.18b, 1.19, 1.23c, 1.24, and 1.25b. Some of these claims were initiated before the prohibition plea defendants' wager of law, some after.

[72] Case no. 1.23b. Records of the church court proceedings are printed in *Canterbury Cases*, 633–89. These do not include reference to the writ of prohibition.

[73] Case no. 1.23c. There was no allegation of caption and imprisonment.

which was the prohibition plea in which he had been acquitted; in effect, there could be no wrong in proceeding to judgment and sanctions if there was no wrong in disobeying the writ of prohibition. The king's representative responded that the judge had been ordered not to proceed further while the prohibition plea was pending—by means of 'the king's writ of judgment' (*breve de judicio*)[74]—and therefore should answer to the king for this contempt, a claim triable by jury. Rather than ruling on this question of law, the court adjourned the case to the next term. On that date it was adjourned again, and then again three times after that. Nothing is recorded after the final adjournment in 1302, so the question remained undecided. While this issue was pending a jury in another proceeding found that the church court plaintiffs' claim in the same ecclesiastical action was illegitimate,[75] so the question of a potential conflict between the judge's successful wager of law and a verdict in the contempt action was especially problematic.

Another contempt action raised the same question and was also left undecided. A prohibition plea plaintiff alleged that the church court judge and suitor proceeded with their case against him after wager of law had been assigned by the king's court, resulting in his excommunication.[76] They later made their law during the same term in which the parties appeared on the plaintiff's contempt action. The church court suitor denied proceeding after his wager of law and proof by jury was assigned. The subsequent verdict stated that he had in fact proceeded against the complainant both before and after his wager of law and explained in detail why the ecclesiastical action was illegitimate, essentially retaliation for an earlier secular complaint brought against the church court suitor. Again, then, Common Pleas was presented with a verdict that contradicted an earlier wager of law. Again the court did not decide the issue.[77]

Year Book cases from the reign of Edward II reveal that this question was eventually resolved, in a manner that preserved the integrity of wager of law in prohibition procedure. A defendant who had waged his law but had been accused of further proceedings pending its completion made his law on the prohibition plea.[78] The court then refused to hear the jury's verdict on the contempt suit, because it might have contradicted the wager, which would have been tantamount to attaint.[79] A contradictory jury verdict thus would not be allowed to call into question a judgment based on a prohibition plea defendant's successful wager of law. Another case further demonstrates the royal courts' determination not to allow contempt actions triable by jury to replace compurgation. Here the plaintiff asked that his contempt suit be decided before the defendant was admitted to complete his wager of law, because the contempt would otherwise go unpunished.[80] Justice Stanton rejected this argument on the ground that a mere allegation of contempt should not prevent

[74] No other references have been found to a writ of this kind. It is possible that when the prohibition plea plaintiff initiated his case the writ of attachment issued against the defendant included an order to halt proceedings in the church court. Whether that was typical practice is unknown.

[75] Case 1.23a.

[76] Case no. 1.25b. The prohibition plea, with the defendants' wager of law, is Case no. 1.25a.

[77] A prohibition plea plaintiff could not avoid this problem by dropping the prohibition plea (and thereby avoiding wager of law) but proceeding with a contempt action triable by a jury. Unless he or she continued to prosecute the prohibition plea, the contempt suit would be dismissed: YB 32 & 33 Edw. I, 15–17.

[78] YB 2 & 3 Edw. II, 138–139.

[79] Chief Justice Bereford said, 'L'atteynt n'est mye grantable in ceo case'.

[80] YB 5 Edw. II, 118–119.

decision of the principal issue in such cases, the prohibition plea itself. In other words, the prohibition plea and its customary mode of proof were to retain priority over contempt actions. Failure to preserve this distinction would have significantly altered the prohibition process, but these cases show that the royal justices were aware of this fact and took steps to prevent that result.

It thus was settled that contempt actions challenging abuse of ecclesiastical sanctions, triable by jury, would not be a way to avoid the consequences of the availability of wager of law in prohibition pleas. (Plaintiffs did, however, have access to final prohibitions against further prosecution by defendants acquitted following compurgation.) Contempt actions still might make it somewhat more difficult for the church courts to employ sanctions against users of prohibitions abusively, by providing for the possibility of punishment in cases in which for some reason prohibition plea defendants were unable to clear themselves. Otherwise, as long as the church court judge and suitor could clear themselves by wager of law after disobedience of a prohibition, they would not be subject to liability for having resorted to excommunication and caption. While the king's courts would protect a church court defendant against further proceedings after wager of law, they would not allow complaints about ecclesiastical sanctions to provide a vehicle for re-trial—by jury—of defences already proved by compurgation.

Before leaving the matter of canonical sanctions it is necessary to consider a suggestion offered by Helmholz.[81] Referring to the copious evidence of non-compliance with writs of prohibition found in the common law plea rolls on the one hand and the lack of evidence of disobedience in the church court records on the other,[82] he proposes that the common law prohibition pleas may in fact have concealed a 'two-stage' process whereby the ecclesiastical tribunals halted proceedings in response to prohibitions but then allowed the suitor to commence a personal action against the user of the prohibition on account of his or her resort to secular authority for the purpose of impeding ecclesiastical justice. One objection to this explanation is the wording of the prohibition plea itself: the plaintiff simply alleged ecclesiastical cognizance of a secular matter in defiance of a prohibition, the suit proceeding until he or she was suspended and excommunicated (*spreta prohibitione secutus fuit quousque suspensus fuit et postea excommunicatus*). The typical entry says nothing about a separate ecclesiastical proceeding aimed at punishing the church court defendant for resorting to a writ of prohibition. Helmholz's point, however, is that the formal, formulaic allegations recorded in the plea rolls may have masked more complex sequences of events. Probably it is impossible to settle this question definitely, but there is reason to view Helmholz's hypothesis with a measure of skepticism. For one thing, he himself notes that there is limited direct evidence in the church court records of ecclesiastical proceedings to punish users of prohibitions.[83] Further, common law court records indicate that such proceedings were considered an offence separate from the mere refusal to defer to a prohibition.

[81] See Helmholz, *Canon Law*, 77–99.

[82] In his thorough survey of the surviving records of the medieval church courts he found no examples of refusal to defer to royal prohibitions. Helmholz, *Canon Law*, 85–86. This phenomenon is discussed below, pp. lxxxii–lxxxiv.

[83] He cites only a few examples, from records spanning over 200 years, in which church courts applied sanctions because 'the interference involved the use of secular legal process'. See Helmholz, *Canon Law*, 90–91.

The plea rolls include entries that observe a distinction between those cases in which the church court simply failed to obey a prohibition and chose instead to proceed with the cause before it and those extraordinary cases in which the ecclesiastical tribunal actually took positive steps to punish the person who resorted to a writ of prohibition. Evidence from the common law records is limited; taken together with the scant ecclesiastical evidence this may mean that these things did not happen very often. Nevertheless, several cases make explicit reference to the sort of two-stage process that Helmholz has suggested, thereby setting them apart from the numerous prohibition pleas in which there was no such indication. In these unusual cases it was necessary for the defendant to reply to the charge of having sued the complainant on account of resort to the writ of prohibition, rather than to the allegation of proceeding contrary to prohibition. This is most obviously apparent in a sequence of two consecutive entries on the Common Pleas rolls, one alleging disobedience of a writ of prohibition and the other refusal to vacate sentences of excommunication issued on account of having used the writ.[84] In other cases the distinction between ignoring a prohibition and taking action against its user is equally clear. In one, the king (nominally the plaintiff) alleged that, whereas a church court defendant produced a prohibition, the ecclesiastical judge immediately excommunicated all those honoring it including the king himself and proceeded to prosecute the defendant and pronounced sentence upon him '*ratione predicti brevis* [*de prohibitione*] *impetrati*'.[85] It was alleged further that the judge ignored subsequent orders from the sheriff of Norfolk on behalf of the king that he revoke the sentences of excommunication. The judge denied issuing these sentences on account of the prohibition and these denials were submitted to different forms of proof. Wager of law was assigned as to the sentences allegedly imposed on the user of the prohibition and those deferring to it and the judge immediately made his law. The claim that the judge had included the king himself in his initial sentence of excommunication was treated separately and was tried by a jury, presumably because the court was unwilling to allow wager of law against the king. Several terms later, a jury appeared and found the church court judge guilty as charged. He was then jailed '*pro contemptu*'. There was no suggestion in this case that the possible invalidity of the original writ of prohibition might have been a defence to charges of having punished the church court defendant for making use of it. Nor was there any attention paid to the inconsistency between the successful wager of law and the jury's verdict.

Another case similarly indicates that a prosecution in church court based on resort to prohibition was viewed as a distinct offence. The defendant in a prohibition plea was also accused specifically of a second ecclesiastical suit against the church court defendant for having used a prohibition.[86] The defendant denied having sued the initial allegedly

[84] The first entry includes an allegation 'de placito quare cum pluries mandavit dominus rex quod [defendants] non tenerent placitum in curia christianitatis de laico feodo ipsius Johannis in Kyngesbrigge et quod sentencias excommunicationis in ipsum ea occasione latas revocarent, prefati episcopus, Ricardus, et Henricus sentencias illas hactenus revocare non curarunt, in regis contemptum et prefati Johannis dampnum gravissimum etc.': CP 40/27, m. 133 (1278) (process entry). The entry immediately following and distinct from this one is the prohibition plea de laico feodo between the same parties, in standard form.

[85] Case no. 1.3. The person who brought the writ of prohibition is not identified as a clerk. The king's status as nominal plaintiff in this case therefore cannot be explained on that ground, as in the ex relatu plurium cases. It probably instead reflects the magnitude of the offence to the king's crown and dignity.

[86] Case no. 1.13.

non-spiritual plea and in addition pleaded that he had not then sued the plaintiff 'on account of any plea brought in the lord king's court or prohibition directed to him'.[87] Jury trial was assigned.

We can never be certain what really lay behind the formulaic plea roll entries, but the fact that some entries departed from standard form may well indicate that differences in substance necessitated special treatment to distinguish them from typical prohibition pleas. At the very least it is clear that an ecclesiastical judge or suitor who yielded to a prohibition but then impleaded the church court defendant again for having obtained it would be liable to answer for a particular common law offence, as would a judge who issued a sentence of excommunication simply because a defendant had produced a prohibition. Given the availability of special remedies for use in such situations, it may be an exaggeration to conclude that ecclesiastical sanctions represented a 'real weapon' for the protection of individual suitors or the church's jurisdictional authority.[88] Instead, Fitzherbert's statement regarding prohibition and excommunication—that 'a Man shall not be punished for suing forth Writs in the King's Courts, whether he have Right or Wrong'—seems an accurate summary of the protection offered by the common law.[89]

* * * * * * * *

Despite certain structural weaknesses—such as the ready availability of writs of prohibition even under false pretenses, wager of law as the usual mode of proof in prohibition pleas, and the liability of prohibition plea plaintiffs to ecclesiastical sanctions and imprisonment—the prohibition process generally functioned in such a way as to protect the legitimate interests of ecclesiastical judges and suitors on the one hand and prohibition plea plaintiffs on the other. The royal courts accepted the spiritual nature of the ecclesiastical suit in question as valid ground for ignoring a writ of prohibition and continuing proceedings against the church court defendant even to the point of excommunication

[87] On the return day, the defendant was acquitted without a verdict being taken because it had somehow become clear that the defendant had not offended the king. The basis for this judgment may have been that no proceedings were taken or sentence issued against the king himself. The record includes nothing further about whether church court proceedings were taken against the real party in interest, the abbot of Winchcomb, and about whether he might have been entitled to a remedy despite the absence of an offence to the king. Case no. 1.3, however, indicates that the wrong in cases like these was not simply to the king but also to the party retaliated against. For another case alleging excommunication in retaliation for use of a writ of prohibition, see CP 40/149, m. 205 (1304). This claim was distinct from separate ones between the same parties alleging disobedience of the prohibition and continued proceedings in church court while the prohibition plea was pending. See Cases nos. 1.25a and 1.25b.

[88] Cf. Helmholz, *Canon Law*, 98.

[89] *New Natura Brevium*, 94. Litigants who had resorted to various common law remedies complained that they were proceeded against in church court on that account. As in the cases in which litigants were sued in church court for obtaining writs of prohibition, here too the church court proceedings were viewed as actionable wrongs in themselves, regardless of the validity of the common law action that gave rise to the church court retaliation. For example, in one case a complainant brought a case in Common Pleas alleging that he was sued in Court Christian for obtaining and then acting on a royal writ of replevin. The church court was alleged to have issued sentences of excommunication against those who replevied the complainant's animals and also against the king, the chancellor, and the chancery clerks: CP 40/70, m. 58 (1288) (process entry). See also CP 40/59, m. 22d (1285) (alleging church court proceeding to punish use of a writ of trespass); KB 27/162, m. 65d (1300) (alleging retaliation in church court for bringing trespass action); CP 40/156, m. 107 (1305) (alleging church court suit to impede land claim brought before king's justices itinerant).

and caption. At the same time, a complainant unjustly impleaded in a church court was protected from further prosecution upon completion of his prohibition plea by means of final prohibitions and the royal justices did not tolerate the use of ecclesiastical sanctions simply to impede the prohibition process or to punish those who resorted to prohibitions.

Perhaps, then, it is unfair to criticize a system that was capable of a fair degree of substantive justice on account of inefficiency. Yet the many procedural steps required for the adjudication of the competing interests must have had a detrimental effect on the way the system functioned in at least some cases. Although judge or suitor could ultimately vindicate non-compliance with an illicit prohibition, the time and expense required to do so may well have encouraged some simply to drop their actions upon receipt of the prohibition rather than contest its validity. Church court records generally do not include evidence of proceedings after receipt of prohibitions, though there may have been reasons why such evidence did not find its way into formal records. The development of writs of consultation to compel judges to hear cases prohibited but actually within the church's jurisdiction probably attests to a certain amount of informal pressure not to disobey even illicit prohibitions. These pressures may also explain the otherwise odd fact that many prohibition pleas were not pursued to a conclusion; cessation of the church court suits against the plaintiffs was probably sufficient in many cases to alleviate the desire for further prosecution of the common law damages claim, which was unlikely to succeed anyway because of wager of law.[90]

The problem was that the system required those wishing to defend themselves from prohibitions to establish their jurisdictional right through litigation in a royal court. In order to secure compensation for this burden the clergy requested that unsuccessful prohibition plea plaintiffs pay damages to defendants who had been vexed unjustly. In fact, it was not current practice in any other kind of litigation for unsuccessful plaintiffs to compensate defendants. Even if that were not the case, however, prohibition procedure could not readily accommodate this request because it must have been clear to all concerned that the availability of wager of law meant that many defendants acquitted were not necessarily 'innocent'. Perhaps the ease with which prohibition plea defendants were able to clear themselves, combined with the common law's acknowledgment of their right to proceed with legitimately spiritual causes despite prohibitions, counterbalanced the troublesome necessity of justifying their activities before the king's justices.

Probably too it should be remembered that prosecution of a common law suit imposed burdens on the patience and finances of suitors. This, combined with the likelihood of amercement for a false claim, may accordingly have imposed informal pressures on church court defendants not to resort to litigation when their prohibitions were disobeyed, pressures corresponding to and counterbalancing those encouraging deference to prohibitions by ecclesiastical judges and suitors.

[90] There are many plea roll entries of various stages in mesne process against prohibition plea defendants that never resulted in actual trial of the dispute. In addition, there are numerous examples of cases in which the parties appeared, joined issue, and had proof assigned, but no reappearance for completion of the proof was recorded and accordingly no final judgment issued. Where they were entered, such reappearances begin with the word 'Postea'. Only about 60 percent of those prohibition pleas to be decided by compurgation have postea's; for jury cases the figure is around 15 percent. Instead of a postea there is only the blank space reserved for its enrollment.

Even if the sum of all these informal pressures and checks and balances was a reasonably just system—at least for those determined to pursue their interests—the prohibition process was not an efficient one if compared to an ideal model capable of accomplishing its aims in a straightforward manner. Initial inquiries into the validity of requests for prohibitions—perhaps by requiring presentation of the libel—could have diminished the need for subsequent litigation. Replacement of wager of law by jury trial in all prohibition pleas would have eliminated a largely perfunctory exercise, although trial by jury could be cumbersome and presented reliability issues of its own. Such sweeping reforms would no doubt have elicited cries of protest from one quarter or another and were probably never seriously considered anyway. So, despite its inefficiency, we should perhaps recognize the achievement of a system that developed so as to offer reasonably effective protection to those who needed it and were willing to persevere in securing it, without unreasonably infringing upon the rights of others.

A final point might be made before turning to the substantive rules that determined the limits of the royal and ecclesiastical jurisdictions in relation to each other. The prohibition process was not itself a 'church and state' controversy. The writ of prohibition was available only to individual litigants at their own discretion; the king did not interfere with ecclesiastical administration of justice unless asked to do so. Decisions to obtain prohibitions were therefore the decisions of individuals. Moreover, the users of prohibitions were clerks as well as lay people. Hence, for example, the need for the *ex relatu plurium* writs designed to relieve clerks of the special pressures discouraging their resort to prohibitions. It was not one's status as clerk or lay person that governed decisions to obtain prohibitions. Rather, it was a matter of the particular circumstances in which individual church court defendants found themselves. Their main concern probably being to avoid conviction, prohibition was simply one of the various available options, an alternative to acquiescence in the church's jurisdiction. Other options included contesting the merits of the church court suitor's claim or taking advantage of procedural protections offered by canon law. The choice of option depended on practical considerations such as a prediction of how the judge would react to a prohibition and, if it were necessary to initiate one, how much a prohibition plea would cost and how it would likely turn out. Ideological considerations—opinions concerning the liberties of the church or the judicial prerogatives of the crown—probably played an insignificant role in such decisions. Particular church court judges might take offence at royal interference and the clergy as a group might object to the constitutional position of the church courts as subject to secular regulations governing the scope of their jurisdiction, but these were broader questions, largely separate from the day to day mechanics of prohibition procedure.

3

PROHIBITION: SUBSTANTIVE LAW

Having considered the writ of prohibition's procedural aspects, it is now appropriate to turn to the substantive rules that defined the writ's scope. This section therefore examines the applicability of prohibitions to various sorts of ecclesiastical causes, as a means by which the royal courts defined the boundaries between the two jurisdictions. The state of the law during the reign of Edward I will be explained, in order to allow an assessment of the extent to which the law applied during the last quarter of the thirteenth century was a departure from previous practice as revealed in case records and in the *Bracton* treatise. Separate discussions of the various forms of prohibition provide the organizational structure, but one area of ecclesiastical jurisdiction subject to prohibition—tithe causes—that does not fall neatly under one such heading will be considered on its own.

Ecclesiastical suits for annual rents will also receive separate treatment, but in the context of the common law writ available for claimants. This discussion forms a part of the next section, on the availability of common law actions for the trial of ostensibly spiritual matters. In fact sections 3 and 4 are complementary: a full picture of the jurisdictional relations of church and state requires not only an understanding of the scope of direct secular intervention—via prohibitions—but also of the indirect impact of available common law actions on the activity of the church courts. It must be stressed that the primary focus of this section is law, not practice. The important question of the extent to which the rules described below actually succeeded in restricting the functioning of the church courts on a daily basis is a separate question, considered at the end of this section.

Prohibitions de laico feodo

The common law forbade the church's exercise of jurisdiction over land and other real property, with the exception of disputes concerning consecrated land known as *elemosina*. *Bracton* defines this as the land granted to a church 'in the name of dower' at its dedication. It was *res sacra*, the property of God, and included churches, chapels, monasteries, and church yards, as well as buildings such as dormitories and refectories necessary to the function of a religious foundation. *Bracton* distinguished such property from other lands or structures held by churches or their personnel in frankalmoin tenure, a species of feudal tenure requiring spiritual service (such as prayers for the donor) instead of military or rent service. Disputes concerning lands of this sort did not enjoy jurisdictional immunity.[91] In order to give effect to this distinction the Constitutions of Clarendon established the assize utrum, whereby a lay inquest stated whether land contested by a layperson and a

[91] See *Bracton*, 4:265, 266, 3:128.

clerk was *elemosina* or *feodum laicum* as preliminary to the settlement of the dispute in the appropriate forum.[92]

While recognizing the church's jurisdiction over this special class of real property the crown refused to allow ecclesiastical cognizance of claims concerning feudal tenure, including claims by clerks to hold land in frankalmoin. Writs to halt suits in church courts *de laico feodo* were among the earliest forms of prohibition, probably instituted in conjunction with the introduction of the assize utrum.[93] *Glanvill* includes both the prohibition and a writ of attachment for non-compliance.[94] *Bracton* cites a prohibition plea heard in 1235 or 1236 to distinguish between an ecclesiastical claim for a church's endowment and one for land held in frankalmoin tenure. The defendant argued that the land pertained to a church as *libera elemosina* but did not assert that it was part of the church's endowment. Therefore the ecclesiastical suit for spoliation was illicit.[95] In contrast, in a prohibition plea heard a few years earlier a chaplain clearly stated that his church court action had not concerned the plaintiff's lay fee but instead was an attempt to recover 'lands which were of the demesne and dower of his church' (*terre que est de dominico ipsius ecclesie et unde ecclesia sua dotata fuit*). A jury was summoned; if it had corroborated his claim the verdict would have served to acquit him of the prohibition plea.[96] Another earlier prohibition plea included in the *Note Book* explained the conceptual basis for the church's jurisdiction in such cases: when the prohibition plea plaintiff took ash-trees from the church yard of a chapel pertaining to the defendant's church, the latter brought suit in church court 'because he had committed sacrilege within his sanctuary'.[97]

Probably the clergy did not insist on wider competence to judge land disputes, at least where churches held property by feudal tenure, because there was no explicit canonical warrant for such a claim. For example, Pope Innocent III, though he elsewhere made statements that by implication claimed the broadest possible jurisdictional authority for the church courts,[98] in his famous decretal *Novit* specifically exempted disputes concerning feudal tenures (*de feudo*) from ecclesiastical cognizance.[99]

There was a possible basis for ecclesiastical jurisdiction over land transactions in the canonical concept of *fidei laesio*: the enforcement of agreements arguably pertained to the church because of its supervision of the sanctity of oaths. This doctrine was of greater importance with regard to agreements involving movable property—it will be discussed more fully in that context—but attempts were made to apply it to certain land disputes

[92] Const. Clar. c. 9, printed in *Select Charters*, 165–166. According to Douglas, Maitland and those who have followed his conclusions 'failed to discriminate between tenure in elemosina, rooted in the particular spiritual quality of the service, and a class of property termed elemosina, to which jurisdictional privilege was attached.': Douglas, 'Frankalmoin and Immunity', 27–28. Cf. Pollock & Maitland, 1:240–251. The point is that a clerk could hold land by frankalmoin tenure (i.e., in elemosina, for prayers or other divine service) but only his church's elemosina was immune from secular jurisdiction. The confusion arose from the medieval use of the term libera elemosina to refer to a church's endowment, a species of tenement, and to a species of tenure (frankalmoin).

[93] See Flahiff, 'Prohibition I', 270–271.

[94] *Glanvill*, 146–147.

[95] *Bracton*, 4:266; see *BNB*, 3:163–164.

[96] *BNB*, 2:424–425.

[97] *BNB*, 2:576–577.

[98] As in Per venerabilem, X 4.17.13. On the broad scope of this jurisdictional pronouncement, which has been subjected to differing interpretations, see Tierney, '*Per venerabilem*'.

[99] X 2.1.13.

during the early thirteenth century. One case from the reign of John suggests that this jurisdictional question had then not yet been settled,[1] but by 1219 breach of a promise was clearly insufficient to confer jurisdiction upon a church court in a land dispute. A prohibition plea decided that year, as well as another decided a year later, resulted from ecclesiastical actions against tenants of land for terms of years who refused to vacate the tenements upon the expiration of their terms. The defendants in both prohibition pleas denied that their suits had concerned lay fee, citing instead the termors' promises to restore the land to them, but in each case the prohibition was upheld.[2] Thereafter, through the reign of Edward I at least, there are no further prohibition pleas in which *fidei laesio* was pleaded as ground for ecclesiastical cognizance of a land dispute. At no time was breach of faith offered as relevant to the contractual aspect of the feudal tenurial relationship, although it centered on an especially sacred oath.

The sacramental aspect of one species of action did, however, extend the church's jurisdiction over real property beyond those claims concerned only with consecrated land. During the middle ages the custom developed that land and other real estate held by burgage tenure—the mode of landholding peculiar to boroughs—were devisable by will, that is, not subject to the general common law rule against testamentary bequests of real property. Claims based on legacies were therefore within the church's testamentary jurisdiction; prohibition did not lie against them.[3] The extent of the tenant's freedom to devise varied from place to place, some boroughs enjoying an unrestricted freedom, others allowing devise of purchased land but not that acquired by inheritance.[4] In some towns no testamentary devise was licit.[5] The question of whether citizens of a particular town enjoyed the privilege—and consequently whether the claim made in an ecclesiastical court for a testamentary bequest of real property was subject to prohibition—was decided in the royal courts. For example, in 1285 a prohibition plea plaintiff accused a woman of suing for 10 shillings not concerned with testament or marriage.[6] She answered that the plaintiff was

[1] *Plac. Abbr.*, 31.

[2] *BNB*, 2:47, 3:402–403. We can perhaps better understand why these disputes went before ecclesiastical tribunals if it is noted that the termor's interest was more personal than real. The lessee, though in possession of the land, did not enjoy a freehold interest (the lessor did); hence novel disseisin and the other real actions were not available. The second case just cited reveals the typically financial purpose of these arrangements, which 'was a matter of commercial contract, not of subinfeudation, . . . so the natural legal remedy of the lessee was a writ of covenant against his lessor rather than a real action': Baker, *Legal History*, 299. If the lessee's remedy was contractual it is not hard to see that the lessor seeking to recover the land after expiration of the term might likewise resort to a contractual action in a church court, even though the proper remedy at common law was a real action.

[3] *Bracton*, 4:273–274. But cf. the addicio at fol. 412b that contradicts this view. On Bracton's confusion, see below, note 4. For burgage tenure generally, see Hemmeon, *Burgage Tenure*, and 'Burgage Tenure'. For devisability of land, see Sheehan, *Will*, 274–281; Bateson, *Borough Customs*, 2:xcii–xciv; Hemmeon, 'Burgage Tenure', 27:43–47 and *Burgage Tenure*, 130–144.

[4] See Hemmeon, 'Burgage Tenure', 27:44–45. Of London *Bracton* says in one place that inherited land is not devisable (4:268), but elsewhere that it could be bequeathed ut catallum whether acquired through inheritance or purchase (3:295). The latter statement according to Thorne was a subsequent interpolation. Hemmeon stated that in London 'there was certainly complete freedom of devise in [Bracton's] day, and no doubt long before' ('Burgage Tenure', 27:43), but Thorne has argued that the 'additions' to the original were inserted after 1236. The later interpolation—and Bracton's treatment of the problem—may reflect the fact that the 'development of freedom of devise proceeded at different rates in different boroughs', in the direction of 'the removal of restraints'. Perhaps changes were occurring in London while *Bracton*'s author was at work on the treatise. See Sheehan, *Will*, 275–276.

[5] Hemmeon, *Burgage Tenure*, 135–138.

[6] Case no. 1.12.

her husband's executor and because her husband had bequeathed to their son 10 shillings in rental income '*prout bene potuit secundum consuetudinem ville de Staundford*' she brought suit before the local dean to effect execution of the testament. The prohibition plea plaintiff denied that it was legitimate to devise 'lands, tenements, or rents' in that town, so a jury was summoned.[7]

While the king's courts reserved the authority to rule on the existence of the privilege, they did not challenge the church' s jurisdiction over testamentary claims for real property in this case or elsewhere if the testator's right to devise that property was established. Cases from the later thirteenth century involving prohibitions *de laico feodo* indicate that by 1272 the jurisdictional arrangement governing real property was well settled. Prohibitions *de laico feodo* during the reign of Edward I reached a wide variety of real property disputes besides simple claims for land,[8] but the litigation resulting from these prohibitions was not complex in comparison, for example, to that involving tithes. The typical attachment suit resulted in the defendant's brief denial of proceeding contrary to prohibition.[9] Occasionally he or she raised an exception to a particular feature of the plaintiff's allegation, but this never resulted in complicated legal arguments recorded in the plea rolls.[10] The legal principles seem instead to have been clear. Moreover, prohibitions *de laico feodo* led to relatively few attachment suits, probably indicating general knowledge and acceptance of the common law's definition of 'lay fee' and its assertion of jurisdiction over it. In the area of real property the boundary between the two jurisdictions was clearly defined prior to Edward I's accession and remained so during his reign.

Prohibitions de advocatione

The Constitutions of Clarendon opened with a statement of the crown's claim to hear all disputes over ecclesiastical patronage in its own courts.[11] In spite of canon law

7 The question could also arise in connection with a real action, as in a mort d'ancestor case in 1291. The tenants denied that tenements in Newcastle had ever been subject to the assize. The claimant admitted that it did not apply to bequeathable tenements, but argued that those which descended by inheritance were not devisable in Newcastle. (Bequeathable land could not be subject to mort d'ancestor. Cf. *Bracton* 3:295.) The claimant later withdrew his writ before judgment was issued, but clearly the court's decision as to whether the assize lay would also have been a decision regarding devisability in Newcastle: KB 27/128, m. 21d (1291), printed in *King's Bench Cases*, 2:51–53.

8 Ecclesiastical claims for rents or services due from freehold lands were also subject to prohibitions *de laico feodo*: Case no. 1.12. See also Case no. 1.7a; CP 40/33, m. 36 (1280); CP 40/64, mm. 61, 64 (1286). Prohibitions de laico feodo likewise lay against claims for pasturage (JUST 1/485, m. 2 (Lincolnshire, 1280) (suit 'de pastura ad centum oves')); easements (CP 40/27, m. 103d (1278) ('de quodam chimino habendo'), CP 40/52, m. 9d (1284)); and for suit to court. CP 40/55, m. 83d (1284) (archbishop of Canterbury allegedly sued the plaintiff in church court 'petendo ab eo quod faceret sectam ad hundredum suum de Canehull pro manerio de Pyninton, quod est laicum feodum suum').

9 E.g., CP 40/9, m. 9d (1275); CP 40/27, m. 165 (1278); JUST 1/1074, m. 17d (Yorkshire, 1279); KB 27/104, m. 17d (1287).

10 E.g., CP 40/54, m. 27d (1284) (acknowledging earlier suit for tithes but denying land claim). Similar is CP 40/80, m. 59 (1289).

11 Const. Clar. c. 1, printed in *Select Charters*, 164. On the jurisdictional arrangement governing patronage, see Gray, 'Ius Praesentandi'.

provisions to the contrary,[12] writs of prohibition were available from the later twelfth century to enforce this determination. *Glanvill* included church court actions concerning patronage as the only causes subject to prohibitions besides those *de laico feodo*. The treatise gave two varieties of prohibition *de advocatione*. One was available to patrons of clerks whose incumbency was the subject of an ecclesiastical suit brought by another clerk claiming to hold the same church at the presentation of another patron. This writ, in the *Indicavit* form, ordered the ecclesiastical judges to halt proceedings until a royal court had decided the question of to whom the right of presentation pertained, 'because disputes concerning advowsons belong to the king's crown and dignity'.[13] The ecclesiastical actions subject to this prohibition did not seek to settle the question of the right of advowson per se—the dispute between the rival clerks was technically for possession only—but they did pose an indirect threat to the true patron's right to present. If the church court awarded possession of the church to a clerk presented by the patron's rival, this possession might ultimately create a new 'right' prescriptively detrimental to the old one.

Because the church courts might also entertain a suit concerned directly with advowson rights, in which the patron was sued by a rival claiming the right to present, another prohibition, in standard form, was available to the patron.[14] Either the *Indicavit* or the standard prohibition *de advocatione* could lead to a writ of attachment and a prohibition plea if ignored by the ecclesiastical judge or suitor. The record might refer to the royal prohibition '*que dicitur Indicavit*',[15] but otherwise it made no difference as far as the prohibition plea was concerned which sort of writ had originally been used against the ecclesiastical suit.

While the lay courts decided disputes concerning the right to present (*jus patronatus*), the actual possession of ecclesiastical benefices was under the jurisdiction of the church; admission, rejection, or deprivation of the patron's candidate were left to the authority of the local bishop.[16] This jurisdictional relationship was well-established by the later thirteenth century. Church courts seem at least occasionally to have attempted to exercise jurisdiction over causes brought by clerks claiming the right to hold a particular benefice, actions that clearly threatened the right of the patron who had presented the incumbent. There was no doubt that according to common law these suits were subject to prohibition.[17] At the same time, only one prohibition plea even suggests that the royal justices were willing on occasion to intrude upon a matter usually supervised by the church. In 1297 prohibition plea plaintiffs accused the defendants of hearing an ecclesiastical suit against a rector presented by the plaintiffs.[18] A rival presentee to the same benefice had initiated the action and allegedly persisted in spite of two successive *Indicavit* prohibitions. The defendants answered that the church court suit had merely concerned accusations of canonical irregularities

[12] See especially X 2. 1. 3, a decretal of Pope Alexander III directed specifically to England: 'Causa vero iuris patronatus ita coniuncta est et connexa spiritualibus causis, quod non nisi ecclesiastico iudicio valeat definiri, et apud ecclesiasticum iudicem solummodo terminari'. But cf. Hostiensis' comment on English practice: 'hanc decretalem non servat curia illustris regis Anglie: immo quicquid dicat papa, ipse cognoscit; vel is cui committit' (quoted in Gray, 'Ius Praesentandi', 487 n. 3).

[13] *Glanvill*, 52. See also *Bracton*, 4:253.

[14] See *Glanvill*, 53, where the prohibition is combined with a writ of attachment. *Bracton*'s example is in standard form, similar to the *de laico feodo*: *Bracton*, 4:252–253.

[15] E.g., CP 40/121, m. 285 (1297).

[16] For discussion, see below, p. cii.

[17] E.g., KB 27/144, m. 15d (1295); CP 40/161, m. 273 (1306).

[18] CP 40/121, m. 285 (1297).

rendering the incumbent unsuitable to occupy a benefice (*super quibusdam criminibus adulterii et incestus et defectus susceptionis ordinum*). The plaintiffs argued that the ecclesiastical action had sought not only the deprivation of their clerk but also the admission of their rival's candidate. Thus this prohibition plea actually involved two distinct issues: the possible loss of the living by the incumbent and the admission of another clerk in his place. Only the second necessarily threatened the plaintiff's advowson right; the first was purely ecclesiastical and should have been recognized as such. But, instead of allowing the church court judges to proceed with it subject to the proviso that the plaintiffs might present a successor if the incumbent were deprived, the royal justices avoided the jurisdictional question by suggesting that the form of the writ of attachment was improper—it was an *ex relatu plurium* but the plaintiffs were lay persons—and adjourned the case. Although no final judgment was issued and there is no other similar evidence of secular interference in this aspect of the church's jurisdiction, the justices may in this case have evaded an unambiguous acknowledgment of the spiritual nature of at least one part of an ecclesiastical action because it seemed to threaten the interests of lay patrons.

The division between the jurisdictions with respect to patronage was not the subject of innovation during the reign of Edward I, but in one instance the crown gave a precise definition to a previously vague rule. Writs of prohibition *de advocatione* lay against ecclesiastical suits that might deprive a church of a substantial part of its tithe income, because the value of the patron's right to present to that living would thereby be diminished. This subject will be discussed more fully below in connection with tithe litigation, but here let it suffice to say that in 1286 *Circumspecte agatis* laid down that the church courts could hear disputes concerning a benefice's right to tithes only if the amount claimed did not exceed one-fourth of its value. The general principle was already well-established and the fraction may have been as high as one-third previously, though the exact limit was uncertain. In the wake of this clarification attempts were made to extend the one-fourth rule to claims for annual rents due from church revenues by means of prohibitions *de advocatione*, but no firm ruling on this question had emerged by the end of Edward I's reign.[19]

There is no evidence in the plea rolls or the clerical *gravamina* that either crown or clergy sought to increase the scope of its jurisdiction over ecclesiastical patronage during the reign of Edward I. By 1272 the canonical basis for such a claim on the part of the church no longer made any difference. Nor did the crown seek for pretenses to alter the jurisdictional arrangement, in place for over a century, that recognized both the spiritual nature of disputes over idoneity and the secular, proprietary aspect of lay patronage.

Prohibitions de catallis et debitis

This writ of prohibition ordered the ecclesiastical judge or suitor to halt prosecution of a cause 'concerning chattels or debts that are not testamentary or matrimonial' (*de catallis et debitis que non sunt de testamento vel matrimonio*). The object of this prohibition was thus a spiritual claim for movable rather than real property, the 'chattels or debts' referring to disputes over goods or money respectively. The implication of the prohibitory clause is that any such suit not based upon the two named sacramental matters was beyond the church's

[19] See below, pp. xciv–xcv.

jurisdiction. In fact, however, the ecclesiastical courts enjoyed a competence over movable property claims that extended beyond these categories to include customary religious payments such as tithes and mortuaries. The church also claimed jurisdiction over oaths and therefore potentially over all sorts of contractual disputes, whether arising from loans or commercial agreements, but these were subject to prohibition if there were no other spiritual basis for the cause. The royal courts also forbade ecclesiastical suits for the collection of pecuniary penances from convicted sinners. Although the scope of the prohibition *de catallis et debitis* was otherwise settled prior to the reign of Edward I, the writ played an important role in the crown's formal assumption early in that reign of jurisdiction over debt claims brought on behalf of as well as against the estates of deceased testators.

The prohibition for chattels and debts was not as old as those concerned with lay fee or advowson. It does not appear in *Glanvill* but was probably available on a routine basis from around the 1220's.[20] *Bracton* discusses the scope of the prohibition *de catallis et debitis*, noting that a prohibition plea defendant's claim that the church court action had actually been a claim for a testamentary legacy or for chattels due as part of a marriage settlement was if proved ground for acquittal.[21] In one case from 1239 a woman produced church court records in support of her assertion that her ecclesiastical suit had concerned goods bequeathed to her in her husband's will.[22] Defendants in another prohibition plea, heard in 1230, argued that the church court action had actually been a claim for four marks promised on the occasion of his daughter's marriage. The royal justices recognized the spiritual nature of this dispute, granting leave for it to go forward in the church court.[23]

The common law courts did not challenge the jurisdictional arrangement discussed in *Bracton* and applied in the cases just cited during the reign of Edward I. In fact the very rarity of prohibition pleas from the later thirteenth century in which such testamentary or matrimonial claims were explicitly at issue strongly suggests that the rule was so well established as to be taken for granted by litigants. There are, however, many attachment cases in which the plaintiff simply alleged that the ecclesiastical suit was for some sum of money or item of property, perhaps a beast or simply some unspecified 'lay chattel', that was not connected with testament or marriage. It is possible that in some of these cases the church court defendant was attempting to halt a legitimate ecclesiastical dispute by misrepresenting its subject matter, but there are no instances in which a royal court refused to accept a defendant's plea stating the true nature of the action. In a case heard during the Norfolk eyre of 1286, for example, a widow, in effect pleading that her ecclesiastical suit had been both testamentary and matrimonial, asserted that the goods at issue had been granted to her by her husband as part of her marriage portion and then left to her in his will. She offered proof by compurgation but the plaintiff dropped his suit against her.[24]

[20] Flahiff, 'Prohibition I', 277.

[21] *Bracton*, 4:249–250, 267.

[22] KB 26/120, m. 23 (1239), printed in Flahiff, 'Prohibition II', 242 n. 78. See also KB 26/130, m. 18 (1243), printed in Flahiff, 'Prohibition II', 285–26.

[23] *BNB*, 2:353–254. The annotator of the Note Book remarked in the margin that prohibition did not lie in the case of money promised in maritagium but did if land was promised.

[24] 'Et [Alicia] bene cognoscit quod ipsa secuta fuit placitum in curia christianitatis versus predictum Rogerum de predictis catallis et debitis, set dicit quod quidam Hugo quondam vir suus die quo ipsam disponsavit concessit ei predicta catalla nomine maritagii et postea in ultima voluntate sua legavit ei predicta catalla, unde dicit quod ipsa implacitavit predictum Rogerum de predictis catallis in curia christianitatis tanquam de illis que fuit [sic] de testamento': JUSTl/578, m. ll (Norfolk, 1286).

Complementary to the rule upon which the widow's defence was based was a judgment issued in a common law debt action heard in Suffolk, also in 1286 by the same justices itinerant.[25] The claimant produced a deed according to which the defendant was one of the pledges (*fidejussores*) for payment of 40 marks due from the father of the claimant's wife on account of a marriage agreement (*pro contractu matrimoniali*). The defendant argued that because the cause was clearly matrimonial the plaintiff's suit pertained to the church's jurisdiction; if he had demanded the money in a church court prohibition would not lie against his claim. Moreover, the defendant continued, if the royal court entertained this claim the plaintiff might recover twice by bringing suit also before an ecclesiastical tribunal. The justices, accepting the defendant's arguments, dismissed the case and invited the claimant to sue in a church court if he wished.

An elaborate case from 1297 suggests that under certain circumstances the common law justices may have been willing at least to consider upholding a prohibition against an ecclesiastical suit for a testamentary legacy, though no final judgment was actually issued.[26] The detailed jury verdict reveals that the defendants had sued a plea in church court for a legacy due them according to their father's will. But this will had been revoked by the testator following recovery from his illness and another one later drawn up instead. The jury stated that the legacies from the more recent testament had been paid. One would assume that the nature of this dispute, clearly involving a claim for a testamentary bequest and the corollary question of the validity of a will, would have provided the necessary grounds for Common Pleas to acquit the prohibition plea defendants. The justices did not do this. After the jury's verdict final judgment was postponed and this aspect of the case, according to the record, left unresolved. Further proceedings on a collateral issue survive. The plaintiffs had also alleged contempt in conjunction with their prohibition plea, on account of the continuation of the cause in church court leading to excommunication pending appearance in Common Pleas on the writ of attachment. On this question another jury said that the defendants had indeed proceeded pending the common law suit against them. Final judgment was again postponed, presumably because the justices could not decide the contempt suit until they had ruled on the principal plea.[27] (As we have seen, acquittal on the ground that the ecclesiastical suit was legitimate was sufficient to excuse the alleged contempt.) Why the justices did not settle the principal matter is not clear. Perhaps they were reluctant to dismiss the testamentary question because of the evident possibility of fraud. At any rate, while this case seems to represent a failure to respect the jurisdictional rule regarding claims for testamentary legacies, neither here nor in any other prohibition plea from the reign of Edward I did the royal justices issue a judgment explicitly ignoring the rule. Nor did they consider claims for testamentary legacies sued at common law.

Writs and pleadings usually spoke as though the church's jurisdiction over claims for money or other chattels included only those based on a testamentary bequest or a marriage agreement. In fact the ecclesiastical courts enjoyed a general competence over disputes concerning religious dues and offerings, prohibitions *de catallis et debitis* notwithstanding.

[25] Case no. 2.6.

[26] Case no. 1.23a. For the extensive records of the church court proceedings, see *Canterbury Cases*, D.19.

[27] Case no. 1.23d. The ecclesiastical judge in these proceedings acquitted himself by wager of law. The contempt action against him was left unresolved (Case no. 1.23c), presumably because a jury verdict would have amounted to attaint of his wager. For discussion of this point, see above, pp. xlvii–xlix.

Of greatest importance was jurisdiction over claims against parishioners for failure to pay tithes. The relation of this form of prohibition to tithe litigation will be discussed in a separate section below. As to other sorts of religious payments, several cases survive in which the prohibition plea plaintiff alleged unsuccessfully that a rector had brought suit before an ecclesiastical tribunal, claiming a cow or other beast, contrary to a writ of prohibition. In response the rector stated that his claim had been for a mortuary rather than the plaintiff's 'lay chattel'.[28]

The common law courts did exercise control over mortuary claims in one respect. The rights of rectors to beasts from the estates of their deceased parishioners was based upon local custom, which varied widely.[29] If the plaintiff in a prohibition plea denied the defendant's right, the royal courts used local inquests to determine whether local custom did in fact support the rector's claim. This question arose in a case heard in Common Pleas in 1291.[30] The defendant stated that he had prosecuted a claim for two bulls in his capacity as executor of a recently deceased rector to whom the animals pertained as mortuaries due from two deceased parishioners. The prohibition plea plaintiff countered that according to local custom he and his ancestors had always received the best beast of a deceased tenant as a heriot; he therefore claimed the animals in question as his own. The defendant in turn alleged that it was customary for the best beast to go to the rector and offered to prove this fact by a jury verdict. The jurisdictional arrangement was here similar to that governing disputes over tithes or testamentary bequests of real property. When the legitimacy of a claim depended upon local custom, the royal courts assumed the authority to decide what was customary. Once this was settled the claim itself was left to the church courts for adjudication.

In addition to the church's jurisdiction over tithes or mortuaries the common law allowed ecclesiastical courts to hear suits for goods or money claimed as oblations or obventions. So, for example, in a prohibition plea *de catallis et debitis* heard in 1285 the defendants stated that they had resorted to canonical sanctions to compel certain parishioners to contribute bread for distribution as alms (*panis benedictus*). The plaintiffs' suit was dismissed when they were unable to show that this was not legitimately a matter for the church's jurisdiction.[31] This rule was at least as old as the mid-thirteenth century.[32] Again, questions of local custom were reserved for the common law courts, as in a case from 1263 in which the prohibition plea plaintiff asserted that an offering claimed as obligatory by the defendant was actually strictly voluntary.[33]

[28] E.g., Case no. 1.26a. In another case, a rector was accused of suing a plea 'de quodam bove ipsius Laurencii precii unius marce'; he replied 'quod ipse nuncquam secutus fuit placitum in curia christianitatis de laycis catallis predicti Laurencii etc., set dicit quod quidem Robertus le Chapeleyn parochianus ipsius Fulconis obiit, ratione cuius mortis idem Fulco de consuetudine etc. habuisse debuit de catallis predicti Roberti etc. Et quia quedam bona et catalla predicti defuncti ad manus predicti Laurencii devenerunt et dicebatur idem Fulco de mortuario habendo de catallis predicti defuncti traxit eum in placitum in curia christianitatis et per consultationem inde habitam per G. de Thornton tunc justiciarium ad placita regis etc. placitum illud secutus fuit in eadem curia etc. Et quod nullum aliud placitum secutus fuit in curia christianitatis de laycis catallis predicti Laurencii petit quod inquiratur per patriam': CP 40/121, m. 268d (1297). For similar cases, see CP 40/68, m. 20 (1287); CP 40/87, m. 115d (1291); CP 40/91, m. 59d (1291); CP 40/102, m. 174 (1293).

[29] See *Canterbury Cases*, 80.

[30] CP 40/91, m. 81d (1291). This case, incorrectly ascribed to the Middlesex eyre of 1294, is reported at YB 21 & 22 Edw. I, 588–591. We are indebted to Dr Paul Brand for this reference. See also YB 30 & 31 Edw. I, 440–447.

[31] CP 40/60, m. 50d (1285), printed in Flahiff, 'Prohibition II', 288–289.

[32] See cases cited in Flahiff, 'Prohibition II', 261 n. 85.

[33] Prynne, *Records*, 3:120–121. According Dr Paul Brand, this case came from the 1263 Sussex eyre.

While recognizing the church's competence to judge claims for goods or money claimed as testamentary legacies, gifts made in connection with marriages, or customary religious payments, the royal courts refused to allow ecclesiastical jurisdiction over commercial contracts, debts, fines, and certain pensions and annual rents.[34] These matters could potentially come before a church court for several reasons, including the clerical status of one or both of the parties, prior recording of an obligation before a local ordinary, the sealing of an agreement with an oath, or the arguably spiritual nature of the obligation or exaction. The practical question of the extent to which the crown actually succeeded in removing such matters from the church courts is considered below. Here it is necessary to consider how prohibitions *de catallis et debitis* provided the opportunity for the restriction of ecclesiastical jurisdiction in these areas.

There are numerous prohibition pleas in which a plaintiff alleged a suit in church court '*de debito*' of a certain sum not connected with marriage or testament.[35] Rather than attempting to justify resort to ecclesiastical jurisdiction the defendant usually made a general denial of having proceeded contrary to the prohibition. In such cases the record rarely indicates the circumstances of the debt, because it was only necessary for the plaintiff to allege that the ecclesiastical suit was for a sum '*quod non fuit de testamento vel matrimonio*', to which a general denial was sufficient reply. Sometimes, however, we see that the church court suit was an attempt to compel the repayment of a loan[36] or to collect money due for goods sold.[37] Prohibitions *de catallis et debitis* also lay against actions in church courts for goods claimed as the result of an unperformed commercial contract. This probably accounts for some at least of the many prohibition pleas heard during the reign of Edward I in which the defendant was said to have brought suit in church court claiming some specific chattel, although the precise nature of the obligation upon which the claim was based was not explained.[38]

The church's claim to judge such cases was based on two separate principles. One centered on the ecclesiastical status of the parties to the dispute, or at least of the defendant, and was accordingly less broadly applicable than the other. The clergy complained in 1285 that clerks and other *religiosi* who made recognition of loan agreements before their ordinaries were being prevented from bringing attempts to enforce repayment before ecclesiastical tribunals.[39] Similarly, a petition presented in 1295 or thereabout asked that church courts hear all pecuniary causes between two clerks or between layman and clerk if the latter were the defendant.[40] Both statements reflected the belief that suits against

[34] For detailed consideration of pensions and annual rents, see below, pp. lxxxviii–ci.

[35] E.g., CP 40/19, m. 39d (1277) (15m.); CP 40/41, m. 80d (1281) (20*s*.); CP 40/80, m. 19d (1289) (10m.). Many other cases cite sums of money 'not concerned with testament or marriage' without mentioning a specific amount.

[36] E.g., the defendant was accused of suing the plaintiffs in church court 'petendo ab eis viginti libras ex cause mutui': CP 40/89, m. 58 (1291).

[37] E.g., CP 40/79, m. 74 (1289) ('de quodam debito quinque solidorum pro blado eidem Jocelino vendito'); CP 40/98, m. 130 (1293) ('de debito triginti solidorum pro quodam equo ab eisdem Simone et Thoma empto ut ipsi asseruerunt').

[38] E.g., CP 40/61, m. 49 (1286) (65 sheep); CP 40/79, m. 76 (1289) ('de una tunica'); CP 40/89, m. 130d (1291) ('unum plumbum staunticium precii sex solidorum et octo denariarum et unum manuale molendinum precii trium solidorum'). Sale contracts were not, of course, the only possible basis for ecclesiastical suits for chattels such as these.

[39] *Councils & Synods*, 971–972.

[40] *Councils & Synods*, 1143.

clerks were better heard by the church, all the more so if both parties had voluntarily submitted to its jurisdiction. Nevertheless the common law stoutly resisted such assertions.[41] According to *Bracton*, debt actions were for secular determination, on account either of the secular nature of the object of the action, a debt, or of the cause of the action, a contract (*ratione rei* [*quae petitur*] *vel contractus*); the clerical status of one or both of the parties did not alter the lay forum's competence.[42] Nor did a prior agreement to submit to the church's jurisdiction exempt an ecclesiastical suit from prohibition: the parties could not by their own consent alone renounce recourse to secular justice because this was prejudicial to another interested party, the crown.[43] There is no evidence that the crown retreated from these positions during the reign of Edward I.

The more widely applicable basis for ecclesiastical jurisdiction over contract was the canonical concept of *fidei laesio*, which gave the church potentially far-reaching competence over all manner of agreements in which a contracting party—lay or ecclesiastic—pledged an oath to perform some obligation and then broke the pledge by failing to do so. As Maitland wrote, one 'who pledges his faith, pawns his Christianity'.[44] The crown acknowledged that correction of the sin of perjury was the church's responsibility, but the ecclesiastical courts might also attempt to go further, applying sanctions to compel specific performance of promises confirmed by oaths.[45] William of Drogheda, the author of a treatise on canon law procedure left unfinished by his death in 1245,[46] stressed the connection between the church's penitential duty and the enforcement of contracts, while warning that the crown would not readily condone the latter. He advised that the advocate seeking to recover a debt compose the libel carefully, without mentioning the sum of money claimed by the plaintiff. If the defendant were found liable the judge would assign penance for the sin of perjury, which would not be absolved until the guilty party had paid the amount due. Thus would the claimant recover the debt indirectly and avoid a writ of prohibition.[47] Presumably a similar indirect course would be required for recovery of goods where the claim was unconnected with marriage or testament.

Advice such as Drogheda's notwithstanding, the crown rejected the church's authority to enforce promises to pay money during the reign of Henry II. The Constitutions of Clarendon included a statement that pleas concerning debts were for royal justice, regardless of whether there had been a pledge of faith.[48] A case included in *Bracton*'s *Note Book* reveals the rule in operation in the early thirteenth century. In 1220 a woman accused a man of suing her unjustly in ecclesiastical court, claiming four marks not related to

[41] Canonical claims to jurisdiction ratione personae was rejected in England from an early date. See Helmholz, *Canon Law*, 110.

[42] *Bracton*, 4:249–250.

[43] *Bracton*, 4:251.

[44] Pollock & Maitland, 1:128.

[45] See X 1.35.3 ('Studiose agendum est [per judices ecclesiasticos], ut ea, quae promittuntur, opere compleantur') and Sext. 2.2.3, referring specifically to jurisdiction over laymen ratione iuramenti. Informal words of consent were sufficient to create a sacramental obligation. X 1.35.3 (with the rubric 'Pacta quantumque nuda servanda sunt'). Hostiensis stressed this point: 'Ut modis omnibus servetur, etiamsi sit nudum secundum canones . . . quia inter simplicem loquelam et iuramentum non facit Deus differentiam.' Quoted in Pollock & Maitland, 2:195 n. 2. See also C. 22 q. 5 c. 12. See generally *DDC*, 7:993–1001; Esmein 'Serment Promissoire'.

[46] On Drogheda and his work, see de Zulueta, 'Drogheda'.

[47] Drogheda, *Summa Aurea*, 66–67.

[48] Const. Clar. c. 15, printed in *Select Charters*, 167.

testament or marriage. He attempted to justify his suit on ground of breach of faith (*de fide lesa pro predictis marcis*). Although the plaintiff's prohibition plea was dismissed—because she was not answerable without her husband—the defendant was nevertheless ordered to proceed no further with his ecclesiastical action.[49] Over a half century later Edward I declared that '*cognitio contractus de debito*' had always pertained to the secular courts and even if he wished to do so the barons would not allow him to decree that prohibitions should not issue against church court actions of that kind.[50]

Another early case shows the common law's opposition to the application of breach of faith doctrine to promises to deliver goods. Following a recovery of land in a royal court the successful party agreed to hand over to the former tenant the next crop to be harvested from the land (*fidem dedit de restituenda ei investitura in autumpno*). The promise was breached, prompting a church court action, but a prohibition plea resulted in judgment against the claimant and an order to refrain from further prosecution.[51] *Bracton* states that a claim for 'any secular article' based on a commercial agreement pertained to the secular courts.[52] Since it is elsewhere said that the very fact of sale changes chattels such as tithes from spiritual to temporal,[53] any claim for goods resulting from a sale was necessarily secular. As far as the common law was concerned, pledge of faith did not alter the secular nature of contract disputes.[54] The royal courts continued during the reign of Edward I and thereafter to apply this principle to contract disputes involving debts and chattels.

Another aspect of ecclesiastical justice subject to prohibitions *de catallis et debitis* was the imposition of pecuniary penance by the church courts. The competence of the church over such an obviously spiritual matter as the assignment of penance for the correction of sin was not directly questioned, but the common law forbade assignment of any but corporal penance, just as it objected to the enforcement of contracts under colour of correction of sin. In 1280 the crown stated that the church courts could not impose '*penam pecuniariam*'; if an attempt were made to exact the money by ecclesiastical sanctions prohibition would lie. If, however, the guilty party willingly agreed to substitute a money fine prosecution to collect it would not be subject to prohibition.[55]

Cases from *Bracton*'s *Note Book* indicate that the rule against involuntary pecuniary penance was an old one. In a prohibition plea from 1233 a prior claimed that contrary to the plaintiffs' allegations he had sued them in church court for a spiritual offence (violence against his clerks) and upon conviction had assigned no pecuniary penance.[56] Another

[49] *BNB*, 3:335. Cf. a prohibition plea arising from an ecclesiastical suit in which a judge 'fecit citari eundem Nicholaum quod esset responsurus de lesione fidei sue per quam se obligavit ad solucionem predictorum denariorum faciendam'. The judge pleaded as warrant for proceeding 'de debito' an agreement between the parties submitting to the church's jurisdiction, on account of which the royal justices dismissed the prohibition plea. The annotator of the *Note Book* wrote 'Error' beside this entry; *Bracton*'s disapproval of the judgment is at 4:268–269.

[50] This statement resulted from a papal nuncio's query as to the validity of a prohibition. He had been ordered by the papal curia to proceed with a rector's appeal in an action of debt despite a prohibition. See *Councils & Synods*, 1090–1091.

[51] *BNB*, 2:516–517.

[52] *Bracton*, 4:265.

[53] *Bracton*, 4:282.

[54] 'si in foro seculari agatur de aliquo placito quod pertineat ad coronam et dignitatem regis, et fides fuerit apposita in contractu, non propter hoc pertinebit cognitio super principali ad iudicem ecclesiasticum': *Bracton*, 4:249.

[55] *Councils & Synods*, 875.

[56] 'non fuit eis inflicta aliqua pena pecuniaria, immo quod disciplinas haberent in diebus festinis': *BNB*, 2:585–586.

entry records a prohibition plea defendant's undertaking to wage his law that he had not attempted to exact 15 marks '*nomine pene*' from the plaintiff.[57]

Circumspecte agatis seemingly modified the crown's stand on pecuniary penance in 1286 by allowing that some mortal sins could be punished either by fine or corporal penance. In practice, however, the older rule seems to have remained in force. In a prohibition plea heard in 1295 the defendants, accused of suing and holding a plea for a one mark debt, put themselves upon a jury, which reported that the plaintiff had been convicted in church court of fornication and been sentenced to corporal penance.[58] The Common Pleas justices then asked the jurors if the ecclesiastical judge had attempted to exact any money (*aliquam pecuniam numeratam*) from the church court defendant. He had not, so the defendants were released. Similarly, a suit on a prohibition *de transgressione*—this form will be discussed below—resulted in a jury's verdict that the ecclesiastical cause had actually been '*de adulterio*'.[59] Again the court asked specifically if a money fine had been demanded of the plaintiff. It is possible that some of the many prohibition pleas from throughout the reign of Edward I that alleged illicit suits for small sums of money resulted from attempts to exact money involuntarily in lieu of corporal penance. There are no instances from before or after *Circumspecte agatis* of attempts to justify such exactions explicitly.

The crown's policy toward pecuniary penance may have been based on a similar attitude expressed on occasion by the English episcopacy.[60] Papal legates also condemned the practice in English church councils, in accordance with canonical doctrine.[61] It may therefore be misleading to interpret the common law's objection to pecuniary penance as an intrusion upon the church's penitential authority. Some members of the clergy probably supported the royal policy.

While there was no expansion of the scope of the prohibition *de catallis et debitis* during the reign of Edward I in the areas so far discussed, in one important respect there was a potentially significant jurisdictional innovation. *Bracton*, following cases decided earlier in the reign of Henry III, states that an executor could bring an ecclesiastical action to claim a debt owed to the testator if the debt had been clearly recognized or proved (*recognitum sit et probatum*) during the testator's lifetime; as such it could legitimately be considered already among his or her assets.[62] In addition, it would seem, an executor could be sued by a creditor in church court for a debt under the same condition. If the claim for or against the estate of the deceased were contentious a secular court was to hear it. The alleged debt would be claimed by or against the heir, not the executor.

By early in the reign of Edward I the jurisdictional situation had changed, in the direction of greater competence for the secular authority and a correspondingly restricted sphere for the ecclesiastical. In 1280 the clergy complained that prohibitions were preventing

57 *BNB*, 2:679.
58 Case no. 1.18c.
59 Case no. 1.19.
60 E.g., synodal statutes for Exeter diocese, 1287, cc. 5, 31, printed in *Councils & Synods*, 994, 1028; statutes for Winchester diocese, ca. 1295, c. De penitencia, printed in *Reg. Pontissara*, 1:222.
61 See legatine council of Otto, 1237 c. 20, printed in *Councils & Synods*, 254, where acceptance of money in lieu of penance is described as simoniacal. This statute was confirmed by the legatine council of Ottobuono held in 1268 c. 19, printed in *Councils and Synods*, 768. The latter included a reference to a text of Isidore incorporated in the Decretum as C. 11 q. 3 c. 72. See also X 5.37.3.
62 *Bracton*, 4:267–268. For early cases, see *BNB*, 2:132, 620–621.

executors from bringing claims in church courts for debts owed to deceased testators. Neither this complaint nor the royal response mentioned the distinction between recognized and unrecognized debts stated in *Bracton*. The crown replied that legacies of money or other chattels 'in the hands' of the deceased could be claimed in ecclesiastical courts; but if not the executor or the legatee was to make the claim against the debtor in the lay forum, just as the deceased would have done while alive. The reason given was concern that the debtor not be in a worse position vis-à-vis his or her creditors than would have been the case prior to the testator's death. The implication was that the obligation might be proved more easily before an ecclesiastical tribunal.[63] The royal statement suggests an unqualified stand against ecclesiastical actions for debts brought by executors.

Again in 1285 the clergy urged that the church's testamentary jurisdiction not be divided by the reservation of debt cases to the royal courts; it was often not possible to implement the deceased's will because of the expense and inconvenience of suing at common law. On this occasion the crown answered succinctly that cognizance of debts owed to deceased testators would not be granted to the church courts.[64] Such claims were no longer within the church's jurisdiction. Moreover, the common law courts now treated the executor as the proper representative of the testator, at least as far as collection of debts was concerned.

The clerical complaints of 1280 and 1285 and the crown's responses suggest that exclusive royal jurisdiction over debt claims brought by executors was a novel development. Maitland wrote that chancery made available common law writs of debt for executors some time during the early years of Edward I.[65] This would have been a necessary complement to a new policy denying the church's jurisdiction in such cases. The earliest example of executors using the writ of debt during Edward's reign is from Hilary term, 1279.[66] In fact, there are instances of such claims from the reign of Henry III.[67] So, while the 1279 action could have provoked the clergy's grievance, it is more likely that newly issued writs of prohibition against debt claims brought by executors in church courts were the actual provocation. No pre-1280 prohibition pleas involving such writs can be identified, but it is possible some are hidden behind the formulaic statement of the prohibition plea plaintiff's claim (alleging a suit in church court for a debt that was not testamentary or matrimonial) and the defendant's opaque general denial and wager of law.

The clergy's complaints did not refer to debt claims brought *against* the estates of deceased persons. The earliest example of such a claim from Edward I's reign also appears on the roll for Hilary term, 1279.[68] That roll also records a claim in which executors of one man sued those of another.[69] Later that year a creditor recovered 10 marks by writ of

[63] See *Councils & Synods*, 875–876. The crown's statement included a reference to a novel distinction introduced by Walter de Merton, chancellor from 1272 to 1274, that recognized ecclesiastical jurisdiction over claims for chattels in the hands of the testator's debtors but bequeathed by name (specialiter et nominatim alteri legetur). The crown disapproved of this but expressed an intention to look into it further.

[64] *Councils & Synods*, 958. There was no further mention here or elsewhere of Walter de Merton's distinction referred to in 1280.

[65] Pollock & Maitland, 2:347. Maitland did not explain why this may not have occurred earlier, that is, after *Bracton* but before 1272. He cited cases from early Year Books, but the earliest of these dates only from 1292.

[66] CP 40/28, m. 47 (1279) (process entry).

[67] Dr Paul Brand has found several examples.

[68] CP 40/28, m. 50 (1279) (process entry).

[69] CP 40/28, m. 72d (1279) (process entry).

debt from the executors of a deceased debtor.[70] These claims too were not novel; there are instances of debt actions brought against executors from the reign of Henry III.[71] However, also in 1279, we find a prohibition plea in which the plaintiff alleged that the illicit ecclesiastical suit had been a debt claim against executors of the bishop of Norwich.[72] All of this seems to indicate a determination by the crown, early in the reign of Edward I, to assert exclusive jurisdiction over litigation involving debts owed by or to deceased testators.

A Common Pleas case decided early in 1280 suggests that the jurisdictional innovation was then still recent and potentially destabilizing. A plaintiff in a common law debt action asserted a claim based on a bequest included in a will.[73] As such, the claim differed from those brought against executors arising out of obligations incurred prior to a testator's death. The royal justices ruled that debt did not lie against executors if the money sought was a testamentary legacy and dismissed the claim to the church courts. This restatement of the traditional rule was necessary to preserve the jurisdictional distinction recently blurred by the introduction of common law debt actions against executors. The claimant in this case had in effect been attempting to determine how far the common law courts intended to go in extending the scope of their jurisdiction over claims against executors. In a 1285 case, justices itinerant accepted a prohibition plea defendant's plea that her church court action had been for a testamentary legacy and allowed her to wage her law.[74] In another case, King's Bench told the king's attorney to sue in Court Christian if he wished to obtain implementation of a testamentary bequest to support a chantry in honor of the royal family.[75]

Thus, while preserving the church's jurisdiction over claims based on testamentary bequests, the royal courts appear to have assumed exclusive jurisdiction over claims involving debts owed by or to deceased testators during the 1270's.[76] This was the only innovation in the scope of the prohibition *de catallis et debitis* during the reign of Edward I.[77] Though potentially significant, in fact this development was of limited practical significance, as will be seen below.

Tithe litigation and prohibitions

Before considering the other forms of prohibition it is necessary to treat the extent to which the church's jurisdiction over tithes was subject to prohibitions *de catallis et debitis* and *de*

[70] CP 40/31, m. 12d (1279). This case, based on a claim arising out of a sale of goods transaction, was decided by a jury because the executors were barred from waging law on behalf of the deceased. Also on this roll are process entries for debt claims against executors (m. 101) and by executors (m. 99d).

[71] Again, we are indebted to Dr Paul Brand for this information.

[72] CP 40/31, m. 118d (1279) (an *ex relatu plurium* case).

[73] Case no. 2.2.

[74] Case no. 1.14.

[75] KB 27/124, m. 70 (1290), printed and translated in *Parl. Rolls*, 352, 398. Subsequent proceedings may be found at pp. 352–354 and 398–400.

[76] The second Statute of Westminster laid down that bishops were to answer at common law for the debts of intestates, just as executors would if the deceased had made a will: Stat. West. II, c. 19, printed in *SR*, 1:82. This development was the logical extension of the common law's assumption of jurisdiction over debt claims brought by or against executors, a development initiated by the judges rather than by parliament.

[77] The crown further strengthened the executor's position as representative of the deceased at common law by making available the writ of account in 1285 to compel a bailiff to render an accounting of a receivership. St West. II c. 23, printed in *SR*, 1:83. See Baker, *Legal History*, 363–364. With regard to movable property, the executor, in Sheehan's phrase 'the creature and darling of the ecclesiastical courts' (*Will*, 230), replaced the heir in the common law courts by the end of the thirteenth century.

advocatione. This problem gave rise to often complex litigation in the royal courts during the reign of Edward I, but the justices maintained the necessary distinction between those tithe disputes purely spiritual and those that because of some secular aspect were justiciable at common law. The latter included suits for money due in return for tithes sold and claims for tithes of sufficient magnitude to affect substantially the value of an advowson. The common law's jurisdiction over trespass also brought certain tithe disputes before the royal courts, but as this did not involve prohibitions discussion in detail is reserved for section 4 below.

There are numerous instances in the plea rolls from throughout the thirteenth century in which a defendant accused of suing or holding a plea in a church court for goods or money '*que non sunt de testamento vel matrimonio*' denied that the suit had involved the plaintiff's lay chattels and claimed instead that its subject had been tithes. In most of these cases the common law records tell us little about the precise nature of the tithe action, but it is apparent that they typically involved causes in which a parson had cited a resident of his parish for refusal to pay his or her tithes. This was spoliation, a wrong punishable by excommunication.[78]

Bracton states that prohibition did not lie against actions for spoliation of tithes heard in church courts.[79] Because they aimed only at the recovery of property possessed by established right without themselves raising the issue of right they did not threaten the interests of other potential claimants. Moreover, the possible right of another patron to present a clerk to a benefice with a right to receive that income would not be implicated or impaired. Accordingly, *Bracton* emphasizes that the spoliation must be recent: clearly if tithes had been withheld for a long enough time a prescriptive right against their payment would develop, especially if in the meantime the parishioner had been paying the tithes to someone else. If the rector had not recently been in possession he could not claim spoliation; his action would instead be an assertion of a competing right and therefore be of potential concern also to the patron of the church whose rector had meanwhile been receiving the tithes in question.[80]

The common law courts during the reign of Edward I continued to accept pleas of spoliation of tithes in defence of allegations that church court suits had concerned lay chattels and therefore were subject to writs of prohibition *de catallis et debitis*. For example, the prior of Farley stated that 'he is parson of the church of Chippenham, in whose parish Nicholas (the prohibition plea plaintiff) has two mills, and because Nicholas detained his tithes from one of these he sued him in a church court'.[81] In another case an ecclesiastical judge asserted that the church court suitor, a rector, had brought an action for tithes due on the increase from a parishioner's woodland and poultry (*decimas provenientes de proficuo bosci et pullorum*).[82] He justified proceeding despite the prohibition by virtue of a consultation stating that '*in huiusmodi placitis de decimis licite posses procedere*'. In other cases defendants indicated

[78] See X 3.30.5, 6.

[79] *Bracton*, 4:269.

[80] Flahiff discusses the distinction between possessory and proprietary actions, citing cases from before 1272 in which prohibition plea juries were to say whether the defendant had been receiving the tithes at issue. If so the ecclesiastical suit was legitimately de decimis, being concerned with spoliation, and a matter for a church court. If, however, the claim was for tithes that had previously pertained to the prohibition plea plaintiff's church the dispute was usually justiciable at common law because patronage rights were at stake. See Flahiff, 'Prohibition II', 273 n. 53, and the case quoted at 274 n. 58. For early cases in which spoliation claims were allowed to the church courts, see *BNB*, 2:170–171, 679–680.

[81] CP 40/38, m. 21 (1281).

[82] JUST 1/1089, m. 17 (Yorkshire, 1293).

clearly that withholding of tithes was the basis for their causes in church court, sometimes mentioning spoliation explicitly.[83]

Disputes about the manner of tithing were also granted to the church's jurisdiction.[84] For example, a parishioner objected to a parson's demand that tithes of grain be set aside in the form of shocks rather than garbs and brought writs of prohibition against the parson and the judge when he was sued in church court.[85] The judge deferred to the writ until he had received a consultation acknowledging the church's jurisdiction over the manner of tithing (*de modo decimandi*). In Common Pleas the parishioner initially stood on his claim of right to pay his tithes in the form of garbs rather than shocks and requested a jury on this question. The court initially summoned a jury but later reversed itself, recognizing that the issue as framed by the parishioner was actually for the church court to decide.[86]

Prohibition pleas in which the plaintiff was not the defendant's parishioner sued for detention of tithes but rather a rival claimant were of a different nature. In such situations one might find a rector at law with his fellow in a neighbouring parish over whether tithes from certain fields were owed to one or the other. Here the rights of their respective patrons were also at issue, because if the recipient lost the cause not only did he and his successors lose that income but the patron and his or her heirs lost the right to present their clerks to that income. Tithes might comprise the entire revenue of a church, so loss of some portion through proprietary litigation could seriously damage the value of the advowson to its owner.[87] Accordingly, prohibitions to halt such proceedings were available both to the rector whose right to certain tithes was being challenged and to his patron, in either the *Indicavit* or standard forms. In contrast to spoliation causes, in which patronage rights were not at risk and the *de catallis et debitis* form was used, the attachment cases involving proprietary claims typically alleged that a suit in a church court was concerned with the advowson (*de advocatione*) of a particular church or with some part of the advowson.[88]

83 Cases nos. 1.4, 1.11, 1.21, and 1.29. See also CP 40/80, m. 27d (1289) (suit for tithes pertaining to defendant's church 'et de spoliatione earumdem decimarum'); CP 40/91, m. 136d (1291) (church court action 'de spoliatione decimarum et non de laicis catallis'); CP 40/159, m. 5 (1306) (action 'pro decimis lane sue ad ipsum et ecclesiam suam predictam spectantibus quam decimam ei solvere contradixit'). In another case King's Bench annulled an earlier judgment that had not recognized the spiritual nature of what was in fact a spoliation dispute. A jury heard by justices in eyre had stated that a parson's ecclesiastical suit for tithes allegedly due from a parishioner had been illicit because according to long-standing custom he held a meadow as his tithe, having no right to tithe from the prohibition plea plaintiff's land. King's Bench overruled this judgment because the eyre record indicated clearly that the defendant had only sued for tithes pertaining to his church. Case no. 1.15.

84 Later in the middle ages the crown claimed authority to decide disputes about local tithing customs, which had the effect to diminishing the church's jurisdiction over tithe disputes. Helmholz, *History*, 455.

85 Case no. 1.28. A shock is defined by the *Oxford English Dictionary* as 'a group of sheaves of grain placed upright and supporting each other in order to permit the drying and ripening of the grain before carrying'. In contrast, a garb was simply a sheaf, that is, a large bundle of grain bound together after reaping.

86 The prohibition plea plaintiff then repleaded, claiming that the church court suit was for his lay chattels. The church court suitor denied and wager of law was assigned. He immediately made his law and he and the church court judge were acquitted.

87 E.g., plea that 'Nichil pertinet ad capellam illam nisi ille decime, et ita si amitteret decimas, per consequens amitteret illam advocationem'. *CRR*, vol. 11, no. 2666 (1224).

88 The *de catallis et debitis* form might, however, be used if the complainant were a parson deprived of tithes rather than his patron. For example, in one case a church court judge defended having proceeded despite prohibition because the case involved a claim by a parson 'super quibusdam decimis eisdem persone subtractis per ipsum abbatem infra limites predicte ecclesie prout continetur in quodam libello ipsius persone quem profert': Case no. 1.29. While it is possible that the church court action was brought against a recalcitrant parishioner withholding tithes, it appears instead that the abbot had taken tithes himself as a rival claimant (substraxit). He may have been rector of a neighbouring church appropriated to his house. The judge halted proceedings until he had obtained a consultation, which in this case referred to the one-fourth rule discussed below, relevant in cases involving disputed rights to receive tithes from certain land.

The plaintiff then revealed that tithes were the real issue in the oral elaboration of the accusation.

The prohibition against claims for tithes affecting advowson interests was not absolute. *Circumspecte agatis* allowed the church courts to hear suits for tithes between rival claimants as long as the amount claimed did not exceed one-quarter of the value of living. In other words, this was considered the limit beyond which a patron's interests might suffer substantial injury. If the claim did implicate the patron's interests, the dispute was not for a church court to decide. Instead, a claim for the right to the tithes was actionable at common law by the patron of the rival claimant. The second Statute of Westminster provided a special writ of right of advowson for claiming tithes when the value amounted to at least 'one-fourth or one-third'.[89] In an early case on the statute it was argued that the action lay only for the patron after his clerk had been prevented from suing by a prohibition.[90] The claimant, an abbot, identifying himself as '*patronus et persona*' of the church to which the tithes were allegedly due, replied that this was not a valid reason for quashing his writ because if this writ were quashed he would be without a remedy, since an action in church court for more than one-fourth of a church's revenues would be subject to prohibition. Beginning during the 1290's, consultations authorised church court suits for tithes 'both major and minor as long as the tithes demanded did not extend to a quarter part of the value of the whole church'.[91]

For example, in 1288 the patron of Ainderby Steeple in Yorkshire brought a prohibition against a suit in which the rector of that church was being sued by an abbot for tithes previously collected by the rector. In the subsequent prohibition plea the abbot admitted that the tithes claimed issued from land within the rector's parish (the basis for the abbot's own claim is not recorded), but denied that they amounted to one-fourth of Ainderby Steeple's income.[92] Rather, he argued, they were worth only 100 shillings, while the benefice was valued at 100 marks annually. The patron denied the abbot's assessment and offered to prove by jury that the amount was actually a quarter. The jury's verdict thus would determine the appropriate forum for resolution of this dispute.

Circumspecte agatis rapidly attained statutory authority as the basis for the one-fourth rule. The earliest such reference in the Common Pleas rolls was a case in which two clerks were accused of suing a plea in church court concerning 'the advowson of one-half of the church of Brockton-near-Leigh' contrary to a prohibition delivered during Lent, 1288.[93] They admitted having sued but claimed that the value of the tithes did not amount to one-fourth of the church's revenues; therefore, they argued, their suit was 'licit according to the statute' (*sicut eis bene licuit per statutum*). An attempt was made in 1295 to establish that the 'statute' did not bind the king in regard to the one-fourth rule (that is, that suits for less than that amount should be subject to prohibition if the advowson were held by the king), but the justices of Common Pleas adjourned the case on this point of law and left it unsettled.[94]

[89] St West. II c. 5, printed in *SR*, 1:75–76.
[90] Case no. 2.10.
[91] Case no. 1.21. See also Case no. 1.29.
[92] Case no. 1.17. For similar claims, see CP 40/91, m. 208d (1291); CP 40/110, m. 120d (1295).
[93] CP 40/80, m. 210 (1289).
[94] Case no. 1.20.

Earlier in the reign of Edward I the maximum amount seems to have been as high as a third,[95] but *Bracton*'s discussion indicates that the figure was previously lower. The treatise states that rival claims to tithe involving 'one-sixth, one-fifth, or one-fourth' of a church's value should be heard at common law and gave as an example a writ of prohibition in which the amount mentioned was one-sixth.[96]

During the latter half of the reign of Edward I attempts were made to apply the one-fourth rule to suits for spoliation of tithes. In fact the rule had no relevance to such actions because they did not involve rights of patronage, but in a few cases prohibitions *de advocatione* were used against spoliation actions. The clergy complained that this was an unjust intrusion upon the church's jurisdiction, but the records indicate that the problem was one of confusion rather than a deliberate change in policy.

In a case heard by justices in eyre at Canterbury in 1293, the abbot of Lewes priory brought a prohibition plea '*de advocatione quarte partis ecclesie Sancti Thome Martiris*' against a church court judge and suitor, the rector of St John's, Lewes.[97] The defendants pleaded that their action had actually been '*de spoliatione quarumdem decimarum*' pertaining to the rector's church. Upon receipt of the writ of prohibition, they had obtained a consultation endorsed on their libel recognizing the spiritual nature of their cause: '*Licitum est judicibus ecclesiasticis cognoscere in foro ecclesiastico de spoliatione decimarum, regia prohibitione non obstante*'. The abbot insisted on his allegation as originally stated, but the king's court ruled against him because he had not shown that the church court cause was unconcerned with spoliation. The entry does not record the abbot's grounds for claiming that the suit had concerned advowson rights but it seems probable that he had collected tithes previously received by St John's, claiming them for St Thomas'. If St Thomas' was one of the churches appropriated to the priory, it would have been both patron and rector and the contest over the tithes in question would have implicated the value of the benefice. So, when sued for spoliation by the rector of St John's the abbot in turn alleged that his rights of patronage were threatened and obtained a writ of prohibition *de advocatione*. However, if St Thomas' had not previously exercised its supposed claim, an action for spoliation was the proper remedy for the rector of St John's. Had the priory brought a claim of right to the tithes in church court, then patronage rights would have been at issue, because the proprietary rather than merely possessory right to the tithes would have been contested. In that case, however, the patron of St John's would have been the one to resort to the prohibition *de advocatione*.[98]

A similar prohibition plea heard in Common Pleas shows clearly how the theoretically unambiguous distinction between actions for spoliation and for right might be blurred in practice.[99] The patron of Iver church accused the abbot of Osney of suing in church court for tithes pertaining to Iver amounting to one-fourth of its value. The defendant acknowledged his suit but asserted that the tithes actually belonged to a chapel held by his house. He and his predecessors had been accustomed to receive those tithes until despoiled of them by the rector of Iver for the last two years (*quousque iam duobus annis elapsis* . . .

[95] *Councils & Synods*, 875 (royal response to clergy's complaint).
[96] *Bracton*, 4:254.
[97] JUST 1/375, m. 62d (Kent, 1293).
[98] For a case apparently arising from a similar situation, see CP 40/91, m. 305d (1291).
[99] CP 40/69, m. 28 (1287).

ipsum de predictis decimis spoliavit). The prohibition plea plaintiff emphasized that the abbot had not denied that the tithes amounted to a quarter of Iver's value. The ecclesiastical suit therefore threatened the proprietary right of Iver to the tithes—that is, the right upon which the rector had acted in assuming possession two years ago—as well as the possessory right established by the rector through his collection.[1] Perhaps predictably, the justices adjourned the case at this point and it was not reopened. The difficult legal problem was where possessory rights ended and proprietary ones began: could the abbot claim that he was despoiled of his right to tithes if his rival had himself been in possession for the last two years? Did that two-year possession confer a prescriptive right on the rector of Iver, a right to which his patron was entitled protection? While the defendant in a typical spoliation action would have been a parishioner, here he was another claimant whose patron asserted a proprietary interest in the despoiled tithes because his clerk had been in possession of them. *Bracton* states that allegations of spoliation must allege a recent spoliation. Here we see a prohibition plea plaintiff in effect arguing that two years was not recent enough. This question did not receive a definite answer during the reign of Edward I, though a ruling in favour of the prohibition plea plaintiff would have resulted in a significant extension of royal jurisdiction by broadening the patron's ability to assert a proprietary interest in tithe disputes.

The question of the applicability of the one-fourth rule to spoliation actions was a further source of confusion in a Common Pleas case of 1295, in which a royal justice had issued a consultation relevant to suits touching advowson rights although the ecclesiastical action had been for spoliation.[2] Here the problem was evidently simple error rather than an actual question of law. The prohibition plea accused a vicar of suing the master of St Nicholas' Hospital, York concerning 'debts and chattels not related to testament or marriage', namely a quantity of wool and a sum of money. The defendant pleaded that the hospital had raised a hundred sheep in his parish and had refused to pay his tithes on them, on account of which he sued before the local ordinary. Met with a prohibition he obtained a consultation allowing the suit to proceed as long as it did not concern a quarter of the church's value—which church is not specified. In fact, the ecclesiastical suit was obviously for spoliation, an alleged detention of tithes. This was why the prohibition had not been in the *de advocatione* form; the complainant had not intended to suggest that rights of patronage were at risk. Nevertheless the pleadings resolved themselves around the one-fourth question as presented in the consultation and the defendant offered proof by jury. A later plea roll entry, however, records the reissue in standard form of a writ to the sheriff ordering him to summon the jury and rehearsing the question to be put to it. Here there was no mention of the one-fourth rule. Instead the question was in terms of a standard defensive plea that the ecclesiastical suit had concerned spoliation. The jury was to say whether 'the vicar sued the master in church court for wool worth 20 shillings and for the sum of 20 shillings and four marks, which goods and money did not concern

[1] 'Et Robertus dicit quod ipse tenet integraliter predictum manerium de Evere cum omnibus pertinenciis suis ad quod advocatio predicte ecclesie mere pertinet tamquam jus suum et desicut predictus abbas non dedicit quin secutus fuit predictum placitum in curia christianitatis de predictis decimis que excedunt valorem quarte partis advocationis predicte ecclesie et idem Robertus tam in possessoria quam in petitorio posset jacturam advocationis predicte ecclesie incurrere si contigerit ipsum abbatem in causa ista in curia christianitatis optinere, petit judicium etc.'

[2] Case no. 1.21.

testament or marriage, as the plaintiff alleges, or if the vicar sued a plea for tithes from a hundred sheep raised in his parish, as he alleges'.[3] In other words, if the vicar's suit was for tithes the plaintiff would lose his prohibition plea and the dispute be returned to the church court for decision there. Advowson rights were not at issue. The consultation probably took the form it did because, with the head of a religious house as church court defendant, the ecclesiastical suit resembled a dispute between rival claimants to tithes rather than an action against a recalcitrant tithe payer.

The royal courts did not use the availability of the two forms of prohibition as the occasion for an expansion of royal jurisdiction over spoliation actions. Suggestions to the contrary in the clerical *gravamina* evidently resulted from cases such as those discussed above, reflecting either legitimate confusion or a difficult legal dilemma. With respect to tithes sold the jurisdictional arrangement was clear. The resultant debt could not be claimed in an ecclesiastical court. According to *Bracton*, tithes became lay chattels through sale.[4] This rule was restated in royal responses to clerical grievances presented in 1280, 1300, and 1301[5] and was included in *Circumspecte agatis*. An example of its application is a case from the Norfolk inquest of 1286, in which a plaintiff alleged that he was sued in ecclesiastical court for 130 marks.[6] The defendant, a clerk, pleaded that he had sold the revenues of his church to a third party for that sum and then sued the plaintiff, as the debtor's pledge for payment, in a church court. The jury stated that the defendant had indeed continued his action after delivery of a prohibition, so the court ruled that because the money claimed '*non fuit de testamento vel matrimonio*' his failure to defer to the prohibition was illicit. The uncontested fact that the money was due in return for tithes and other ecclesiastical income was not a legitimate defence.

Transactions involving tithes were also claimed by the crown when tithes from one location were exchanged for those owing from another. In one case, the parson of Holbeach accused the abbot of Croyland of taking grain located in his, the parson's, parish.[7] The abbot replied that he had only collected tithes pertaining to the church of Whaplode, of which he was parson. The jury's verdict revealed that predecessors of the parties had entered into a composition whereby all tithes of sheaves issuing from lands in Holbeach cultivated by men domiciled in Whaplode would pertain to the parson of Whaplode and his successors. On account of this agreement Common Pleas issued judgment against the plaintiff. The other half of the agreement stipulated that the parson of Holbeach was to receive tithes from land in Whaplode cultivated by men of Holbeach parish. The royal courts' competence to hear suits arising from tithe compositions thus was not limited to cases of sale. It also encompassed exchanges. Here too the transaction in question transformed chattels from spiritual to lay.

[3] CP 40/111, m. 15 (1296).

[4] *Bracton*, 4:282. See also *BNB*, 2:244–245, 3:518–519.

[5] *Councils & Synods*, 875, 1209.

[6] Case no. 3.17. For a common law action of debt based on a sale of tithes, see CP 40/70, m. 26d (1288): 'Et unde dicit quod cum idem Johannes de Wyntereshulle habuisset et recepisset ex emptione sue totam decimam bladi parochialis ipsius magistri Petri capelle sue de la Sele pro triginta duabus marcis sterlingorum . . . predictus Johannes de Wynetereshull' et alii semper hucusque predictam pecuniam ei detinuerunt et ei reddere contradicunt'. See also CP 40/153, m. 157d (1305) (executors sue on agreement whereby deceased parson sold tithes to defendants for six-year term).

[7] Case no. 2.9.

Money could be claimed in church court in lieu of tithes in one special case, that of a suit for arrears in payment. As such, a pecuniary estimate of the value of the overdue goods was in some situations the only reasonable means of compensation. The royal responses to the *gravamina* of 1280, 1300, and 1301 included this exception to the general rule.[8] Thus, in a prohibition plea from 1283 alleging an illicit suit for 100 pounds a clerk defended himself by claiming that his action had been for arrears in tithes (*de arreragiis predictarum decimarum*) and offered proof by a jury.[9]

Questions of the liability to tithes of particular goods or of lands from which tithes had not previously been collected were obviously subject to contention. There is evidence that the royal courts claimed the authority to decide such disputes,[10] but the common law records do not support that conclusion with regard to the reign of Edward I. Litigation in church courts concerning refusals to pay tithes from newly cultivated land or on goods not previously titheable would, if the crown was in fact asserting its right of jurisdiction over these matters, have been natural subjects for writs of prohibition and prohibition pleas. There is, however, no evidence that special forms of prohibition '*de decimis unconsuetis*' were devised or that other forms were applicable against ecclesiastical suits concerning such matters. Liability of land not previously tithed, though a matter of right, was obviously beyond the reach of prohibitions *de advocatione* because no patron could allege that his or her church's income was threatened by a rival's attempt at collection. The *de catallis et debitis* form might have been useful for parishioners sued in either situation but there are no prohibition pleas in which such matters were at issue. Nor is there any royal legislation on titheability from the thirteenth century comparable to the extensive ecclesiastical statutes on the subject.[11]

The common law records indicate that, with respect to the potentially highly contentious issue of the jurisdictional arrangement governing tithe litigation, Edward I and his justices continued to maintain a reasonable and consistent policy and resisted whatever temptation there may have been to expand the crown's judicial competence. Clerical *gravamina* are an especially poor guide to actual practice in the courts in this area.

Prohibitions de transgressione

During the thirteenth century common law actions of trespass developed against the background of the general principle that what we would call tort disputes between private parties were for local courts to decide. The royal justices claimed to hear only those in which some public interest was involved, primarily breach of the king's peace. Hence the formula '*vi et armis et contra pacem regis*' that typically supplemented the plaintiff's allegation of wrongdoing and served to distinguish the complaint from those more properly heard in county or manorial courts. The tendency was for the scope of royal jurisdiction over trespass to expand to include non-violent wrongs but the Statute of Gloucester issued in 1278 reaffirmed the jurisdictional distinction by ordaining that as previously sheriffs

[8] *Councils & Synods*, 875, 1209.

[9] CP 40/51 m. 85 (1283). See also Case no. 3.20.

[10] See Maitland, *Roman Canon Law*, 84, and sources there cited.

[11] See *Councils & Synods*, 511–512, 623–624, 795–796, 818–819, 1052–1055.

were to hear pleas of trespass in the counties unless there really had been violence or the goods taken were worth at least 40 shillings.[12] By the end of the thirteenth century all general common law writs of trespass—alleging assault and battery, carrying off of goods, the breaking of a close, or some combination of these—included the *vi et armis* phrase to bring the complaint within the crown's jurisdiction. In fact this allegation was at times fictitious but the royal interest requirement as defined in 1278 was not openly abandoned until the third quarter of the fourteenth century, with the admission into the royal courts of purely private trespass suits by means of actions 'on the case'.[13]

In its technical sense trespass obviously had no place in the church courts. It seems unlikely that an ecclesiastical tribunal would have claimed the right to hear a personal action grounded on the assertion that the defendant's conduct had constituted breach of the king's peace. In fact, however, it is equally clear that some wrongs, while they could be dressed up as a matter for the royal courts, might also find their way into a church court on different grounds. For example, a woman claimed she was sued in church court for 'beating and mistreating' another woman (*Ricardus et Amicia traxissent eandem Ivettam in placitum . . . querendo quod eadem Ivetta eandem Amiciam verberasset et male tractasset*).[14] The record does not allow us to see with certainty what the actual cause of the ecclesiastical action was. Perhaps it was simply a heated argument between the two women, the subsequent action aimed not at compensation for a physical injury—this would be the purpose of a common law trespass action—but simply at redress of some verbal humiliation through public penance. Clearly, though, the prohibition plea plaintiff described the ecclesiastical suit in terms of the comparable common law wrong, in order to establish that it was not justiciable in a church court.

Besides its common law meaning, trespass *(transgressio)* had a broader, non-juridical meaning of wrongful action or sinful conduct generally. So, we find a prohibition plea plaintiff, who had alleged that a church court had heard a suit '*de transgressione contra pacem*' against him, contradicted by a jury's report that the *transgressio* had not been a trespass pertaining to royal justice but merely a prosecution for the sin of adultery.[15] Here it seems as though the plaintiff attempted unsuccessfully to take advantage of the generality of the term 'trespass'. In both of these cases the choice between the royal or ecclesiastical forum depended on an evaluation of the conduct that was the cause of the action.

Probably because of the term's conceptual and semantic ambiguity the writ of prohibition specifically *de transgressione* did not appear until common law trespass had attained a precise meaning. In his treatment of the writ's origins Flahiff wrote that this form was first devised for use against ecclesiastical suits brought by clerks against royal officers who had arrested them for alleged crimes. Such a writ is found in *Bracton* and cases arising from it were common by around 1260.[16] In fact, however, this particular sort of prohibition

[12] St Glouc. c. 8, printed in *SR*, 1:48.

[13] For the origins of trespass, see Milsom, *Studies*, 1–90. A briefer account is Baker, *Legal History*, 60–64.

[14] CP 40/110, m. 9ld (1295). The common-law writ of trespass for battery included the allegation that the defendant 'ipsum verberavit, vulneravit et male tractavit.' For an example, see Baker, *Legal History*, 544.

[15] Case no. 1.19.

[16] See Flahiff, 'Prohibition I', 279–280 and *Bracton*, 4:258–259. The earliest case cited by Flahiff is from 1240; his statement that the prohibition issued to halt an ecclesiastical suit de transgressione contra pacem is misleading. Nor is there any reason to believe that the plaintiff was a clerk. See *CRR*, 16:251; and Flahiff, 'Prohibition I', 279 n. 94.

had nothing to do with trespass except in a most general sense and made no use of the word *transgressio*. The alleged wrong was a judicial proceeding against a royal officer attempting to perform his duty. The ecclesiastical suit—though it was *contra pacem* in that it impeded law enforcement—could not be construed as a plea of trespass *contra pacem* in the usual sense of an act of violence in disturbance of law and order. The contrast is clear if we look at those cases that arose from prohibitions more properly concerned with trespass suits in church courts. The earliest instances occur only during the reign of Edward I.

One case involved an accusation by a layman and his three brothers that a prior had sued them for trespass in a church court.[17] The plaintiffs' recitation of their writ included a *cum*-clause, employed in all writs of prohibition *de transgressione*, stating that 'pleas concerning trespass done against the king's peace pertain to the king's crown and dignity'. According to the plaintiffs the defendant had cited them for beating and mistreating his men and had proceeded with his suit in spite of a prohibition. A jury later found for the plaintiffs. Prohibition lay against the prior's suit because actions of that sort—alleging the secular wrong of battery—had no place in a church court.

Other cases resulting from prohibitions *de transgressione* typically contained similar allegations that the defendant had brought an ecclesiastical suit for battery. The earliest such cases are from the late 1270's.[18] Both the specific content of these allegations—actions for battery—and their dates may have been due to the same cause. As we have seen, the Statute of Gloucester gave a precise definition of the crown's jurisdiction over trespass in 1278, allowing only suits in which the goods allegedly taken were worth at least 40 shillings or the plaintiff had actually been beaten. The new species of prohibition and the cases arising from it probably related to the second half of this limitation.[19] The statute did not state that actions for battery were to be heard exclusively in the royal courts but the words of the prohibition *de transgressione*—explicitly declaring that wrong against the king's peace were matters for his courts—provide strong evidence that this was in fact intended.[20] Thus, these prohibitions became available only after the crown had issued a clear statement as to what sorts of trespass were and were not justiciable at common law.

This may explain why prohibitions issued against ecclesiastical suits for battery but it may then be asked why no prohibitions *de transgressione* were used in the wake of

[17] Case no. 1.7b.

[18] The following entries record the appearance and pleadings of both parties; they were therefore initiated by writs of attachment issued a few terms previously, pursuant to writs of prohibition issued a few terms earlier still, probably during the later 1270's: Case no. 1.6 (Hilary 1280); CP 40/41, m. 3d (Trinity 1281). For other prohibition pleas de transgressione, see CP 40/78, m. 82 (1289); CP 40/111, m. 69d (1296); CP 40/115, m. 33d (1296); CP 40/116, m. 58 (1297); CP 40/123, m. 84d (1298); CP 40/150, m. 23 (1304); CP 40/159, m. 180 (1306).

[19] Flahiff may have found a writ of prohibition de transgressione in a register of writs dating from before the statute. The register's date is doubtful, however. At one point he referred to it as dating from 'around 1272' but elsewhere it is said simply to date from 'the early years of Edward I's reign': 'Prohibition I', 280, 267 n. 32. E. de Haas and G. D. G. Hall said only that it is later than 1275 but before Edward II: *Early Registers*, xxiii. It is probably not safe to conclude that this register and its contents predate the Statute of Gloucester. Another register includes a good example of the writ but though it is based on material compiled in the 1260's it contains many later additions and in its present form is also probably post-1275: *Early Registers*, xxiv, lv, 107.

[20] Cf. Beckerman, 'Forty-Shilling Limit', where it is shown that the 40-shilling rule limited the jurisdiction of the royal courts but not the local ones; that is, suits for over that amount might be heard either locally or by the royal courts. In contrast the words of the prohibition de transgressione indicate that, not only were suits for trespass contra pacem beyond the competence of the church courts, but they were not triable elsewhere than in the royal courts.

the 1278 statute against pleas in church courts involving the equivalent of common law actions of trespass *de bonis asportatis* exceeding 40 shillings. It may be that the need was not there or that the statute did not intend to limit the church's jurisdiction in this regard. More likely the new prohibition *de transgressione* was not necessary in such cases because the older, more common form *de catallis et debitis* lay against any ecclesiastical suit for goods or money unless the chattels sought concerned marriage or testament or were claimed as ecclesiastical payments. There was therefore no need to use the newer prohibition against attempts to obtain compensation for or compel restitution of stolen property in church courts. If this is so, such suits may lie behind some of the many prohibition pleas in which the church court plaintiff's claim was allegedly for some item of property.

Despite the creation of the prohibition *de transgressione* the church retained jurisdiction over violence against clerks and their property. Here the sin was sacrilege, an attack on the church's personnel being akin to an attack on its property.[21] From at least the early thirteenth century the common law recognized the sanctity of the clerk's person and the church's authority to punish violators.[22] The Statute of Gloucester did not alter this situation. For example, in a prohibition plea heard in 1289 the defendants—each described by the plaintiff as *laicus*—were accused of suing a plea 'concerning battery' (*de verberationibus*) in a church court.[23] Two of the three replied that they were actually clerks and had sued 'because of defamation and violence done them, as was licit' (*pro defamatione et violencia eis facta . . . sicut eis bene licuit*). They offered to prove this by jury.[24] Another case shows clearly that an action for theft of property belonging to an ecclesiastic was not subject to prohibition.[25] A layman accused the prioress of Easebourne of suing in church court *de transgressione* and *de advocatione*. The substance of her suit was evidently an allegation that he had taken certain obventions and oblations due to a chapel. The theft element probably provided the plaintiff with his trespass charge, while the advowson allegation suggests that the actual source of the dispute may have been a patronage controversy. She pleaded in defence that he had 'maliciously carried off the payments, thus committing sacrilege,' and produced a consultation acknowledging the spiritual nature of her suit. She then offered proof by jury.

There is only one apparent instance of the successful use of a prohibition against such suits from the reign of Edward I, but in fact the royal justices did not claim jurisdiction on the ground that the suit was justiciable as common law trespass. Instead, the prohibition plea plaintiff claimed that as a bailiff he had impounded two horses *damage feasant*.[26] He was sued by the owners, who were clerks, in a church court '*super captionem dictorum equorum*', and brought a prohibition because the dispute was subject to the common law of distraint and replevin. In this case the bailiff might have used a prohibition *de catallis et debitis* instead of *de transgressione*. Either way, the basis for the prohibition was not the

[21] See especially C. 17 q. 4 c . 29 (Si quis suadente diabolo . . .). See also *DDC*, 3:865–866.

[22] *Bracton*, 4:266. For early cases, see *BNB*, 3:470 and KB 26/115B, m. 14d (1234).

[23] KB 27/121, m. 26d (1289).

[24] The third said nothing as to whether he was a clerk. Instead he denied suing after prohibition, perhaps because he was a layman.

[25] CP 40/113, m. 58 (1296).

[26] KB 27/94, m. 42 (1285). For distraint and replevin, see Pollock & Maitland, 2:575–578.

church's jurisdiction over seizure of property belonging to clerks but rather interference with the lawful means for recovery of distrained property.

The prohibition *de transgressione* was a creation of Edward I's reign, closely related to the rise of the common law tort remedy. It is difficult to see these developments as a serious intrusion upon the church's judicial authority. The jurisdictional area that the new prohibition was designed to protect was probably not an important source of business for the church courts. Some prohibition plea plaintiffs may have strained the limits of the common law concept to the detriment of ecclesiastical suitors, but the royal courts did observe the concept's narrow scope. At any rate the number of cases in which prohibitions *de transgressione* interfered with church court litigation was very small. Of greater importance to the church was the continued recognition of the church's competence to punish acts of violence against clerks.

Prohibitions concerning defamation and other special cases

In addition to the four *de cursu* prohibitions already discussed—for lay fee, advowson, lay debts and chattels, and trespass—other *de precepto* forms were available on an ad hoc basis for particular situations as they arose. Defamation was ordinarily a matter for the church courts,[27] but ecclesiastical actions accusing appellors, plaintiffs, or jurors of false assertions in royal courts were not tolerated. Writs of prohibition *de diffamatione* for halting such actions appear in the registers of writs beginning around the middle of the thirteenth century, though the policy underlying them dates from as early as 1230. In addition prohibitions were available to prevent ecclesiastical prosecutions of royal officers attempting to carry out their duties or against private parties who resorted to extrajudicial distraint according to customary practice. All of these forms of prohibition followed from the principle, as formulated by Flahiff, that 'What transpires in the king's court or what is done by his order or that of his justices or according to recognized custom may not be the grounds of an action in church court'.[28]

Prohibition pleas concerning defamation from the reign of Edward I are rare. Writs of attachment in these cases alleged illicit suits *de catallis et debitis* rather than defamation specifically.[29] The reason for this is apparent in a case in which the prohibition plea plaintiff stated that after she had brought an appeal of homicide against the alleged killer of her husband, the accused sued her in church court *de diffamatione* presumably on the ground that her accusation had been false.[30] As a result of this suit she was made to pay either a fine or compensation (*per quod . . . catalla sua amisit*), which was the basis for her resort to a prohibition plea in the *de catallis et debitis* form. Similarly, in 1294 a man alleged that he recovered 40 shillings in a trespass action heard in a county court but was subsequently sued for defamation by the convicted party.[31] Here the prohibition plea plaintiff

[27] For defamation, see *Defamation Cases*. See also Baker, *Legal History*, ch. 25; Milsom, *Historical Foundations*, 332–344.

[28] 'Prohibition I', 282. On these forms of prohibition and their history, see id. at 281–283.

[29] The earliest prohibition plea concerning defamation found by Flahiff was also in the de catallis et debitis form, a case dating from 1230: 'Prohibition I', 281 n. 104.

[30] Case no. 1.8.

[31] CP 40/104, m. 133d (1294).

stated clearly that the object of the ecclesiastical suit had been recovery of the 40 shillings: 'et exigisset ab eo predictos quadraginta solidos, imponens eidem Roberto quod ipsam Margeriam de predicta transgressione maliciose defamasset'.[32]

There is no evidence during the reign of Edward I of any prohibition plea specifically *de diffamatione*—and therefore no direct evidence for the use of that writ of prohibition. In one prohibition plea *de catallis et debitis* the plaintiff made no reference to money, claiming only that he had been accused of defamation in a church court. When the defendants replied that a mere allegation of a defamation suit was insufficient to support a prohibition plea the case went no further and the plaintiff was amerced for a false claim.[33] It seems possible therefore that though the special form of prohibition was available—the registers attest to this—litigants preferred to use the standard *de catallis et debitis* form because it was necessary to allege a claim for money. Merely to allege a defamation action in church court ran the risk of dismissal on the ground that such actions were properly for the church to decide. Accordingly, other defamation actions may lie behind some of the numerous prohibition pleas that simply alleged an illicit attempt to collect a sum of money in a church court.[34]

In addition to the cases concerning ecclesiastical allegations of defamation there is a handful in which the basis for the ecclesiastical suitor's claim is not clear. In one case a jury affirmed the complainant's assertion that he was sued in a church court because he had sued a common law plea of trespass in King's Bench.[35] It is possible that in some of the other cases such as this[36] the church court action was for defamation but because the limitations on prohibition pleas suggested above discouraged mention of this, the plaintiffs instead emphasized the punitive purpose of the ecclesiastical suit without referring to defamation as such. This was itself treated as a common law offence.

One case reveals that the church courts at times prosecuted common law suitors on the ground that their plea in the royal court was properly a matter for the church's jurisdiction. Perhaps this explains some of the allegations in which the reason for the ecclesiastical suit

32 In a plaint sued before justices itinerant in 1293 the defendant pleaded that, contrary to the plaintiff's allegation that he had sued 'de laycis catallis', his action had actually been 'de quadam diffamatione': JUST 1/1094, m. 16d (Yorkshire, 1293).

33 CP 40/96, m. 198d (1292): 'Et dicunt quod non debent ei inde ad hoc breve respondere, quia dicunt quod predictus Robertus per breve suum asserat ipsos tenuisse placitum in predicta curia christianitatis de catallis et debitis que non sunt de testamento vel matrimonio etc. et in narratione sua dicat ipsos tenuisse placitum de diffamatione etc. que mere spectat ad curiam christianitatis etc., petit sic judicium etc. Et Robertus non potest hoc dedicere. Ideo consideratum est quod predictus Robertus nichil capiat per breve suum set sit in misericordia pro falso clamore'.

34 But compare the case of a clerk who lost a real property dispute and then accused the jurors of canonical defamation. There was no suggestion that the basis for the resultant common law action was a claim by the clerk for money damages. Rather, the fact of an ecclesiastical suit against a common law jury was itself a serious offence against the crown, requiring that the defendant answer both the king and the wronged individuals: *Plac. Abbr.*, 269–270.

35 Case no. 2.19.

36 E.g., a common-law action 'de placito quare cum idem Reginaldus prout moris est in regno Anglie inplacitet predictum Hugonnem coram domino rege in curia regis per breve suum de quadam transgressione eidem Reginaldo per predictum [Hugonem] illata ut dicitur idem Hugo eadem occasione trahit eum in placitum in curia christianitatis in lesionem corone et dignitatis sue et contra prohibitionem etc.': CP 40/53, m. 15d (1284) (process entry only). For other examples, see CP 40/31, m. 84d (1279) (process, alleging church court suit to impede land claim in Common Pleas); CP 40/59, m. 22d (1285) (process, alleging church court action on account of trespass suit in Common Pleas); KB 27/162, m. 65d (1300) (church court action brought on account of action for trespass contra pacem); *Plac. Abbr.* 299.

was not clearly stated. A clerk complained that when he sued a trespass action in King's Bench an ecclesiastical judge ordered him to halt proceedings and then excommunicated him because he refused to do so. The church court then itself proceeded to consider the dispute that had been the cause of the common law trespass suit, despite a writ of prohibition.[37] The ecclesiastical order followed by the court's own assumption of jurisdiction was comparable to the common law's provision of prohibitions and actions for settling the principal matter. This case demonstrates that a special common law remedy was available to prevent and punish such church courts proceedings.

Other attempts to subject the crown's legal process to ecclesiastical supervision were likewise subject to prohibition. Examples from Edward I's reign include church court suits brought against sheriffs by those accused of common law crimes and arrested pending trial.[38] In one case, a under-sheriff was sued in Court Christian and excommunicated, supposedly because of his execution of the king's mandate on behalf of the sheriff of Kent.[39] The archbishop of Canterbury responded that the church court action was in response to acts of violence and sacrilege committed by the under-sheriff against two clerks. A jury found for the under-sheriff and the court of King's Bench awarded him 40 pounds compensation and ordered the archbishop's arrest.[40]

Various church court prosecutions concerning distraint and replevin also gave rise to occasional prohibition pleas, such as a case dealing with canonical sanctions issued against those who had replevied animals detained by the bishop of Rochester[41] and another already discussed resulting from a suit against a bailiff who had impounded two horses *damage feasant*.[42] The canonical basis for such prosecutions is generally not clear. It may be that cases such as these were instances of abuse of ecclesiastical justice even by the church's own standards. In one case, for example, the complainant in a trespass action accused the defendant of excommunicating him as soon as he learned that the common law suit had been initiated against him and also refused him last rites when gravely ill until he should swear to drop the trespass suit.[43] Similarly, refusal to release animals and chattels upon offer of gage and pledge was wrongful, even where the basis for the distraint

[37] CP 40/31, m. 2 (1279): 'cum predictus Henricus implacitasset coram domino rege quemdam Robertum le Sauvage de bonis et catallis suis per ipsum Robertum captis et asportatis contra pacem et idem magister Simon prefato Henrico mandasset quod de predicto placito prosequendo coram domino rege cessaret, prefatus Simon pro eo quod in prosecutione predicti placiti non cessavit predictum placitum de predictis bonis et catallis in curia christianitatis una cum predicto Roberto tenuit et ipsum excommunicationis sentencia innodavit'.

[38] E.g., 'Simon de Rybbeford attachiatus fuit ad respondendum regi de placito quare secutus est placitum in curia christianitatis de eo quod, cum Walterus de Bokkyng' nuper subvicecomes regis in comitatu Glouc' prout ad officium suum pertinuit de receptamento latrocinii indictati capi et apud Glouc' imprisonari fecisset donec per justiciarios regis ad gayol regis ibidem deliberanda assignatos deliberatus fuisset, predictus Simon secutus est placitum in eadem curia christianitatis contra prohibitionem etc.': CP 40/11, m. 55 (1275) (process entry). For similar examples, see CP 40/9, m. l0d (1275); CP 40/105, m. 140 (1294) (process entry, alleging church court suit against county 'ballivus et minister' for arrest of clerk appealed for homicide); CP 40/121, m. 43d (1297) (process, alleging church court suit against coroner).

[39] Case no. 1.27.

[40] The case was part of one chapter in the contentious relationship between king and archbishop. See Denton, *Winchelsey*, 181–183.

[41] CP 40/70, m. 58 (1288) (process entry).

[42] Above, p. lxxviii. For a case concerning distraint for debts owed the royal exchequer, see CP 40/9, m. 44d (1275), printed in part in Flahiff, 'Prohibition I', 282 n. 108.

[43] Case no. 2.13.

was a spiritual matter, such as demise of a church for a term in return for money that has not been paid.[44]

The cases discussed here all indicate that the crown, during the reign of Edward I as previously, provided remedies for individuals who incurred ecclesiastical prosecution because of their involvement in common law proceedings either as suitors or royal officials. It was argued in section 2 that ecclesiastical sanctions probably were not very effective in deterring or punishing resort to writs of prohibition. Helmholz has also noted examples of church court proceedings against those who sued allegedly spiritual causes in royal courts.[45] The availability of common law remedies, however, must have discouraged these prosecutions as well, and indeed any attempts by the church courts to impede the ordinary functioning of the secular legal system. Evidence for their efficacy from the church court records is itself limited,[46] and the infrequency of resort to the common law remedies would seem to indicate that they were not often needed. Direct efforts by the church courts to prevent or retaliate against proceedings in the royal courts were probably as uncommon as prosecutions of those who used writs of prohibition.

Prohibition in the church courts

Having considered the substantive and procedural aspects of the writ of prohibition in some detail, it may be appropriate at this point to say a few more general words about the impact of prohibition on the functioning of the church courts. Church court records survive in large volume for most of the English dioceses during the pre-Reformation period, though what survives represents only a small part of the whole. Very little of this has been edited.[47] Two remarkable facts pertinent to this study emerge from the work of those who have examined these records. One is the low numerical frequency of direct evidence of the use of writs of prohibition. Also noteworthy is the apparent absence of any instances in which the courts disobeyed prohibitions.

Helmholz, in a thorough examination of ecclesiastical court records from ten dioceses spanning the years 1293 to 1501, found not a single case in which a church court failed to defer to a writ of prohibition.[48] This confirmed the earlier conclusions of Woodcock for Canterbury diocese[49] and Donahue for York.[50] Evidence from Canterbury province during the thirteenth century only slightly modifies these conclusions.[51] The discussion of the Statute of Consultation presented above complements the view that ecclesiastical judges were often compliant when faced with writs of prohibition. The 1290 statute provided that

[44] Case no. 2.14.

[45] Helmholz, *Canon Law*, 93–94.

[46] Helmholz, *Canon Law*, 95.

[47] For a list, see Helmholz, *History*, 647–648. Especially important studies include Adams and Donahue's *Canterbury Cases* and Helmholz's *Defamation Cases*. See also Helmholz, *History*; Helmholz, *Canon Law*; Helmholz, *Marriage Litigation*; Woodcock, *Canterbury Courts*; Donahue, 'Roman Canon Law'.

[48] Helmholz, *Canon Law*, 85–86.

[49] *Canterbury Courts*, 107–108.

[50] 'Roman Canon Law', 663–664.

[51] *Canterbury Cases* includes no instances in the records of the church courts for disobedience of prohibitions but the editors have found external evidence for two such cases: see Cases D.6 and D.19.

ecclesiastical suitors were to have a remedy out of chancery ordering judges to proceed with legitimately spiritual cases in which the suitor had no alternative action at common law. Ecclesiastical judges evidently were deferential toward prohibitions even when there was no legal necessity.

In an obvious but crucial respect, the common law court records contradict evidence of regular compliance with writs of prohibition. During Edward I's reign in Common Pleas alone there were slightly more than 300 prohibition pleas that resulted in appearance of the parties and trial of the alleged refusal to obey the prohibition. King's Bench and the justices itinerant in the counties also heard occasional prohibition pleas. In addition, an undetermined number of prohibition pleas were commenced but dropped prior to appearance of the parties. So, there is substantial evidence in the common law records that church courts often proceeded with ecclesiastical suits despite writs of prohibition ordering them to halt.

There are two possible solutions to this paradox. The allegations of disobedience contained in the attachment writs may have been false, or the church court records did not register prohibitions that were disobeyed, containing only references to compliance. The first explanation is unlikely. If an ecclesiastical judge or suitor actually did defer to a prohibition, it is hard to see why the church court defendant would nevertheless have then proceeded to initiate a common law action alleging refusal to obey. The purpose of the writ of prohibition was relief from an allegedly illicit ecclesiastical suit, while the prohibition plea sought damages for continued prosecution of the suit. Surely the cessation of proceedings would ordinarily have been a sufficient remedy. Some attachment suits may have been vexatious, but the necessary expense and effort, plus the likelihood of defeat by wager of law and the resultant fine for the false claim, must have deterred all but the most contentious from using writs of attachment in this manner.

Rather, it is probably the church court records that offer an inaccurate picture. They seem only to have mentioned prohibitions that were in fact obeyed or for which disobedience was warranted. Perhaps this is to be expected: if the judge thought little enough of a royal prohibition to ignore it, it seems unlikely that he would have ordered the court clerk to include it in the official record, which might have later been introduced in evidence against him in a prohibition plea. Instead, the clerk probably recorded receipt of a prohibition only when the judge or suitor decided to respect it, in which case it would be necessary to record some reason for the cessation of proceedings. If so, the absence of clear indications of disobedience in the church court records tells us nothing about the actual rate of disobedience.

There are six cases from the Court of Canterbury during the period 1292–94 in which litigants obtained prohibitions. In the three ecclesiastical case records that include references to prohibitions, the judge deferred to the prohibition in each.[52] Twice the church court ignored writs of prohibition, but in neither case does the church court record itself provide the evidence of the prohibition.[53] The sixth case was an appeal from trial in the

[52] *Canterbury Cases*, Cases D.7, D.12, and D.18. Consultations were obtained in Cases D.7 and D.12; in the latter there were further prohibitions after the consultation, but the court acta refer to the consultation as warrant for proceeding.

[53] *Canterbury Cases*, Cases D.6 and D.19. The evidence for prohibition is in the common law records. The entries bearing on Case D.19 are printed in this volume as Cases nos. 1.23a - 1.23e.

Court of Arches, where a prohibition was ignored.[54] The trial court record has not survived, however, so we do not know whether a prohibition was enrolled or included among the *acta*. Probably it was not. If these cases are typical, the church courts did not record disobedience of prohibitions among the records of their proceedings. Such evidence must be sought in the common law rolls. The lack of evidence of non-compliance in the church court records probably is misleading.[55]

In addition to the question of compliance or non-compliance with prohibitions, it is necessary to consider the frequency with which litigants resorted to prohibitions. This is important because it indicates the extent to which the church courts operated independently of crown interference. Frequent use of prohibitions would also be evidence of sharp disagreement regarding the proper spheres of secular and spiritual justice. Finally, knowledge of the number of prohibitions employed allows a judgment to be made about the importance of the prohibition process in determining the limits of the church's legal authority. The church court records themselves are not an accurate guide to the frequency of resort to prohibition, but when considered with the common law evidence it appears that the frequency was low.

Helmholz found a total of only 52 instances of prohibitions received among several thousand ecclesiastical suits surviving from 14 dioceses during the period 1293 to 1501, 'a minute percentage of the total'.[56] This confirmed Woodcock's earlier conclusion for Canterbury diocese.[57] Donahue's thorough study of the 232 cases surviving from York during the fourteenth century turned up only eight in which prohibitions were registered. Based on his conclusion that what survives is a random sample comprising two to four percent of the total number of cases heard,[58] we can conjecture that a complete set of records would have contained approximately 200 to 400 prohibitions, or 20 to 40 per decade for the diocese. These figures would indicate prohibitions obeyed and therefore recorded for one diocese. In contrast, the common law records for Edward I's reign yield an average of approximately 10 cases per year that actually resulted in the parties' appearances in Common Pleas for the entire country; most if not all of these would have been cases in which prohibitions where disobeyed. Certainly there were more writs of prohibition delivered that never resulted in a prohibition plea or that led to prohibition pleas dropped before the parties' appearances. Even so, the composite picture is one in which writs of prohibition, though not insignificant in number, seem not to have figured in a large number of ecclesiastical cases. Clearly the number of cases in which prohibitions were obeyed is very small in relation to the total number of cases heard in the church courts. Factoring in the instances of alleged disobedience does not alter the general impression of low frequency. Maitland's remark that prohibitions were 'always buzzing about the ears'[59] of church court judges during the thirteenth century seems unwarranted.

[54] *Canterbury Cases*, Case D.11.

[55] A further reason why disobedience of prohibitions did appear in the church court records may be that attachment suits were sometimes initiated only after the church court had decided the principal cause. The losing party might have resorted to prohibition in order to avoid enforcement of an adverse judgment.

[56] Helmholz, *Canon Law*, 81–85.

[57] Woodcock, *Canterbury Courts*, 107–108.

[58] 'Roman Canon Law', 663–664.

[59] Pollock & Maitland, 2:200.

Of course, the more important question is the number of prohibitions in relation to the number of cases actually subject to prohibition, rather than in relation to the total number of cases regardless of subject matter. Here statistical precision is even less feasible, but again prohibitions do not appear to have played a significant role in defining the scope of the church's jurisdiction. Helmholz and Donahue have argued that a large number—perhaps a very large number—of prohibitable cases escaped prohibition. Thus, the low frequency of prohibition allowed the church courts to hear several sorts of cases that the common law regarded as beyond their jurisdiction. It is clear that one large and important legal subject—actions to enforce promises—comprised a significant part of church court activity despite the availability of prohibitions, but there is in fact little reason to believe that the church courts enjoyed a more general freedom from secular interference.

Church courts routinely entertained *fidei laesio* actions for the enforcement of promises to pay money of deliver chattels made by or to deceased persons, with little apparent interference from writs of prohibition.[60] The common law's position on these matters thus seems to have had little effect. Woodcock and Helmholz both discovered that breach of faith comprised a very considerable portion of church court business—perhaps the single most frequent type of case—during the fifteenth century.[61] Debt claims by and against executors were also a 'staple part of medieval probate jurisdiction' by at least the mid-fourteenth century.[62]

Beyond these promissory disputes, however, there is little reason to believe that the church courts heard significant numbers of cases that the common law regarded as beyond their jurisdiction.[63] In cases involving tithes, ecclesiastical patronage, and annual rents, all areas in which there was significant shared jurisdiction, the church courts seem to have kept largely within the bounds set by common law. Cases on other subjects claimed by common law, such as land or trespass, seem to have occurred infrequently. It is thus not surprising that only around 20 percent of the prohibition pleas heard during Edward I's reign resulted from prohibitions *de laico feodo*, *de advocatione*, or *de transgressione*.

Many more people used the *de catallis et debitis* form of prohibition than the other forms because the large number of church court suits claiming money and chattels gave them greater opportunity to do so. Even so, there were still far too few prohibitions to prevent the church from continuing to hear promissory cases. Common law jurisdictional rules notwithstanding, it was the litigants themselves who decided what sorts of cases came before the church courts and how often prohibitions were introduced. They initiated the large numbers of claims for debts and chattels while generally refraining from suing actions asserting real property or advowson rights or alleging trespass. Likewise,

[60] See Helmholz, *Canon Law*, 263–289, 307–321; Woodcock, *Canterbury Courts*, 85, 89–90; Owen, 'Ecclesiastical Jurisdiction', 218–219.

[61] According to Woodcock, breach of faith actions for debts 'provided the bulk of the Instance business of the [Canterbury] Consistory Court during the fifteenth century': *Canterbury Courts*, 90. See also Helmholz, *Canon Law*, 263–264. A roll from the Lincoln consistory court for 1430–31 included 28 cases of breach of faith out of 90 cases recorded: Morris, 'Consistory Court', 157 n. 4. Most were debt actions. According to the church court records, none was prohibited.

[62] Helmholz, *Canon Law*, 310.

[63] This argument is developed more fully in Millon, 'Ecclesiastical Jurisdiction'.

the litigants themselves decided when to obtain writs of prohibition and to sue attachment actions against violators. They apparently chose not to do so very often because the same attitudes that led people to accept the church's authority to decide promissory claims presumably discouraged resort to prohibition, which amounted to invocation of the crown's monopoly over such cases. Of course, the church court defendant who otherwise took for granted the church's jurisdiction might have found himself or herself in a situation that encouraged casting aside of these assumptions and resort to common law. But this did not happen very often, at least not often enough to curtail the church's ability to offer effective remedies to promisees. An extra-legal consensus that the church was the proper forum for the coercion of those who did not keep their promises was evidently more important than the common law jurisdictional rules in this area.

Aside from whatever moral or theological considerations were at work, there were sound practical reasons why litigants should have continued to sue breach of promise actions in the church courts while pursuing other secular claims at common law. As is well known, medieval common law contractual remedies—the writs of covenant and debt—were of very limited utility, especially as to informal agreements.[64] This meant that most contract litigation was conducted in local courts, secular as well as ecclesiastical, where facts could be readily determined and sanctions were enhanced by powerful reputational considerations. In contrast, the king's courts offered sophisticated and comprehensive remedies for claims to real property, including advowson rights, and the common law's monopoly discouraged efforts to obtain judgments that could be overturned in the king's courts. In theory contract too was secular, but effective contract remedies were the necessary complement to prohibition if litigants were to abandon the church courts for Westminster. Not until the sixteenth century, when assumpsit replaced first the writ of covenant and then the writ of debt, did the common law offer a unified and efficacious contract remedy for unsealed agreements.[65] It is therefore no coincidence that there was a sharp decline in breach of faith cases in the ecclesiastical courts during the first half of the sixteenth century and a virtual disappearance by mid-century. As Helmholz has shown, the decline in the one reflected the rise of the other.[66]

In order to understand the impact of prohibitions on the jurisdictional competence of the church courts it is necessary to consider not only the scope of the various forms of prohibition but also the extent to which alternative remedies to prohibitable causes of action were available at common law. Litigants did not make extensive use of prohibitions unless corresponding remedies were available in some other forum. Once the common law attempted to consolidate its authority over a particular cause of action, the church courts were powerless to resist. The ultimate factor was the political relationship between the two jurisdictions in England. The crown successfully asserted the authority to decide which forum was competent to decide a particular class of dispute. In practice this meant its discretion to provide new common law remedies and to adjudicate prohibition pleas in ways that further limited the church's jurisdiction. The latter were important only when related to the former, but in combination they were capable of effective enforcement of

[64] See, e.g., Baker, *Legal History*, 318–326.
[65] Baker, *Legal History*, 329–345.
[66] Helmholz, *Canon Law*, 283–285.

the crown's jurisdictional determinations. It is notable that Edward I chose to make limited use of this power.

* * * * * * * * *

Writs of prohibition did not provide the vehicle for an extensive redefinition of the boundaries between the two jurisdictions during the reign of Edward I. For the most part the royal courts continued to apply substantive rules developed earlier in the century and chancery continued to issue writs already well established in practice. The creation of a new form of prohibition—*de transgressione*—followed from common law trespass' attainment of conceptual maturity but did not itself entail an intrusion upon the church's judicial authority because of its narrow scope. Potentially more important was the crown's assumption of exclusive jurisdiction over debt claims by or against executors beginning around 1279. Intelligible as an effort to rationalize the common law's jurisdiction over debt litigation, the boldness of this development is apparent, though its practical impact was slight.

4

COMMON LAW ACTIONS AND ECCLESIASTICAL INTERESTS

This section continues the discussion of the substantive rules governing the relations between the royal and ecclesiastical jurisdictions, but from a different point of view. The focus is on common law actions that had an indirect impact on the church's judicial competence by bringing disputes before the royal courts that might otherwise have been settled by church courts. Prohibitions played a complementary role by preventing the church courts from entertaining those disputes; they are treated below to the extent they were not in section 3 .

The main theme of the previous section was the general lack of jurisdictional innovation during the reign of Edward I. That theme will also be evident in what follows, but as in section 3 there is an exception. The common law action for recovery of annual rents brought a significant amount of arguably spiritual business into the king's courts. A creation of the later thirteenth century, the development of this remedy took place largely, though not exclusively, during Edward's reign. In other areas of the law, however, things remained much as before.

The topics treated herein aim not at a comprehensive discussion of all those areas in which there was a potential jurisdictional conflict between the two fora, but rather at the analysis of a few that deserve special attention because they involved particularly significant ecclesiastical interests. The large amount of litigation in the common law courts attests to their importance to contemporaries. In addition to annual rents, the following discussion will include the jurisdictional arrangement governing ecclesiastical patronage, which comprised a complex set of rules and remedies. The availability of common law trespass for certain tithe disputes resulted in a surprisingly large number of cases, a phenomenon that has not previously been investigated in detail. The system of benefit of clergy was an important feature of the criminal law and one that, for historical reasons, was especially important to the English church. In each of these areas it will be seen that, though the crown obviously intruded on the church's jurisdiction to the extent that limitations were placed upon it, the operation of the common law during Edward I's reign nevertheless preserved the distinctions between the respective spheres of competence of the two legal systems.

Annual rents

Annual payments, in cash or in kind, from religious foundations (such as parish churches or abbeys) or individuals to other foundations or to individual laymen or clerks were an important feature of daily affairs in thirteenth-century England. A particular church might be obliged to pay a part of its revenues to another church or monastic foundation in perpetuity or to some individual for his or her lifetime. Religious institutions or individual prelates might retain clerks as attorneys to represent their interests before ecclesiastical or royal tribunals. Another sort of annual rent was the corrody, whereby a lay person

surrendered property to a religious house in return for food, lodging, and other necessities for the remainder of his or her life.

Although such obligations were at least arguably spiritual—in regard to the status of one or both of the parties or to the purpose or source of the payments—the crown claimed jurisdiction over many of them. The common law writ for recovery of arrears of an annual rent was available to enforce certain secular obligations and also certain spiritual ones. Writs of prohibition complemented this action, by providing the means for the restriction of the church's jurisdiction over matters claimed for the royal courts. This common law action, in conjunction with prohibition, allowed the crown to make substantial inroads on the church's competence to judge disputes involving rents. The action itself was not much older than the reign of Edward I, so for the most part this development was a product of the last quarter of the thirteenth century. Royal jurisdiction over annual rents was not absolute, however, because the justices were reluctant to assert exclusive authority over a particular species.

The common law action for recovery of an annual rent (*de annuo redditu*) dates from late in the reign of Henry III.[67] It was available for recovery of several varieties of payment. According to Chief Justice Weyland, speaking in 1284, 'Annual rent can only exist in one of three forms: as something payable from a chamber for life; as an obligation payable from a manor or tenement; as an assignment of the rent due to a lord from his tenant'.[68] Thus, an obligation might arise from a personal agreement between grantor and grantee, said to issue simply from the deliberately vague grantor's 'chamber' (*camera sua*), rather than from some fixed and specific land or foundation. As Maitland wrote, these arrangements appear to us as 'merely personal annuities, unsecured annuities; the grantee has nothing to trust but the grantor's honesty and solvency'.[69] Alternately, a holder of land might impose a charge upon it for the benefit of another party, perhaps as repayment of a loan or as a charitable gift motivated by piety.[70] Or a lord might convey rent service owed by a tenant to a third party.[71] In contrast to these various forms of 'non-tenurial' rent, recoverable by the writ *de annuo redditu*, a lord seeking to recover rent service owed by a tenant—'tenurial' rent—could use a real action because the obligation was thought to arise from the land itself.[72]

Only the first of these three—personal annuities payable from the grantor's chamber—potentially raised a jurisdictional question. Most notable were agreements between church officials and clerks in which annual payments were granted in return for legal advice and representation in the church courts. Despite the arguably spiritual nature of these arrangements, the crown claimed authority to decide claims based on them. The writ of annual rent was also available where a prelate had promised to provide a pension until he presented the recipient to a benefice. In addition to these cases involving personal annuities, a

[67] Pollock & Maitland, 2:134. A justicies form of the writ had been created earlier.

[68] *Earliest Law Reports*, 1:145.

[69] Pollock & Maitland, 2:133. See generally id., 2:129–134, 143.

[70] Pollock & Maitland, 2:130.

[71] Pollock & Maitland, 2:130.

[72] Pollock & Maitland, 2:131–132. Lords also possessed the power of distraint—seizure of personal property—against their tenants in cases of non-payment. See Pollock & Maitland, 2:576–577. Blackstone refers to rent issuing from land as a 'rent-charge', to distinguish it from an annuity, 'a yearly sum chargeable only upon the person of the grantor': *Commentaries*, 2:40.

fourth category of annual rent not mentioned by Chief Justice Weyland—permanent obligations owed by one religious foundation to another or to an individual—also presented a potential jurisdictional controversy. Here the question was complex and seems not to have been decided until the last years of Edward I's reign.

The king's courts asserted jurisdiction over cases involving personal annuities even when the status of the parties to the agreement and its subject matter seemed clearly to be spiritual. In one Common Pleas case the actual deed of grant, made by the bishop of Coventry and Lichfield, was produced in evidence: 'we have granted an annuity of six marks to our esteemed clerk master John Lovel to be paid as long as he provides diligent and faithful legal representation as our advocate in the court of Canterbury'.[73] John brought suit for arrears amounting to 62 marks against the bishop's executors. They in turn produced documentary proof that 12 marks had been paid for two year's service, after which the bishop had died; therefore, the defendants argued, John had no longer been able to perform the service upon which the payment of the annuity was contingent. They asked for a ruling on this point, '*unde cum predictum scriptum . . . sit conditionale etc. et predictus magister Johannes non tenuit conditionem illam, que est causa actionis sue in hoc casu*'. Acknowledging that the obligation was personal in nature, the plaintiff countered that the bishop had been alive for several years after the cessation of payment, during which he continued in dutiful service, but here the case was adjourned and eventually left undecided.

In addition to cases involving payment for legal counsel and representation,[74] similar kinds of agreements were made in connection with other kinds of professional services.[75] Failure to perform the condition—the provision of the specified services—was the standard defence. The royal justices therefore might find themselves inquiring into events in ecclesiastical courts and referring these questions to lay juries. Thus, in one case the defendant acknowledged the agreement but asserted that in the course of a matrimonial cause the plaintiff had first assisted him but had later gone over to the other party.[76] The jury agreed with the plaintiff, who recovered his arrears and 40 shillings damages. In a similar case, a jury rejected a parson's contention that the plaintiff had actually pleaded against him in an attempt to deprive him of his benefice, first in the Court of Arches and later before the bishop of Exeter's official.[77]

The common law action of annual rent was also available in the case of another sort of personal annuity arrangement often entered into by ecclesiastics. These were the cases in which a promise was made to provide a pension until the recipient should be presented to

[73] CP 40/123, m. 40 (1298): 'damus et concedimus dilecto clerico nostro Johanni Lovel sex marcas annue pensionis . . . solvendas . . . quamdiu idem clericus in curia Cantuariensis in officio advocationis in negotiis nos et officium nostrum tangentibus nobis patrocinium prestiterit diligens et fidele'. Note that in this case and in others the agreement referred to the annual rent as a pension. 'Annual rent' appears to be the common law term for these arrangements. See also CP 40/60, m. 15 (1285).

[74] See also cases cited below, notes 76 and 77.

[75] E.g., CP 40/146, m. 85d (1303) ('phisicus' was engaged 'pro servicio . . . in labore medicinali').

[76] CP 40/72, m. 39 (1288).

[77] CP 40/87, m. 115 (1291). For other cases in which similar defences were presented, see CP 40/60, m. 15 (1285); CP 40/104, m. 105d (1294); CP 40/142, m. 48d (1302). In one case, the claimant, engaged 'pro patrocinio suo', was said to have represented adversaries in Court Christain and also before the king's justices intinerant: CP 40/89, m. 76 (1291).

a 'competent ecclesiastical benefice'. These agreements reflected the perennial problem in medieval England of an insufficiency of benefices in relation to the number of ordinands and the consequent canonical obligation of the ordinary to support his ordinands pending presentation to livings.[78]

Occasionally the defendants in these cases attempted to deny their responsibility for the acts of their predecessors,[79] but more typically they pleaded performance of the condition to which the obligation was subject, namely presentation to a competent benefice. Responding to such pleas the plaintiffs often raised questions of fact that again might have been better suited to decision by ecclesiastical authorities than by lay juries. For example, a plaintiff admitted he had been presented to a benefice by the defendant but asserted that this had occurred before the making of the pension agreement; the defendant was therefore still obliged to pay the annuity.[80] Or, in another case, it was argued that the plaintiff received a living not from the defendant but from a different patron.[81] Another possibility was the plaintiff's admission that he had been presented by the defendant but his denial that the living was '*competens*', as when a clerk objected that he had received a prebend worth no more than 10 pounds annually while he had been promised a benefice worth 20 pounds.[82] In another case, the defendant argued that he had presented the plaintiff, who had later resigned the benefice to the use of another clerk.[83] In yet another case, a defendant acknowledged his obligation but declared that the plaintiff was married and therefore had disabled himself from holding an ecclesiastical benefice (*per quod inhabilis est ad beneficium ecclesiasticum obtinendum*), thereby extinguishing the obligation (*sic annuitas predicta per factum ipsius Johannis est extincta*).[84] The clerk admitted that he was married but persisted in his claim, arguing that the deed stated simply that he was to receive his pension until provided with a living. He was prepared to prove that he had not yet been presented and asked whether, the condition of the agreement being unperformed, any other not mentioned in the deed should relieve the grantor of his obligation to pay the arrears, at least for the period during which he was a bachelor. The justices ruled that the right to arrears of the annuity was forfeited because the plaintiff had by his own act rendered performance of the condition impossible.[85]

Although it is clear that the common law action of annual rent was frequently used during the reign of Edward I by clerks claiming payments for legal or other professional services or pending presentation to a living, the extent to which similar disputes brought before ecclesiastical tribunals were subject to prohibition is a separate question that was not treated in section 3 and is more difficult to answer. Direct evidence is limited but it

[78] Rodes, *Ecclesiastical Administration*, 115.
[79] E.g., CP 40/18, m. 39 (1277).
[80] CP 40/91, m. 309 (1291).
[81] CP 40/83, m. 74d (1290).
[82] CP 40/127, m. 48d (1299). In other cases the obligor did not commit himself to provision of a benefice of a stated value. Competence therefore could not be determined by reference to the obligation's terms. E.g., CP 40/31, m. 137d (1279); CP 40/64, m. 35 (1286). In 1309 Stanton, J. said that in such cases the benefice must amount to at least the value of the annual payment and be tenable for life in order to extinguish the obligation. YB 2 & 3 Edw. II 125–126.
[83] CP 40/63, m. 22d (1286).
[84] CP 40/113, m. 15 (1296).
[85] For additional cases, see *Earliest Law Reports*, 4:404–406; CP 40/150, m. 97 (1304) (jury verdict for plaintiff).

appears that prohibition was available against these kinds of cases if brought in church courts. In one prohibition plea, a clerk allegedly prosecuted a claim in church court for an annual rent of two marks (*duas marcas annuas*) against a parson; the basis for the obligation was not specified.[86] In another prohibition plea, a judge was accused of hearing a claim brought by a clerk against an abbot and a prior for 60 marks owed him for expenses incurred 'in handling their affairs and for damages sustained on account of their failure to present him to a certain church'.[87] Perhaps the action sought compensation for legal services rendered, although there is no express mention of an on-going relationship and an annual payment obligation. The claim may also have involved a right to an annuity pending presentation to a benefice, although it could also have been based on an agreement to present with a promise of compensation for failure to do so. The defendant denied having held the plea. The implication is clear that the king's court considered the claim outside the church's jurisdiction. It is certainly possible that some of the many prohibition pleas concerning unspecified claims for money unrelated to testament or marriage involved church court suits for annual obligations of these kinds.

While the jurisdictional arrangement governing personal annuities was well settled, at least as far as the competence of the king's courts was concerned, another broad class of annual rent raised difficult questions that were not resolved until late in Edward I's reign. These cases involved annual payments issuing from ecclesiastical foundations such as parish churches, either permanently to another ecclesiastical foundation or to an individual for life. Church court suits appear not to have been subject to prohibition except under special circumstances. The royal courts were initially hesitant to admit claims based on these obligations and the jurisdictional question took some time to be resolved. These arrangements differed from the purely personal annuities discussed above—to be paid from some individual grantor's 'chamber'—because the obligor was an entity rather than a natural person. They also differed from obligations arising out of particular land, which were enforceable by means of common law real actions.[88] *Bracton*'s discussion of a particular sort of annual rent in this class—the corrody—in the treatment of novel disseisin explains why such payments were initially thought to be exempt from the assize. Rents issuing from religious foundations, such as abbeys or priories, originated in spiritual property, not in the chattels of some private individual (*in bonis dei et non alicuius hominis privati vel singularis personae*). As 'quasi-spiritual or annexed to spiritualities', the proper forum for their recovery was, according to *Bracton*, the ecclesiastical.[89]

One area in which the royal courts did claim jurisdiction over rent obligations assumed by ecclesiastical foundations was claims based on tithe compositions. As we have seen, the common law held that tithes were converted from spiritualities to temporalities by the fact of an exchange transaction. Farming of tithes, whereby the recipient of certain tithes granted them to another party in return for annual money payments, was therefore a secular matter; arrears in the annual obligation were recoverable at common law and prohibition

[86] CP 40/61, m. 52d (1286).

[87] CP 40/48, m. 14 (1283) (suit was allegedly 'tam pro expensis suis in negotiis expenditis quam pro dampnis suis que habuit occasione quod eum non presentaverit ad ecclesiam').

[88] Pollock & Maitland, 2:131–132.

[89] *Bracton*, 3:60. Canon law required episcopal approval of pensions attached to benefices because of their potential burden on a living's resources: see X 3.5.10.

lay against attempts to bring such claims in church courts. Common Pleas cases from 1286 and 1287 resulted in clear statements of the rule that, even though the basis of the agreement was tithes, a claim for money due was to be brought in a royal court.

In the 1286 case, the abbot of St Evroult brought an annual rent action against the abbot of Leicester, claiming arrears based on an agreement entered into by their predecessors in 1241.[90] Tithes from certain demesne lands of the earl of Leicester, previously due to St Evroult, were thenceforth to be taken at perpetual farm (*ad perpetuam firmam*) by the abbot and convent of Leicester in return for 20 marks annually. The abbot of Leicester argued in his defence that the royal courts should proceed no further with the case because the plaintiff's deed clearly showed that his action was based on tithes, a matter pertaining to the church's jurisdiction. His adversary replied that he was not claiming tithes but an annual payment due according to a contract (*per contractum*); even though tithes were involved, the royal courts had jurisdiction because claims for annual rents pertained to the lay forum. After an adjournment the court ruled for the plaintiff on the ground that he was seeking arrears in an annual rent, not tithes, and such claims were justiciable at common law according to custom (*secundum consuetudinem regni*).

In the 1287 case the parties were again two heads of religious houses, the priors of Huntingdon and of St Andrew's, Northampton.[91] Here Common Pleas again claimed jurisdiction over obligations based on tithe compositions and also made clear that the royal courts would admit no church court interference with the enforceability of such agreements. The prior of St Andrew's produced a deed recording an agreement entered into by their predecessors whereby the canons of Huntingdon were to receive *imperpetuum* certain tithes previously due to St Andrew's in return for annual money payments. As in the case just discussed, the defendant objected to Common Pleas' jurisdiction, arguing that, as the deed showed, 'the origin and principal cause of the rent are tithes' and 'a plea concerning tithes or those matters that are accessory to tithes is not to be determined in this court'. He argued further that the agreement had been the subject of a dispute heard by ecclesiastical judges and later on appeal by the Roman Curia, where it had been annulled as a 'corruption' and the prior of Huntingdon and his successors thereafter discharged of their obligation. Presumably this was the reason for the cessation of payment 14 years previously. In reply the plaintiff claimed that Common Pleas had jurisdiction 'in all pleas except pleas concerning testament, marriage, and tithes', but by composition the action for tithes was cancelled and an action for arrears in an annual rent justiciable at common law accrued to him. The court accepted this view, granting him arrears and damages, 'because the prior of Huntingdon does not deny the writing . . . nor that he owes him the arrears'. The justices thus completely ignored the defendant's second argument, that the agreement was void, apparently on the ground that once the original agreement was entered into, its enforcement was a matter for the royal courts and it was not to be meddled with by the church, which had no authority over it. The judgment is particularly interesting in light

[90] *Earliest Law Reports*, 2:245–248; see also 3:125–130. Apparently the abbot of St Evroult initially brought this claim in Court Christian but stopped when met by a writ of prohibition. When the abbot then proceeded to sue at common law instead, the abbot of Leicester allegedly had him cited before the archbishop of Canterbury, who eventually issued a definitive sentence against the abbot of St Evroult in the amount 200 pounds 'nomine expensarum'. The abbot of Leicester denied and a jury was summoned but no verdict is recorded: KB 27/94, m. 1d (1285).

[91] Case no. 2.5.

of the substantial body of ecclesiastical legislation explicitly directed against farming of tithes, here disregarded by the crown.[92]

While the special circumstance of a tithe composition rendered an otherwise spiritual obligation secular, the general common law rule at least during the first half of Edward I's reign was as stated in *Bracton*—annual rents issuing from ecclesiastical foundations such as monasteries or parish churches were spiritual and as such were for the church courts. *Circumspecte agatis* in 1286 endorsed this principle, as least as to pensions owed by rectors to prelates.[93] Toward the end of the thirteenth century, however, the crown broadened its jurisdiction to include claims for such payments in certain cases, including those apparently referred to in *Circumspecte agatis*. Legal arguments presented in the course of litigation indicate that this development was a departure from previous practice. The crown's eventual assumption of jurisdiction took some time to work itself out. Meanwhile, the separate but related question of whether claims for such payments might be subject to prohibition if brought in church court remained unresolved at the end of Edward I's reign.

One theory that might have supported prohibition in some cases was the possible prejudice to rights of patronage. For example, if it was determined that a parish church owed an annual rent, the value of the church's advowson to the patron could be diminished accordingly. This question was first addressed in Common Pleas in two prohibition pleas in 1290. In the first case, the bishop of Worcester attempted to halt a claim for an annual rent in the Court of Arches, where the prior of Kenilworth had brought suit against the rector of Halford.[94] The advowson of Halford had previously belonged to the priory but by a written agreement it had been yielded to the bishop and his successors in return for an 'annual pension' of five marks to be paid by Halford church to the priory. So, the prior argued, his ecclesiastical suit was a purely spiritual one. The bishop defended the prohibition on the ground that the prior's attempt to collect the annual rent threatened his interest in the advowson because the amount claimed allegedly exceeded one-fourth of the church's annual income. His writ of prohibition, in the *de advocatione* form used to block disputes involving rival claims to tithes,[95] was delivered in January 1290. Even though the bishop's predecessor had been a party to this arrangement, the bishop now seems to have been attempting to apply the one-fourth rule stated in *Circumspecte agatis* to claims for annual rents owed by parish churches.[96] The argument is especially interesting because the 'statute' mentioned that rule only in connection with tithe disputes and expressly reserved to the church jurisdiction over annual rents payable by parish churches. The case was adjourned, presumably to consider this question of law, and not decided.

Another prohibition plea from the same year again raised the issue and seemed initially to result in a clear recognition of the patron's interest but the judgment was reversed on a writ of error to King's Bench. A patron had presented two clerks to the same benefice. In order to resolve the resultant confusion all parties agreed to submit to the ruling of the local

[92] See Mansi, *Conciliorum*, 21:387 (1129, c. 4), 22:135 (1172, c. 7), 22:141 (1173, c. ll), 22:150 (1175, c. 10); *Councils & Synods*, 769 (1268, c. 20).

[93] Printed in *SR*, 1:101.

[94] CP 40/83, m. 90 (1290).

[95] See above, p. lix.

[96] As discussed in section 3, Circumspecte agatis recognized the church's jurisdiction over disputed claims to collect tithes as long as the amount involved did not reach one-fourth of value of the church in possession.

bishop, who declared that one clerk should assume possession of the living while the other should receive a pension for life from the church's income, payable by the current incumbent whomever he should be. Since the bishop's ruling the advowson of the church had changed hands; the current patrons now brought a prohibition plea *de advocatione* against a claim for arrears in the pension, on the ground that the pension amounted to one-third of the value of the church from which it was due.[97] The defendant in this prohibition plea—who had ceased to receive his pension when a clerk presented by the prohibition plea plaintiff had succeeded the rector originally party to the settlement—argued that the pension was a spirituality not recoverable at common law. Moreover, he produced a deed attesting to the pension agreement sealed by the local bishop and the then patron. A jury later found in support of the plaintiffs' allegation that the patron's assent had been illegitimate: it had been given without the assent of his co-patron, who was now the wife of the prohibition plea plaintiff. Common Pleas then entered judgment for the prohibition plea plaintiff and ordered the defendant to proceed no further with his claim in ecclesiastical court. Soon after, however, the Common Pleas record was called before King's Bench on a writ of error.[98] The pension claimant seems to have argued that there was no basis for the judgment against him because there was no finding that his claim had been for one-third of the value of the church in question as had been alleged against him. Instead, the pleadings and jury verdict had gone off on a different point, whether there was a valid assent by the patron to the pension arrangement. There being no finding as to the value of the amount claimed in relation to the church's income, there was no basis for the Common Pleas judgment and King's Bench therefore reversed it. This dispute, which seemed initially to resolve the question of the patron's interest in a claim for an annual rent brought against his or her church by applying the one-fourth rule otherwise applicable to tithe controversies, thus again ended up with that question left undecided.[99]

Aside from the possible application of the one-fourth rule raised but not resolved in these prohibition cases, there is no further reason to conclude that, during the reign of Edward I, the crown sought to restrict the church's jurisdiction over claims for annual rents owed by ecclesiastical foundations. Nevertheless, during the 1290's the royal justices indicated some willingness to allow claims for annual rents owed by ecclesiastical foundations to be brought at common law. In the course of the two prohibition pleas from 1290 in which the one-fourth rule was relied upon it had been pointed out that there was no common law remedy for recovery of an annual rent payable by a parish church. This was

97 Case no. 1.16a.

98 Case no. 1.16b.

99 A later case also might have raised that question but again the issue was not clearly presented. This case involved a writ of prohibition presented in 1306 to halt a church court suit brought on behalf of the prior of Rochester cathedral priory against the parson of All Hallows Barking 'exigendo unam marcam annue pensionis nomine prioris de Roff'': CP 40/161, m. 504d (1306), also enrolled at CP 40/164, m. 203d (1307) but without the jury verdict. Rochester cathedral priory had previously held the advowson of the church, but at least by 1302 or 1303 it seems to have been transferred to the abbess and convent of Barking. Harben, *Dictionary of London*, 13. Assuming the priory was no longer perpetual rector, the basis for its claim is unclear. In any event, while its suit threatened the value of the advowson to the convent, the convent does not seem to have brought the writ of prohibition, which was in the de catallis et debitis form rather than the de advocatione suitable for asserting patronage interests. Further, the prohibition plea defendant denied proceeding contrary to prohibition rather than attempting to defend the church's juridiction, so the question of the one-fourth rule's potential application to claims for annual rents was not presented. Nor was Common Pleas called upon to decide whether prohibition was appropriate despite *Circumspecte agatis*'s apparent authorization of ecclesiastical suits like this.

to be expected, given that *Circumspecte agatis* had recognized the church's jurisdiction in such cases and that there was apparently no writ of prohibition to prevent its exercise. Even so, during the last decade of the thirteenth century ecclesiastical litigants attempted to bring common law actions on several occasions. This development may have reflected the increasing popularity of the writ of annual rent—still a relatively new creation—and concern over the uncertain possibility that church court actions might be subject to prohibition if the amounts involved were high enough, a risk left open by the unresolved prohibition pleas just discussed. Although the defendants in the cases heard during the 1290's argued strenuously that the royal courts had no basis for jurisdiction over such matters, they did not fully succeed in preventing the extension of the common law remedy. The result was concurrent royal and ecclesiastical jurisdiction over similar claims.

In spite of a 1292 ruling that assumed their competence, the justices of Common Pleas seem to have wavered on the matter of their jurisdiction in subsequent annual rent cases heard during the 1290's in which the jurisdictional question was raised directly. In the 1292 case the defendant, a rector, did not raise that question but the fact of a judgment for the plaintiff, also a rector, on a claim for a non-personal annual rent indicates the willingness of the royal justices to admit such claims for determination at common law.[1] The plaintiff produced a document showing that the obligation resulted from the settlement of a dispute between the parties' predecessors decided during Becket's archbishopric, according to which payments were thenceforth due from one parish church to another. The defendant did not deny this or that the plaintiff and his predecessors had received the payments continuously since the reign of Richard I until his own incumbency. Instead, he argued that agreements of this kind could not impose a permanent obligation on a church without the assent of the patron and the local ordinary. The court acknowledged that this was the case with regard to more recent arrangements (*modernis temporibus*), but ruled that 'seisin as long and continuous as the time from whence the writ of right runs' was sufficient to render the patron's formal assent unnecessary.[2] This judgment was therefore a refinement of the court's ruling in the second of the 1290 prohibition pleas that invalid assent of the patron might be ground for prohibition against an annual rent action in a church court. Not only were claims based on especially long seisin enforceable regardless of the patron's assent, but Common Pleas would itself adjudicate them.

Common Pleas also exercised jurisdiction on several other occasions during the 1290's when defendants pleaded against the validity of the original agreement rather than challenging the court's authority directly. An interesting example is a claim brought against the prior of St Swithin's for 13 years' arrears in an annual rent of 40 marks allegedly granted by the priory during the incumbency of a predecessor of the prior.[3] He denied that the

[1] This case was first heard during Easter term 1292, when it was adjourned pending summons at the defendant's request of patron and ordinary. CP 40/93, m. 27 (1292). Neither appeared, so the court proceeded to judgment without them: CP 40/96, m. 114 (1292).

[2] The emphasis on long seisin may have echoed similar arguments heard in cases on annual rents issuing from manors rather than ecclesiastical foundations. See *Earliest Law Reports*, 1:144–146, 175–177. The reference to the writ of right was in reply to the plaintiff's assertion of seisin since the reign of Richard I; Richard's accession (in 1189) had recently been fixed as the legal limitation beyond which parties to actions on writs of right could not plead. St. West. I, c. 39, printed in *SR*, 1:36. In 1290 it was ordained that user of a franchise since 1189 was sufficient answer to a writ of quo warranto. St. 18 Edw. I, printed in *SR*, 1:107.

[3] CP 40/92, m. 95 (1292).

deed proffered by the plaintiff was the legitimate act of his house (*non est factum predicti conventus*). A jury, closely interrogated by the justices on this question, stated that the prior's predecessor had been removed from his office by the bishop-elect of Winchester during the 1250's. After his deprivation, the four monks entrusted with custody of the conventual seal applied it to a piece of blank parchment (*parcamenum album*), which was sent to Rome where the grant of the annuity was written on it. Because neither the use of the seal nor the grant of the annuity was approved by the convent the jurors believed that the document was not 'good or legal'. Asked if it was customary practice for the custodians of the seal to use it 'without the consent or knowledge of the chapter', the jurors replied that it was not. This would have been sufficient to discharge the priory of its obligation at common law,[4] but the parties instead reached a compromise: the prior acknowledged the plaintiff's right in return for remission of the claim for arrears. This case is instructive not only for the evidence it provides of the lay jurors' detailed knowledge of the priory's internal affairs but also because it shows that, if the defendant did not plead against its jurisdiction, Common Pleas apparently was prepared to decide the claim on its merits.[5]

These cases did not address the fundamental jurisdictional question directly, apparently because the defendants did not raise it. When in 1293 a litigant did argue it directly, the justices were indecisive. In this case, discussed earlier in another context,[6] patronage rights were not discussed at all, although given the nature of the dispute they might have been. A clerk sued a parson in Common Pleas for arrears in an annual rent pursuant to a settlement of a dispute that had been submitted to the arbitration of the local bishop several years previously. The clerk was thenceforth to receive 40 shillings twice a year for life from the parson 'on behalf of his parsonage' (*per manus . . . nomine personatus*). The defendant objected that the nature of the obligation exempted it from secular jurisdiction. The claim was against his church, not him personally. If he were to die or resign his adversary could still bring his claim against the next incumbent. Moreover, another royal court had earlier ruled that this very claim was a purely spiritual matter. When he had brought the annual rent claim before royal justices itinerant in Norfolk that court had dismissed it and invited him to sue in an ecclesiastical court if he wished. Before Common Pleas could

[4] Cf. the writ of entry for recovery of church land alienated by a bishop or prior without the assent of his chapter or convent. Like the other forms of the writs of entry, this one alleged a specific defect in the tenant's title, here based on an invalid alienation. See Pollock & Maitland, 2:68.

[5] See also a case in which a clerk claimed an annual rent from the prior of Holy Trinity, York based on an agreement made with the defendant's predecessor. He had evidently held the office illegally, as an intruder, so the question was whether his act in granting the rent was valid. The bench asked the jury whether others of his acts had been treated as valid. No judgment is enrolled, but the jurisdiction of the royal court was unchallenged. JUSTI/1091, m. 26 (Yorkshire, 1294).

In another case a clerk sued a prior for 14 robes, the arrears in his annuity of one 'roba' decens de secta clericorum per year for life based on a sealed deed. The prior pleaded that the seal was not that of his convent. The jury stated that the seal had not been in use when the deed was allegedly made, 23 years previously, so the plaintiff was amerced for a false claim. CP 40/130, m. 85d (1299).

Yet another example of the king's court deciding an annual rent claim against a religious foundation was a case first decided in 1296 and then heard again in 1307 when an action was brought to enforce the earlier judgment. In this case too the plaintiff, a prior, pleaded long seisin by his predecessors. The defendant, a parson, said he could not answer without the king, who held the advowson of his church, or the local bishop. The king authorised the case to proceed and the bishop did not appear after being summoned. The defendant therefore denied the plaintiff's assertion of long seisin and put himself upon a jury, which later found for the plaintiff. CP 40/163, m. 48 (1307).

[6] Case no. 2.12.

rule on this jurisdictional question, however, the plaintiff raised a collateral issue that diverted the justices' attention. Following the ruling of the justices itinerant, he brought his action before an ecclesiastical tribunal but the defendant produced a writ of prohibition. Had he proceeded in spite of the prohibition and an attachment suit followed, again the jurisdictional question would have been raised. Instead, he obeyed the prohibition (or perhaps the judge did) and instituted the annual rent action now before Common Pleas. The justices accordingly turned to the question of whether the defendant had in fact brought a prohibition after a royal court had declared the cause to be within the church's jurisdiction. He refused to answer this and went on to make the telling point that, even if he had, that would not necessarily confer jurisdiction on Common Pleas to decide a 'purely spiritual' matter. The case was here adjourned and not resumed, leaving unresolved the contradiction between the judgment of the justices itinerant endorsing the church's jurisdiction and the willingness of Common Pleas to decide a similar claim a year previously.

Common Pleas avoided settling the jurisdictional question in at least three more attempts to use writs of annual rent to enforce non-personal ecclesiastical obligations during the 1290's. These cases were all analogous to the 1292 one, in that prescriptive right was alleged in the absence of evidence of assent of the patron of the church from which the money was due. In each case the defendant argued that there was no basis for Common Pleas' jurisdiction, but in none did the justices issue a ruling on that point. For example, in 1296 the prior of Loders brought an annual rent action against the vicar of St Pancras, pleading seisin of the annual payment by his predecessors since the reign of King John.[7] According to the original agreement the plaintiff's house was to receive 20 shillings from the vicar of St Pancras, whoever he should be (*qui pro tempore fuerit vicarius*).[8] The defendant objected to the court's jurisdiction, on the ground that the plaintiff offered no 'deed of the patron or other title whose cognizance pertains to the secular forum'. The plaintiff replied that he claimed the annuity as the right (*ut jus*) of his house, in the seisin of his predecessors since time out of mind. This prescriptive right was, he argued, by its very nature a *jus laycum* and therefore enforceable at common law.[9] The view that a spiritual claim became a temporal depending on its evidentiary basis is difficult to grasp,

[7] CP 40/115, m. 105 (1296).

[8] St Pancras was evidently appropriated to Loders priory. The usual procedure in such situations was for the religious house, as perpetual rector, to receive the church's or chapel's income directly, while appointing a vicar supported by a stipend to undertake the parochial duties. The balance between the income and the stipend would be profit for the religious house. By 1300 at least half of the parish churches in England had been appropriated. See generally Hartridge, *Vicarages*. For some examples of pensions due from appropriated churches to religious houses, see Thompson, *English Clergy*.

[9] 'Et predictus Thomas [the defendant] venit. Et dicit quod non debet de predicto annuo redditu in curia respondere seculari etc. Dicit enim quod idem prior predictam annuytatem ab eo exigit ut provenientem de ecclesia sua predicta Sancti Pancracii absque hoc quod per factum alicuius patroni aut alium titulum cuius cognitio ad forum pertinent seculare predictum annuum redditum sibi deberi alleget etc. Et ex quo cognitio de factis predictorum episcopi et archiepiscopi ad forum spectat ecclesiasticum ut de re spirituali etc. dicit quod videtur ei quod cognitio istius placiti ad forum spectat ecclesiasticum. Et petit judicium etc.

'Et Prior dicit quod ipse exigit predictum annuum redditum ut jus ecclesie sue predicte de seisina predecessorum [illegible word] a tempore quo non extat memoria etc. Et ex quo predicta annuytas per tanti temporis prescriptionem ecclesie sue predicte tamquam jus laycum est annexa, dicit quod cognitio inde ad forum seculare pertinet etc.'.

The case ended in compromise: the defendant acknowledged the plaintiff's right and the latter remitted his claim for arrears.

but certainly the argument here was an echo of the plaintiff's successful plea in the 1292 case discussed above.

Similar arguments were made in another case a year later.[10] Here the record reveals clearly that the dispute was between a religious foundation and the vicar of a parish church appropriated to it. Because the claimant was also the patron, there was no issue as to whether an adverse judgment would diminish the value of the benefice to the owner of the advowson. In this case too, the jurisdictional question was left unresolved.[11]

The question may finally have been settled in a case pleaded in 1301 but actually decided early in 1303.[12] As part of a settlement of a dispute over an advowson, the patron of the church agreed that it would pay an annual rent of two marks to another religious foundation, Stone priory. When the incumbent parson stopped paying, the prior sued a writ of annual rent and pleaded a fine levied in the king's court early in the reign of Henry III that memorialized the settlement. The parson first objected to Common Pleas' jurisdiction on the ground that the claim was purely spiritual because the payments were alleged to issue from a church. The court rejected this argument and the parson then argued that the fine was void because it did not include the assent of the parson at the time. The justices rejected this argument too and entered judgment for the prior. The parson's effort to challenge the validity of the fine suggests that perhaps an otherwise spiritual claim was rendered secular by the special status of a final concord. This way of thinking would have paralleled the argument heard in 1296 that long seisin could transform a spiritual claim into a *jus laicum*. The record of the 1301 case reveals nothing of whether the justices intended to make a broader assertion of jurisdiction over all annual rents payable by religious foundations regardless of the evidentiary basis for the plaintiff's claim.

Another Common Pleas case more clearly suggests an assertion of general jurisdiction but again there is no clear judicial statement. A prior brought a claim on behalf of his priory against the parson of St John's, Wenham, for an annual rent granted to the priory by the bishop of Norwich.[13] This was memorialized in a deed. The parson claimed that his church was called All Saints' and the issue went to a jury, which found that it had been called St John's at the time of the grant and had been so called during the incumbencies of four succeeding parsons and only thereafter was renamed All Saints'.[14] Without stating a reason, Common Pleas gave judgment for the claimant. Here there was no fine or claim of prescriptive right. The court's willingness to decide the case thus seems to suggest that the king's justices had assumed jurisdiction over annual rents payable by parish churches. The fact that there was no jurisdictional objection may indicate that that issue was now settled.

The claims in these cases were for rents issuing from permanent locations and regular revenues and therefore could be thought of as analogous to rents issuing from real property. As such they differed from personal annuities due from individuals. Plaintiffs claiming from religious foundations accordingly tended to describe their rights as analogous to real property rights, as such entitled to the common law's protection. Hence the emphasis where possible on long seisin or a fine. The common law's apparent inclination to view

[10] CP 40/116, m. 12d (1297).
[11] For yet another case raising the jurisdictional question but not deciding it, see CP 40/110, m. 124d (1295).
[12] Case no. 2.15.
[13] CP 40/150, m. 128 (1304).
[14] Today there is an All Saints' church in Little Wenham, Suffolk and a St John's in Great Wenham.

rents due from ecclesiastical foundations as analogous to real rents had in fact been partially embodied in a statute of 1285. The second statute of Westminster granted the protection of novel disseisin to corrodies.[15] Prohibition was available to keep these claims out of the church courts.[16] Earlier *Bracton* spoke of corrodies as matters for ecclesiastical jurisdiction, being payments of spiritual property.[17] Maitland, however, was incorrect in suggesting that the statute brought about the removal of corrody suits from the church's competence.[18] The common law plea rolls from earlier in Edward's reign reveal numerous instances of claims for corrodies allegedly withheld unjustly, so the crown's assumption of jurisdiction predated the statute.[19] The significance of this statutory provision was not that it redefined the appropriate forum before which such claims were to be made. Rather, it brought such claims within the scope of the real action of novel disseisin.

The common law presumably chose to treat corrodies like real rents because they were due from a certain, fixed place. This may seem to have warranted extension of novel disseisin. So too, probably, the fact that they typically included a right to reside in a particular place; interruption was similar—in fact if not in theory—to dispossession of a free tenement. Corrodies therefore could be distinguished from more purely personal obligations between individuals. Other obligations owing from churches—as entities rather than from their incumbents as individuals—were actually closer in substance to corrodies as far as their source was concerned. The tendency embodied in the statute probably encouraged the king's justices to think in real terms in other cases of rents due from ecclesiastical foundations, even though such claims were outside the scope of the statute and the remedy.

Despite the conceptual similarity, the non-personal aspect of these obligations arguably took them outside the scope of the writ for recovery of annual rents, which was intended to enforce personal contractual obligations rather than those issuing from specific land or religious foundations. Moreover, the absence of secular patronage interests in many of these disputes—arguably at least the basis for prohibition of some ecclesiastical suits for annual rents owed by parish churches—was an additional ground for exempting them from secular jurisdiction. It was probably this tension, between the quasi-real nature of the obligations and the personal nature of the remedy, that caused the reluctance of the Common Pleas justices during the 1290's to dismiss the claims to the ecclesiastical forum but prevented them from boldly extending the scope of the relatively recently instituted annual rent action beyond the realm of the purely personal. Why the judges seem finally to have changed their minds is unclear, if in fact they did.

To sum up, it is clear that during the reign of Edward I there was a marked tendency to bring certain annual rent claims under common law jurisdiction, claims based on arrangements that were arguably matters for church courts to adjudicate because of the ecclesiastical status of the parties as individuals or institutions and of the property at issue. The writ of annual rent, developed during the later years of the reign of Henry III, included within

[15] St. West. II, c. 25, printed in *SR*, 1:84–85. For cases, see, e.g., CP 40/81, m. 72d (1290); CP 40/91, m. 147d (1291); CP 40/98, m. 78 (1293).

[16] E.g., CP 40/134, m. 58 (1300).

[17] *Bracton*, 3:60.

[18] Pollock & Maitland, 2:134–135.

[19] The writ commanded the defendant to answer 'quare subtraxit corrodium'. See, e.g., CP 40/19, m. 62d (1277); CP 40/30, m. 21 (1279); CP 40/31, m. 118 (1279); CP 40/44, m. ld (1282); CP 40/48, m. 41 (1283).

its scope personal obligations such as agreements concerning the salaries of advocates or pensions of unbeneficed ordinands, which fell under the broad heading of annuity arrangements between individuals, the payments not issuing from some specific real property. At some point in the later years of Henry III or early years of Edward I the common law went further, extending its jurisdiction over an important class of annual rent—corrodies—and then, by statute, allowing claims to be made by means of the assize of novel disseisin. The apparent reason was that corrodies were conceptually similar to possessory rights in rent issuing from land. Moreover, Common Pleas admitted claims by writ of annual rent for payments due from religious foundations that were not personal, probably under the influence of the concept embodied in the statutory rule. Efforts were made to bring annual rents within the mantle of the *Circumspecte agatis*' one-fourth rule, but prohibition may not have been available to halt church court claims against religious foundations where there was no partronage interest at stake. Common Pleas did not during the reign of Edward I issue a firm statement of its jurisdiction over non-personal obligations, but even so the royal justices decided several cases in which their jurisdiction was not challenged. The limited scope of prohibition together with Common Pleas' liberal exercise of jurisdiction meant that the legal boundary between the two fora in this area was not exclusive and probably was somewhat vaguely defined. The church courts apparently were active in this area.[20] While the common law's treatment of annual rents during Edward I's reign thus appears to have included some notable innovation, the actual impact on the church's jurisdiction probably was not great.

Ecclesiastical patronage

The law governing ecclesiastical patronage was an important aspect of the crown's jurisdiction during the middle ages, a fact attested by the large volume of litigation it generated and its resultant complexity. In general the common law courts during the reign of Edward I respected the jurisdictional arrangement inherited from his predecessors and continued to apply already established rules to disputes within their competence. The *jus patronatus* was the right of a patron, lay or ecclesiastic, to present a candidate to the local bishop for admission to and institution in a benefice in the patron's gift,[21] and the Constitutions of Clarendon included it among those matters reserved to the royal courts.[22] In the years that followed the common law developed a set of remedies that protected these rights, including the assize of darrein presentment (*de ultima presentatione*) and the writ of right of advowson. The first protected the possessory right of the person most recently seised of the advowson—seisin being defined as the exercise of the right to present—while the latter was concerned with title rather than mere recent possession. Both corresponded to real actions because an advowson was considered an item of real property (a species of 'incorporeal hereditament'), typically appurtenant to a manor though detachable from it by grant.

[20] Helmholz, *History*, 369.
[21] See generally Gray, 'Ius Praesentandi'; Pollock & Maitland, 2:136–140; Holdsworth, *HEL*, 3:24–25, 138–143.
[22] Const. Clar. c. 1, printed in *Select Charters*, 164.

By the reign of Edward I the clergy no longer challenged the crown's claim to decide disputes concerning rights to ecclesiastical patronage. The one exception recorded in the plea rolls was a case in which the defendant, tacitly recognizing the general jurisdictional rule, sought exemption from it. A woman recovered the advowson to a church in Wales in an action against the bishop of St Asaph heard by royal justices of assize.[23] She won her claim as the result of his repeated defaults and he subsequently ignored the writ of judgment ordering him to admit her candidate to the living. Attached to answer for this refusal in Common Pleas, the bishop declared that 'the advowson of a church is something purely spiritual, the jurisdiction over which in Wales pertains wholly to the local ordinaries'. The court refused to consider this objection and ordered that the bishop be compelled by distraint to admit the plaintiff's clerk.[24] One also finds occasional prohibition pleas indicating that church courts may have attempted to exercise jurisdiction in some cases, but there does not seem to have been any doubt about their impropriety in the eyes of the common law.[25]

Secular jurisdiction over advowson extended only as far as disputes over the right to present a clerk to the local bishop for admission and institution. Actual possession of the benefice by the candidate was subject to the local ordinary's approval, according to canonical regulations applied at an ecclesiastical inquest. Upon presentation of the candidate the bishop authorised a local panel to determine whether the benefice in question was in fact vacant, the clerk suitably qualified to occupy it, and his patron the true holder of the right to confer it.[26] Typically the panel consisted of 12 men, half clerks, half lay.[27] If the last question was disputed the inquest informed the bishop that the right of advowson was litigious and no further action was taken by him until a royal court had settled the matter.[28] As a rule the royal courts respected the church's jurisdiction over questions of voidance and idoneity, acknowledging that '*huiusmodi cause cognitio ad forum spectat ecclesiasticum*'.[29]

Refusal to institute an appropriate candidate was an offence at common law. In one noteworthy case, the king had recovered the advowson in King's Bench and then claimed that the archbishop of Canterbury and others were interfering with the bishop of Worcester's

[23] Case no. 2.3a.

[24] Case no. 2.3b. It is possible that this case was the basis for the clergy's complaint to the king in 1285: 'Item, quod ecclesie Wallie sue libertati pristine dimittantur'. The crown responded, 'Rex intellegit quod sunt plus libere quam fuerint ab initio': *Councils & Synods*, 958; see also id. at 961, 963. On Edward I's subjugation of Wales and the Welsh church, see Powicke, *Thirteenth Century*, 433–444.

[25] E.g., a case in which it was alleged that a clerk sued for admission to a church before the archbishop of Canterbury and succeeded in gaining institution to the benefice despite a writ of prohibition: CP 40/161, m. 273 (1306). See also KB 27/144, m. 15d (1295) (suit in church court concerning prebend in the king's gift).

[26] Gray, 'Ius Praesentandi', 490–494. For some early fourteenth-century examples of forms used in inquests *de jure patronatus*, see id. at 508–509. A Common Pleas jury describes the procedure in CP 40/90, m. 20 (1291).

[27] Helmholz, *History*, 484.

[28] A writ to the bishop, Ne admittas, was available pendent lite. If he ignored it, after settlement of the patronage dispute the patron could sue a writ *quare incumbravit* against the bishop. Gray, 'Ius Praesentandi', 495–496.

[29] E.g., CP 40/144, m. 244 (1302); CP 40/145, m. 189 (1303); CP 40/150, m. 177d (1304), all involving questions of vacancy, and CP 40/150, m. 84d (1304) (patron's candidate said to be 'minoris . . . etatis, illegitimus, et insufficienter litteratus'); CP 40/152, m. 79d (1304) (candidate said to be unsuitable because 'plura beneficia tenuit etc. et etiam illegitimus est').

institution of his clerk.[30] The archbishop had brought an action in the court of Arches against the bishop, who had appealed to Rome. Meanwhile, a writ of prohibition had been introduced, and it was now alleged in vivid terms that the archbishop's clerk had shown great contempt to the king. Surprisingly, a jury verdict heard before the king's council at Westminster cleared the dean of Arches and the allegedly defiant clerk of all the purported contemptuous behavior. The larger question of the archbishop's interference with the king's advowson right was apparently resolved by compromise.[31]

Advowson cases in which the head of a religious house was defendant were numerous. This reflects the widespread incidence of appropriation, whereby religious houses obtained advowsons from donors and ordained themselves perpetual rector while appointing vicars to reside in the parishes. In litigation resulting from these circumstances an abbot or prior often pleaded plenarty in defence: the church to which the claimant asserted the right of presentation was not vacant but 'full and provided for by the abbot and convent' (*plena et consulta de abbate et conventu suo*). The royal justices routinely submitted this plea to the local ordinary, requesting him to investigate and inform the court.[32] Occasionally the bishop reported simply that the church in question had been appropriated 'since time out of mind',[33] while other returns include a statement that an earlier lay patron had granted the advowson to a religious house, which had since held it to its own uses.[34] Attempts by common law plaintiffs in advowson cases to require that defendants pleading plenarty due to appropriation produce written evidence of the original grant by a patron were unsuccessful. The adoption of such a requirement would have provided the occasion for royal restriction both of the church's authority to decide the validity of the exception and of the prescriptive rights of religious houses, but Common Pleas in a conclusive ruling in 1283 declined to do so.[35]

Canon law required certain qualifications for the admission of a candidate to an ecclesiastical benefice, including minimum age, legitimate birth, good morals, literacy, and

[30] Case no. 2.18. This episode, involving the advowson of the church of Dodderhill, Worcester diocese, is discussed in detail in Denton, *Winchelsey*, 215–218. The earlier case in which the king recovered the advowson from the prior and convent of Worcester is found at KB 27/175, m. 19 (1304), printed in *King's Bench Cases*, 3:125–127.

[31] Denton, *Winchelsey*, 217.

[32] According to an argument presented in a Common Pleas case, an exception of plenarty raised three points for episcopal verification: 'necesse habet verificare tria, scilicet de quo plena etc. et ad cuius presentationem etc. et a quo tempore. Et super istis tribus necesse est scribere loci ordinario etc.': CP 40/95, m. 195 (1292). In the case of an appropriated benefice the answer to the first two would have been the religious house itself. For additional examples, see CP 40/144, m. 244 (1302); CP 40/145, m. 189 (1303); CP 40/150, m. 177d (1304). Cf. a case in which a bishop twice responded to Common Pleas' queries in too much detail, by explaining that the defendant, a religious house, had occupied the church in question illegally. A third time the justices wrote ordering the bishop to state simply (precise) whether the church was vacant and no more. The defendant then appealed to the Court of Canterbury for an order halting the bishop's inquiry; Common Pleas ruled that it thereby lost the right to episcopal verification and put the question to a lay assize instead: CP 40/89, m. 157 (1291).

[33] E.g., KB 27/37, m. 29d (1278).

[34] E.g., CP 40/13, m. 7d (1276); CP 40/58, m. 26 (1285).

[35] In a lengthy case the claimant insisted that the defendant's exception of plenarty be supported by written evidence of a grant of the advowson from a patron. The Common Pleas justices, after many delays and a writ of certiorari from King's Bench, finally ruled that the local ordinary would determine whether the church was vacant: CP 40/49, m. 32 (1283). In another case, the question was raised whether a plea of plenarty should simply be referred to the bishop where it was alleged that the religious house had wrongfully gained possession of the advowson. According to a report of the case, this issue was not resolved. See Brand, *Making of the Common Law*, 465–472.

ordination at least at the level of subdeacon.[36] Although restricting the patrons' freedom of appointment and therefore potentially in conflict with their interests, the crown did not challenge the substance of these regulations. If the question of idoneity arose in the course of common law litigation, the royal justices left it to the local bishop for resolution. Thus, in one case the archbishop of Canterbury confirmed the bishop of Norwich's assertion, in defence of his refusal to admit the plaintiff's candidate, that the clerk was a 'notorious adulterer and simoniac'.[37] In other cases, bishops stated that the candidate was not ordained[38] or was illiterate.[39] These facts would have been revealed in the course of the ecclesiastical inquests convened after the patron's presentation of the candidate to the bishop. There is no evidence to suggest that king's courts failed to respect such findings during the reign of Edward I.

A potentially problematic cause for disqualification was pluralism, the simultaneous possession without dispensation of more than one benefice with cure of souls. Canon law condemned the practice—a clerk receiving a second benefice was *ipso jure* deprived of the first[40]—because of the obvious tendency for the pluralist to neglect his parochial duties, but it persisted nonetheless because of its utility to patrons as a means of rewarding deserving clerks or relatives.[41] The status of the pluralist at common law arose twice in the course of advowson litigation during the reign of Edward I, but Common Pleas declined to issue a definite ruling on both occasions, thus avoiding a potentially difficult jurisdictional conflict. In one case the bishop of Worcester argued that he had not admitted the plaintiff's candidate because he himself had previously conferred the living upon another clerk by virtue of his authority to collate to benefices vacant for over six months through the neglect of their patrons.[42] This case therefore turned on whether the benefice had been vacant when the plaintiff attempted to make his presentation. He alleged that he had presented the last incumbent, who had died in 1289, and then presented his successor. The bishop, however, claimed to have deprived the incumbent because of pluralism over a year previously, in January 1288.[43] The legal question was accordingly whether

36 For the canonical requirements, see *DDC*, 2:735–747, especially pp. 735–738. All were subject to papal dispensation. An early fourteenth-century English inquest included the following questions 'circa personam': 'Utrum fuit legitime etatis et libere conditionis. Utrum fuit de legitimo matrimonio procreata. Utrum fuit laudibile vite et conversationis. Utrum fuit sufficiente literata. Utrum fuit infamia notata. Utrum alibi beneficiata' (Gray, 'Ius Praesentandi', 509).

37 The bishop first pleaded that the plaintiff's candidate 'non est idonea persona nec fuit die presentationis facte et dicit enim quod idem Radulfus pupplice infamis est et irregularis et sic inhabilis ad quodlibet beneficium ecclesiasticum optinendum'. In response to the plaintiff's objection that this plea was too general, the bishop stated that the candidate was a 'notorious adulter et simoniacus': CP 40/125, m. 22 (1298). Simony—an appointment made in exchange for a money payment—was a ground for disqualification under canon law: X 5.3.8.

38 E.g., a candidate was admitted 'in corporalem possessionem' of the church in question but not instituted as rector until he had been ordained: CP 40/83, m. ld (1290). The distinction was between the approval of the candidate by the bishop as suitable and the actual commission of the cure to him. See Phillimore, *Ecclesiastical Law*, 1:350. See also CP 40/106, m. l9 (1294).

39 E.g., CP 40/150, m. 84d (1304).

40 X 3.5.28 (De multa). Earlier twelfth-century legislation included X 3.4.3; X 3.5.7; X 3.5.14. See also Sext. 1.16.3. For English provincial legislation, see *Councils & Synods*, 774–780, 873–881, 916–917.

41 See Moorman, *Church Life*, 28–30. See also Waugh, 'Pecham and Pluralities'.

42 CP 40/83, m. 18d (1290).

43 'Et episcopus dicit quod quia predictus Remundus optinuit plura beneficia etc. sine dispensatione citari fecit ipsum coram eo . . . ostensurus si quod haberet per quod pluralitatem beneficiorum posset optinere, quo die ipsum Remundum ecclesia illa sententialiter privavit'.

this deprivation was valid in the eyes of the common law. If so, the bishop's collation was legitimate; if not, he had usurped the plaintiff's right to present. No judgment was issued.

In another case, the claimant referred directly to a conciliar statute on pluralism according to which a church to which his predecessor had last presented was legally vacant.[44] The defendant answered simply that the church was not vacant, but still in the possession of the clerk named as the deprived pluralist. The claimant acknowledged that the clerk was in possession, but stated that, following his denunciation as a pluralist by the local bishop, another clerk had been presented. A cause between the two presented candidates was now pending in church court. The defendant argued simply that his adversary's common law suit—an assize of darrein presentment—was inappropriate because the church in question was not vacant.[45] Again, the question of vacancy turned on the canonical issue of deprivation due to pluralism. The defendant recommended that his plea of plenarty be referred to the local ordinary, which would have allowed the church to settle the issue of vacancy according to its own rules, but Common Pleas did not rule on the defendant's request and the case remained undecided.

It is tempting to see in Common Pleas' hesitation in these two cases disapproval of the church's legislation regarding pluralism, which had the effect of limiting patrons' freedom to provide for clerks of their choosing. Nevertheless, there is no clear evidence from the reign of Edward I of the royal courts ignoring vacancies created by operation of canon law or challenging the bishops' jurisdiction over deprivations on account of pluralism. The unwillingness of the king's justices to act boldly on this issue is notable when compared with the crown's attempt a half century later to apply directly and to its own advantage another papal constitution against pluralism. By treating benefices as automatically vacant at common law by virtue of the canon without episcopal certification, the royal courts were able to usurp the church's jurisdiction over plenarty and voidance.[46] In contrast, the royal courts refrained from any such innovation during the reign of Edward I.

Two Common Pleas cases concerning a different question reveal an ambivalent attitude toward papal legislation on the part both of the royal justices and ecclesiastical litigants. According to the Lateran Council of 1179, the authority to collate to a benefice devolved to the patron's superior if the patron were an ecclesiastic and the benefice vacant for over six months due to the patron's failure to present.[47] The common law courts accepted

[44] CP 40/106, m. 244d (1294).

[45] The claimant stated that his predecessor had last presented a clerk, 'qui quidem Henricus post ultimum concilium Lugdunensi plura admisit beneficia ecclesiastica curam animarum habentia absque dispensatione, inde optenta etc. per quod eadem ecclesia modo vacat etc.'. The reference is to a statute of the Council of Lyons (1274) that established that those holding plural benefices were to exhibit their dispensations before their ordinaries. Sext. 1.16.3. The claimant seems to have acted pursuant to the earlier canon De multa, X 3.5.28, in presenting the second clerk. The defendant was arguing that pending the church court action, in which the accused pluralist was presumably defending himself, the church was not yet vacant; the assize did not lie because 'ecclesia non vacet per mortem, cessionem, resignationem, sive privationem persone'.

[46] The constitution was Execrabilis, issued in 1317. Extrav. Joh. XXII 3.cap. un. Maitland suggested that the reason for the royal policy was the patronage that would accrue to the crown, including advowsons in the king's hand on account of wardships or episcopal vacancies, by operation of the papal constitution if it were enforced directly by the common law courts: Maitland, *Roman Canon Law*, 148–157.

[47] X 3.8.2. See also X 1.10.2; X 1.10.3.

this general principle throughout the thirteenth century, but a specific point requiring clarification arose in 1276. An abbot brought a writ of *quare non admisit* against the bishop of Norwich, who stated that he had not admitted the abbot's candidate because the church had not been vacant.[48] He himself had presented a clerk to it, '*auctoritate concilii post lapsum tempus semestre*', because the abbot had neglected to do so following the death of the last incumbent. The abbot explained that he had been abroad and unaware of the vacancy. Common Pleas ruled that the six months were only to be reckoned against the patron from the day on which he learned of the vacancy. Here the royal justices not only followed the law of the church, but cited it as authority.[49]

When, however, a year later the court was again faced with the need to interpret another aspect of the six-month rule, it made no reference to canon law in handing down its decision. In this case, in which Eleanor the Queen Mother was plaintiff, the bishop of Lincoln argued that the semester began on the day of the rector's death, thereby ignoring the canonical rule and the recent Common Pleas judgment.[50] His statement that the death had occurred within the realm while the plaintiff was likewise within the realm suggests that he may have been testing the applicability of that ruling. More important, he asserted that a church council (*in concilio apostolico*) had ordained that the semester was to be computed 'by days and weeks, not by months of the year'. He had presented his clerk on 9 March 1277, twenty-six weeks inclusive from the week of 17 September 1276, when the rector had died. The plaintiff argued that six months had not elapsed from the day she received notice, 13 October. Moreover, she stated that the period was to be reckoned by months. The king and his council endorsed both her arguments in ruling in her favour.[51] The bishop's defence, in relation to canon law, is noteworthy in several respects. Not only did he ignore the specific common law precedent requiring the patron's knowledge of a vacancy, he seems also to have cited a non-existent conciliar canon; it is not to be found it among the enactments of the Third or Fourth Lateran Councils or in the *Decretum* or *Decretales* of Gregory IX. Additionally, he failed to present his best available argument: among the *Decretales* were ordinances stating specifically that lay patrons were required to present within four months rather than the six available to ecclesiastical patrons.[52] We can only guess how Common Pleas would have reacted to that argument—which if accepted would have defeated the queen mother's suit, perhaps an unlikely possibility in itself—in the light of its earlier explicit recognition of another canon on the same subject. This case would seem to reveal either

[48] CP 40/17, m. 85d (1276).

[49] 'Et etiam quia tempus sex mensium auctoritate concilii non incipit currere patrono nisi a tempore scientie mortis persone'. The canon, X 3.8.5, actually was not the product of a council but was instead a decretal letter from Innocent III to a legate.

[50] CP 40/21, m. 100 (1277).

[51] 'Postea a die Pasche in quindecim dies anno regni regis nunc sexto veniunt predicte partes et recitata fuit loquela predicta coram domino rege et eius consilio plenario coram quo consideratum fuit quod tempus semestris durat et durare debet per dimidium annum et computari debet per menses anni et non per ebdomadas. Et quod idem tempus computari debet a die quo noticia mortis vel cessionis ultimi rectoris pervenit ad patronum vel per rationabiles dietas computandas potuit pervenisse'.

[52] X 3.38.22; X 3.38.27. See also Sext. 3.19. cap. un., issued several years after this case was decided. The question was settled as far as the common law was concerned by a 1350 statute establishing that lay as well as ecclesiastical patrons were entitled to six months. St 25 Edw. III, St 4, printed in *SR*, 1:316.

ignorance on the part of the bishop's counsel or lack of faith in the authority of papal law in the king's courts.[53]

Before leaving the subject of the jurisdictional arrangement governing ecclesiastical patronage during the reign of Edward I, it is necessary to take a brief look at a problem that raised important questions about the church-state relationship during the fourteenth century. Canon law gave the pope wide powers to provide clerks to vacant benefices, in derogation of the true patron's right to present.[54] In England provisions were not made to benefices in the gift of lay patrons.[55] Even as to ecclesiastical patrons, however, papal provisors could under certain circumstances be prejudicial to the rights of the crown. Cathedral prebends, of which the bishop was patron, were a staple of papal patronage. This was a source of friction because the crown claimed the right to present to livings in episcopal patronage when the temporalities of a bishopric were in royal custody due to a vacancy.[56] During the fourteenth century a combination of popular opposition to foreign provisors and the crown's desire to maintain or increase its ability to provide for its own servants led to legislative and judicial action against papal provisions.[57]

In contrast to these developments, the reign of Edward I was not a period of major innovation. The plea rolls do not reveal opposition to papal provision.[58] Nor is there evidence of an attempt on the part of the popes to enlarge the scope of their activities to include provisions to English benefices in the gift of lay patrons. A case from 1300 resulted in a statement of the priority over a papal provision of the crown's right to present to a

[53] For another case in which the six-month rule was cited, see CP 40/39, m. 58d (1281). An abbot claiming an advowson brought an assize of darrein presentment before justices itinerant. He stated that he had presented the last rector, but when he attempted to appoint a successor found that the archbishop of Canterbury had presented a clerk of his own, before lapse of the six-month period. The archbishop responded that he had done so pursuant to the Council of Lyons (ratione concilii Lugdon'). Asked 'per quem articulum eiusdem concilii' he conferred the benefice, he refused to answer: 'dicit quod ipse est archiepiscopus et primas Anglie et quod non vult nec debet ad hoc respondere in curia ista'. Later, in Common Pleas the archbishop again refused to justify his actions and because he did not deny that the abbot was the 'verus patronus' and that he had presented a candidate within eight days of the previous parson's death and because 'consuetudo regni Anglie sit quod nullus patronus debet ad presentatione ecclesie sue excludi auctoritate concilii nisi negligens sit et remissus in presentando infra tempus semestre', the court gave judgment for the abbot, ordering that the abbot's candidate be admitted and any incumbent be removed.

[54] See Sext. 3.4.2; Extrav. commun. 1.3.4; Extrav. commun. 3.2.13; Extrav. John. XXII 3.cap. un. Papal authority to dispose of benefices the patrons of which were ecclesiastics was grounded on the doctrine of plenitudo potestatis. See generally Barraclough, *Papal Provisions*; Pantin, *English Church*, ch. 4.

[55] YB 3 & 4 Edw. II, 170–172. See also Deeley, 'Papal Provision', 505–506.

[56] See generally Howell, *Regalian Right*.

[57] St 25 Edw. III, St 4, printed in *SR*, 1:316; St 13 Ric. II, St 2, c. 2, printed in *SR*, 2:69. For parliamentary petitions, see *Rot. Parl.*, 1:220, 1:207, 2:141, 2:144, 2:162, 2:172–73, 2:228. See Deeley, 'Papal Provision'; Cheyette, 'Statute of Provisors'; McKisack, *Fourteenth Century*, 272–283; Stubbs, *History*, 2:155–156.

[58] Case records indicate recognition that intervening papal provisions did not prejudice an ecclesiastical claimant's right based on presentation by a predecessor, as in a darrein presentment case in which the assize stated that the defendant's ancestor granted the advowson to the claimant's predecessor, the abbot of Bardney. He then presented, but the next two vacancies were filled by papal provision. Nevertheless, the assize found for the current abbot, because 'possessio ecclesie de Bardeney presentandi ad predictam ecclesiam de Magna Hale hucusque continuatur sine interuptione, cum provisio pape fuit possessio [presentandi] predicte ecclesie de Bardeney'. That is, papal provision was deemed equivalent to the abbots' own exercise of the right to present: CP 40/92, m. 74 (1292). For other cases in which Common Pleas tacitly accepted the validity of papal provision, see CP 40/70, m. 44 (1288); CP 40/93, m. 132d (1292). In one Common Pleas case, a lay patron's effort to present his clerk seems to have been impeded by a papal provision but the case was adjourned pending judgment and not decided. CP 40/46, m. 82d (1281).

cathedral prebend during an episcopal vacancy, but the king also gave way in two similar contemporary disputes.[59]

During the last year of his reign King Edward succeeded in obtaining recognition of the retroactive applicability of the crown's prerogative exemption from the six-month rule, in a case in which an asserted royal right to present to the treasurership of York cathedral was based on the simultaneous vacancy of benefice and archbishopric—to which the right to present would otherwise have pertained—nearly ten years previously. Despite two intervening provisions, the king's council ruled that the canonical rule requiring presentation within six months did not bar the king's presentation.[60] The case may perhaps be a sign that the crown's position was beginning to change during the last years of Edward I's reign, but royal opposition to papal provisions began in earnest only under his son and grandson.

In its particular details as well as general principles the jurisdictional arrangement governing ecclesiastical patronage continued in operation during the reign of Edward I largely as it had under his predecessors. The plea rolls do not reveal a widespread campaign or even a tendency to expand royal authority at the expense of English or Roman ecclesiastical interests.

Trespass and tithes

The common law action of trespass in the '*quare bona et catalla cepit et asportavit*' form[61] played a significant role in tithe litigation in medieval England. Nevertheless, the crown did not during the reign of Edward I use its jurisdiction over trespass as the pretense for secular determination of proprietary rights to tithes. The courts interfered with tithe disputes by means of their jurisdiction over trespass only insofar as the plaintiff's clearly established possession of tithes was intruded upon or the manner of collection was sufficiently irregular to constitute an offence against public order. There is no evidence that the application of these rules during Edward's reign was a departure from earlier practice, but they are worth detailed consideration because they have not previously been studied.[62]

As we have seen, claims brought by parsons against parishioners for non-payment of tithes were justiciable in the church courts as spoliation.[63] No corresponding remedy was available at common law, and it was a valid defence to a prohibition plea that the cause in church court was for withholding of tithes.[64] Disputes between rival claimants to tithes were also to be decided in Court Christian, as long as the value of the tithes in question did not implicate patronage interests, defined as exceeding one-fourth of a church's

59 Deeley, 'Papal Provision', 506–507.

60 *King's Council Cases*, 18–27.

61 On the various forms of trespass writs, see Baker, *Legal History*, 60–64. For a thorough account of the conceptual and doctrinal development of trespass, see Milsom, *Studies*, 1–90.

62 Cf. Adams's statement that the royal courts sought 'consistently' to appropriate the church's jurisdiction over tithes during the thirteenth and fourteenth centuries. Adams, 'Tithes', 1.

63 See above, pp. lxix–lxx.

64 E.g., Cases nos. 1.4, 1.11, 1.15, 1.21 (consultation referring to one-fourth rule), and 1.29 (consultation referring to one-fourth rule). See also CP 40/38, m. 21 (1281); CP 40/80, m. 27d (1289); CP 40/91, m. l36d (1291); JUST 1/1089, m. 17 (Yorkshire, 1293); CP 40/159, m. 5 (1306) (defendant obtained consultation).

revenues.[65] In contrast, disputes between rival claimants to tithes and attempts by unwilling parishioners to contest collection of tithes from their lands came before the royal courts under colour of allegations of forcible taking of the plaintiff's property. In the typical case, one party accused the other of violently taking his goods. The plaintiff then named them, assigning a monetary value, recited the circumstances of the wrong, and claimed money damages. The defendant denied the wrong, stating instead that he had only carried off his own tithes and identifying himself as a parson to whom the tithes were due or, occasionally, as the parson's servant. The plaintiff countered the defendant's plea by reiterating that the goods in question were his or her own property—*catalla sua propria*—and not the defendant's tithes. In these cases as in all trespass suits a jury was summoned to decide the issue.

The plaintiff generally did not elaborate on these allegations by describing the circumstances in which the alleged wrong occurred. Nor did the initial count assert that the goods in question were in fact the plaintiff's tithes, presumably because the royal courts would reject claims for tithes as beyond the scope of the common law's jurisdiction and send the complainant to a church court. The royal courts could not, however, dismiss a simple *de bonis asportatis* claim in standard form. And, in responding to the defendant's plea that he was only taking his tithes, it was not necessary for the plaintiff to say anything more than that the goods taken were simply 'his own chattels'. The denial of the defendant's plea was sufficient for joinder of an issue triable by a jury. So, although trespass was of broad enough scope to encompass disputes that were obviously concerned with tithes, this was not due to a conscious policy aimed at drawing such disputes away from the church courts. Instead, the concept of trespass brought an important group of tithe cases before the royal justices. The common law rules applied for their settlement, however, preserved the integrity of the church's jurisdiction over tithes, while recognizing and protecting interests defined as secular.

Two broad classes of tithe disputes were litigated by writs of trespass. In the first the plaintiff had already collected a tenth part of the crop in the field where it had been harvested.[66] Either before or after the plaintiff had been able to carry it away to be stored the defendant came and seized it, perhaps claiming it as his or her tithes, but not necessarily. On account of this taking the plaintiff brought the trespass action. The second type of case did not result from the plaintiff's own collection of tithes. Rather, the defendant took tithes from property belonging to the plaintiff; the trespass action therefore required the defendant to justify having done so. In these cases plaintiffs argued either that they were not the defendant's parishioner subject to tithe collection or that the defendant's manner of taking tithes was irregular and therefore amounted to trespass.

The first class of cases turned on a straightforward rule. Unless the plaintiff who had collected the tithes had also deposited them in a barn or other certain place within or without the field where the grain was harvested or at least carried it away from the field, he or she could not successfully prosecute a common law action for trespass if the defendant made off with them. Thus in one case the defendant, a parson, argued that the grain

[65] See above, p. lxxi.

[66] Typically, after reaping and binding into sheaves, a landholder physically segregated each tenth sheaf of wheat, oats, etc. in the field where it was harvested, to be carted away by the rector's servants. Ault, 'Village Church', 207.

in question was his tithe, which he had carried away after it had been set apart from the rest of the harvest by his parishioners.[67] The plaintiff, a prior, reiterated that the grain was his, 'gathered and placed in his seisin', until taken forcibly by the defendant and his accomplices. The jury's verdict indicated that the dispute arose from the prior's and parson's conflicting claims to tithes from a third party. The parson's predecessors had received part of the tithes in return for a yearly money payment to the priory. When the current parson assumed the living, the prior collected some sheaves in the field where the grain had been set aside as tithes. The parson then came and had them carried off as his own tithes. The justices, revealing their criteria for determining whether a wrong justiciable at common law had been committed, then asked the jurors if the prior had stored the grain in a barn (*grangia*) or 'other certain place outside the field'. He had not; just as he was about to do so the parson's men had taken the grain away. The court therefore ruled that this tithe dispute was for the church courts to decide and dismissed the plaintiff's suit. Because the prior had not sufficiently taken possession of the grain, his claim was in fact an assertion of a right to tithes wrongfully collected by the parson. This was a matter of the parties' respective rights to the tithes in question and as such a matter for ecclesiastical determination.[68]

In a similar case heard a few years later, King's Bench applied the converse of the rule used above. Again the parties—an abbess and a parson—were contesting tithes that each claimed from a third party.[69] Here the jury stated that the plaintiff had collected the tithes and put it in heaps (*in montellis*) in a barn located within the fee in which the grain had been harvested. When she tried to carry these tithes away to her house the defendants seized her carts. Because the tithes had actually been collected and stored by the plaintiff, King's Bench exercised jurisdiction, awarding damages to the plaintiff and fining the defendant. By implication, then, trespass would also lie in the case of seizure of grain removed as tithes and taken to the plaintiff's property.[70]

The king's courts thus defined the point at which tithes became property entitled to common law protection in terms of possession. Once someone had clearly established possession, by storage in a barn or removal from the field, the action of trespass was available just as it was to anyone else whose chattels were unjustly seized. In such cases the common law could assume jurisdiction without prejudice to the church's jurisdiction over proprietary right to tithes because the king's courts were concerned only with unjust disturbance of possession. In contrast, if the harvesters had simply separated sheaves from the rest of the crop in the field where it had grown, no claimant to tithes had yet established

[67] Case no. 2.7.

[68] Possibly the parson held his living as the vicar of a church appropriated to the priory and, as was usual, each was entitled to a portion of the parochial income. Disputes of this sort seem often to have come before the royal courts under colour of trespass. For example, in one case the defendants 'dicunt quod vicarius de Wendover habere debet terciam garbam decime ecclesie de Wendover et predictus prior [plaintiff] duas partes decime predicte, unde dicunt quod ipsi nomine ipsius vicarii colligere et asportare fecerunt portionem garbarum ad vicariam predictam pertinenciam et non blada ipsius prioris': KB 27/116, m. 5 (1289). See also KB 27/163, m. 14 (1301); KB 27/166, m. 45 (1301); JUST 1/589, m. 4 (Norfolk, 1305).

[69] KB 27/118, m. 33 (1289).

[70] See, e.g., a plaintiff's assertion that the grain in question was 'blada sua propria et non decime ecclesie de Grenewyk' and that 'ipse Petrus blada illa colligere et adunare et tassiare fecit in villa predicta. Et quod predictus prior [defendant] et alii postea venerunt et blada predicta ceperunt et asportaverunt': KB 27/114, m. 39 (1288).

possession so trespass would not be available, even if someone had come to the field and identified the sheaves as his or her tithes. In such a case, if a rival claimant carried away those sheaves, the common law courts would not recognize that a wrong had been committed. At that point the dispute was still between two rival claimants to tithes, each asserting a right to the goods in question but the aggrieved party not yet having taken possession of them. That person's claim amounted to a claim of proprietary right to tithes collected by another and therefore was for a church court to settle.[71]

The second broad class of trespass cases resulted from tithe disputes of a different sort. While in the first group the basis of the plaintiff's suit was the alleged intrusion upon possession of tithes already collected, in other cases the plaintiff had not collected tithes at all. Rather, the plaintiff sought to establish that the defendant's taking of tithes was an intrusion upon his or her right to the chattels at issue. Because, however, the plea was only that '*catalla sua propria*' had been taken, it is often impossible to ascertain whether the plaintiff's interest in those chattels was simply one of a landholder whose crop was unjustly tithed or whether the defendant's collection of tithes was an usurpation of the plaintiff's right to the same goods as his or her own tithes.[72] Only unusually detailed jury verdicts reveal the actual circumstances of these disputes and allow us to determine the underlying jurisdictional principles.

In those cases in which the plaintiff's trespass suit was actually an assertion of a rival claim to the goods in question as tithes the rule coincided with the one applied in the possessory cases discussed above. Because there was no disturbance of actual possession of the items named in the writ, the dispute pertained to the church courts. A mere assertion that the defendant took goods to which the plaintiff was entitled as his or her tithes—but which had not been collected and stored or carried away—was not sufficient ground for a trespass action. Accordingly such cases are very rare, but one finds occasional examples in which such an assertion was evidently the basis for the action. In one case, the parson of Great Fransham brought a trespass claim against several lay persons.[73] The jury stated that he had collected tithes from the land in question during the first two years of cultivation but thereafter the defendants had taken those tithes, acting on behalf of the rector of Beeston. Questioned by the bench, the jurors said the land was wholly within the plaintiff's parish. Although the pleadings do not reveal it, it is evident that this case arose from a dispute between two rival parsons—Great Fransham and Beeston are within about two miles of each other in Norfolk—each claiming ownership of tithes from newly cultivated waste or common land. Accordingly, the court ruled that this was a dispute entirely about

[71] Accordingly, in a number of trespass cases the plaintiff alleged carrying off of goods and the defendant reponded that he or she had merely taken tithes owed from the land in question. The plaintiff then reiterated that the goods in question were 'catalla sua propria' and requested a jury. That plea would require proof either that the plaintiff had collected and stored tithes only to have them taken by the defendant or, as discussed below, that the defendant took tithes from the plaintiff's land but did so improperly

[72] For example, a parson as defendant 'dicit quod ipse predicta blada et fenum tanquam decimas ad predictam ecclesiam suam pertinentes cepit et asportavit set non contra pacem'; the jury said that the defendant took the plaintiff's goods and chattels, but 'sine armis'; the plaintiff recovered damages and the value of the goods: CP 40/122, m. 23 (1288). In another case, the jury stated that 'Johannes et alii [defendants] non ceperunt blada ipsius Hervicii persone sicut queritur, set decimas ipsius abbatis de quibus ipse et predecessores sui a tempore quo non extat memoria fuerunt in seisina de predictis decimis percipiendis': CP 40/113, m. 78d (1296).

[73] Case no. 2.4.

the right to certain tithes—there was no secular interest implicated—and told the plaintiff he should sue before an ecclesiastical tribunal.[74]

In other cases plaintiffs brought trespass actions not because they claimed goods taken from a third party as their own tithes, but because the defendant allegedly collected tithes from the plaintiff's property unjustly. According to these complaints the defendants—though they claimed only to have taken tithes due them—actually carried off the plaintiff's lay chattels. These cases therefore appear to have turned on the question of whether the defendant had a right to the goods in question as tithes. If there was no such right, the goods were simply the plaintiff's lay chattels unlawfully taken. So, at first glance at least, several trespass cases from the reign of Edward I seem to be trials in royal courts of a parson's right to collect tithes from his parishioner. Without more than that, these cases properly belonged in Court Christian.

In fact there are no cases from this period in which the king's justices unambiguously decided a matter of right to tithes in a case of this sort. Instead, the issue was whether the defendant's manner of collecting the tithes constituted a trespass. Did he or she act in such a manner that, regardless of a right to the goods as tithes, a breach of peace was committed in taking them? This was clearly the issue in a case heard by royal justices itinerant in Kent in 1292, in which the master of St Bartholomew's Hospital, Hythe, accused the parson of Saltwood of trespass against his wheat, barley, and peas, every year since 1278.[75] The parson replied that his adversary was his parishioner and he had merely taken tithes from lands within his parish, after the crop had been 'tithed' (*decimavit*), that is, the tenth part assessed and set aside from the other nine parts in the field at the time of harvest. The plaintiff denied that the crops in question had been tithed (*blada illa non decimata*) and this question was put to a jury, which confirmed the plaintiff's accusations. The parson had annually entered the master's barn forcibly (*vi et armis*) and there counted off his sheaves from those stored there. In addition, he himself had seized sheaves in the fields in the manner alleged by the plaintiff, that is, without their having been counted and set aside as tithes. On account of these trespasses the justices awarded damages for the plaintiff. It is not clear from the record whether the parson had no right at all to take the goods in question as his tithes, or whether he took more than was due him. In any event, the court did not consider the question of the defendant's right at all, even though two issues bearing

[74] The case indicates that royal courts did not assume jurisdiction over right to tithes from newly cultivated land. Cf. Adams, 'Tithes', 4. In another case, a parson attempted to use trespass for what appears to have been a claim of right. The defendant was an abbot who pleaded that the goods at issue were 'his tithes, separated from the other nine parts and collected in a field' (decime ipsius abbatis separate a novem partibus etc. et collecte in campo) from which he and his predecessors had always taken their tithes. The parson replied simply that the goods were 'taken from his possession' (extra seisinam ipsius Johannis). This was an insufficient response: the justices inquired further as to the nature of his possession. Were these his, the parson's, tithes pertaining to his church? How was he seised of the goods—in the field where they had grown, was he in the process of carrying them off, or had he stored them within his close? Were they still growing in his church's field or his free tenement? The court here was attempting to discern whether the claim implicated possessory interests protected by trespass or was instead a dispute over right to tithes between two rival claimants. When the parson refused to answer, the court entered judgment for the abbot: CP 40/131, m. 67d (1300). In another case, the defendant said goods taken where not the plaintiff's (a prior) but rather that she (a prioress) 'colligere fecerat decimas garbas ipsius prioresse pertinentes . . . separatas a novem partibus et adunare'. This was a defence either to a rival claim of right or to an assertion of improper taking of the plaintiff's property: CP 40/135, m. 267d (1301)

[75] Case no. 2.13.

directly on that question were raised by his claim that the land from which the tithes were taken was within his parish and the fact that he had been receiving tithes from the plaintiff for the last 14 years. Instead, the judgment was based on his conduct in collecting the plaintiff's goods, the use of force in taking them from the barn and collection in the field before they had been separated and expressly set aside as tithes. In another trespass claim brought by a lay person against a parson who claimed to have taken the goods in question as his tithes, the jury said that the parson took the goods 'against the plaintiff's will' (*contra voluntatem*).[76] The implication is that the parson was not supposed to collect his tithes until the tithe-payers had set them aside for him.

In another case the abbot of Cirencester brought an action of trespass against the parson of Rushton and several accomplices.[77] They defended themselves by pleading that the goods in question—grain and hay—were tithes owed to Rushton church, properly tithed and not collected forcibly. The abbot replied that these were his goods (*propria catalla*), taken from places not previously tithed by the parson. The jury stated that the parson's predecessor had earlier recovered the right to those very tithes in a church court and had afterwards successfully collected them. The jury also gave additional information concerning the parson's right: the grain was collected from lands of the abbot's free tenants and therefore could not have been his chattels and, as to the hay, the church court had condemned the abbot for his unwillingness to allow tithes to be taken. Rather than focusing on the question of right to collect the tithes in question, Common Pleas instead concerned itself with a different matter. The justices, having inquired concerning the manner in which the rectors of Rushton had previously collected their tithes of hay (*qualiter . . . percipere debeant*), learned that after the hay had been mowed (*falcata*) the parson, by the view of reliable men (*per visum legalium hominum*), had had the meadow measured and a reasonable tenth separated from the rest of the crop. The justices also asked if the lands in question were within the defendant's parish but, informed that they were, adjourned the case pending further information on the local custom of tithing hay. Ample information was provided concerning the defendant's right to tithes—in particular the references to the church court judgment and the location of the abbot's lands within the parish of Rushton—should the justices have sought a basis for a ruling on that issue. Instead, the alleged trespass was a question of whether tithes had been assessed properly, that is, according to the local custom. Perhaps the church court in issuing judgment against the abbot had granted

[76] KB 27/164, m. 10 (1301). Cf. a case in which the defendant seems to have attempted to establish that the dispute was really over right to tithes, as a plea against the jurisdiction of Common Pleas. The defendant, a parson, argued that he had earlier won in church court the right to collect the goods in question as his tithes due from a third party. Moreover, he said, the plaintiff, an abbot, held no lay fee or other land in the area, so he could only claim the goods at issue as tithes owed to himself but collected by the defendant. The abbot's claim, the parson said, thus was an assertion of a right to tithes, therefore a matter for a church court to settle. The jury's verdict contradicted the defendant's reference to a church court judgment. Instead, the abbot and his predecessors had always received 'sheaves' from the lands in question. The jury did not explain the nature of this right and did not describe the sheaves as tithes. Apparently the goods in question were simply part of a crop owned by the abbot and the defendant's description of the dispute as one over right to tithes was an unsuccessful plea against common law jurisdiction. Here too the key fact was that the defendant had used force against the abbot in taking goods as tithes. This constituted a trespass and Common Pleas found for the plaintiff: CP 40/93, m. 135d (1292). The abbot brought a similar action against the same parson two years later: CP 40/104, m. 55 (1294) (no verdict recorded).

[77] Case no. 2.11. See also CP 40/102, m. 204d (1293) (trespass suit by same abbot against tithe collectors of parson of Rushton).

a mandate to the parson that was in breach of local custom. This case thus indicates that the manner in which tithes were assessed and collected could constitute a common law trespass if done contrary to custom, independent of the question of use of force. A decision on that point would not, however, have necessarily prejudiced the question of right to the tithes in question.[78]

We have seen in several of the trespass cases discussed above that the plaintiffs were heads of religious houses. This fact gives us a clue to the probable basis for some of these disputes. Much if not most monastic land in thirteenth-century England was exempt from tithes.[79] The law governing these exemptions was complex, however, and presumably subject to litigation since significant financial interests were at stake.[80] As we have seen the royal justices concentrated on whether the parson's conduct in collecting tithes was tortious according to common law conceptions of trespass, but nevertheless disputes concerning monastic claims that lands belonging to their houses were exempt from payment may have been the source for some of the trespass suits in which religious houses were plaintiffs.[81] Some of these may have been litigated by means of common law writs of trespass rather than canonical libels because the plaintiffs had already been unsuccessful in church court actions. In the case of the abbot of Cirencester and the parson of Rushton discussed above[82] the jury stated that the parson had already obtained a judgment from an ecclesiastical court in his favour. Therefore the abbot, unable to reopen the question of the parson's right to tithes before the king's justices, sought to adjust his complaint in accordance with common law trespass principles in order to continue his resistance to the parson's efforts to collect tithes from his abbey's land. In another case the parson of Hadham defended himself against the prior to Ely's trespass suit by reference to a previous judgment in a church court recognizing his right to tithes from the prior's land. Unfortunately the jury's verdict and the judgment of the royal court if any are illegible, so the facts at issue cannot be determined in greater detail.[83]

A reason has been suggested for the many trespass cases concerning tithe disputes between the heads of religious houses and parsons. Though these complainants may have been attempting to use common law actions of trespass to resist their tithe obligations, the royal courts confined themselves to questions of improper methods of collection, avoiding canonical questions of right or monastic exemption. Lay persons seem rarely to have used trespass actions to contest tithe collections although it would have been possible to contest a parson's right to tithes by suing a trespass claim alleging force or failure to observe local custom.[84] The apparent infrequency of trespass suits brought by lay persons probably

[78] For two cases involving local custom, one concerning method of tithing, the other right to a mortuary, see YB 32 & 33 Edw. I, 408–411; YB 30 & 31 Edw. I, 440–447.

[79] Moorman, *Church Life*, 116.

[80] The subject of religious houses as payers and recipients of tithes during the earlier middle ages is treated in vast detail in Constable, *Monastic Tithes*.

[81] Besides the cases discussed so far in this section, see KB 27/118, m. 19 (1289); CP 40/130, m. 30d (1299); CP 40/134, m. 139d (1300); KB 27/167, m. 41 (1302); CP 40/145, m. 28 (1303).

[82] Case no. 2.11.

[83] CP 40/96, m. 1 (1292).

[84] Some tithe disputes between lay persons and their priests are probably hiding behind trespass cases in which the defendant answered by a general denial, without any reference to tithes. For example, a parson accused another of trespass vi et armis against his blada. Only the jury's verdict revealed that tithes were the subject of the dispute. CP 40/107, m. 76 (1295).

indicates that arguments between lay parishioners and their priests over tithe obligations were less likely to be controversial than efforts to collect from monastic foundations. The farmer's duty to set aside a tenth of his or her crop at harvest surely was taken largely for granted. Evidently disputes that did require adjudication typically went before the ecclesiastical courts, where suits for spoliation of tithes between parsons and their parishioners are the single largest category of causes to be found in the English records.[85]

Before leaving the subject of trespass and tithes, it is necessary to consider the closely related question of common law actions to claim another typical religious payment, the mortuary. In 1289 Avelina, the widow of Richard of Whatfield, accused the local parson of abducting a horse from her, *vi et armis et contra pacem*.[86] In his defence the parson asserted that the horse pertained to him as a mortuary on the occasion of the death of the plaintiff's husband. She replied that the parson received an ox as mortuary, but later took the horse by force. As in several of the tithe cases, this trespass suit seems to be a challenge to the parson's right to a mortuary, which would be for the church courts to decide. The actual substance of the trespass suit, however, was the parson's alleged use of force against the plaintiff. Thus the jury stated that the parson seized the horse '*vi et armis . . . in regia strata contra pacem*'. In such cases the king's courts claimed jurisdiction and could exercise it without interfering with questions of right. The parson might in fact have had a right to the horse, as he might have a right to tithes, but if he took it violently or even against the will of his parishioner it was a common law wrong.[87] The proper course of action would have been an ecclesiastical suit for detention of a mortuary, corresponding to a canonical action of spoliation for refusal to pay tithes.[88]

To sum up, although many disputes involving tithes came before the royal courts through writs of trespass the justices did not treat this as an opportunity to expand temporal jurisdiction at the expense of the spiritual. This is especially noteworthy in light of the nature of pleadings in these trespass cases, which often reduced the dispute to a question of whether the goods taken were the defendant's tithes (or mortuary) or the plaintiff's lay chattels. This ostensible question of fact actually raised the legal question of the legitimacy of the defendant's right to claim the property at issue as tithes, but the royal justices did not concern themselves with matters of right. Instead, they defined common law trespass in terms of possession. Had the plaintiff clearly established possession of the tithes by removal from the field or storage in a barn? If so, he or she was entitled to the common law remedy. Were the goods collected by the defendant still in the plaintiff's possession, that is, not obviously separated as tithes from the other nine parts of his or her crop? If

[85] Helmholz, *History*, 444.

[86] Case no. 2.8. In the same year one Robert de Furneus brought a trespass action against the same parson in King's Bench alleging taking of a horse together with 'unum aketum, unum capellum ferreum, unum collarium': KB 27/121, m. 20d (1289). As in the Common Pleas case, the defendant said that these chattels came to his church as a mortuary owed by Richard of Whatfield. A different jury said that the parson took the horse and other items 'vi et armis et sicut idem Robertus queritur et non nomine mortuarii'. Damages were assessed at eight marks. Neither of these cases refers to the other, even though they both seem to deal with the same wrong.

[87] The defendant's plea provides a colourful description of typical practice, which involved a voluntary handing over of the animal in question, said to have been received 'ex liberatione' of the deceased's son.

[88] For other trespass cases involving mortuaries, see KB 27/125, m. 46d (1290); CP 40/109, m. 117d (1295). Other cases probably are recorded as standard trespass claims met with general denials of the alleged wrongful taking without reference to the defendant's right to the animal in question as a mortuary. If there were a legitimate claim of right, the defendant could simply deny having wrongfully taken the plaintiff's property.

so, trespass lay against the taker. In neither situation did the question of right necessarily arise; the royal courts looked only at the disturbance—sometimes violent, though not necessarily—of possession. If someone wished to assert a right to chattels in the possession of another as tithes or a mortuary, the proper course was a claim for spoliation in a church court. The common law courts during the reign of Edward I treated tithes in general as subject to ecclesiastical jurisdiction. Only if secular interests were involved—breach of the king's peace, conversion of tithes to lay chattel by sale or exchange, or significant impact on rights of patronage—did the royal courts intrude.

Crime

The idea that clerks should enjoy immunity from secular criminal proceedings was older than the clash between Henry II and Becket, which brought the jurisdictional issue sharply into focus.[89] The *Decretum* had earlier collected several texts that amounted to a statement of general clerical immunity.[90] The Constitutions of Clarendon, published in 1164, ordained that clerks accused of serious crime in a royal court were to be handed over without trial to an ecclesiastical court for trial there, and, if convicted, degraded from holy orders and returned to the secular authorities for punishment as laymen.[91] In the aftermath of the Becket dispute, however, the church gained recognition of complete clerical immunity in criminal cases, excepting only the crown's powers to arrest and detain accused clerks pending delivery to the ordinary and to seize their chattels if convicted by the church.

During the thirteenth century the royal justices introduced an important modification of the general principle and the resultant arrangement continued in use for the remainder of the middle ages. A clerk accused of violent crime in a royal court who pleaded his clergy was claimed by his bishop. This privilege was unavailable in trespass cases, even where physical force was alleged. Thus, when a layperson accused two clerks of a bloody assault, they refused to answer without their bishop.[92] Common Pleas therefore convicted them because the case against them involved a 'personal trespass' (*transgressio personalis*) rather than life and limb (*non tangit vitam et membrum*) and awarded massive damages that were later compromised. Where benefit of clergy was available, the king's court empanelled a lay jury to rule on the substance of the accusation, in order to determine '*pro quali*' the accused should be handed over.[93] If the jury found him guilty he was delivered to the church as '*clericus convictus*', to be tried according to canon law. If he failed to clear himself before the church court, he forfeited his chattels to the crown but was not otherwise subject to secular punishment. Royal courts accepted the church's judgment,

[89] On the legal issues, see Fraher, 'Becket Dispute'; Duggan, 'Becket Dispute'. Both authors take issue with the traditional view—that Becket's position was ungrounded in canon law—presented in Maitland, *Roman Canon Law*, 132–147. On the general subject of clerks and secular criminal law, see Gabel, *Benefit of Clergy*; Helmholz, *History*, 511–514.

[90] Immunity from civil as well as criminal secular proceedings: see C. 11, q. 1, passim.

[91] Const. Clar. c. 3, printed in Select Charters 164–165. The text is not entirely clear, but see Maitland, *Roman Canon Law*, 133–136 and Duggan, 'Becket Dispute', 3–4.

[92] Case no. 2.1.

[93] See Case no. 2.17.

however, even if it contradicted the earlier conviction by the lay jury, a significant factor considering the notorious ease with which criminous clerks exonerated themselves by purgation. A finding of not guilty by the lay jury resulted to the accused's acquittal and delivery to the bishop as *clericus quietus*. The royal courts took no further notice of him.[94]

The important developments—secular trial prior to delivery and forfeiture of chattels if convicted in church court—occurred well before Edward I's accession, probably around the middle of the thirteenth century.[95] Edward was an important innovator in some areas of the criminal law,[96] but benefit of clergy was not among them. His reign did not produce significant changes in the procedural or jurisdictional arrangements for the treatment of clerks accused of crime.

An interesting footnote to the subject of benefit of clergy during the reign of Edward I is a case heard in 1300. It provides an insight into the crown's stance toward papal legislation, at least regarding the question of the scope of the category *clericus* as it applied to immunity. Ralph accused William in a county court of strangling his—William's—wife, who was Ralph's relative. The case was evoked into Common Pleas on petition of the defendant, who there pleaded his clergy.[97] Because of unspecified doubts as to whether he was a clerk (*quia curia hic quibusdam certis de causis non est ad plenum certiorata utrum predictus Willelmus tanquam clericus debeat ad curiam ecclesiasticam remitti vel tanquam laicus in curia hic respondere*), he was remanded in custody. Over a year later no bishop had claimed him, but he again pleaded his clergy. At this point the record states:

> And because the Roman curia has promulgated a new constitution regarding cases of this sort, which evidently distinguishes between those cases in which such wrongdoers who have pleaded their clergy before secular courts ought to be handled over to an ecclesiastical court and those cases in which they should answer before the secular judge, and it is not clear to this court whether the king wishes to observe this constitution in his realm, this case is adjourned until Easter term.[98]

The constitution referred to was a decretal of Pope Boniface VIII included in the *Liber Sextus*, the authoritative compilation promulgated in 1298. This canon established that married clerks must be tonsured and dressed in clerical habit if they were to enjoy jurisdictional immunity when accused of crimes or delicts before secular courts.[99] The quoted statement indicates that the royal justices attributed to the king the discretion to recognize or ignore this papal pronouncement, of direct relevance to the common law governing benefit of clergy. In the event, the question of recognition was not addressed directly. Instead, the court noted that the defendant had been arrested untonsured and in secular dress and accordingly was presumed to have been living as a lay person. Therefore, he

94 See Gabel, Benefit of Clergy, especially ch. 2. If found guilty by the church, a clerk would have no standing at common law until he had purged himself of the crime in question. CP 40/153, m. 112d (1305).

95 Gabel, Benefit of Clergy, 36–37.

96 Particularly in the area of enforcement and other procedural matters: see Plucknett, *Edward I and Criminal Law*, especially ch. 4.

97 CP 40/131, m. 21d (1300).

98 'Et quia curia Romana novam in huiusmodi casu edidit constitutionem que evidenter distinguit quo casu huiusmodi malefactores qui coram judice seculari se dicunt esse clericos etc. curie ecclesiastice tradidebent, et quo casu coram judice seculari respondere, nec constet curie hic utrum dominus rex constitutionem illam in regno suo observare voluerit etc., datus dies eis hic a die Pasche in unum mensem'.

99 Sext. 3.2.cap. un. This decretal probably dates from between 1295 and 1297. Genestal, *Privilegium Fori*, 100.

was not to be delivered until he had proved himself to be a clerk before his ordinary in the presence of a royal justice.[1] The additional requirement was not included in the papal edict,[2] but the royal court could deny William the privilege attached to clerical status without explicitly endorsing the edict because to do so would not contradict it. Moreover, no ordinary had claimed him as a clerk so the court's ruling was unlikely to be challenged. Eventually, William was evidently pressed to plead as a layman. He put himself upon a lay jury, which found him guilty as charged, and he was hanged.

The record of this case speaks of endorsement or rejection of the papal edict as a matter of royal discretion. Earlier during Edward's reign the crown had given explicit recognition to a canonical rule limiting the scope of clerical immunity in a different context. In 1275 or 1276 a royal statute endorsed a canon promulgated by the Council of Lyons of 1274, which stipulated that a clerk who married a second time or married a widow was *bigamus* and therefore no longer privileged.[3] Significantly, the royal statute also attributed retroactive force to this rule in endorsing it, again revealing the crown's exercise of discretion in regard to the scope of clerical immunity. In light of the crown's apparently ambivalent posture toward canon law in this area, it is noteworthy that there were no major attempts during the reign of Edward I to limit the privilege or otherwise to reform the system of shared jurisdiction over criminous clerks.

* * * * * * * * *

Many spheres of medieval life involved issues of importance to the laws of both church and state. Crime and ecclesiastical patronage, tithes, and annual rents due to or from ecclesiastical persons or foundations all posed potentially difficult jurisdictional problems. Yet during the earlier thirteenth century the two legal systems managed to devise rules and procedures that accommodated spiritual and royal concerns of policy and principle while producing a minimum of jurisdictional conflict. In these areas Edward I's reign reveals continuity rather than change, the sole significant exception being the tentative development of a common law remedy for annual rents owed by religious foundations. Aside from this, neither the king's judges nor his parliament attempted to enlarge the scope of the crown's judicial competence by creating new remedies or expanding old ones.

[1] 'testatum est hic etc. quod predictus Willelmus tempore quo captus fuit inventus fuit in habitu seculari et sine tonsura clericali et ex hoc curia presumit quod pro laico ante captionem suam se communiter gerebat et non pro clerico, et in casu illo curie ecclesiastice liberari non debet antequam coram ordinario suo in presencia judicis secularis probaverit se fuisse clericum etc.'.

[2] Perhaps a reference to a reading test, which was usually conducted by the ordinary in doubtful cases. It was applied rarely during the reign of Edward I, coming into widespread use only during the fourteenth century. Gabel, *Benefit of Clergy*, 64–74.

[3] The canon was Sext. 1.12.cap. un. The royal statute was St. 4 Edw. I, printed in *SR*, 1:42–43.

5

CIRCUMSPECTE AGATIS AND THE NORFOLK EYRE OF 1286

During the reign of Edward I the royal courts generally continued to apply jurisdictional rules established under his predecessors. Some of these rules date from the Constitutions of Clarendon, others originated not in royal ordinances or statutes but in the common law courts. With the few exceptions discussed above, the substantive law applied during Edward I's reign did not differ from that described in *Bracton*. This conclusion conflicts, however, with standard views on the significance of the writ *Circumspecte agatis*. Published in 1286 and very soon after cited as a statute,[4] it has been described as 'a landmark defining the boundary between the royal and ecclesiastical jurisdictions'.[5] Others have also seen the writ as a definitive settlement of boundaries that were previously perhaps only vaguely articulated and subject to ad hoc decisions by the royal justices as to which cases were spiritual and which secular.[6] Historians who have written that Edward I embarked on a policy of major curtailment of ecclesiastical jurisdiction over lay persons to testimonial and matrimonial causes only interpret *Circumspecte agatis* as a retreat from this policy, allowing a broader scope of authority for the church courts.[7] The actual purpose of the writ can only be appreciated in the context of political events of 1285 and 1286. In relation to these—and to the substantive jurisdictional rules evident in the common law plea rolls—it is clear that Edward did not attempt to limit significantly the church's jurisdiction, which was already subject to established, definite rules and procedures. This being the case, views on the significance of *Circumspecte agatis* merit reevaluation.[8]

The Easter Parliament of 1285 opened on 4 May.[9] The clergy presented grievances, which resulted in discussions with a committee of representatives of the king headed by the chancellor. Royal responses to these complaints have survived, together with clerical criticisms and further responses.[10] In addition, *gravamina* concerning selected chapters of the second statute of Westminster—published during this parliament on 28 June—led to further replies and criticisms.[11]

Meanwhile, the crown issued an edict concerning the church's jurisdiction. Although this has not survived, references in other documents from the parliament attest to its existence and also offer suggestions of its contents. On 1 July a writ addressed to the clergy

[4] See above, p. lxxi.

[5] Graves, 'Circumspecte Agatis', 1. This article is essential for the date, text, and circumstances of *Circumspecte agatis*.

[6] E.g., Baker, *Legal History*, 129. Graves referred to 'the indeterminate boundary between the two jurisdictions, royal and ecclesiastical. Writs of prohibition sporadically checked the aggressions of ecclesiastical judges within this borderland; but it was not clear in what cases such writs of prohibition lay': 'Circumspecte Agatis', 2. Powicke described *Circumspecte agatis* as aimed at 'closer definition': *Thirteenth Century*, 482.

[7] See, e.g., Stubbs, *History*, 2:119; Flahiff, 'Prohibition I', 308, 309; Jones, 'Relations', 164; Jones, 'Gravamina', 221; Hyams, 'Norwich Inquiry', 620.

[8] This subject is considered in greater detail in Millon, 'Circumspecte Agatis'.

[9] For the following events, see Douie, *Pecham*, ch. 8. See also Graves, 'Circumspecte Agatis'; Richardson & Sayles, 'Easter Parliament'; Powicke, *Thirteenth Century*, 481–483. The relevant documents are printed in *Councils & Synods*, 955–975, with the writ itself printed at 969–972 and also in *SR*, 1:101–102.

[10] *Councils & Synods*, 956–963.

[11] *Councils & Synods*, 964–967.

of Norwich diocese rehearsed a long list of pleas beyond the jurisdiction of the church courts. The writ declared that a royal commission of inquiry was to investigate complaints against infringements upon royal jurisdiction since Edward's coronation and cite offenders to appear at Westminster.[12] In January 1286 the king replaced this commission of inquiry with a general eyre possessing the judicial authority to try offences against the crown's jurisdiction by ecclesiastical judges. A further set of clerical grievances (its precise date is unclear) resulted from the 1 July writ and perhaps also from the conduct of the royal justices in Norfolk.[13] These complaints led directly to *Circumspecte agatis*, an executive order in the form of a writ issued in June or July 1286 by the king to the justices itinerant in Norfolk. It ordered them to 'proceed circumspectly' against the clergy of Norwich diocese. The justices were not to punish them for hearing legitimately spiritual causes, a list of which was included in the writ.[14]

The most thorough analysis of the relations between crown and clergy during the year leading up to the issue of *Circumspecte agatis* is Douie's account, in her biography of John Pecham, archbishop of Canterbury from 1279 to 1292.[15] She concluded, from an analysis of the 1 July writ and the subsequent *gravamina*, that the lost edict was a 'wholesale and indiscriminate limitation of the church's jurisdiction to testamentary and matrimonial cases'; while previously the boundary between the jurisdictions had been vague, the new 'policy of limitation by definition' claimed certain 'border-line cases . . . entirely for the State'.[16] The clergy's complaints, however, led Edward to grant, by means of *Circumspecte agatis*, a return to the status quo current at his coronation. This represented an abandonment of the lost edict's 'frontal attack on the Church courts'. In addition, *Circumspecte agatis* erected a barrier against further pursuit of 'the tactics of piecemeal encroachment', employed successfully by the royal courts during Henry III's reign.[17]

Douie offered her theory on Edward's policy toward the church courts without the benefit of a thorough study of the common law court records. Such a study was not germane to her biography of Archbishop Pecham, but the result was a misunderstanding of royal policy. In fact, despite the assumption of debt claims by and against executors and the development of writs of annual rent and prohibitions *de transgressione*, neither Edward I nor his father pursued a policy of 'piecemeal encroachment'. The rules applied by the royal courts during Edward's reign were, in general, the same as those applied previously. Moreover, there is no evidence that the law on these matters was vague. The boundary between the two jurisdictions prior to 1285 was not ill-defined; it was at times the subject of controversy, but the rules governing it were by 1272 well established and applied consistently. Most important, the lost edict probably was not a 'frontal attack' at all. Rather than a reordering of the substantive rules defining the boundary, it probably was aimed only at procedural reform. *Circumspecte agatis* was in fact only a necessary explication of the edict's purpose rather than a substantive grant to the clergy.

[12] *Councils & Synods*, 967–969.

[13] *Councils & Synods*, 969–972.

[14] Circumspecte agatis was issued from Paris, where Edward was to do homage to the new French king, Phillip IV, and to resolve a dispute over lordship of certain French lands. Powicke, *Thirteenth Century*, 290–291.

[15] Douie, *Pecham*, ch. 8.

[16] Douie, *Pecham*, 314.

[17] Douie, *Pecham*, 318–319. See also Richardson & Sayles, 'Easter Parliament', 222; Jones, 'Relations', 95.

The *gravamina* presented in the Easter Parliament prior to the 1 July writ, the writ itself, and the complaints presented after the issue of the writ all provide information bearing on the content of the lost edict. The tenth item in the initial list of grievances requested that 'laymen litigating in ecclesiastical courts should not be bothered (*graventur*) on account of this until a prohibition has been produced and it has been determined whether the cause pertains to the ecclesiastical forum'.[18] The usual prohibition procedure did not operate in this way; there was no inteference with ecclesiastical suits unless the church court defendant obtained a prohibition. The grievance suggests that this had changed: now lay persons suing in church courts were subject to prosecution by the crown even if no prohibition were produced against them. The royal response makes this clear, while indicating that this general prohibition applied only to suits outside the church's jurisdiction. A note on further discussions also states that the king would not allow the church to hear any case pertaining to his court, whether before prohibition or after; all offenders were to be punished.[19]

The royal response to the grievances also suggests that the substantive sphere of the church's jurisdiction had been narrowed: 'The king's court maintains that the prelates know well that they may take cognizance only of pleas concerning testament and marriage'.[20] The lost edict, which was probably published or at least discussed during the Easter Parliament, therefore appears to have laid down that ecclesiastical cognizance of all cases besides testamentary and matrimonial ones was a wrong regardless of whether a prohibition was produced. Offenders would be punished by a prosecutorial process rather than the ordinary civil procedure of attachment available to church court defendants but only if they initiated it themselves. The edict thus apparently had two aspects, one procedural, the other substantive.[21]

The text of the 1 July writ itself provides further clues to the contents of the lost edict and allows us to evaluate it in terms of the two aspects that emerge from the *gravamina* and the royal responses. The writ opened with a lengthy and comprehensive catalogue of pleas that were outside the church's jurisdiction and prohibited ecclesiastical cognizance of them. It then ordered Richard de Boyland and the sheriffs of Norfolk and Suffolk to announce this general prohibition on the king's behalf and to 'inquire who has been holding and suing pleas listed above in church courts contrary to the aforesaid prohibition, and cite them to answer before the king's justices at Westminster'.[22] The writ thus stipulated in detail those cases that pertained to the crown and mandated prosecution of offenders of the general prohibition regardless of whether the litigants in such cases had attempted to

18 *Councils & Synods*, 958.

19 *Councils & Synods*, 963.

20 *Councils & Synods*, 958.

21 The first of the grievances presented after the 1 July writ referred to both aspects in terms similar to the earlier complaint: 'Inprimis, cum a tempore cuius memoria non existit fuerit ecclesia in possessione pacifica cognoscendi de omnibus causis spiritualibus et pluribus civilibus donec inhibitio regia porrigeretur iudici vel prelato, hiis temporibus ministri regie magestatis inhibent ordinariis generali edicto ne cognoscant de aliquibus causis, nisi tantum de matrimonio vel testamento; et sic est ecclesia libertate pristina spoliata': *Councils & Synods*, 969. This was not the only specific reference to the 'general edict'. The clergy's replies to the crown's responses to their original set of gravamina objected to a 'public edict' ('cum sit edicto puplico promulgatum ut prelati cognoscant tantum de causis testamentariis et matrimonialibus . . .'): *Councils & Synods*, 959–960. This reference, made prior to 1 July, makes it clear that the lost edict was not the writ issued on that date.

22 *Councils & Synods*, 967–969.

halt them by means of writs of prohibition. This writ sought to implement the procedural innovation described in the *gravamina* as having been announced in the edict.

But did the edict also intend to restrict the church courts' authority over lay persons only to testamentary and matrimonial causes? Were such matters as withholding of tithes and mortuaries and correction of sin no longer to be justiciable in church courts? Despite the clergy's reaction to the edict, there is good reason to believe that this was not the case. The 1 July writ listed about two dozen items pertaining to the royal courts. These included pleas concerning feudal tenures and liberties, distraints, trespasses against the king's peace, contracts (*conventionibus*), advowsons, and pecuniary matters. Being a description of the scope of royal jurisdiction, the writ did not specify those causes legitimately ecclesiastical. There was also no statement that the church's jurisdiction was henceforth purely testamentary and matrimonial. Perhaps this was to be inferred from the inclusion of pleas concerning 'other chattels and debts not related to testament or marriage' among the list of matters subject to the crown's jurisdiction. If so, this was a surprisingly vague means for removing from the church courts disputes over tithes, mortuaries, and other religious payments, ecclesiastical annuities, prosecutions for correction of sin, and other matters previously recognized as spiritual. If the crown intended to implement such a radical policy, it seems reasonable to assume that the writ would also have included these matters in its long list of pleas exclusively for the royal courts, or at least have made an explicit, positive statement of such a crucially important innovation.

If the writ designed to implement the edict is unconvincing evidence for a 'frontal attack', the records of the Norfolk inquest themselves indicate clearly that no such policy was enforced, suggesting further that none was intended. These records, bound with the rolls for the 1286 general eyre of Norfolk,[23] include several allegations of non-compliance with prohibitions, all similar in form and substantive content to those found in the Common Pleas rolls.[24] One such case resulted in a writ of caption and imprisonment on account of the complainant's excommunication; he was only released after paying a fine of 10 shillings.[25] In addition there are many instances on each membrane of alleged violations of royal jurisdiction that contain no reference to prohibition. These cases, tried by juries, accordingly are examples of the new procedure mandated by the lost edict and the 1 July writ, whereby ecclesiastical adjudication of matters outside the church's authority became a punishable offence even in the absence of a writ of prohibition. The majority of the cases falls into this category.

While the records reveal this important procedural innovation, none of the Norfolk cases provides any indication that the crown had modified the jurisdictional rules circumscribing the activities of the church courts in any way. Rather, they involve standard complaints, such as several examples of ecclesiastical suits for the enforcement of obligations, some

[23] The fullest record is Boyland's roll, JUST 1/575. The complaints against ecclesiastical judges begin at m. 101, headed 'Inquisitiones capte coram R. de Boylund et W. de Royng' vicecomes, de transgressionibus factis laycis et comitatui Norwic' dioc' per clericos totius dioc'', and continue through m. 109d. Boyland's roll for the Suffolk eyre of that year includes only one membrane headed 'Rotulus de querelis conquerentis de clericis in Com' Suff''. See JUST 1/829, m. 58. Evidently the inquest was not pursued in that county. Selections from the Norfolk inquest are printed here as Cases nos. 3.1 to 3.25.

[24] E.g., Cases nos. 3.7, 3.8, 3.10, 3.13, 3.16, 3.17, 3.18, and 3.21.

[25] Case no. 3.13.

being commercial agreements,[26] others claims for debts.[27] One complainant referred to an action in church court for a 'lay contract'.[28] Allegations of suits for unspecified debts or chattels not concerned with marriage or testament probably also refer to contract cases.[29] One defendant, a subdean, admitted that he had summoned the plaintiffs before him to compel payment of a sum of money based on pledge of faith (*pro fidei datione*).[30] Complainants accused ecclesiastical judges of hearing claims for debts owed by deceased persons, one brought against an executor[31] and another against the debtor's heir.[32] In one case a widow was sued for an unpaid fine assessed against her husband on account of adultery, even though she was not her husband's executor.[33] There is a case in which the defendant admitted that he had heard a claim for an 'annual rent' that pertained to royal jurisdiction,[34] and another in which the suit in church court was against a pledgor on another's debt.[35] Two complainants, one lay, the other a prior, alleged church court actions against them for battery[36] and another complained of being cited to answer in a land plea.[37] Many of the complaints are accusations of pecuniary exactions for correction of sins, including fornication,[38] adultery,[39] sabbath and feast-day offences,[40] usury,[41] and violence against a clerk.[42] It is likely that none of these cases belonged in the spiritual forum according to established common law rules.

A number of cases seem to have involved nothing more than harrassment by ecclesiastical officials designed to extort money. One judge was convicted of citing the complainant to appear in Yorkshire and elsewhere on what proved to be a nonexistent claim.[43] A subdean caused two lay persons to be cited in church court because they had attempted

[26] Case no. 3.6. See also JUSTl/575, m. 104 (complaint of William But concerning church court claim for a 'dolium vini'), m. l09d (complaint of Alexander le Bucher, sued in church court 'pro quodam contractu inter eos habito pro quodam vitulo quod non fuit de testamento vel matrimonio').

[27] Cases nos. 3.2, 3.6, 3.7, and 3.15. See also JUSTl/575, m. l0ld ('Cum idem magister Henricus mutuo tradidisset predictis Rogero et Simoni [complainants] x marcas idem magister Henricus citari fecit ipsos coram commissario episcopi Norwic'').

[28] Case no. 3.21. See also JUSTl/575, m. 101d (complaint of Edmund de Swatfend regarding church court suit 'de contractu'), m. 109d (complaint of Alexander le Bucher regarding church court suit 'pro quodam contractu').

[29] E.g., JUSTl/575, m. 101 (complaint of Margaret Man), m. l0ld (complaints of William Isonde and Walter Kyde), m. 103 (complaint of William Brimman), m. 105d (complaints of Simon fitz Thomas and Benedict Gentil).

[30] Case no. 3.2.

[31] Case no. 3.22.

[32] Case no. 3.14.

[33] Case no. 3.9. See also JUSTl/575, m. 102 ('Convictum est per Juratatam in quam Alicia Colyn de Swanton'querens et Walterus clericus se posuerunt quod idem Walterus citare fecit ipsam Aliciam coram Johanne de Fereby exigendo ab eadem tria quarteria ordei precii xii solidorum de debito Nicholai Colyn quondam viri sui ipsius Alicie et quod quidam debitum non fuit de testamento vel matrimonio').

[34] Case no. 3.11.

[35] Case no. 3.17.

[36] Cases nos. 3.13 and 3.25.

[37] JUSTl/575, m. 103d (complaint of Thomas de Feltewell regarding church court suit 'de quodam tenemento in Lenn'').

[38] Cases nos. 3.4 and 3.23.

[39] Cases nos. 3.5 and 3.9.

[40] Cases nos. 3.1 and 3.3. See also JUSTl/575, m.105d (exaction of three shillings from Theobald le Tayllur 'pro halidayeswerk iniuste et per extorsionem').

[41] Case no. 3.19. See also JUSTl/575, m. 107 (complaint of Lucia widow of Adam de Silvestre).

[42] JUSTl/575, m. 102 (complaint of John Baldewyne).

[43] Case no. 3.24.

to collect a debt from him due on a sale of wine.[44] Another ecclesiastical official seized an executor's documents of account.[45] A tenant whose goods were distrained by his lord for nonpayment of rent caused him to be cited in church court and, when a writ of prohibition was produced, the judge threw it against a wall and continued with the case.[46] A papal official appointed to collect offerings for the Holy Land proceeded against a lay person despite a writ of prohibition and had him excommunicated.[47] Some cases involved retaliation for use of writs of prohibition,[48] including one in which a church court judge instituted proceedings against a clerk on account of his resort to prohibition.[49]

None of these cases suggests an alteration of standard jurisdictional boundaries. Each of these matters—contract and debt, pecuniary fines for sin, trespass, lay fee—was by 1286 established as beyond the scope of the church's legal authority. There were no instances during the Norfolk inquest of prosecution for church court actions previously recognized as spiritual. The wrong alleged in every one of the sin cases was the exaction of money fines; there were no suggestions that the king's justices were willing to consider the legitimacy of the grounds on which the ecclesiastical suits were founded, even though some seem to have been excessively harsh.[50] Likewise, the various contract and debt cases, obviously based on the common law's objection to ecclesiastical settlement of such disputes, reveal no signs of intrusion upon the church's penitential authority over the sin of perjury. Given the alacrity with which the complainants stepped forward, a new ruling restricting the church courts solely to testamentary and matrimonial causes alone would doubtless have resulted in a chorus of objections to collections of ecclesiastical payments and dues. Yet the justices explicitly affirmed the church's jurisdiction over tithes; a lay person's claim was dismissed because the church court suit complained of, for six marks, was for arrears of tithes owed to a parish church.[51] In another case, a clerk was convicted of disobeying a prohibition even though the cause in question was for spoliation of tithes, but in fact the parishioner had paid his minor tithes and according to local custom was not obliged to harvest the corn owed as major tithes.[52] It seems therefore that that the clerk's offence was not prosecution of a spoliation action but rather his vexacious use of ecclesiastical process to compel his parishioner to scythe corn designated as tithes when it was in fact the parson's responsibility to do so himself. No one alleged that a mortuary, obvention, oblation, or other legitimate customary payment had been unjustly collected. The court did condemn, after consultation with the king's council, tolls exacted by the dean and subdean of Norwich on certain commercial activities conducted during feast days, but these had

[44] Case no. 3.12.

[45] Case no. 3.22.

[46] Case no. 3.18

[47] Case no. 3.8.

[48] Case no. 3.7.

[49] Case no. 3.21

[50] E.g., JUSTl/575, m. l0ld (Richard atte Dam fined half mark 'eo quod predicta Margar' non potuit concipere de predicto Ricardo viro suo infantem'), m. 104 (subdeacon of Norwich 'cepit et extorsit de laicis catallis suis [i.e., of the complainants] vi denarios eo quod predictus Galfridus calefecerit aquam per diem festinum').

[51] Case no. 3.20. If the church had jurisdiction over claims against parishioners for money equivalents of arrears in tithes, a fortiori suits for the tithes themselves must have been licit.

[52] Case no. 3.10. See also JUSTl/575, m. 101 (subdean of Norwich prosecuted John de Rollisby 'eo quod idem Johannes quadam die tempore fenationis negavit ad cariandum fenum ipsius decani et ad acommodandam cartatam suam').

been found by the jury to have been unprecedented.[53] Clearly the Norfolk inquest of 1286 was not the occasion for a new policy of limitation directed against the church courts.

If the crown did not intend a redefinition of the substantive rules governing the boundary between the two jurisdictions and the reform was only procedural, why did the clergy interpret the edict as a restriction of its judicial competence purely to matters testamentary and matrimonial? The evidence is not decisive, but it seems likely that the clergy's reaction was based on a misunderstanding, perhaps due to imprecise drafting of the edict. It has been noted already that the wording of the writ of prohibition *de catallis et debitis* strictly speaking forbade all ecclesiastical suits concerning chattels or debts unless they were '*de testamento vel matrimonio*'. In fact, the royal courts throughout the thirteenth century recognized that the church's jurisdiction included other claims for chattels, notably tithes and other religious dues, prohibitions *de catallis et debitis* notwithstanding. If the aim of the lost edict was to declare that ecclesiastical cognizance of matters pertaining to secular justice was *ipso facto* a wrong subject to prosecution and the edict was phrased in terms of the standard prohibition *de catallis et debitis*, lacking the common law qualifications observed in practice, then it might well have appeared that the innovation was substantive as well as procedural.

Several of the complaints presented after the 1 July writ support this interpretation. They are specific claims for ecclesiastical jurisdiction over cases involving debts and chattels not testamentary or matrimonial—such as tithes, customary obligations to maintain the fabric of local parish churches, spiritual annuities, debts recognized before ordinaries in which the parties were clerks[54]—on the ground that these have customarily been settled in church courts. In addition, the clergy complained that they would be unable to correct sins such as violence against clerks, defamation, and breach of faith.[55] Since it seems especially unlikely that the crown intended to put a stop to the church's penitential function, probably instead the issue here was pecuniary penance, the imposition of which was long since denied to the church courts but nevertheless pertinent to an apparent general prohibition on all non-testamentary or matrimonial money claims.

Circumspecte agatis itself was a direct response to several of the grievances presented after the 1 July writ,[56] an attempt to clear up the misunderstanding caused by the writ and the edict. It recognized the spiritual nature of correction of mortal sins such as fornication and adultery, and even admitted that in certain cases the church courts might impose pecuniary rather than corporal penance. (The only reservation was the fining of unfree persons, who owned no property in their own right.) Exactions of money for the maintenance of church property was also licit, as were claims for tithes and mortuaries brought against parishioners. Questions of right to tithes contested by two rectors were for the church, unless the amount at stake amounted to a fourth of the value of the church in possession of the tithes. In what was probably a reference to a common feature of appropriation arrangements, *Circumspecte agatis* endorsed the right of a 'prelate' who was patron of a church to bring an ecclesiastical action for a pension due from the 'rector' of the church. As for

[53] Case no. 3.1.
[54] *Councils & Synods*, 970–972 (nos. 4, 8, 14, and 15).
[55] *Councils & Synods*, 970 (no. 4).
[56] See *Councils & Synods*, 970–971, especially nos. 4, 8, 13, and 14.

violence against clerks and defamation, these had already been grantd to the church courts as long as correction of sin rather than monetary compensation was the object of the suit. (The reference here was evidently to the lengthy royal response to a clerical *gravamen* presented and answered in 1280.[57] The tone of the passage in *Circumspecte agatis* suggests that rehearsal of this fact was felt to be unnecessary, that is, there had been no change in the crown's views on the church's jurisdiction since then.) Likewise, the church could hear breach of faith actions aimed at correction of sin. There is nothing in *Circumspecte agatis* that did not address directly an issue raised in the clerical grievances; as a positive statement, it referred only to jurisdictional matters involving claims for debts or chattels that the crown was willing to admit pertained to the church.

Circumspecte agatis was by no means a comprehensive description of ecclesiastical jurisdiction or even of all the areas of competence that most frequently conflicted with the common law. There was no consideration of the scope of the prohibitions *de laico feodo* or *de transgressione*. The complex legal arrangements governing ecclesiastical patronage were treated only in relation to the one-fourth rule. The writ did not even mention the church's extensive testamentary or matrimonial authority. What *Circumspecte agatis* did provide was a catalogue of all those causes concerning goods or money that were justiciable in church courts, prohibitions *de catallis et debitis* notwithstanding. Every clause related to an ecclesiastical action for goods or money, whether tithes, for example, or pecuniary penance, and each recognized the church's jurisdiction '*non obstante regia prohibitione*'. Because the royal prohibition here referred to was the one *de catallis et debitis*, it was not necessary to mention that ecclesiastical suits for testamentary legacies or marriage portions were licit: the writ of prohibition said that itself. It was because the document aimed to define the scope of that particular form of prohibition that other aspects of the church's jurisdiction potentially subject to other forms of prohibition—such as disputes over elemosinary land or the suitability of clerks to hold benefices to which they were presented by their patrons—were ignored. The scope of those forms of prohibition did not require explication.

It thus appears that the crown issued *Circumspecte agatis* because of the clergy's objections to the lost edict. That edict was not, however, a radical restriction of the church's jurisdiction only to testamentary and matrimonial matters. The 1 July writ designed to implement the edict, and containing a lengthy list of pleas claimed by the royal courts, omitted any direct reference to those areas of the law that were supposedly the object of a 'frontal attack'. The records of the inquest set in motion by the 1 July writ reveal no signs of battle. But nevertheless the edict did require clarification; probably it was based in form on the prohibition *de catallis et debitis* but neglected to include the qualifications on that writ's statement of jurisdiction observed at common law. The clergy's understanding of it was such that the publication of *Circumspecte agatis* was necessary. Under the circumstances, the clergy regarded this as a victory, despite the fact that the writ was a purely conservative document containing no substantive grants at all.

The misplaced emphasis on the substantive importance of the lost edict and *Circumspecte agatis* has resulted in failure to appreciate the true significance of Edward's policy during 1285 and 1286. The edict and 1 July writ announced a new enforcement procedure

[57] *Councils & Synods*, 874–875.

for ecclesiastical infringements on royal jurisdiction. A prosecutorial process, based on lay inquests, was to replace the older system of writs of prohibition enforceable by civil actions, which depended on the initiative of individual complainants.

In the event, however, the new procedure proved to be of very little significance in church-state jurisdictional relations during the reign of Edward I. It was not implemented throughout the country and was used only sporadically after 1286. The *gravamina* presented after the 1 July writ made no specific reference to Norfolk (concerned instead generally with 'wrongs committed against the churches of Canterbury province')[58] and another copy of the writ announcing the inquest was addressed to the clergy of Somerset and Dorset[59] but there is no evidence of an actual inquest into jurisdictional offences in those counties or in any others. Eyres were conducted in several counties within a few years of 1285—including one in Dorset in 1287—but the records of the proceedings against ecclesiastical judges included in the Norfolk eyre rolls are unique.[60]

Later in the reign there is very little evidence of the procedure announced in 1285. An eyre roll from Kent, dated 1292, includes an entry in which an executor complained that a clerk had impleaded him in a church court concerning a non-spiritual matter.[61] The case was argued and decided without any reference to a writ of prohibition, suggesting that the prosecution of the ecclesiastical suit was treated as itself a wrong at common law even absent an allegation of refusal to honor a prohibition. A King's Bench case heard in 1297 referred to an inquiry at a sheriff's tourn into ecclesiastical suits contrary to prohibition.[62] This may have been an indictment procedure aimed at discovering violators of prohibitions, but there is no further evidence of similar practices during Edward's reign. Another King's Bench case, from 1298, included an allegation that a royal bailiff went before an 'an inquisitor and auditor of complaints against clerks' in Suffolk (*adivit inquisitorem et auditorem querelarum conquerentium de clericis*) and falsely accused a clerk of excommunicating him unjustly.[63] The reference suggests the sort of inquisitorial procedure mandated in 1285, but this and the other cases noted here are isolated instances. There is no reason to believe that a prosecutorial procedure was implemented on regular, general basis after the Norfolk eyre of 1286.[64]

If the purpose of the lost edict of 1285 was to establish a new procedure for policing the boundary between the two jurisdictions, it is necessary to consider why it was not pursued after 1286. The eyre system itself—the omnicompetent tribunals that were supposed to

58 *Councils & Synods*, 969.

59 Graves, 'Circumspecte Agatis', 2 n. 3.

60 Bartholomew Cotton's *Historia Anglicana* includes this passage: 'Eo anno [i.e., 1286] fecit inquiri rex qui clerici implacitaverant quoscumque de feodo seu laicis catallis in curia Christianitatis, et de praelatis, qui graviter punierant excessus laicorum pecuniariter; et clericos, praelatos, et eorum ministros de hujusmodi [culpa] convictos graviter vinxit et incarceravit'. Although this statement may seem general enough to suggest a broad campaign, its context and the author's parochial background (a Norwich monk, whose original contributions to the history concerned mainly Norwich and Yarmouth) indicate that the reference is probably to Norfolk alone. Note that the jurisdictional offences mentioned were all well established ones, without indication of a newly restrictive policy.

61 JUST 1/375, m. 81 (Kent, 1292).

62 Case no. 1.22. This case came from Norfolk, so perhaps the inquiry was a survival of the 1286 inquest.

63 KB 27/156, m. 23 (1298). This case is from Suffolk and therefore could have referred to the 1286 inquest. There is no notation of the events alleged in the 1298 complaint among the 1286 records, however.

64 The eyre of London of 1321 included an indictment procedure for the prosecution of jurisdictional complaints against ecclesiastical judges: *YB Eyre of London 1321*, 1:38.

visit each county at least once every decade and the vehicle by which the procedure was implemented in Norfolk—ceased after 1294, possibly because other institutions had been develop to fill the void created by the intinerant justices' intermittent appearance.[65] This does not explain why the crown did not devise some other method for hearing complaints against the church courts on a local level. Perhaps the commitment to reform was simply insufficient to overcome the inertia of customary patterns of interaction between ecclesiastical and secular legal systems at the local community level.[66] Or perhaps the real grant to the clergy in 1286 was not in the area of substantive law defining the boundary between the two jurisdictions—the problem that attracted the attention of the clergy at the time and of historians since then—but rather a quiet decision, not expressed in *Circumspecte agatis* or observed until after the Norfolk eyre, to proceed no further with the new enforcement procedure. This itself was of relatively less importance, because even if abandoned the standard prohibition procedure remained in place as a vehicle for policing the church's exercise of its jurisdiction. So, the crown could avoid possible opposition to a new procedure without giving up too much. Meanwhile, the boundary between the two jurisdictions, defined initially during the reign of Henry III, remained for the most part intact under Edward, unaffected by *Circumspecte agatis*.

[65] The eyres were replaced by specialized commissions of limited authority and, later, by local justices of the peace. See Burt, 'Demise of the General Eyre'. See also Crook, 'Later Eyres'.

[66] Compare the incomplete success of Edward's ambitious quo warranto campaign, also intended to be implemented through the eyre system. See Sutherland, *Quo Warranto*, especially 184–189. Hyams suggests a parallel between the quo warranto inquiries and what he sees as a policy of pressure on the church's jurisdiction. In each area, the aim was to subordinate these 'external jurisdictions' to the common law: 'Norwich Inquiry' 621.

PROHIBITION CASES

1.1a

CP 40/6, m. 46.
Common Pleas, Michaelmas term 1274

Leyc'. Robertus prior sancte Marie de Pratis Leyc' attachiatus fuit ad respondendum magistro hospitalis sancti Lazari de Burton' de placito quare tenuit placitum in curia christianitatis de advocatione quarte partis ecclesie de Galby contra prohibitionem etc.

Et prior venit et defendit vim et injuriam quando etc. et bene defendit quod non tenuit predictum placitum de advocatione predicta contra prohibitionem predictam sicut ei inponit et hoc paratus est verificare sicut curia consideraverit. Ideo consideratum est quod vadiat ei legem se xij^{ma} manu. <Postea fecit ei legem. Ideo consideratum est quod predictus prior inde sine die. Et magister in misericordia. Et inhibitum est predicto priori ne teneat predictum placitum etc.>[1]

1.1b

CP 40/11, m. 6
Common Pleas, Michaelmas term 1275

Leyc'. Robertus prior sancte Marie de Pratis Leyc' attachiatus fuit ad respondendum magistro hospitalis sancti Lazari de Burton de placito quod, cum predictus Robertus attachiatus esset in curia regis ad respondendum eidem magistro de placito quare tenuit placitum in curia christianitatis de advocatione quarte partis ecclesie de Walby contra prohibitionem regis et idem prior venisset in eadem curia et vadiasset quamdam legem quod [nuncquam][2] tenuit predictum placitum in prefata curia christianitatis contra prohibitionem predictam et eandem legem in eadem curia se duodecima manu fecisset per quod consideratum fuisset quod predictus prior iret inde sine die et predictus magister esset in misericordia et insuper in prefata curia regis per prefatos justiciarios prohibitum esset predicto priori ne predictum placitum extunc ulterius teneret, predictus prior spreta predicta prohibitione predictum placitum in predicta curia christianitatis postea tenuit et adhuc tenet contra predictam prohibitionem, in ipsius magistri prejudicium et sui juris gravissimam lesionem. Et unde predictus magister queritur quod, cum idem prior in crastino

[1] The 'postea' appears to be in the same hand as the rest of the record, apparently written at the same time.
[2] MS. reads nucquam

PROHIBITION CASES

1.1a.

MASTER OF BURTON LAZARS v. PRIOR OF ST MARY-OF-THE-MEADOWS

Leicestershire. Robert, prior of St Mary-of-the-Meadows, Leicester, was attached to answer the master of the hospital of Burton Lazars concerning a plea that he held a plea in Court Christian concerning the advowson of a quarter part of the church of Gaulby contrary to prohibition etc.

And the prior appears and denies force and wrong whenever etc. and completely denies that he held that plea concerning the advowson of that church contrary to prohibition as is alleged against him. And this he is prepared to prove as the court shall adjudge. Therefore it is adjudged that he is to wage his law twelve-handed. Later he made his law. Therefore it is adjudged that the prior go without day. And the master is in mercy. And the prior is ordered not to hold that plea etc.

1.1b

MASTER OF BURTON LAZARS v. PRIOR OF ST MARY-OF-THE-MEADOWS

Leicestershire. Robert, prior of St Mary-of-the-Meadows, Leicester, was attached to answer the master of the hospital of Burton Lazars concerning a plea that, whereas Robert was attached to answer to the master in the king's court on a plea concerning why he held a plea in Court Christian concerning the advowson of a quarter part of the church of Gaulby contrary to royal prohibition and the prior came into the king's court and waged his law that he never held that plea in Court Christian contrary to prohibition and made his law twelve-handed in the court whereby it was adjudged that the prior go without day and the master be in mercy and moreover in the king's court the prior was ordered by the justices not to hold the plea thereafter any further,[1] scorning the prohibition the prior afterwards held and is still holding the same plea in Court Christian, to the prejudice of the master and most grievous offence to his right. And the master complains that, whereas on the morrow of All Souls just past[2] the prior made his law before the justices here and then was enjoined that he hold the plea no further, scorning that injunction the prior afterwards held the plea

[1] Case no. 1.1a.
[2] 2 November 1274.

Animarum proximo preterito coram justiciariis hic fecisset predictam legem [d]<ita quod>[d] et [d]<tamen>[d] inhibitum esset predicto priori ne ulterius placitum predictum teneret, idem prior spreta <inhibicione>[1] predicta postea tenuit predictum placitum et ipsum excommunicavit et condempnavit. Unde dicit quod deterioratus est et dampnum habet ad valenciam centum marcarum. Et inde producit sectam etc.

Et predictus prior venit et defendit vim et injuriam quando etc. Et bene defendit quod ipse nuncquam post inhibitionem predictam predictum placitum tenuit. Et quod ita sit ponit se super patriam. Et magister similter. Ideo preceptum est vicecomiti quod venire faciat hic in octabis sancti Hillarii nisi R. de Seyton prius etc. xij etc. per quos etc. Et qui nec etc. ad recognoscendum in forma predicta. Quia tam etc.

1.2a

CP 40/17, m. 73
Common Pleas, Michaelmas term 1276

Glouc'. Beatrix que fuit uxor Ricardi regis Alem' in misericordia pro pluribus defaltis versus Edmundum comitem Cornub'.

Eadem Beatrix attachiata fuit ad respondendum predicto Edmundo de placito quare secuta est placitum in curia christianitatis de debitis et catallis que non sunt de testamento vel matrimonio contra prohibitionem etc. Et unde predictus comes queritur quod cum Willelmus le Brun procurator eius die Martis proxima ante diem Palmarum anno regni domini regis nunc tercio in ecclesia b[eate][2] Marie de Arcubus Lond' porigisset et tradidisset procuratori predicti regine breve domini regis de prohibitione ne p[redictum][2] placitum de catallis et debitis que non sunt de testamento vel matrimonio ulterius sequeretur nomine predicte regine, p[redictus][3] procurator spreta predicte prohibitione nomine predicte regine domine sue et postquam certa noticia ad personam predicte regine de prohibitione domini regis pervenit sequebatur placitum in curia christianitatis scilicet coram decano de Arc[ubus][2] Lond' in ecclesia beate Marie de Arcubus predicta de debito quinquaginta et duarum mille marcarum ad grave dampnum [pre]dicti[2] comitis et contra prohibitionem predictam. Unde dicit quod deterioratus est et dampnum habet ad valenciam sexaginta mille marcarum. Et inde producit sectam.

Et Beatrix per attornatum suum per breve domini regis nunc venit et defendit vim et injuriam quando etc. Et bene def[endit][2] quod nunquam post predictam prohibitionem ei factam [secuta][3] fuit aliquod placitum in curia christianitatis de catallis et debitis que non sunt de testamento vel matrimonio etc. sicut predictus comes in brevi suo queritur. Et hoc offert defendere contra ipsum et sectam suam. Ideo consideratum est quod vadiat ei legem se duodecima manu. Et veniat cum lege sua die Pasche in quindecim dies. Plegii

[1] Altered from prohibicione
[2] MS. damaged.
[3] MS. reads sequta

and condemned and excommunicated him. He says he is thereby harmed and damaged to the value of 100 marks. And he produces suit etc.

And the prior appears and denies force and wrong whenever etc. And he denies that he ever held the plea after the injunction. And that it is so he puts himself upon the country. And the master likewise. Therefore the sheriff is ordered to cause to appear here on the octave of Hilary, unless Roger de Seaton earlier etc., 12 men etc. by whom etc. and who are not etc. to give their verdict on this matter etc. Because both parties etc.

1.2a

EARL OF CORNWALL v. BEATRICE, QUEEN DOWAGER OF GERMANY

Gloucestershire. Beatrice, widow of Richard king of Germany,[1] in mercy for numerous defaults against Edmund, earl of Cornwall.[2]

Beatrice was attached to answer Edmund concerning a plea as to why she sued a plea in Court Christian concerning debts and chattels that are not testamentary or matrimonial, contrary to prohibition etc. And in this regard the earl complains that, since William le Brun his proctor presented the king's writ of prohibition to the queen's proctor on Tuesday preceding Palm Sunday in the third year of this king's reign[3] in the church of St Mary-le-Bow, London that he cease suing a plea in the queen's name concerning chattels and debts that are not testamentary or matrimonial, scorning the prohibition and after certain notice of the lord king's prohibition to the queen herself the proctor sued the plea in Court Christian before the dean of Arches, London in the church of St Mary-le-Bow concerning a debt of 52,000 marks, to the earl's grave damage and contrary to the prohibition. He says he is thereby harmed and damaged to the value of 60,000 marks. And he produces suit.

And Beatrice by her attorney appointed by a writ of the present lord king now appears and denies force and wrong whenever etc. And she completely denies that she ever sued any plea in Court Christian concerning chattels and debts that are not testamentary or matrimonial after prohibition as the earl alleges in his writ. And she offers to prove this against him and his suit. Therefore it is adjudged that she is to wage her law twelve-handed. And let her come with her law on the quindene of Easter. Pledges for her law Grimald de Pauncefot and John de Bocking. And her attorney is told that he should cause his lady to

[1] The second son of King John and younger brother of Henry III, Richard was crowned king of Germany in 1257. He married Beatrix von Falkenburg, his third wife, in 1269 and died in 1272.

[2] Edmund of Almain, second earl of Cornwall, was Richard's son and heir born in 1249. His mother was Sanchia, Richard's second wife and sister of Henry III's queen Eleanor of Provence.

[3] 2 April 1275.

de lege Grimbaldus de Pauncefot et Johannes de Bocking'. Et d[ictum][1] est attornato predicte regine quod faciat venire dominam suam ad prefatum terminum ad faciendum legem in p[ropria][1] persona sua. Et similiter inhibitum est eidem regine ne pendente placito predicto aliquod placitum in curia christianitatis sequatur.

Postea in octabis sancte Trinitatis venit predicta Beatrix et fecit legem suam et datus est cis dies apud Salop' in crastino Animarum de audiendo judicio suo super lege ista.

1.2b

CP 40/20, m. 14
Common Pleas, Trinity term 1277

Midd. Magister Robertus Trillawe decanus de Arcubus London' attachiatus fuit ad respondendum Edmundo comiti Cornub' de placito quare tenuit placitum in curia christianitatis de catallis et debitis que non sunt de testamento vel matrimonio contra prohibitionem regis etc. Et unde predictus comes per attornatum suum queritur quod cum Beatrix que fuit uxor Ricardi regis Alemann' inplacitasset ipsum coram predicto magistro Roberto petendo ab ipso medietatem omnium bonorum que fuerunt predicti Ricardi estimatam ad medietatem quinquaginta mille marcarum que non sunt de testamento vel matrimonio et quidem Willelmus de Brun procuratur ipsius comitis detulisset eidem magistro Roberto regiam prohibitionem die Martis proxima ante festum Palmarum anno regni regis nunc tercio in ecclesia beate Marie de Arcubus London' ne predictum placitum teneret idem magister Robertus spreta predicta prohibitione tenuit predictum placitum predictis die et anno. Et similiter postea die Lune proxima post festum sancti Dunstani archiepiscopi. Unde dicit quod deterioratus est et dampnum habet ad valenciam quinquaginta mille librarum. Et inde producit sectam etc.

Et magister Robertus venit et defendit vim et injuriam quando etc. Et bene defendit quod nunquam post predictam prohibitionem ei ex parte predicti comitis per predictum procuratorem suum exibitam tenuit aliquod placitum de catallis et debitis que non fuerunt de testamento vel matrimonio et hoc paratus est defendere contra ipsum et sectam suam sicut curia consideraverit. Et si hoc non sufficit dicet aliud.

Et predictus comes dicit quod [i]<idem Robertus>[i] non debet ad aliquam defensionem per legem suam ad presens admitti quia dicit quod predictus Robertus predicto die Martis ante Dominicam Palmarum postquam predicta prohibitio ei porrecta fuit et similiter die Lune post festum sancti Dunstani tenuit predictum placitum et pronunciavit esse procedendum in eodem placito non obstante predicta prohibitione et profert acta inde confecta et sigillo ipsius magistri Roberti signata que hoc idem testantur. Unde petit judicium si predictus [i]<Robertus>[i] possit seu debeat se per legem suam contra factum suum proprium defendere vel acquietare.

Dies datus est eis de audiendo judicium suum in crastino Animarum apud Salop' etc.

[1] MS. damaged.

appear on that date to make her law in person. And likewise the queen is enjoined not to sue any plea in Court Christian while this plea is pending.

Later on the octave of Trinity[1] Beatrice appears and makes her law. And day is given to the parties on the morrow of All Souls at Shrewsbury to hear judgment on this wager of law.

1.2b

EARL OF CORNWALL v. DEAN OF ARCHES

Middlesex. Master Robert Trillawe, dean of the Arches, London, was attached to answer Edmund earl of Cornwall concerning a plea as to why he held a plea in Court Christian concerning chattels and debts that are not testamentary or matrimonial, contrary to the king's prohibition etc. And in this regard the earl by his attorney complains that, whereas Beatrice widow of Richard king of Germany sued him before master Robert seeking from him half of all the goods that belonged to Richard estimated to be worth half of 50,000 marks that are not testamentary or matrimonial, and one William le Brun the earl's proctor delivered a royal prohibition to master Robert on Tuesday preceding Palm Sunday in the third year of this king's reign[2] in the church of St Mary-le-Bow, London, that he should not hold that plea, scorning that prohibition master Robert heard that plea on that day and year and likewise on Monday after the feast of St Dunstan.[3] He says he is thereby harmed and damaged to the value of 50,000 marks. And he produces suit etc.

And master Robert appears and denies force and wrong whenever etc. And he completely denies that he ever held any plea concerning chattels and debts that were not testamentary or matrimonial after the prohibition was shown to him on behalf of the earl by his proctor. And he is prepared to prove this against him and his suit as the court should adjudge. And if this is not sufficient he will say something else.

And the earl says that Robert ought not now be admitted to any denial by wager of law because on Tuesday preceding Palm Sunday after the prohibition had been delivered to him and likewise on Monday after the feast of St Dunstan he held the plea and pronounced that the plea ought to proceed notwithstanding the prohibition. And the earl proffers *acta* compiled on this matter and sealed by master Robert that attest to this. And he prays judgment whether Robert may or should defend or acquit himself by wager of law against his own deed.

Day is given to the parties to hear their judgment on the morrow of All Souls at Shrewsbury etc.

[1] 31 May 1277.
[2] 2 April 1275.
[3] 20 May 1275.

1.2c

CP 40/20, m. 14d
Common Pleas, Trinity term 1277

Berks. Edmundus comes Cornub' questus est domino regi quod cum Beatrix que fuit uxor Ricardi regis Alem' attachiata esset in curia regis hic in crastino Animarum anno regni regis nunc quarto ad respondendum eidem Edmundo de placito quare secuta fuit placitum in curia christianitatis de catallis et debitis que non sunt de testamento vel matrimonio contra prohibitionem etc. ad quem diem eadem Beatrix venisset per attornatum suum et in eadem curia vadiasset inde legem suam et eidem ex parte regis inhibitum fuisset et prohibitum ne pendente predicto placito in prefata curia regis aliquod placitum in curia christianitatis ulterius sequeretur eadem Beatrix postea post predictam inhibitionem ei factam dictum placitum in prefata curia christianitatis postposito inde precepto regis secuta fuit ita quod ad sectam suam idem placitum iam devolutum est et positum in curia Romana in regis contemptum et dignitatis regis et corone [i]<sue>[i] lesionem manifestam necnon et dicti Edmundi dampnum gravissimum et gravamen etc. Et unde dominus rex per Alanus de Walkyngham qui sequitur pro eo queritur cum predicta Beatrix attachiata esset in crastino Animarum anno predicto ad respondendum predicti comiti de placito quare secuta fuit placitum in curia christianitatis de catallis et debitis que non sunt de testamento vel matrimonio videlicet de medietate omnium bonorum et catallorum que fuerunt predicti Ricardi quondam viri sui quorum summa estimatur ad quinquaginta et duas mille marcarum contra prohibitionem domini regis etc. et ad diem illum eadem Beatrix vadiavit legem suam quod nullum placitum secuta fuit in predicta curia christianitatis versus eundem comitem de catallis et debitis que non fuerunt de testamento vel matrimonio post prohibitionem ei inde liberatam et ex parte domini regis eidem Beatrici inhibitum fuisset ne aliquod placitum in prefata curia christianitatis pendente predicto placito in curia regis hic inter eos amplius sequeretur prefata Beatrix postea post predictam defensionem ei ex parte domini regis factam per suos justiciarios hic predicto die Jovis proximo post festum sancti Martini in Hyeme anno eodem in capitulo sancti Pauli Lond' coram magistris Johanne de Derby, Ade de Fyleby, Andrea de Kylkenny, et Alano de Crepping commissariis [archidiaconorum][1] Lond' et Midd' judicum a domino papa delegatorum. Et similiter die Lune proxima post festum sancte Lucie et Purificationis beate Marie in predicto capitulo coram eisdem judicibus contra preceptum regis et defensionem suam secuta fuit, ita quod idem placitum positum est in Curia Romana ad sectam suam in contemptum regis et dignitatis sue et corone sue lesionem centum mille librarum necnon ad grave dampnum predicti Edmundi sexaginta mille librarum. Et hoc paratus est verificare per recordum et testimonium magistri Radulfi de Freningham justiciarii de Banco missi in propria persona ad predictam curiam christianitatis ad audiendum, testificandum, et recordandum si predicta Beatrix post inhibitionem predictam predictum placitum in predicta curia christianitatis prosecuta fuisset in cuius presencia ipsa per procuratorem suum idem placitum sequebatur ita quod devolutum est ad predictam curiam Romanam ut predictum est et etiam per acta inde

[1] MS. reads ardiachid

1.2c

THE KING AND THE EARL OF CORNWALL v. BEATRICE, QUEEN DOWAGER OF GERMANY

Berkshire. Edmund earl of Cornwall complained to the king that, whereas Beatrice widow of Richard, king of Germany, was attached in the king's court here to appear on the morrow of All Souls' in the fourth year of this king's reign[1] to answer Edmund concerning a plea as why she sued a plea in Court Christian concerning chattels and debts that are not testamentary or matrimonial, contrary to prohibition etc., on which day Beatrice appeared by her attorney and waged her law in that court and was enjoined and prohibited on behalf of the king not to sue further any plea in Court Christian while the plea in the king's court was pending,[2] after that injunction Beatrice sued that plea in Court Christian, disregarding the king's order on this, such that at her suit it has devolved to the court of Rome, in contempt of the king and his dignity and manifest harm to his crown and also to the most serious damage and wrong to Edmund. And in this regard the lord king through Alan de Walkyngham who sues for him complains that, whereas Beatrice was attached to appear on the morrow of All Souls' to answer the earl concerning a plea as to why she sued a plea in Court Christian concerning chattels and debts that are not testamentary or matrimonial, namely concerning half of all the goods and chattels that belonged to her late husband Richard estimated to be worth 52,000 marks, contrary to the lord king's prohibition etc. and on that day she waged her law to the effect that she sued no plea in Court Christian against the earl concerning chattels and debts that were not testamentary or matrimonial after the prohibition delivered to her and on behalf of the lord king she was enjoined from continuing to sue any plea in Court Christian while the plea was pending in the king's court between them, Beatrice later, after that injunction issued on behalf of the king by his justices here, on Thursday after the feast of St Martin in hyeme in the same year[3] in the chapter of St Paul's, London before masters John de Derby, Adam de Fyleby, Andrew de Kylkenny, and Alan de Crepping, commissaries of the archdeacons of London and Middlesex, judges delegate of the pope, and likewise on Monday following the feast of St Lucy[4] and on the Purification of Mary[5] in that chapter before the same judges, continued her suit contrary to the king's precept and injunction, such that it was removed to the court of Rome at her suit, in contempt of the king and offending his crown and dignity in the amount of 100,000 pounds and also to the grave damage of Edmund in the amount of 60,000 pounds. And he is prepared to prove this by the record and testimony of master Ralph de Farningham, justice of the Bench,[6] sent in person to the Court Christian to hear, testify, and record whether Beatrix prosecuted the plea there after the injunction and in whose presence she sued that plea by her proctor such that it has devolved to the court of Rome as has been said and also by the *acta* compiled on the matter that he proffers and

[1] 2 November 1276. [2] Case no. 1.2a. [3] 12 November 1276.

[4] 14 December 1276. [5] 2 February 1277.

[6] Farningham was appointed justice of the Common Bench in 1275 and served until 1278. He may have been trained in civil or canon law and was sent to the court of Rome twice on the king's business and may have represented clients in the church courts in England. *Earliest Law Reports*, 1:cxxxix–cxl. These qualifications may explain his selection for the office performed in this case.

confecta que profert et hoc testantur. Et si hoc non sufficiat ad illud verificandum producit sectam. Et idem comes paratus [i]<est>[i] tam pro domino rege quam pro ipso illud verificare sicut curia consideraverit.

Et predicta Beatrix venit. Et dicit quod non habet hic diem ad hoc breve eo quod ipsa non est attachiata ad inde respondendum et petit judicium si antequam attachiata debeat ad illud respondere. Et quia ipsa Beatrix secuta fuit idem placitum in curia christianitatis contra inhibitionem et defensionem domini regis ei inde factam in contemptum eiusdem domini regis et ipsa reperitur presens in curia, consideratum est quod respondeat domino regi.

Et predicta Beatrix defendit vim et injuriam quando etc. et dicit quod non tenetur ad hoc breve respondere eo quod non est returnabile nec sufficiens in se cum non contineatur in eodem quod vicecomes illud habeat hic ad hunc diem. Dicit etiam quod idem breve nuncquam emanavit de curia ista eo quod magister Rogerus de Seyton est testis in eodem brevi dato apud Westm' sextodecimo die Maii hoc anno quo die idem Rogerus non fuit in curia ista eo quod per quatuor dies antea versus [i]<partes>[i] Shocie iter suum arripuerat. Unde petit judicium si debeat ad huiusmodi breve respondere.

Dies datus est eis de audiendo judicio suo in crastino Animarum apud Salop'.

1.3

CP 40/19, m. 15d
Common Pleas, Easter term 1277

Norf'. Magister Nicholaus de Capella attachiatus fuit ad respondendum domino regi de placito quare, cum Gilbertus de Thychewell' tanquam nuncius domini regis breve suum de prohibitione predicto magistro Nicholao in pleno capitulo apud Docking' porrigi fecisset ne tenerent placitum in curia christianitatis de catallis et debitis que non sunt de testamento vel matrimonio, in personas illud breve [i]<regis>[i] differencium, auxilium, consilium, et favourem eidem brevi prestantium in eodem pleno capitulo sentenciam excommunicationis non excipiendo personam regis minus provide fulminavit trahens dictum Gilbertum ad loca remota inde in placitum coram eo in curia christianitatis ut sic eum gravius [fatigare][1] posset laboribus et expensis et eum ex causa predicta excommunicatum denunciari fecit in corone [i]<et>[i] regie dignitatis lesionem et domini regis contemptum manifestum nec non et predicti Gilberti preiudicium et non modicum gravamen etc. Et unde dominus rex per predictum Gilbertum qui sequitur pro eo queritur quod cum idem Gilbertus breve suum de prohibitione predicto Nicholao die Jovis proximo post festum sancti Marci ewangeliste anno regni regis nunc tercio in pleno capitulo apud Docking' per quemdam Thomam Tristrem porrigi fecisset ne placitum de catallis et debitis que non sunt de testamento vel matrimonio contra prohibitionem domini regis [teneret][2],

[1] MS. reads fatiga
[2] MS. reads tenerent

that attest to this. And if this does not suffice for proof he produces suit. And the earl is ready for the lord king and for himself to prove this as the court may adjudge.

And Beatrice appears and says that she does not have a day here on this writ because she has not been attached to answer thereon and prays judgment whether she ought to answer it before she has been attached. And because Beatrice sued the plea in Court Christian contrary to the injunction and prohibition of the lord king issued to her in contempt of the lord king and she is found present in court, it is adjudged that she should answer the king.

And Beatrice denies force and wrong whenever etc. and says that she is not held to answer this writ because it is not returnable and is insufficient because it does not say that the sheriff is to have it here on this day. She says also that the writ never issued from this court because master Roger de Seaton[1] is named a witness in the writ dated at Westminster on 16 May of this year[2] on which day Roger was not in this court because he had started on a journey to Scotland four days earlier. She prays judgment whether she ought to answer this sort of writ.

Day is given to the parties to hear their judgment on the morrow of All Souls at Shrewsbury.

1.3

THE KING AND GILBERT DE THYCHEWELL v. NICHOLAS DE CAPELLA

Norfolk. Master Nicholas de Capella[3] was attached to answer the lord king concerning a plea as to why, whereas Gilbert de Thychewell' acting as the lord king's messenger caused the king's writ of prohibition to be delivered to master Nicholas in the full chapter at Docking that he should not hold a plea in Court Christian concerning chattels and debts that are not testamentary or matrimonial, in the full chapter Nicholas indiscreetly fulminated a sentence of excommunication upon those persons bringing that king's writ, and giving aid, counsel, and favour to the same writ, not excepting the person of the king, drawing Gilbert to remote places in a plea before him in Court Christian so that he might thus gravely harass him with labor and expense and on account of that cause he caused him to be denounced as excommunicate, to the wrong of the crown and royal dignity and manifest contempt of the lord king and also to the prejudice and significant oppression of Gilbert etc. And in this regard the lord king through Gilbert who sues for him complains that, whereas Gilbert caused the king's writ of prohibition to be presented to Nicholas by one Thomas Tristrem on the Thursday first following the feast of St Mark the Evangelist

[1] Appointed justice of the Common Bench in 1268 and served as chief justice from 1274 until his retirement in 1278.
[2] 1277.
[3] Perhaps the same person involved in Case no. 1.4.

prefatus Nicholaus post predictum breve per eos receptum in personas illud breve differentium et eidem favourem prestantium sentenciam excommunicationis non excipiendo personam regis fulminavit et per [i]<decem>[i] capellanos sibi subiectos de decanatu de Hecheham ipsam sentenciam solempniter predictis die et loco pulsatis campanis et accensis candelis puplicari fecit, trahens ea occasione predictum Gilbertum in placitum in curia christianitatis coram eo apud Brakedene die [sabbati][1] proxima post festum sancti Barnabe anno predicto denuncians ipsum ratione predicti brevis impetrati in sentenciam generalem incidisse et postquam ipsum per diversos labores et expensas per diversa loca fatigasset cum eadem de causa esse excommunicatum die Veneris proximo ante festum Exaltationis Sancte Crucis anno predicto [d]<et denuncians ipsum ratione predicti brevis>[d] apud Docking' denunciari fecit de die in diem. Et similiter ubi vicecomes Norff'ex parte domini regis et per eius preceptum in propria persona die Dominica proxima ante festum sancti Nicholai anno quarto efficaciter monuit quod sentencias et huiusmodi errores sine mora revocaret, idem Nicholaus predictas sentencias et errores ad mandatum domini regis et vicecomitis monitionem non revocavit immo prosequebatur in corone et regie dignitatis lesionem et regis contemptum mille librarum et predicti Gilberti dampnum centum marcarum. Et inde producit sectam etc.

Et magister Nicholaus venit et defendit vim et iniuriam quando etc. [i]<et quicquid etc.>[i] Et bene defendit quod ipse numquam excommunicationis sentenciam in predictum Gilbertum nec in aliquem breve domini regis predictum defferentem, auxilium, consilium, vel favourem prestantes fulminavit nec ipsum Gilbertum ea de causa ad loca remota in curia christianitatis ad placitum [d]<traxit>[d] nec excommunicatum eadem de causa denunciavit. Et hoc offert defendere contra ipsum et sectam suam sicut curia consideraverit. Ideo consideratum est quod vadiat ei legem se xij^{ma} manu. Et predictus Nicholaus instanter fecit legem suam. Ideo ipse inde quietus et predictus [Gilbertus][2] in misericordia.[3]

Et quo ad hoc [i]<quod>[i] predictus [Gilbertus][2] dicit [i]<ipsum Nicholaum>[i] sentenciam excommunicationis non excipiendo personam domini regis in omnes consilium, auxilium, et favourem prestantes fulminasse dicit quod ipse nunquam hujusmodi sentenciam fulminavit. Et quod ita sit ponit se super patriam. Et [Gilbertus][2] qui sequitur pro domino rege similiter. Ideo preceptum est vicecomiti qoud venire faciat hic in octabis sancte Trinitatis nisi J. de Lovetot prius etc. xij^{cim} etc. per quos etc. qui nec etc. ad recognoscendum in forma predicta. Quia tam etc. Postea ad diem illum predictus Gilbertus qui sequitur pro domino rege optulit se iiij^{to} die versus magistrum Nicholaum. Et ipse non venit. Et habuit diem ad hunc diem ut patet superius. Ideo preceptum est vicecomiti quod distringat eum per omnes terras etc. Et quod de exitibus etc. Et quod habeat corpus eius a die sancti Michaelis [i]<in xv dies>[i] apud Salop' ad audiendum predictam juratam. Et preceptum est vicecomiti quod habeat corpora recognitorum ad prefatum terminum etc. Postea in octabis sancti Johannis Baptiste anno regis nunc sexto venerunt juratores qui dicunt super sacramentum suum quod predictus Nicholaus die quo predictum breve ei porrectum fuit in pleno capitulo de Docking' per predictum Thomam de Tristrem ne predictum placitum teneret statim post

[1] MS. reads sabati

[2] MS. reads Girebertus

[3] In the margin at this point are written lex and 12 dots.

in the third year of this king's reign[1] in the full chapter at Docking that he should not hold a plea concerning chattels and debts that are not testamentary or matrimonial, contrary to the lord king's prohibition, after they had received the writ Nicholas fulminated a sentence of excommunication upon those persons bringing the writ and giving favour to it, not excepting the person of the king, and caused the sentence to be proclaimed on that day at that place by 10 chaplains of Heacham deanery subject to him with bells tolling and candles burning, and on that account drew Gilbert into a plea in Court Christian before him at Bracon Ash on the first Saturday after the feast of St Barnabas in the same year[2] denouncing him as incurring a general sentence by reason of having obtained a writ of prohibition and later harassed him by various expenses and travels to various places when he caused him to be denounced as excommunicate for the same cause on the Thursday preceding the feast of the exaltation of the Holy Cross in the same year[3] at Docking from day to day. And likewise, when the sheriff of Norfolk on behalf of the lord king and by his command officially admonished Nicholas in person on the Sunday preceding the feast of St Nicholas in the king's fourth year[4] that he should revoke these sentences and errors without delay, Nicholas did not revoke these sentences and errors according to the king's command and the sheriff's warning but instead prosecuted them, in violation of the king's crown and royal dignity and in contempt of the king to the value of 1000 pounds, and to the damage of Gilbert to the value of 100 marks. And he produces suit etc.

And master Nicholas appears and denies force and wrong whenever etc. and anything etc. And he completely denies that he ever fulminated a sentence of excommuniction upon Gilbert or anyone bringing the lord king's writ or gave deference, aid, counsel, or favour to it, or that he drew Gilbert into a plea in Court Christian to remote places on that account, or denounced him as excommunicate for that reason. And this he offers to prove as the court shall adjudge. Therefore it is adjudged that he is to wage his law twelve-handed. And Nicholas immediately makes his law. Therefore he is acquitted and Gilbert is in mercy.

And insofar as Gilbert says that Nicholas fulminated a sentence of excommunication upon all who gave counsel, aid, and favour, not excepting the person of the lord king, he says that he never fulminated this sentence. And that it is so he puts himself upon the country. And Gilbert who sues for the lord king likewise. Therefore the sheriff is ordered to cause to appear here on the octave of Trinity, unless J. de Lovetot earlier etc., 12 men etc. by whom etc. and who are not etc. to give their verdict on this matter etc. Because both parties etc.

Later on that day Gilbert who sues for the lord king appeared on the fourth day against master Nicholas. And he did not appear. And he was given a day to this day as appears above. Therefore the sheriff is ordered to distrain him by all his lands etc. and as to the issues etc., and that he should have his body at Shrewsbury to hear this jury. And the sheriff is ordered that he should have the bodies of the jurors at that time etc.

Later on the octave of St John the Baptist in this king's sixth year[5] the jurors appeared and said on their oath that, on the day that the writ of prohibition was delivered to him

[1] 25 May 1275.
[2] 15 June 1275.
[3] 12 September 1275.
[4] 1 December 1275.
[5] 6 July 1278.

receptionem eiusdem per quosdam presbiteros quos ad hoc deputavit in omnes illos breve illud deferentes et consilium, auxilium, et favourem eidem prestantes in eodem capitulo sentenciam excommunicationis fulminavit non excipiendo personam regis. Ideo mandatum est episcopo Norwic' quod faciat eum venire hic in octabis sancti Michaelis auditurus inde recordum et judicium suum. Postea venit predictus magister Nicholaus et committitur gayole pro contemptu.

1.4

CP 40/20, m. 29
Common Pleas, Trinity term 1277

Norff'. Magister Nicholaus de la Chapele attachiatus fuit ad respondendum domino regi de placito quare, cum placita de catallis et debitis que non sunt de testamento vel matrimonio ad dominum [i]<regem>[i] et ad coronam et dignitatem suam et non ad alium pertineant in regno suo, idem Nicholaus ut ex relatu plurium accepit secutus fuit placitum in curia christianitatis de catallis et debitis prioris de Bukeham que non sunt de testamento vel matrimonio contra prohibitionem etc. Et unde Ricardus de Hedersete qui sequitur pro rege dicit quod, cum regia prohibitio [i]<procuratori>[i] eiusdem Nicholai tradita fuisset die martis proxima post octabas sancte Trinitatis hoc anno in ecclesia sancti Pauli London' nomine domini regis per quemdam magistrum Adam clericum domini Roberti de Tateshale coram Hugone de Daleby, Petro Mauleun, et Willelmo de Creton ne idem Nicholaus predictum placitum ulterius sequeretur in curia christianitatis etc., idem Nicholaus spreta prohibitione predicta secutus fuit idem placitum in eadem curia contra prohibitionem predictam, in contemptum corone et dignitatis domini regis et dampnum ipsius prioris centum librarum. Et inde producit sectam etc.

Et Nicholaus venit et defendit vim et injuriam quando etc. Et bene defendit quod numquam aliqua prohibitio ei nec procuratori suo super predicto placito porrecta fuit set revera dicit quod [i]<quod [*sic*] ipse prosecutus fuit quoddam placitum in curia christianitatis de decimis suis tantum coram predicto magistro Rogero de Chebenhale et quod>[i] quedam prohibitio liberata fuit eidem magistro Rogero de Chebenhale judici suo. Unde bene defendit quod numquam post predictam prohibitionem predicto Rogero exhibitam secutus fuit aliquod placitum nisi de decimis suis prout predictum est. [i]<Et de hoc>[i] ponit se super patriam et Ricardus qui sequitur pro rege similiter. Ideo preceptum est vicecomiti quod venire faciat apud Salop' a die sancti Michaelis in tres septimanas xii etc. per quos etc. Et qui nec etc. ad recognoscendum in forma predicta. Quia tam etc.

Postea a die sancti Hillarii in xv dies anno sexto venerunt juratores, qui dicunt super sacramentum suum quod nuncquam aliqua prohibitio domini regis exhibita fuit predicto Nicholao nec idem Nicholaus uncquam post predictam prohibitionem predicto magistro Rogero liberatam de eo quod non teneret placitum de catallis et debitis etc. secutus fuit

in the full chapter of Docking by Thomas de Tristrem that he should not hold that plea, immediately after receipt of the writ Nicholas fulminated a sentence of excommunication in the chapter by means of certain priests appointed for this purpose upon all those bearing and giving counsel, aid, and favour to the writ, not excepting the person of the king. Therefore the bishop of Norwich is ordered to cause Nicholas to appear here on the octave of Michaelmas to hear his record and his judgment. Later master Nicholas appeared and is committed to gaol for contempt.

1.4

THE KING AND THE PRIOR OF BUCKENHAM v. NICHOLAS DE LA CHAPELE

Norfolk. Master Nicholas de la Chapele[1] was attached to answer the lord king concerning a plea as to why, since pleas of chattels and debts that are not testamentary or matrimonial pertain to the king's crown and dignity and to no other in his realm, Nicholas, as the king has learned through the relation of many persons, sued a plea in Court Christian concerning the chattels and debts of the prior of Buckenham that are not testamentary or matrimonial, contrary to prohibition etc. And in this regard Richard de Hedersete who sues for the king says that, whereas a royal prohibition was delivered to Nicholas's proctor on the first Tuesday after the octave of Trinity this year[2] in the church of St Paul, London in the name of the king by a certain master Adam, clerk of lord Robert de Tateshale, in the presence of Hugh de Daleby, Peter Mauleun, and William de Creton that Nicholas should should not sue the plea further in Court Christian, scorning the prohibition Nicholas continued to sue in that court contrary to the prohibition, in contempt of the crown and dignity of the king and damage to the prior to the value of 100 pounds. And he produces suit etc.

And Nicholas appears and denies force and wrong whenever etc. And he denies that any prohibition was ever delivered to him or to his proctor in connection with the said plea. He says that in fact he prosecuted a plea in Court Christian concerning only his tithes before master Roger de Chebenhale and that a certain prohibition was delivered to Roger de Chebenhale his judge. Whence he denies thoroughly that he ever sued any plea other than the plea concerning his tithes after the prohibition was presented to Roger. And concerning this he puts himself upon the country and Richard who sues for the king likewise. Therefore the sheriff is ordered to cause to appear at Shrewsbury three weeks after Michaelmas 12 men etc. by whom etc. and who are not etc. to give their verdict in this matter etc. Because both parties etc.

Later on the quindene of Hilary in the sixth year[3] the jurors appear and say on their oath that no prohibition of the king was ever exhibited to Nicholas nor after the prohibition delivered to master Roger that he should not hold a plea concerning debts and chattels etc.

[1] Perhaps the same person involved in Case no. 1.3.
[2] 1 June 1277.
[3] 27 January 1278.

aliquod placitum nisi de decimis suis tantum. Et ideo consideratum est quod predictus magister Nicholaus inde sine die.

1.5

CP 40/28 m. 54
Common Pleas, Hilary term 1278

Norff'. Johannes Puclyng' attachiatus fuit ad respondendum Roberto de Tholthorp de placito quare secutus est placitum in curia christianitatis de catallis et debitis que non sunt de testamento vel matrimonio contra prohibitionem etc. Et unde queritur quod traxit eum in placitum in curia christianitatis coram Gregorio de Kereven decano de Arcubus Lond' petendo ab ipso quindecim libras que non sunt de testamento vel matrimonio et cum idem Robertus detulisset ei regiam prohibitionem die mercurii proxima ante festum Purificationis Beate Marie anno regno regis nunc sexto in ecclesia beate Marie de Arcubus Lond' ne predictum placitum sequeretur idem Johannes spreta regia prohibitione secutus est idem placitum. Unde dicit quod deterioratus est et dampnum habet ad valenciam viginti librarum. Et inde producit sectam etc.

Et Johannes venit et defendit vim et injuriam quando etc. Et bene defendit quod nunquam secutus est aliquod placitum in curia christianitatis versus eum de catallis et debitis que [non][1] sunt de testamento vel matrimonio contra prohibitionem. Et hoc paratus est verificare per sectam suam sicut ei curia consideraverit. Ideo consideratum est quod vadiat ei legem se xii manu. Et veniat cum lege in octabis sancte Trinitatis. Plegii de lege Johannes de Bromholm et Thomas de Gelham. Postea ad diem illum venit predictus Johannes et fecit inde legem suam. Ideo consideratum est quod predictus Johannes inde sine die et predictus Robertus in misericordia pro falso clamore.[2]

1.6

CP 40/32, m. 18d
Common Pleas, Hilary term 1280

Devon'. Magister Ricardus Pace attachiatus fuit ad respondendum Roberto Beaupel, David de Furshull, Willelmo Baghel, Henrico Barri, et Benedicto de la Pille de placito quare, cum placita de transgressionibus contra pacem domini regis factis in regno suo ad ipsum et ad coronam et dignitatem suam et non ad alium pertineant in eodem regno suo,

[1] MS. omits.
[2] In the margin are written lex and 12 dots.

did Nicholas ever sue any plea excepting only a plea concerning his tithes. And therefore it is adjudged that master Nicholas go without day.

1.5

ROBERT DE THOLTHORP v. JOHN PUCLYNG

Norfolk. John Puclyng was attached to answer Robert de Tholthorp concerning a plea as to why he sued a plea in Court Christian concerning chattels and debts that are not testamentary or matrimonial, contrary to prohibition etc. And in this regard Robert complains that John drew him into a plea in Court Christian before Gregory de Kereven, dean of the Arches, London seeking from him 15 pounds that are not testamentary or martrimonial and, when Robert delivered to him a royal prohibition on the Wednesday before the Purification of Mary in the sixth year of this king's reign[1] in the church of St Mary-le-Bow, London that he should not sue the plea further, scorning the prohibition John continued to sue the same plea. He says he is thereby harmed and damaged to the value of 20 pounds. And he produces suit etc.

And John appears and denies force and wrong whenever etc. And he denies that he ever sued any plea in Court Christian against Robert concerning chattels and debts that are not testamentary or martrimonial contrary to prohibition. And this he is prepared to verify by his suit as the court should adjudge. Therefore it is adjudged that he is to wage his law twelve-handed. And let him come with his law on the octave of Trinity. Pledges for his law John de Bromholm and Thomas de Gelham.

Later on that day[2] John came and made his law. Therefore it is adjudged that John go without day and that Robert is in mercy for the false claim.

1.6

ROBERT BEAUPEL AND OTHERS v. RICHARD PACE

Devonshire. Master Richard Pace was attached to answer Robert Beaupel, David de Furshull, William Baghel, Henry Barri, and Benedict de la Pille concerning a plea as to why, since pleas concerning trespasses against the lord king's peace done in his realm pertain to him and to his crown and dignity and to no other in his realm, Richard held a

[1] 26 January 1278.

[2] 20 June 1278.

idem Ricardus tenuit placitum in curia christianitatis super huiusmodi transgressionibus in lesionem corone et dignitatis sue et contra prohibitionem suam etc. Et unde queruntur quod, cum quidam Reginaldus le Erceveske inplacitasset ipsos in curia christianitatis coram predicto magistro Ricardo de verberibus et aliis trangressionibus sibi factis et ipsi die sabbati proxima post festum Omnium Sanctorum anno regni regis nunc septimo in ecclesia sancti Martini Magni Lond' detulissent ei regiam prohibitionem in presencia magistri Walteri Gurdet et Radulfi de Furshull ne diutius predictum placitum teneret, prefatus Ricardus spreta predicta prohibitione tenuit idem placitum in curia christianitatis ad sectam predicti Reginaldi in lesionem corone domini regis et contra prohibitionem suam, ita quod primo fecit ipsos ab ingressu ecclesie suspendi et postea excommunicari. Unde dicunt quod deteriorati sunt et dampnum habent ad valenciam quadraginta marcarum. Et inde producunt sectam etc.

Et magister Ricardus venit et defendit vim et injuriam quando etc. Et bene defendit quod nunquam post predictam prohibitionem ei liberatam [tenuit][1] predictum placitum in curia christianitatis. Et hoc paratus est verificare sicut curia consideraverit. Ideo consideratum est quod vadiat eis legem se duodecima manu. Et veniat cum lege sua cras. Plegii de lege Walterus le Cryur et Hamo de la Bare. Postea venit predictus Ricardus et fecit legem suam. Ideo predictus Ricardus inde sine die et Robertus et alii in misericordia pro falso clamore.[2]

1.7a

CP 40/38 m. 58
Common Pleas, Hilary term 1281

Norf'. Johannes de Clony Prior de Lewes attachiatus fuit ad respondendum Gode que fuit uxor Simonis de Leton' de placito quare secutus est placitum in curia christianitatis de laico feodo ipsius Gode in Hecham contra prohibitionem etc. Et unde queritur quod cum [i]<idem>[i] prior secutus fuisset placitum in curia christianitatis coram magistro Reginaldo [de][3] Cressenhale decano de Suthmallenges versus eamdem Godam exigendo ab eadem quadraginta solidos redditus in Hecham ac eadem Goda die lune proxima post festum Pentecosten anno regni regis septimo [d]<in ecclesia de Hecham>[d] eidem priori in pleno comitatu Norff' in presencia Willelmi de Redham tunc vicecomitis Norff' [i]<et aliorum>[i] detulisset regiam prohibitionem ne ulterius idem placitum versus eam sequeretur idem prior spreta predicta prohibitione secutus est idem placitum in eadem curia versus eam quousque eam ab ingressu ecclesie fecit suspendi et postea excommunicari. Unde dicit quod deteriorata est et dampnum habet ad valenciam centum solidorum. Et inde producit sectam.

[1] MS. reads secutus fuit
[2] In the margin are written lex and 12 dots.
[3] MS. omits.

plea in Court Christian concerning this sort of trespass, offending the king's crown and dignity and contrary to prohibition etc. And in this regard they complain that, whereas one Reginald le Erceveske sued them in Court Christian before master Richard concerning wounds and other trespasses done to him on the first Saturday after All Saints' in the seventh year of this king's reign[1] in the church of St Martin's le Grand, London and they delivered a royal prohibition to him in the presence of Walter Gurdet and Ralph de Furshull that he should not hold the plea further, scorning the prohibition Richard held the plea in Court Christian at Reginald's suit, in violation of the lord king's crown and contrary to his prohibition, such that he first ordered them suspended from entry to the church and then excommunicated them. They say they are thereby harmed and damaged to the value of 40 marks. And they produce suit etc.

And master Richard appears and denies force and wrong whenever etc. And he denies that he ever held the plea in Court Christian after the prohibition was delivered to him. And this he is prepared to verify as the court should adjudge. Therefore it is adjudged that he is to wage his law twelve-handed. And let him come with his law tomorrow. Pledges for his law Walter le Cryur and Hamo de la Bare.

Later Richard came and made his law. Therefore Richard is without day and Robert and the others are in mercy for the false claim.

1.7a

GODA DE LETON v. PRIOR OF LEWES

Norfolk. John of Cluny, prior of Lewes, was attached to answer Goda, widow of Simon de Leton, concerning a plea as to why he sued a plea in Court Christian concerning her lay fee in Heacham contrary to prohibition etc. And in this regard she complains that, whereas the prior sued a plea in Court Christian against Goda before Reginald of Cressenhale, dean of South Malling, claiming from her 40 shillings of rent in Heacham and on the first Monday after Pentecost in the seventh year of this king's reign[2] in the full county court of Norfolk in the presence of William de Redham, then sheriff of Norfolk, and others Goda presented a royal prohibition to the prior that he should not sue the plea against her further, scorning the prohibition the prior sued the plea in Court Christian against her until she was suspended from entry to the church and later excommunicated. She says sher is thereby injured and damaged to the value of 100 shillings. And she produces suit.

And John appears and denies force and wrong whenever etc. And he completely denies that he ever sued the plea in Court Christian after the prohibition was delivered to him as

[1] 5 November 1279.
[2] 21 May 1279.

Et Johannes venit et defendit vim et injuriam quando etc. Et bene defendit quod numquam post predictam prohibitionem sibi inde exhibitam predictum placitum in prefata curia sequebatur sicut ei imponit. Et de hoc ponit se super patriam. Et Goda similiter. Et preceptum est vicecomiti quod venire faciat hic in crastino sancti Johannis Baptiste xii etc. per quos etc. Et qui nec etc. ad recognoscendum etc. Quia tam etc.

Postea ad diem illum vicecomes nichil inde fecit nec breve misit. Ideo sicut prius preceptum est vicecomiti quod venire faciat hic in crastino sancti Martini xii etc. in forma predicta. Et vicecomes sit auditurus iudicium etc. Postea a die sancti Michaelis in xv dies venerunt juratores qui dicunt super sacramentum suum quod predictus prior implacitavit predictam Godam in curia christianitatis de predictis quadraginta solidis eo quod eadem Goda propter suam manifestam contumaciam suspensa fuit ab ingressu ecclesie ita quod ipsa se sentiens inde gravatam impetravit breve prohibitionis super ipsum priorem qui quidem prior non obstante eadem prohibitione prosecutus fuit sentenciam prius latam in ipsam Godam et fecit ipsam ad sectam suam executioni demandari ad dampnum ipsius Gode sex marcaram. Et ideo consideratum est quod predicta Goda recuperet predicta dampna versus eum. Et prior in misericordia.

1.7b

CP 40/38 m. 58
Common Pleas, Hilary term 1281

Norf'. Idem prior attachiatus fuit ad respondendum Albyno de Leton', Andree, Gilberto, Thome fratribus eiusdem Albini de placito quare, cum placita de transgressionibus contra pacem domini regis factis ad dominum regem et coronam et dignitatem domini regis pertineat [*sic*] in regno suo, idem prior secutus est idem placitum in curia christianitatis contra predictam prohibitionem etc. Et unde queruntur quod, cum idem prior secutus fuisset placitum in prefata curia christianitatis coram prefato decano inponendo eis quod homines ipsius prioris verberaverunt et maletractaverunt et plurima enormia eis intulerunt ac idem Aubin et alii predictis die et anno in pleno comitatu Norff' coram predicto vicecomite et aliis detulissent eidem priori predictam prohibitionem ne ulterius idem placitum sequeretur, idem prior spreta regia prohibitione secutus est idem placitum in eadem curia quousque eos ab ingressu ecclesie fecit suspendi et postea excommunicari. Unde dicunt quod deteriorati sunt et dampnum habent ad valenciam centum marcarum. Et inde producunt sectam etc.

Et prior venit et defendit vim et injuriam quando etc. Et bene defendit quod numquam secutus fuit predictum placitum contra predictam prohibitionem sicut ei imponunt. Et de hoc ponit se super patriam. Et Aubin et alii similiter. Ideo preceptum est vicecomiti quod venire faciat hic in crastino sancti Johannis Baptiste xij etc. per quos etc. Et qui nec etc. ad recognoscendum etc. Quia tam etc. Postea ad diem illum vicecomes nichil inde fecit nec breve misit. Ideo sicut prius preceptum est vicecomiti quod venire faciat hic in crastino sancti Martini xii etc. in forma predicta. Et vicecomes sit auditurus judicium etc.

is alleged against him. And concerning this he puts himself upon the country. And Goda likewise. And the sheriff is ordered to cause to appear here on the morrow of St John the Baptist 12 etc. by whom etc. and who are not etc. to give their verdict etc. Because etc.

Later, on that day[1] the sheriff has done nothing and has not sent a writ. Therefore as before the sheriff is ordered to cause to appear here on the morrow of St Martin 12 etc. in the aforesaid form. And let the sheriff be here to hear the judgment etc.

Later, on the quindene of St Martin[2] the jurors appear and say on their oath that the prior sued Goda in Court Christian concerning the 40 shillings so that Goda was suspended from the church for her manifest contumacy such that, feeling herself aggrieved, she sued a writ of prohibition against the prior who, notwithstanding the prohibition, prosecuted the sentence previously imposed on Goda and caused execution to be made against her at his suit, to Goda's damage six marks. Therefore it is adjudged that Goda recover her damages against him. And the prior is in mercy.

1.7b

AUBIN DE LETON AND OTHERS v. PRIOR OF LEWES

Norfolk. The same prior[3] was attached to answer Aubin de Leton, and Andrew, Gilbert, and Thomas brothers of Aubin concerning a plea as to why, since pleas concerning trespasses against the lord king's peace done in his realm pertain to him and to his crown and dignity and to no other in his realm, the prior sued the same plea in Court Christian contrary to the aforesaid prohibition etc.[4] And in this regard they complain that, whereas the prior had sued a plea in the said Court Christian before the aforesaid dean alleging against them that they beat and mistreated the prior's men and perpetrated many other enormities against them and Aubin and the others on the said day and year in the full county court of Norfolk before the said sheriff and others delivered to the prior the aforesaid prohibition that he should not sue the same plea further, scorning the royal prohibition the prior sued the plea in the same court until he caused them to be suspended from entry to the church and thereafter excommunicated. They say they are thereby harmed and damaged to the value of 100 marks. And they produce suit etc.

And the prior appears and denies force and wrong whenever etc. And he denies that he ever sued the plea contrary to the prohibition as is alleged against him. And concerning

[1] 25 June 1281.

[2] 25 November 1281.

[3] This record follows on the plea roll immediately after Case no. 1.7a and refers to parties and events in that case.

[4] The reference appears to be to the suit in Court Christian and prohibition described in Case no. 1.7a but that case involved a claim in Court Christian for 40 shillings of rent.

Postea a die sancti Michaelis in xv dies venerunt juratores, qui dicunt super sacramentum suum quod predictus prior post predictam prohibitionem ei exhibitam secutus fuit predictum placitum in curia christianitatis ad dampnum ipsorum Albini et aliorum quatuor marcarum. Et ideo consideratum est quod predictus Aubin et alii recuperent predictas quatuor marcas versus predictum priorem. Et prior in misericordia.

1.8

CP 40/39 m. 40d
Common Pleas, Easter term 1281

Kanc'. [i]<Henricus>[i] Prior de Folstan et Willelmus de Etlyng attachiati fuerunt ad respondendum Edythe que fuit uxor Philippi le Simple de placito quare predictus prior tenuit placitum in curia christianitatis de catallis et debitis que non sunt de testamento vel matrimonio contra prohibitionem etc. et de placito quare predictus Willelmus secutus fuit idem placitum in eadem curia christianitatis contra eandem prohibitionem etc. Et unde queritur quod, cum ipsa aliquo tempore appellasset predictum Willelmum in pleno comitatu Kanc' coram vicecomite et custodibus placitorum corone domini regis de morte predicti Philippi le Simple quondam viri sui et etiam de roberia et pace regis fracta ac idem Willelmus postea eandem Editham coram prefato priore de diffamatione implacitasset per [i]<quod>[i] eadem Editha catalla sua amisit ac eadem Edytha postea in ecclesia de Folstan die sancti Petri ad Vincula anno regno regis nunc quinto eisdem priori [i]<et Willelmo>[i] regiam prohibitionem detulisset ne [i]<predictus prior>[i] predictum placitum teneret nec predictus Willelmus illud sequeretur, predictus prior spreta predicta prohibitione predictum placitum tenuit et predictus Willelmus illud fuit prosecutus. Unde dicit quod [deteriorata][1] est et dampnum habet ad valenciam centum solidorum. Et inde producit sectam etc.

Et prior de Folstan qui nunc est et predictus Willelmus veniunt et defendunt vim et injuriam quando etc. Et predictus prior dicit quod non debet ei inde ad hoc breve respondere, quia dicit quod ipsa tulit breve istud versus quendam Henricum [i]<quondam>[i] priorem predecessorem suum, qui obiit. Unde petit judicium. Et predicta Editha non potest hoc dedicere. Ideo predictus prior inde sine die. Et Editha in misericordia quo ad hoc, set pardonatur per justiciarios quia pauper.

Et predictus Willelmus dicit quod ipse nunquam aliquod placitum de diffamatione nec catallis vel debitis ipsius Edithe coram prefato priore secutus fuit sicut ei inponit. Et de

[1] MS. reads deterioratus

this he puts himself on the country. And Aubin and the others likewise. Therefore the sheriff is ordered to cause to appear here on the morrow of St John the Baptist 12 men etc. by whom etc. and who are not etc. to give their verdict etc. Because etc.

Later, on that day[1] the sheriff has done nothing and has not sent a writ. Therefore as before the sheriff is ordered to cause to appear here on the morrow of St Martin 12 men etc. in the aforesaid matter. And let the sheriff be here to hear the judgment etc.

Later, on the quindene of Michaelmas[2] the jurors appear and they say on their oath that the prior sued the plea in Court Christian after the prohibition was exhibited to him, to the damage of Aubin and the others four marks. Therefore it is adjudged that Aubin and the others recover four marks against the prior. And the prior is in mercy.

1.8

EDITH LE SIMPLE v. PRIOR OF FOLKESTONE AND WILLIAM OF DETLING

Kent. Henry, prior of Folkestone, and William of Detling were attached to answer Edith, widow of Phillip le Simple, concerning a plea as to why the prior held a plea in Court Christian concerning chattels and debts that are not testamentary or matrimonial, contrary to prohibition etc. and also concerning a plea as to why William sued the same plea in Court Christian contrary to the same prohibition etc. And in this regard she complains that, whereas at another time she appealed William in open session of the county court of Kent before the sheriff and the coroners concerning the death of Phillip le Simple, formerly her husband, and also concerning robbery and breach of the king's peace, and William thereafter sued Edith for defamation before the prior so that Edith later in the church of Folkestone on the feast of St Peter's Chains in the fifth year of this king's reign[3] delivered a royal prohibition to the prior and to William that the prior should not hold the plea and that William should not sue it, scorning the prohibition the prior held the plea and William prosecuted it. She says she is thereby harmed and damaged to the value of 100 shillings. And she produces suit etc.

And the present prior of Folkestone and William appear and deny force and wrong whenever etc. And the prior says that he ought not answer this writ because she brings the writ against one Henry, this prior's predecessor, who has died. And in this regard he prays judgment. And Edith is unable to deny this. Therefore the prior is without day. And Edith is in mercy as to this, but is pardoned by the justices because she is poor.

And William says that he never sued any plea concering defamation or chattels and debts of Edith before the prior as she alleges. And concerning this he puts himself on the country; and Edith likewise. Therefore the sheriff is ordered to cause to appear here three

[1] 25 June 1281.
[2] 13 October 1281.
[3] 1 August 1277.

hoc ponit se super patriam et Editha similiter. Ideo preceptum est vicecomiti quod venire faciat hic a die sancti Michaelis in tres septimas xij etc. per quos etc. et qui nec etc. ad recognoscendum in forma predicta. Quia tam etc.

Postea a die sancte Trinitatis in tres septimas venerunt juratores, qui dicunt super sacramentum suum quod predictus Willelmus secutus fuit predictum placitum in curia christianitatis coram predicto priore de diffamatione ita quod fecit ipsam ad sectam suam excommunicari ad dampnum ipsius Edithe quadraginta solidorum. Et ideo consideratum est quod ipsa recuperet dampna sua quadraginta solidorum versus eum. Et ipse in misericordia.

1.9

JUST 1/181 m. 46
Devonshire Eyre, 1281–82

Henricus Gavel queritur de magistro Johanne de Esse quod, cum idem Henricus alias in curia domini regis coram justiciariis de banco inplacitasset predictum magistrum Johannem de placito quare tenuit placitum in curia [christianitatis][1] de catallis et debitis que non sunt de testamento vel matrimonio contra prohibitionem domini regis ac idem magister Johannes in eadem curia fecisset legem suam quod numquam tenuit placitum in curia [christianitatis][1] contra prohibitionem predictam et prohibitum fuisset [i]<eidem magistro Johanni ne huiusmodi placitum ulterius teneret, idem magister Johannes post predictam prohibitionem in prefata curia ei>[i] factam tenuit placitum predictum et fecit predictum Henricum excommunicari et ab ingressu ecclesie suspendi quousque idem Henricus ei soluisset centum solidos pro expensis suis. Unde dicit quod deterioratus est et dampnum habet ad valenciam viginti librarum. Et inde producit sectam.

Et predictus magister venit et defendit vim et injuriam quando. Et bene defendit quod numquam tenuit huiusmodi placitum post prohibitionem etc. nec ipsum excommunicari fecit nec ab ingressu ecclesie suspendi. Et de hoc ponit se super patriam. Et Henricus similiter. Ideo fiat inde jurata.

Juratores de consensu partium [i]<ad hoc>[i] electi dicunt super sacramentum suum quod predictus magister Johannes numquam post predictam prohibitionem domini regis ei factam in curia domini regis tenuit huiusmodi placitum nec eundem Henricum fecit excommunicari nec ab ingressu ecclesie suspendi. Ideo consideratum est quod predictus magister Johannes inde sine die. Et Henricus in misericordia pro falso clamore.

[1] MS. reads cristianitatis

weeks after Michaelmas 12 men etc. by whom etc. and who are not etc. to give their verdict in the aforesaid matter. Because both parties etc.

Later three weeks after Trinity[1] the jurors come and they say on their oath that William sued the plea in Court Christian concerning defamation before the prior such that he caused Edith to be excommunicated at his suit, to her damage 40 shillings. Therefore it is adjudged that she recover her 40 shillings against him. And he is in mercy.

1.9

HENRY GAVEL v. JOHN DE ESSE

Henry Gavel complains of master John de Esse that, whereas Henry at another time sued master John in the king's court before the justices of the Bench on a plea as to why he held a plea in Court Christian concerning chattels and debts that are not testamentary or matrimonial, contrary to the prohibition of the lord king, and master John in that court made his law to the effect that he never held a plea in Court Christian contrary to the prohibition, and master John was prohibited that he should not hold a plea of this sort further,[2] master John held the plea after the prohibition in that court was issued against him[3] and caused Henry to be excommunicated and suspended from entry to the church until Henry paid him 100 shillings for his expenses. He says he is thereby harmed and damaged to the value of 20 pounds. And he produces suit.

And the master appears and denies force and wrong whenever. And he denies that he ever held a plea of this sort after prohibition etc. or caused Henry to be excommunicated or suspended from entry to the church. And concerning this he puts himself on the country. And Henry likewise. Therefore let a jury be made therein.

The jurors chosen by consent of the parties concerning this matter say on their oath that master John never held this sort of plea nor caused Henry to be excommunicated or suspended from entry to the church after the prohibition of the lord king issued to him in the king's court. Therefore it is adjudged that master John be without day. And Henry is in mercy for the false claim.

[1] 15 June 1282.
[2] This record has not been found.
[3] That is, the prohibition issued by Common Pleas after John's successful wager of law.

1.10

CP 40/47 m. 42d
Common Pleas, Michaelmas 1282

Norhumbr'. Hawisia que fuit uxor Johannis Noger, Thomas le Palmer, et Nigellus filius Gervasii de Pampeden attachiati fuerunt ad respondendum Ade Baret de placito quare secuti sunt placitum in curia christianitatis de laico feodo ipsius Ade in Walker contra prohibitionem etc. Et unde queritur quod, cum predicta Hawisia et alii inplacitassent ipsum [i]<in curia christianitatis>[i] coram magistro Johanne Hok officiali episcopi Dunelm' de laico feodo suo, scilicet de duobus mesuagiis et quatuor bovatis terre cum pertinenciis in Walker, et idem Adam porexisset eis prohibitionem domini regis in ecclesia sancti Cuthberti Dunelm' anno regni regis nunc octavo ne placitum illud ulterius in curia christianitatis exequerentur, iidem Hawisia et alii spreta regia prohibitione secuti sunt idem placitum in eadem curia christianitatis coram prefato officiali. Unde dicit quod deterioratus est et dampnum habet ad valenciam quadraginta solidorum. Et inde producit sectam etc.

Et Hawisia et alii veniunt et defendunt vim et injuriam quando etc. Et bene defendunt quod nuncquam secuti sunt placitum in curia christianitatis coram prefato officiali de laico feodo predicti Ade. Et hoc parati sunt defendere contra ipsum et sectam suam sicut curia consideraverit. Et ideo consideratum est quod vadiant ei inde legem suam se xij^{ma} manu. Et fecerunt inde legem suam. Et ideo consideratum est quod predicti Hawisia et alii inde sine die et Adam in misericordia pro falso clamore etc.[1]

1.11

CP 40/53, m. 28
Common Pleas, Easter term 1284

Norff'. Magister Johannes de Walecote et Willelmus vicarius ecclesie de [Hunstanston'][2] in misericordia pro pluribus [defaltis][3].

Idem magister Johannes et Willelmus attachiati fuerunt ad respondendum Ade de Mostroyl, Hamoni et Joceo filiis eius et Albino de Secheford de placito quare predictus magister Johannes tenuit placitum in curia christianitatis de catallis et debitis que non sunt de testamento vel matrimonio contra prohibitionem etc. Et de placito quare idem Willelmus secutus est idem placitum in eadem curia contra prohibitionem etc. Et unde queruntur quod cum predictus Willelmus implacitasset ipsos in curia christianitatis coram predicto magistro Johanne de laicis catallis ipsorum Ade, <Mathei>[4], et aliorum videlicet de viginti quarteriis frumenti que non sunt de testamento vel matrimonio ac iidem Adam, Matheus, et alii detulissent predicto Willelmo regiam prohibitionem die jovis proxima ante festum sancti Nicholai anno regis nunc decimo in ecclesia Omnium Sanctorum de Len in

[1] In the margin are written lex and 12 dots.

[2] MS. reads Dunstanston' [3] MS. omits. [4] Not one of the named plaintiffs.

1.10

ADAM BARET v. HAWISE NOGER AND OTHERS

Northumberland. Hawise, formerly wife of John Noger, Thomas le Palmer, and Nigel, son of Gervase de Pampeden, were attached to answer Adam Baret concerning a plea as to why they sued a plea in Court Christian concerning Adam's lay fee in Walker contrary to prohibition etc. And in this regard Adam complains that, whereas Hawise and the others impleaded him in Court Christian before master John Hok, official of the bishop of Durham, concerning lay fee, namely two messuages and four bovates of land with appurtenances in Walker, and Adam delivered to them a prohibition of the lord king in the church of St Cuthbert, Durham,[1] in the eighth year of this king's reign[2] that they should not prosecute that plea in Court Christian further, scorning the royal prohibition Hawise and the others sued the plea in Court Christian before the official. He says he is thereby harmed and damaged to the value of 40 shillings. And he produces suit etc.

And Hawise and the others appear and deny force and wrong whenever etc. And they deny that they ever sued a plea in Court Christian before the official concerning Adam's lay fee. And this they are prepared to deny against him and his suit as the court should adjudge. And therefore it is adjudged that they are to wage their law twelve-handed. And thereafter they make their law. And therefore it is adjudged that Hawise and the others are without day and Adam is in mercy for the false claim etc.

1.11

ADAM DE MOSTROYL AND OTHERS v. JOHN DE WALECOTE AND THE VICAR OF HUNSTANTON

Norfolk. Master John de Walecote and William, vicar of the church of Hunstanton, in mercy for numerous defaults.

Master John and William were attached to answer Adam de Mostroyl, Hamo and Joce his sons, and Aubin de Setchford concerning a plea as to why master John held a plea in Court Christian concerning chattels and debts that are not testamentary or matrimonial, contrary to prohibition etc. And concerning a plea as to why William sued the same plea in that court contrary to prohibition etc. And in this regard they complain that, whereas William impleaded them in Court Christian before master John concerning the lay chattels of Adam, Matthew, and the others, namely concerning twenty quarters of wheat that are not testamentary or matrimonial, and Adam, Matthew, and the others delivered a royal prohibition to William on the Thursday before the feast of St Nicholas in the tenth year of this king's reign[3] in All Saints' church, Lynn, in the presence of Richard son of John and

[1] Durham Cathedral. [2] 1279–80. [3] 4 December 1281.

presencia Ricardi filii Johannis et Thome filii Rogeri ne ulterius sequeretur idem placitum in curia christianitatis et eciam eodem die in presencia eorumdem in eadem ecclesia detulissent predicto magistro Johanni aliam prohibitionem regis ne idem placitum teneret, predicti tam Willelmus quam Johannes spretis predictis prohibitionibus videlicet predictus Willelmus secutus fuit illud placitum in curia christianitatis et predictus Johannes illud tenuit in contemptum domini regis etc. Unde dicunt quod deteriorati sunt et dampnum habent ad valenciam quadraginta librarum. Et inde producunt sectam.

Et Willelmus et Johannes veniunt et defendunt vim et injuriam quando etc. Et tam predictus Willelmus quam predictus Johannes bene defendunt quod post predictas prohibitiones eis exhibitas ne predictus Willelmus secutus fuit aliquod placitum in curia christianitatis de laicis catallis ipsorum Ade et aliorum nec predictus Johannes illud tenuit, immo de decimis ecclesie ipsius Willelmi tantum. Et quod ita sit petunt quod inquiratur per patriam. Et Adam et alii similiter. Ideo preceptum est vicecomiti quod venire faciat hic a die sancti Michaelis in tres septimanas nisi T. de Weland prius etc. xii etc. per quos etc. Et qui nec etc. ad recognoscendum in forma predicta. Quia tam etc.

Postea coram J. de Luvetot apud Norwycum venerunt juratores qui dicunt super sacramentum suum quod antecessores Ade Mustroyll semper a tempore quo non exstat memoria consueverunt dare decimas suas omnimodarum terrarum suarum cuicumque voluissent dum tamen esset clericus et idem Adam decimas suas dedit predicto Joceo filio suo sicut antecessores sui eas dare consueverunt ita quod predictus Willelmus vicarius in adventu archiepiscopi in partibus Norff' ostendit archiepiscopo quod quedam decime infra limites parochie sue et que ad vicariam suam pertinebant fuerant alienate per predictum Adam super quibus predictus archiepiscopus concessit ei predictum magistrum Johannem commissarium suum ad audiendum placitum de decimis illis, coram quo predicti Adam de Mustroyll et alii fuerant citati ad respondendum predicto vicario de decimis predictis, cui idem Adam et alii porrexerunt regiam prohibitionem ne placitum illud tenerent qui non obstante regia prohibitione ei postea tenuit predictum placitum. Quesiti si predicte decime umquam fuerunt annexe ecclesie predicte, dicunt quod non. Quesiti si fuerunt infra limites parochie predicte, dicunt quod sic. Quesiti si predictus Adam fuerat patronus eiusdem ecclesie dicunt quod non set dicunt quod ex consensu utriusque partis episcopus loci colligere fecit predictas decimas et eas reponi fecit in loco certo quousque discussum fuisset ad quem illas decimas deberent pertinere et dicunt quod predictus Adam predictas decimas asportavit etc.

1.12

CP 40/58, m. 5d
Common Pleas, Easter 1285

Linc'. Letia de Dene de Staunford attachiata fuit ad respondendum Henrico de Reding de placito quare secuta est placitum in curia christianitatis de catallis et debitis que non sunt de testamento vel matrimonio contra prohibitionem etc. Et unde queritur quod, cum ipsa

Thomas son of Roger that he should not sue the plea further in Court Christian, and also on that day in their presence in the same church delivered to master John another prohibition of the king that he should not hold the same plea, scorning these prohibitions William sued the plea in Court Christian and John held it in contempt of the lord king etc. They say they are thereby harmed and damaged to the value of 40 pounds. And they produce suit.

And William and John appear and deny force and wrong whenever etc. And both William and John deny that William sued any plea in Court Christian concerning Adam's and the others' lay chattels or that John held it after the prohibitions presented to them; to the contrary, the suit concerned only the tithes of William's church. And that it is so they pray may be inquired of the country. And Adam and the others likewise. Therefore the sheriff is ordered to cause to appear here three weeks after Michaelmas unless Thomas de Weland earlier etc. 12 men etc. by whom etc. and who are not etc. to give their verdict in the aforesaid matter. Because both parties etc.

Later, before John de Lovetot at Norwich the jurors appear and say on their oath that the ancestors of Adam Mustroyll have always since time immemorial been accustomed to give tithes from all their lands to whomever they wished as long as he was a member of the clergy and Adam gave his tithes to Joce, his son, just as his ancestors were accustomed to give them, on account of which William, the vicar, upon the archbishop's arrival in Norfolk showed the archbishop that certain tithes within the boundaries of his parish and belonging to his vicarage were alienated by Adam, concerning which the archbishop granted to him that master John should serve as his commissary to hear this plea concerning these tithes, before whom Adam de Mustroyll and the others were cited to answer the vicar concerning these tithes, and to whom Adam and the others presented a royal prohibition that they should not hold that plea, but notwithstanding the royal prohibition he afterwards held the plea. Asked if the tithes were ever annexed to this church, the jurors say no. Asked if the tithes were within the boundaries of the parish, they say yes. Asked if Adam was patron of the church, they say no, but they say that by consent of each party the local bishop caused the tithes to be collected and stored in a certain place until it had been determined to whom those tithes ought to belong and they say that Adam carried off those tithes etc.

1.12

HENRY DE REDING v. LETIA DE DENE

Lincolnshire. Letia de Dene of Stamford was attached to answer Henry de Reding concerning a plea as to why she sued a plea in Court Christian concerning chattels and debts that are not testamentary or matrimonial, contrary to prohibition etc. And in this regard he

implacitasset ipsum Henricum coram decano de Staunford petendo ab ipso decem solidos qui non sunt de testamento vel matrimonio ac idem Henricus detulisset ei regiam prohibitionem ne predictum placitum ulterius sequeretur, predicta Letia spreta prohibitione predicta secuta fuit idem placitum in curia christianitatis contra prohibitionem. Unde dicit quod deterioratus est et dampnum habet ad valenciam centum solidorum. Et inde producit sectam.

Et Letia venit et defendit vim et injuriam quando etc. Et dicit quod quidam Hugo de Tyncote cuius executor testamenti predictus Henricus est legavit cuidam filio ipsius Letie decem solidos annui redditus in villa de Staunford ad sustentationem ipsius filii prout bene potuit secundum consuetudinem ville de Staunford, ita quod ipsa nomine filii sui secuta fuit coram predicto decano executionem predicti testamenti fieri de predicto redditu et quod nullum placitum de laicis catallis ipsius Henrici secuta fuit petit quod inquiratur per patriam.

Et Henricus dicit quod predicta villa de Staunford est gildabilis secundum communem legem Anglie, ita quod nullus de predicta villa potest legare terras, tenementa, aut redditus in eadem villa existencia. Et hoc petit quod inquiratur per patriam. Ideo preceptum est vicecomiti quod venire faciat hic in octabis sancti Michaelis xii etc. per quos etc. Et qui nec etc. ad recognoscendum in forma predicta. Quia tam etc.

1.13

KB 27/90, m. 5
King's Bench, Easter term 1285

Glouc'. Magister Simon de Wymundeham attachiatus fuit ad respondendum [i]<domino regi et>[i] abbati de Wynchecumbe de placito quare blada et separalem [i]<pasturam> ipsius abbatis in Dryemerston' cum averiis suis vi et armis depastus fuit et alia enormia etc. ad grave dampnum etc. et contra pacem etc. Et unde predictus abbas per attornatum suum queritur quod, cum predictus Simon blada et separalem pasturam ipsius abbatis cum averiis suis depastus fuisset et idem abbas averia illa occasione illius transgressionis cepisset et secundum legem et consuetudinem Anglie inparcasset, idem Simon predictum abbatem occasione illius captionis rite et secundum legem facte traxit in placitum in curia christianitatis. Postmodum [i]<cum>[i] dominus rex eidem magistro Simoni per breve suum prohibuisset [i]<ne>[i] huiusmodi placitum sequeretur idem Simon inponens eidem abbati quod ad procurationem suam dominus rex predictum breve [i]<suum>[i] de prohibitione eidem Simoni porexit ob quod idem Simon predictum abbatem iterato in curia christianitatis inplacitavit [i]<asserens ipsum abbatem irregularem et excommunicatum inponens ei quod convolaverat ad vetitum examen>[i] in lesionem regie dignitatis et dampnum ipsius abbatis centum librarum. Et inde producit sectam etc.

Et magister Simon venit et defendit quod nunquam separalem pasturam ipsius abbatis cum averiis suis depastus fuit nec ipsum abbatem in curia christianitatis coram aliquibus judicibus inplacitavit occasione alicuius placiti moti in curia domini regis vel prohibitionis

complains that, whereas she impleaded Henry before the dean of Stamford seeking from him 10 shillings that are not testamentary or matrimonial, and Henry delivered to her a royal prohibition that she should not sue the plea further, scorning the prohibition Letia sued the plea in Court Christian contrary to prohibition. He says he is thereby harmed and damaged to the value of 100 shillings. And he produces suit.

And Letia appears and denies force and wrong whenever etc. And she says that a certain Hugh de Tyncote, the executor of whose testament Henry is, bequeathed to a son of Letia 10 shillings of annual rent in the town of Stamford for the maintenance of her son, as he well could do according to the custom of the town of Stamford, so that in the name of her son she sued for execution of the testament concerning this rent before the dean. And that she sued no plea concerning Henry's lay chattels she prays may be inquired of the country.

And Henry says that the town of Stamford is geldable according to the common law of England, such that no one of the vill may make a will of lands, tenements, or rents existing in that town. And he asks that this be inquired of the country. Therefore the sheriff is ordered to produce here in the octave of Michaelmas 12 etc. by whom etc. and who are not etc. to give their verdict in the aforesaid matter. Because both parties etc.

1.13

THE KING AND THE ABBOT OF WINCHCOMBE v. SIMON OF WYMONDHAM

Gloucestershire. Master Simon of Wymondham[1] was attached to answer the lord king and the abbot of Winchcombe concerning a plea as to why he depastured the abbot's corn and separate pasture in Marston Sicca with his animals and with force and arms and other outrages etc. to the grave damage etc. and contrary to the king's peace etc. And in this regard the abbot by his attorney complains that, whereas Simon depastured the abbot's corn and separate pasture with his animals, and the abbot on account of that trespass seized those animals and impounded them according to the law and custom of England, Simon on account of that seizure done rightly and according to law commenced a plea against the abbot in Court Christian. Soon thereafter, when the lord king by his writ prohibited master Simon that he should not sue this kind of plea, Simon, claiming that the lord king issued his writ of prohibition at the abbot's instigation, on that account again impleaded the abbot in Court Christian, asserting the abbot to be irregular and claiming he was excommunicate because he resorted to a forbidden process, in violation of the king's dignity and to the damage of the abbot 100 pounds. And he produces suit etc.

And master Simon appears and denies that he ever depastured the abbot's separate pasture with his animals or that he impleaded the abbot in Court Christian before any judges

[1] A person of this name also appears in Case no. 1.19.

ei [porrecte][1] [i]<nec aliquam irregularitatem seu excommunicationem ei imposuit>[i]. Et de hoc ponit se super patriam. Et predictus abbas similiter. Ideo preceptum est vicecomiti quod venire faciat coram rege a die sante Trinitatis in xv dies ubicumque etc. xij etc. per quos etc. et qui nec etc. ad recognoscendum in forma predicta. Quia tam etc.

Postea ad diem illum quia constat domino regi quod predictus Simon in nullo [delinquens est][2] versus dominum regem. Ideo dictum est predicto Simoni quod eat inde sine die etc.

1.14

JUST 1/572, m. 12
Norfolk Eyre, 1286

Alicia Grisoun attachiata fuit ad respondendum Rogero le Fraunceys de Thetford de placito quare secuta est placitum in curia christianitatis de catallis et debitis que non sunt de testamento vel matrimonio contra prohibitionem etc. Et unde queritur quod cum predicta Alicia implacitasset eum coram decano de Arcubus London' de quingentis ovibus sexaginta libris sterlingorum sex vaccis et ipse die mercurii proxima ante festum conversionis sancti Pauli hoc anno apud Thetford detulisset ei regiam prohibitionem ne sequeretur placitum in curia christianitis de predictis catallis et debitis que non sunt de testamento vel matrimonio predicta Alicia spreta prohibitione predicta secuta est placitum in curia christianitatis de catallis et debitis predictis quousque idem Rogerus excommunicatus fuit. Unde dicit quod deterioratus est et dampnum habet ad valenciam centum marcarum et inde producit sectam.

Et Alicia venit et defendit vim et injuriam quando etc. Et bene cognoscit quod ipsa secuta fuit placitum in curia christianitatis versus predictum Rogerum de predictis catallis et debitis set dicit quod quidam Hugo quondam vir suus die quo ipsam desponsavit concessit ei predicta catalla nomine maritagii et postea in ultima voluntate sua legavit ei predicta catalla. Unde dicit quod ipsa implacitavit predictum Rogerum de predictis catallis in curia christianitatis tanquam de illis que sunt de testamento. Et quod ipsum aliter [non][3] implacitavit paratus est defendere contra ipsum et sectam suam qualitercumque curia considaverit etc. Et ideo consideratum est quod vadiat legem se xij^{ma} manu. Et veniat cum lege die lune proxima post tres septimanas Pasche etc. Plegii de lege Johannes Grison et Robertus de Brigham. Postea predictus Rogerus non fuit prosecutus ideo predicta Alicia inde sine die. Et predictus Rogerus et plegii sui de prosequendo in misericordia. Querantur nomina plegiorum inter brevia finita.

[1] MS. reads porecte
[2] MS. reads deliquid
[3] MS. omits.

on account of any plea brought in the lord king's court or prohibition directed to him or that he imputed to him any irregularity or excommunication. And concerning this he puts himself on the country. And the abbot likewise. Therefore the sheriff is ordered to produce here before the king on the quindene of Trinity wherever etc. 12 etc. by whom etc. and who are not etc. to give their verdict in the aforesaid matter. Because both parties etc.

Later, on that day, because it is clear to the lord king that Simon is in no way delinquent against the king, it is said to Simon that he go forth without day etc.

1.14

ROGER LE FRAUNCEYS v. ALICE GRISOUN

Alice Grisoun was attached to answer Roger le Fraunceys of Thetford concerning a plea as to why she sued a plea in Court Christian concerning chattels and debts that are not testamentary or matrimonial, contrary to prohibition etc. And in this regard he complains that, whereas Alice sued him in Court Christian before the dean of the court of Arches, London claiming 500 sheep, 60 pounds sterling, and six cows and on the Wednesday before the feast of the Conversion of St Paul this year[1] at Thetford he delivered to her a royal prohibition that she should not sue the plea in Court Christian concerning those chattels and debts that are not testamentary or matrimonial, scorning the prohibition Alice sued the plea in Court Christian concerning these chattels and debts until Roger was excommunicated. He says her is thereby injured and damaged to the value of 100 marks and he produces suit.

And Alice appears and denies force and wrong whenever etc. And she fully admits that she sued a plea in Court Christian against Roger concerning these chattels and debts but she says that a certain Hugh, her deceased husband, on the day he married her granted these chattels to her as her marriage portion and later left them to her in his last will. Whence she says she sued Roger concerning these chattels in Court Christian because they were testamentary. And that she did not otherwise sue him she is prepared to deny against him and his suit as the court should adjudge etc. Therefore it is adjudged that she is to wage her law twelve-handed. And let her appear with her law on the first Monday three weeks after Easter etc. Pledges for her law John Gryson and Robert de Brigham.

Later Roger did not prosecute. Therefore Alice is without day etc. And Roger and his pledges for prosecution are in mercy. Inquire as to the name of the pledges among the finished writs.[2]

[1] 23 January 1286.

[2] Roger le Fraunceys also sued Alice Grisoun of Thetford and John Grisoun for trespass, alleging that they broke into his house and stole his goods valued at 20 pounds. They denied this and asked for a jury. Later Roger defaulted. The record of this case also appears at JUST 1/572, m. 12 (Norfolk, 1286).

1.15

KB 27/103, m. 24d
King's Bench, Hilary term 1287

Cant'. Dominus rex mandavit dilecto et fideli suo Willelmo de Saham quod quia quibusdam certis decausis voluit certiorari super recordo et processu loquele que fuit coram prefato Willelmo et sociis suis justiciariis regis ultimo itinerantibus in comitatu predicto sine brevi regis inter Amiciam de Haukeston' et magistrum Nicholaum de Hegham decanum sancte Marie Linc' de eo quod idem decanus assecutus est placitum in curia christianitatis de catallis et debitis que non sunt de testamento vel matrimonio contra prohibitionem regis etc. mandatum fuit eidem Willelmo quod si judicium inde redditum non sit, tunc recordum illud et processum cum omnibus ea tangentibus regi mitteret. Qui quidem Willelmus misit recordum in hec verba:

Magister Nicholaus de Hegham persona ecclesie de Trumpeton' attachiatus fuit ad respondendum Amicie de Haukeston' de placito quare secutus est placitum in curia christianitatis de catallis et debitis que non sunt de testamento vel matrimonio contra prohibitionem domini regis etc. Et unde eadem Amicia queritur quod cum predictus magister Nicholaus traxisset [eam][1] in placitum in curia christianitatis coram officiale archidiaconi Elyens' et exigisset ab ea catalla scilicet fenum ad valenciam viginti solidorum quod non est de testamento vel matrimonio ac eadem Amicia die martis proxima post festum sancti Petri et Pauli anno regni domini regis nunc duodecimo in presencia quorumdam Alani Collyng' et Herberti de Haukeston' in ecclesia Omnium Sanctorum Cant' prohibitionem domini regis eidem magistro Nicholao detulisset ne ulterius predictum placitum in predicta curia sequeretur, idem Nicholaus spreta inhibitione predicta secutus est nichilominus idem placitum et ipsam iterato fecit citare scilicet die jovis proxima ante festum sancte Trinitatis proximo preteritum infra summonitionem itineris istius et contra prohibitionem regis. Unde dicit quod deteriorata est et dampnum habet ad valenciam quadraginta solidorum. Et inde producit sectam etc.

Et magister Nicholaus venit et defendit vim et iniuriam quando etc. Et bene defendit quod in nullo venit contra prohibitionem domini regis. Dicit enim quod [i]<ipse>[i] nunquam traxit predictam Amiciam in placitum in predicta curia christianitatis et dicit quod predicta Amicia retinuit quandam partem decimarum feni sui pertinentium ad predictam ecclesiam suam de Trumpeton' et de quibus decimis predicta ecclesia sua fuit seysita. Unde dicit quod placitum illud non fuit de laicis catallis vel debitis immo de decimis fuit. Et de hoc ponit se super patriam. Et Amicia similiter. Ideo fiat jurata etc.

Et venit die jovis proxima post quindenam sancti Johannis Baptiste ad quem diem ipsa Amicia optulit iiij die versus predictum magistrum Nicholaum de placito quod esset hic auditurus predictam juratam. Et ipse non venit. Ideo preceptum [fuit][2] vicecomiti quod scire faciat ei quod sit hic die veneris proxima sequenti auditurus juratam illam si sibi viderint expedire. Ideo procedatur ad juratam illam per defaltam ipsius magistri etc. Juratores dicunt super sacramentum suum quod predictus magister Nicholaus secutus fuit

[1] MS. reads eum
[2] MS. reads est

1.15

AMICE DE HAUKESTON v. DEAN OF ST MARY'S, LINCOLN

Cambridgeshire. The lord king commanded his beloved and faithful William de Saham[1] that, because for certain reasons he wished to be informed regarding the record and process of a dispute that was before William and his associates, justices of the king last itinerant in the said county, without the king's writ, between Amice de Haukeston and master Nicholas de Hegham, dean of St Mary's, Lincoln,[2] because he sued a plea in Court Christian concerning chattels and debts that are not testamentary or matrimonial, contrary to the king's prohibition etc., William should send that record and process and all things touching them to the king if judgment had not yet been rendered. William has sent that record in these words:

'Master Nicholas de Hegham, parson of the church of Trumpington, was attached to answer Amice de Haukeston concerning a plea as to why he sued a plea in Court Christian concerning chattels and debts that are not testamentary or matrimonial, contrary to the lord king's prohibition etc. And in this regard Amice complains that, whereas master Nicholas drew her into a plea in Court Christian before the official of the archdeacon of Ely and claimed from her certain chattels, namely hay valued at 20 shillings that is not testamentary or matrimonial, and Amice on Tuesday immediately after the feast of saints Peter and Paul in the twelfth year of this king's[3] reign in the presence of Alan Collyng and Herbert de Haukeston in the church of All Saints, Cambridge, delivered the lord king's prohibition to master Nicholas that he should not sue the plea further in that court, scorning the prohibition Nicholas nevertheless sued the plea and again had her cited on the Thursday before Trinity just past[4] within the summons of this eyre and contrary to the king's prohibition. She says she is thereby harmed and damaged to the value of 40 shillings. And she produces suit etc.

'And master Nicholas appears and denies force and wrong whenever etc. And he denies that he in any way went against the king's prohibition. And he says that he never drew Amice into a plea in the aforesaid Court Christian and says that Amice kept back a certain part of the tithes of hay pertaining to his church of Trumpington, of which tithes his church was seised. In this regard he says that the plea in question did not concern lay chattels or debts but rather was about tithes. And concerning this he puts himself upon the country. And Amice likewise. Therefore let the jury proceed etc.

'And the jury appears on Thursday immediately after the quindene of St John the Baptist,[5] on which day Amice came forward on the fourth day against Nicholas concerning the plea that he be here to hear the jury. And he did not appear. Therefore the sheriff was ordered to inform him that he should be here Friday next to hear the jury if it seems to him expedient. Therefore let the jury proceed by master Nicholas's default etc.

'The jurors say on their oath that master Nicholas sued a plea in Court Christian concerning Amice's lay chattels and not concerning tithes. They say this because master

[1] Served as a justice on several eyres from 1275 until the Cambridgeshire eyre of 1286 and was a justice of King's Bench from 1288 to 1290.

[2] Lincoln Cathedral.

[3] 4 July 1284.

[4] 6 June 1286.

[5] 12 July 1286.

placitum in curia christianitatis de laicis catallis ipsius Amicie et non de decimis quia dicunt quod idem magister Nicholaus est in seysina de tribus dimidiis acris prati nomine decime pro tota decima contingente ecclesiam suam de Trumpeton' de toto prato quod predicta Amicia tenet in eadem villa. Ita quod nec ipse nec predecessores sui a tempore quo non exstat memoria umquam aliquam decimam seu hucusque perceperunt. Et ideo consideratum est quod predicta Amicia recuperet dampna sua que taxantur per juratores ad quadraginta solidos. Et magister Nicholaus in misericordia. Et si presens esset commiteretur gayole etc.

Postea coram rege in crastino Purificationis anno regni regis nunc quintodecimo: Quia compertum est per predictum recordum quod predictus magister Nicholaus nichil petiit nisi nomine decime ecclesie sue predicte pertinentis prout superius manifeste liquet, consideratum est quod predictum judicium pro nullo habeatur. Et predictus magister Nicholaus rehabeat predictos quadraginta solidos.

1.16a

CP 40/82, m. 24
Common Pleas, Easter 1290

Warr'. Magister Adam de Botingdon clericus in misericordia pro pluribus defaltis.

Idem magister Adam attachiatus fuit ad respondendum Roberto de Okovere et Alicie uxori eius de placito quare secutus fuit placitum in curia christianitatis de advocatione tercie partis ecclesie de Frankton contra prohibicionem etc. Et unde [queruntur][1] quod, cum predictus magister Adam traxisset quemdam Nicholaum Lewyn personam ecclesie de Frankton clericum ipsorum Roberti et Alicie in placitum in curia christianitatis coram decano de Arcubus London in ecclesia Beate Marie de Arcubus London de advocatione predicte tercie partis que est de advocatione ipsorum Roberti et Alicie ac ipsi Robertus et Alicia die lune proxima ante festum sancti Edmundi archiepiscopi anno regni regis nunc sextodecimo apud London in predicta ecclesia beate Marie de Arcubus in presencia magistri Philippi Walerand, magistri Roberti de Kinton, magistri Johannis de Melborn, et aliorum etc. porrexissent eidem magistro Ade regiam prohibitionem ne idem magister Adam predictum placitum ulterius sequeretur, idem magister Adam spreta predicta regia prohibitione secutus fuit predictum placitum in prefata curia christianitatis quousque idem Nicholaus ad sectam ipsius magistri Ade ab ingressu ecclesie fuit suspensus et postea excommunicatus, in contemptum domini regis centum librarum et contra prohibitionem etc. Unde dicunt quod deteriorati sunt et dampnum habent ad valenciam centum librarum. Et inde producunt sectam etc.

Et magister Adam venit et defendit vim et injuriam quando etc. Et dicit quod quidam Radulfus de Frankton quondam patronus [ecclesie predicte][2] de Frankton [i]<primo>[i] presentavit predictum magistrum Adam ad predictam ecclesiam et postea quemdam

[1] MS. reads queritur [2] MS. reads ecclesie predicte ecclesie

Nicholas is seised of three half acres of meadow in the name of tithes for all tithes pertaining to his church of Trumpington from the meadow that Amice holds in that vill, such that neither he nor his predecessors from time out of mind until now have ever received any tithes. And therefore it is adjudged that Amice recover her damages assessed by the jurors at 40 shillings. And master Nicholas is in mercy. And if he had been present he would have been committed to gaol'.

Later, before the king, on the morrow of the Purification of Mary in the fifteenth year of this king's reign,[1] because it is found from the above record that Nicholas sought nothing except in the name of tithes pertaining to his church as is manifestly clear from the above, it is adjudged that the judgment be annulled. And let Nicholas have return of the 40 shillings.

1.16a

ROBERT AND ALICE OF OAKOVER v. ADAM DE BOTINGDON

Warwickshire. Master Adam de Botingdon clerk is in mercy for many defaults.

Master Adam was attached to answer Robert of Oakover and his wife Alice concerning a plea as to why he sued a plea in Court Christian regarding the advowson of a third part of the church of Frankton, contrary to prohibition etc. And in this regard they complain that, whereas master Adam drew a certain Nicholas Lewyn, parson of the church of Frankton, and clerk of Robert and Alice, into a plea in Court Christian before the dean of the court of Arches, London, in the church of St Mary-le-Bow, London, concerning the advowson of the third part that is in the patronage of Robert and Alice, and Robert and Alice on Monday last before the feast of St Edmund Archbishop in the sixteenth year of this king's reign[2] at London in the church of St Mary-le-Bow in the presence of master Phillip Walerand, master Robert de Kinton, master John de Melborn, and others etc. delivered to master Adam a royal prohibition that he should not sue that plea further, scorning the royal prohibition master Adam sued the plea in Court Christian until at master Adam's suit Nicholas was suspended from entry to the church and afterwards excommunicated, in contempt of the lord king 100 pounds and contrary to prohibition etc. They say they are thereby harmed and damaged to the value of 100 pounds. And they produce suit etc.

And master Adam appears and denies force and wrong whenever etc. And he says that one Ralph de Frankton, formerly patron of the church of Frankton, first presented master Adam to that church and later presented one Richard of Southam as his clerk to

[1] 3 February 1287.
[2] 15 November 1288.

Ricardum de Sutham clericum suum ad eandem et dicit quod iidem magister Adam et Ricardus ex grante et voluntate predicti Radulfi patroni etc. super istis presentationibus sibi factis totaliter ordinationi Rogeri Coventr' et Lichefeld episcopi se submiserunt, qui quidem episcopus ordinavit quod predictus magister Adam quoad vixerit singulis annis perciperet sexaginta solidos de bonis predicte ecclesie de Frankton per manus predicti Ricardi et cuiuslibet successorum suorum, per quam quidem ordinationem et compositionem idem magister Adam fuit in seisina de predicta annua pensione. Et quia predictus Nicholaus successor predicti Ricardi cessavit a solutione predicte annue pensionis et idem magister Adam nullum breve de cancellaria inpetrare potuit per quod istam annuam pensionem recuperaret eo quod predicta annua pensio ex spiritualibus mere procedit, secutus fuit idem magister Adam predictum placitum in prefata curia christianitatis prout sibi bene licuit et sine regie dignitatis lesione. Et profert quoddam scriptum signatum sigillis predictorum episcopi, Radulfi patroni etc., Ricardi, et ipsius magistri Ade quod predictam compositionem testatur factum apud Rollesham in crastino Resurrectionis Domini anno Domini mcclxx quinto. Profert etiam aliud scriptum sub nomine fratris W. tunc Coventr' ecclesie prior et eiusdem loci conventus sigillo capituli sui signatum, quod predictam compositionem ratam habendo testatur ex auctoritate cathedralis ecclesie sue predicte confirmat factum in predicto capitulo suo die sancte Agathe anno domini mcclxx nono.

Et Robertus et Alicia dicunt quod per compositionem predictam assensum predicti Radulfi patroni etc. testantem idem magister Adam se excusare non potest. Dicunt enim quod predictus Radulfus patronus etc. dedit manerium de Frankton cum pertinenciis cuidam Rogero de Elnhale fratri predicte Alicie et [dicunt][1] quod predicta advocatio est de pertinenciis predicti manerii quod quidem manerium cum pertinenciis idem Rogerus de seisina sua postea dedit predicto Radulfo et predicte Alicie tunc uxori ipsius Radulfi. Unde dicunt quod tempore predicte compositionis non fuit predictus Radulfus solus patronus sine predicta Alicia per quod predictus Radulfus in prejudicium predicte Alicie super jure patronatus predicte ecclesie per se et sine assensu predicte Alicie in aliquo posset consentire. Unde petunt judicium.

Et magister Adam dicit quod predictus Radulfus patronus etc. tempore predicte compositionis fuit solus patronus predicte ecclesie ita quod predicta Alicia tempore illo nichil habuit in jure predicti patronatus predicte ecclesie nec aliquid in eo clamare potuit. Et hoc petit quod inquiratur per patriam. Et Robertus et Alicia similiter. Ideo preceptum est vicecomiti quod venire faciat hic a die sancti Michaelis in xv dies xij etc. per quos etc. Et qui nec etc. ad recognoscendum in forma predicta. Quia tam etc.

Postea a die sancti Hillarii in xv dies anno regis nunc xix veniunt partes et similiter juratores ex consensu partium electi, qui dicunt super sacramentum suum quod die ordinationis predicte ad quam quidem ordinationem predictus Radulfus prebuit assensum fuit predicta Alicia tenens de advocatione predicte ecclesie simul cum predicto Radulfo ex feofamento Rogeri et tantum habuit in eadem advocatione quantum habuit idem Radulfus. Ideo consideratum est quod predicti [Robertus][2] et Alicia recuperent versus predictum magistrum Adam dampna sua que taxantur per juratores ad centum solidos. Et magister Adam in misericordia. Et inhibitum est ei ne ulterius sequatur placitum in curia christianitatis nec aliquam executionem eiusdem etc.

[1] MS. reads dicit [2] MS. reads Radulfus

the same church. And he says that master Adam and Richard according to the grant and will of Ralph the patron etc. submitted themselves fully concerning the presentations made to them to the determination of Roger, bishop of Coventry and Lichfield,[1] who ordered that Adam was to receive 60 shillings from the goods of the church of Frankton for as long as he should live, by the hand of Richard and any of his successors, and according to this decision and agreement master Adam was in seisin of this annual pension. And because Nicholas, Richard's successor, stopped paying this annual pension, and there is no writ out of chancery by which master Adam can recover it because the annual pension arises entirely out of spiritualities, Adam sued the plea in Court Christian as well he might and without offence to the king's dignity. And he proffers a writing sealed with the seals of the bishop, Ralph (the patron), Richard, and this master Adam, which agreement is attested to have been made at Rowsham on the morrow of the Lord's Resurrection[2] in 1275. He also proffers another writing under the name of brother W., then prior of the church and convent of Coventry, sealed by the chapter, which agreement is attested to have been confirmed by the authority of the cathedral church and to have been made in the chapter on the feast of St Agatha[3] in 1279.

And Robert and Alice say that master Adam may not excuse himself by this agreement, which attests to the assent of Ralph, the patron. They say that Ralph, the patron, gave the manor of Frankton with appurtenances to one Roger of Elnhale brother of Alice and they say that the advowson in question is one of the appurtenances to that manor and that Roger from his seisin later gave the manor and appurtenances to Ralph and Alice, then Ralph's wife. In this regard they say that at the time of the agreement Ralph was not the sole patron without Alice and that therefore Ralph could not give his consent concerning the right of patronage to this church to the prejudice of Alice by himself and without Alice's assent. In this regard they pray judgment.

And master Adam says that Ralph the patron at the time of the agreement was sole patron of the church such that Alice at that time had no right in the patronage of the church nor could she claim any. And he prays that this be inquired of by the country. And Robert and Alice likewise. Therefore the sheriff is ordered to cause to appear here on the quindene of Michaelmas 12 etc. by whom etc. and who are not etc. to give their verdict in the aforesaid matter. Because both parties etc.

Later on the quindene of Hilary in the nineteenth year of this king's reign[4] the parties appear and likewise the jurors chosen with consent of the parties. They say on their oath that on the day of the agreement in question, to which Ralph assented, Alice was tenant of the advowson of the church together with Ralph from the feoffment of Roger and had as much right in that advowson as Ralph did. Therefore it is adjudged that Robert and Alice recover their damages against master Adam, which are assessed by the jurors at 100 shillings. And master Adam is in mercy. And he is enjoined not to sue his plea any further in Court Christian nor seek any execution etc.

[1] Roger de Meyland was bishop of Coventry and Lichfield from 1258 to 1295.

[2] 28 March.

[3] 5 February.

[4] 27 January 1291.

Postea mandavit dominus rex breve suum justiciariis hic ut recordum istud ei mitteretur etc. Et ei missum est etc.

1.16b[1]

KB 27/134, m. 39
King's Bench, Michaelmas term 1292

Postea a die sancti Martini in xv dies anno regni regis nunc vicesimo primo veniunt predicti Robertus et Alicia post premunitionem eis factam [i]<videlicet in octabis sancti Michaelis etc.>[i]. Et similiter predictus magister Adam [i]<venit>[i] et quesitum est a predicto magistro Ade in quo erratum est in predicto recordo, dicit quod non est compertum per predictum recordum quod ipse secutus fuit aliquod placitum in curia christianitatis de advocatione tercie partis ecclesie de Fraunkton' super Donnesmore prout breve predictorum Roberti et Alicie requirit et petit quod predictum recordum corrigatur. Et quesitum est a [d]<predicto Ade>[d] predictis Roberto et Alicie quod dicant quicquid voluerint pro predicto recordo manutenendo qui dicunt quod predictus processus satis est sufficiens et petunt quod [predicti][2] processus et recordum stent in suo robore et quesitum est ab eis si predictus Adam aliud placitum secutus fuit in curia christianitatis quam de predicta [d]<advocacione>[d] annua pensione de bonis ecclesie proveniente tantum ad vitam ipsius Ade percipienda, ad quod nichil respondent. Et quesitum est de predicto Ada si quid clamat in predicta advocatione, dicit quod non.

Et inspecto predicto recordo et examinato invenitur quod predicti Robertus de Okovre et Alicia questi fuerunt de predicto magistro Ade de hoc quod ipse secutus fuit placitum in curia christianitatis de advocatione tercie partis ecclesie de Fraunkton' predicte contra prohibitionem regis. Ad quod responsum fuit ex parte predicti magistri Ade quod revera ipse secutus fuit quoddam placitum in curia christianitatis versus Nicholaum Lewyn rectorem ecclesie predicte de quadam annua pensione sexaginta solidorum ad terminum vite sue de bonis eiusdem ecclesie percipienda unde fuit in possessione [i]<sine prejudicio regie dignitatis>[i] et hoc per ordinationem et grantem diocesani et Ricardi de Southam nuper rectoris ecclesie predicte et similiter predicti Radulfi de Fraunkton' qui se gerebat pro patrono. Et de qua quidem pensione petenda ei non competiit actio per breve de cancellaria eo quod predicta pensio mere provenit de spiritualibus [d]<et hoc sine prejudicio regie dignitatis>[d]. Ad quod nichil responsum fuit ex parte predictorum Roberti et Alicie set omissa illa forma placitandi justiciarii et partes se diverterunt ad aliam formam placitandi extra breve et similiter ad inquisitionem quod facere non licuit licet partes ad hoc assensum prebuerint. Et quia nec per confessionem predicti magistri Ade nec per inquisitionem captam sive alio modo convictum sit quod idem magister Adam secutus

[1] This record begins with an enrolled writ of error addressed to John of Mettingham dated at St Andrew's on 2 July 1291 and then follows with a verbatim transcription of Case no. 1.16a.

[2] MS. reads predictus

Later the lord king by writ addressed to the justices here ordered that this record be sent to him etc. And it was sent etc.

1.16b

ROBERT AND ALICE OF OAKOVER v. ADAM DE BOTINGDON

Later on the quindene of St Martin in the twentieth year of this king's reign[1] Robert and Alice appear after the notice given them, namely on the octave of Michaelmas. And likewise master Adam appears. And master Adam, asked in what way error appears in the record, says that it is not clear from the record that he sued any plea in Court Christian concerning the advowson of the third part of the church of Frankton-on-Dunsmore as Robert's and Alice's writ requires, and he prays that the record be corrected. Asked if they have anything they wish to say in defence of the record, Robert and Alice say that the process is sufficient enough and pray that the process and record should stand as valid. And they are asked if Adam sued any plea in Court Christian other than concerning the annual pension owing from the goods of the church to be paid only for the duration of Adam's life, to which they say nothing in response. And Adam is asked if he claims anything in this advowson, to which he says no.

The record having been inspected and examined, it is found that Robert of Oakover and Alice complained of master Adam that he sued a plea in Court Christian concerning the advowson of the third part of the church of Frankton, contrary to the king's prohibition. To this it was responded on behalf of master Adam that in truth he sued a certain plea in Court Christian against Nicholas Lewyn, rector of that church, concerning an annual pension of 60 shillings to be paid to him out of the goods of that church for the term of his life, of which he was in possession, without prejudice to the royal dignity and this was by the order and grant of the diocesan and of Richard of Southam, recently rector of the church, and likewise of Ralph de Fraunkton, who claimed to be the patron. And concerning this pension there was available no action by writ of chancery because the pension arose wholly from spiritualities. To this there was no response on behalf of Robert and Alice, but, abandoning that form of pleading, the justices and the parties took themselves to another form of pleading that was outside the writ and likewise to an inquisition that should not have been taken even though the parties gave their assent to it. And because neither by the confession of master Adam nor by the inquest taken, nor by any other means, was it found that master Adam sued a plea in Court Christian concerning the third part of the church contrary to royal prohibition, as the writ and plaint of Robert and Alice requires, it is adjudged that the process

[1] 25 November 1291.

fuit placitum in curia christianitatis de advocatione tercie partis ecclesie predicte [i]<contra prohibitionem regiam>[i] secundum quod breve et querela predictorum Roberti et Alicie requirunt, consideratum est quod predictus processus pro nullo habeatur et quod predictus magister Adam rehabeat de predictis Roberto et Alicia centum solidos qui eis prius adiudicati fuerunt pro dampnis suis. Et predicti Robertus et Alicia in misericordia pro falso clamore.[1]

1.17

CP 40/87, m. 121
Common Pleas, Hilary term 1291

Ebor'. Simon abbas sancte Marie Ebor' in misericordia pro pluribus defaltis etc. Idem abbas attachiatus fuit ad respondendum Simoni filio Simonis de Furneus de placito quare secutus fuit placitum in curia christianitatis de advocatione quarte partis ecclesie de Enderby Wythe Stepel contra prohibitionem etc. Et unde idem Simon filius Simonis per attornatum suum queritur quod cum quidam magister Henricus de la Neylaund nuper persona ecclesie predicte tenuisset eandem ecclesiam de advocatione sua, predictus abbas secutus fuit placitum in curia christianitatis coram quibusdam magistro Thoma de Abberbyri et Radulfo de Ponthou commissariis archiepiscopi Ebor' de advocatione quarte partis eiusdem ecclesie, scilicet petendo decimas in parochia predicte ecclesie excedentes quartam partem veri valoris eiusdem ecclesie, scilicet duas partes decimarum de dominicis terris Roberti de Furneus et Radulfi de Leck in Eynderby Wythe Stepel et de dominicis terris Radulfi filii Willelmi in Morton super Swaule et de dominicis terris Roberti le Conestable in Thyrnetoft et de dominicis terris Galfridi de Heywyk et participum suorum in Warleby et aliorum tenentium in eadem parochia. Et ipse die veneris proxima post festum sancti Marci Ewangeliste anno regis nunc sextodecimo in aula ipsius abbatis apud Overton juxta Ebor' in presencia Willelmi de Tanefeld, magistri Thome de Burnton, et Johannis le Lardener per quendam Johannem de Waunford predicto abbati regiam prohibitionem porrexisset ne idem abbas placitum illud ulterius sequeretur, idem abbas spreta regia prohibitione secutus est idem placitum coram predictis commissariis quousque idem abbas in placiito illo optinuit etc., in contemptum domini regis etc. et ad dampnum ipsius Simonis centum librarum. Et inde producit sectam etc.

Et abbas per attornatum suum venit et defendit vim et injuriam quando etc. Et bene cognoscit quod ipse secutus fuit placitum in curia christianitatis de quibusdam decimis exeuntibus de quibusdam dominicis infra limites parochie predicte, set dicit quod decime ille non sunt valoris quarte partis veri valoris predicte ecclesie. Dicit enim quod ipse petiit decimas in predicta parochia valentes per annum centum solidos et ecclesia illa valet per annum centum marcas. Et de hoc ponit se super patriam etc.

[1] In the margin are written Misericordia and, underneath, Dampna c. solidi and unde Clericis L solidi (stricken through).

be annulled and that Robert and Alice return the 100 shillings to master Adam that were earlier awarded to them by way of damages. And Robert and Alice are in mercy for the false claim.

1.17

SIMON DE FURNEUS v. ABBOT OF ST MARY'S, YORK

Yorkshire. Simon, abbot of St Mary's, York, is in mercy for many defaults etc.

The abbot was attached to answer Simon, son of Simon de Furneus, concerning a plea as to why he sued a plea in Court Christian concerning the advowson of a fourth part of the church of Ainderby Steeple contrary to prohibition etc. And in this regard Simon, son of Simon, by his attorney complains that, whereas a certain Henry de la Neylaund, formerly parson of that church, held the church of his advowson, the abbot sued a plea in Court Christian before master Thomas de Abberbury and Ralph de Ponthou, commissaries of the archbishop of York, concerning the advowson of a quarter part of that church, namely claiming tithes in the parish of the church exceeding a fourth part of the value of the church, that is, two parts of the tithes from the demesne lands of Robert de Furneus and Ralph de Leck in Ainderby Steeple and from the demesne lands of Ralph, son of William, in Morton-on-Swale, and from the demesne lands of Robert le Constable in Thrintoft, and from the demesne lands of Geoffrey de Heywick and his coparceners in Warlaby, and from other tenants in the same parish. And when, on Friday first after the feast of St Mark the Evangelist in the sixteenth year of this king's reign[1] in the abbot's hall at Overton near York in the presence of William de Tanefeld, master Thomas de Burnton, and John le Lardener, through one John de Waunford he delivered a prohibition to the abbot that the abbot should not proceed further with that plea, scorning the royal prohibition the abbot sued the plea before the commissaries until the abbot prevailed in that plea etc., in contempt of the lord king etc. and to Simon's damage 100 pounds. And he produces suit etc.

And the abbot by his attorney appears and denies force and wrong whenever etc. And he freely admits that he sued a plea in Court Christian concerning tithes issuing from demesne lands within the boundaries of the parish, but he says that those tithes are not a fourth part of the true value of the church. Indeed, he says that he claimed tithes in the parish valued at 100 shillings annually and that church is worth 100 marks annually. And concerning this he puts himself upon the country etc.

[1] 30 April 1288.

Et Simon dicit quod qualitercumque predictus abbas estimat predictas decimas quas ipse petiit, decime ille valent quartam partem veri valoris predicte ecclesie. Et hoc petit quod inquiratur per patriam et abbas similiter. Ideo preceptum est vicecomiti quod venire faciat hic in octabis sancte Trinitatis xii etc. per quos etc. Et qui nec etc. ad recognoscendum in forma predicta. Quia tam etc.

1.18a

CP 40/95, m. 145d
Common Pleas, Trinity term 1292

Lond'. Magister Simon de la Neylond et Hermannus le Somenur attachiati fuerunt ad respondendum Ade Payn de placito quare predictus magister Simon tenuit placitum in curia christianitatis de catallis et debitis que non sunt de testamento vel matrimonio contra prohibitionem et de placito quare predictus Hermannus secutus fuit idem placitum in eadem curia christianitatis contra prohibitionem etc. Et unde queritur quod, cum predictus Hermannus traxisset ipsum in placitum in curia christianitatis coram predicto magistro Simone in ecclesia beate Marie de Aldmanebyr' Lond' exigendo ab ipso Adam unam marcam que non est de testamento vel matrimonio ac idem Adam in vigilia sancti Andrei anno regni regis [i]<nunc>[i] vicesimo in predicta ecclesia in presencia Johannis de Bolington et aliorum porrexisset predicto magistro regiam prohibitionem ne predictum placitum ulterius teneret etc. et similiter predicto Hermanno ne idem placitum ulterius sequeretur in predicta curia christianitatis, idem magister spreta prohibitione etc. nichilominus tenuit predictum placitum etc. et similiter idem Hermannus nichilominus secutus fuit etc. Unde dicit quod deterioratus est et dampnum habet ad valenciam quadraginta solidorum. Et inde producit sectam etc.

Et magister Simon et Hermannus veniunt et defendunt vim et injuriam quando. Et bene defendunt quod predictus magister Simon non tenuit predictum placitum etc. nec idem Hermannus illud placitum secutus fuit in predicta curia christianitatis sicut eis inponitur. Et hoc parati sunt defendere contra predictum Adam et sectam suam sicut curia etc. Ideo consideratum est quod vadiant ei legem unusquisque eorum se xij manu etc. Et veniant cum legibus suis hic in octabis sancti Martini. Plegii predicti magistri de lege etc. Simon de Caumpes de comitatu Cant' et Johannes Herand de comitatu Essex etc. Plegii predicti Hermanni etc. iidem Simon et Johannes etc.[1]

Postea a die Pasche in unum mensem anno xxj venerunt predicti magister Simon et Hermannus le Somenur parati ei inde facere leges suas. Et predictus Adam solempniter vocatus venit et dicit quod predictus Simon postquam justiciarii hic prohibuerunt ei ne predictum placitum teneret etc. fecit ipsum Adam excommunicari in quatuor comitatibus per quod ipse porrexit quoddam bilettum consilio domini regis de predicto contemptu etc. Et quesitus si velit quod predicti Simon et Hermannus faciant ei leges etc., recessit

[1] In the margin at this point is written leges

And Simon says that however the abbot estimates the value of the tithes that he sought, those tithes are worth a fourth part of the true value of the church. And he asks that this be inquired of by the country; and the abbot likewise. Therefore the sheriff is ordered to produce here on the octave of Trinity 12 etc. through whom etc. and who are not etc. to give their verdict in the aforesaid matter, because both parties etc.

1.18a

ADAM PAYN v. SIMON DE LA NEYLOND AND HERMAN THE SUMMONER

London. Master Simon de la Neylond and Herman the summoner were attached to answer Adam Payn concerning a plea as to why master Simon held a plea in Court Christian concerning chattels and debts that are not testamentary or matrimonial, contrary to prohibition, and concerning a plea as to why Herman sued the same plea in Court Christian, contrary to prohibition etc. And in this regard he complains that, whereas Herman drew him into a plea in Court Christian before master Simon in the church of St Mary Aldermanbury, London, seeking from Adam one mark that is not testamentary or matrimonial and, on the vigil of St Andrew in the twentieth year of this king's reign[1] in that church, in the presence of John de Bolington and others, Adam delivered to master Simon a royal prohibition that he should not hear the plea further etc., and likewise to Herman that he should not sue the plea further in Court Christian, scorning the prohibition etc. master Simon nevertheless continued to hear the plea and likewise Herman nevertheless sued etc. He says he is thereby harmed and damaged to the value of 40 shillings. And he produces suit etc.

And master Simon and Herman appear and deny force and wrong whenever etc. And they deny that master Simon heard the plea etc. and that Herman sued that plea in Court Christian as is alleged against them. And this they are prepared to deny against Adam and his suit as the court shall adjudge etc. And it is adjudged that each of them wage is to wage his law twelve-handed etc. And let them appear here with their law on the octave of St Martin. Pledges for the master's law are Simon de Caumpes of Cambridgeshire and John Herand of Essex etc. Pledges for Herman's law are the same Simon and John etc.

Later one month after Easter in the twenty-first year[2] master Simon and Herman the summoner appear ready to make their law. And Adam solemnly called appears and says that Simon, after the justices here prohibited him that he should not hear the plea any further etc. caused Adam to be excommunicated in four counties, on account of which he filed a certain bill[3] in the council of the lord king concerning this contempt etc. And asked if he wishes that Simon and Herman make their law etc., he withdrew in contempt of the

[1] 29 November 1291.

[2] 27 April 1293.

[3] See Case no. 18b, apparently based on this complaint.

in contemptu [i]<curie>domini regis. Ideo predicti magister Simon et Hermannus inde sine die et predictus Adam et plegii sui de prosequendo in misericordia etc. Querantur nomina plegiorum etc.

1.18b

CP 40/96, m. 93
Common Pleas, Michaelmas term 1292

Lond'. Preceptum fuit vicecomiti quod attachiaret magistrum Simonem de la Nelonde et Hermanum le Somenour quod essent hic ad hunc diem ad respondendum tam domino regi quam Ade Payne de eo quare iidem magister Simon et Hermannus, pendente placito in curia regis hic de eo quare secuti sunt placitum in curia christianitatis de catallis et debitis que non sunt de testamento vel matrimonio contra prohibitionem regis etc., predictus magister Simon tenuit placitum et predictus Hermanus secutus est idem placitum in curia christianitatis quousque predictus magister Simon sentencia in ipsum Adam promulgata ad sectam predicti Hermanni ipsum excommunicavit et per totum archideaconatum Lond' pupplice excommunicari fecit. Et postea breve regis de ipso Adam sic excommunicato tamquam claves ecclesie contempnente capiendo iam vicecomitibus porrexerunt, in corone et dignitatis regis lesionem manifestam et curie regis contemptum et predicti Ade dispendium non modicum et gravamen prout ex gravi [querele][1] ipsius Ade accepit rex. Et similiter preceptum fuit vicecomitibus quod si eis constare posset quod predictus Adam occasione predicta et non alia excommunicatus sit tunc ab ipso Adam capiendo per aliquod breve regis ea occasione per predictos magistrum Simonem et Hermannum impetratum seu impetrandum penitus desistant et interim ipsum Adam pacem habere permittant etc. Et vicecomites nichil inde fecerunt set mandaverunt quod predicti magistri Simon et Hermannus clerici sunt et non habent laicum feodum. Et testatum est quod habent ad sufficienciam apud Bassiehawe in parochia sancti Michaelis. Ideo sicut prius preceptum est vicecomitibus quod attachiant eos quod sint hic in octabis sancti Hillarii etc. Et unde etc. Et testatum est etc.

1.18c

CP 40/107, m. 55
Common Pleas, Hilary term 1295

Midd'. Magister Simon de la Leylonde et Hermannus le Somenur attachiati fuerunt ad respondendum tam domino regi quam Ade Payn de placito quare, cum Simon in curia hic

[1] MS. reads quele

lord king's court. Therefore master Simon and Herman are without day and Adam and his pledges for prosecution are in mercy etc. Inquire as to the names of the pledges etc.

1.18b

ADAM PAYNE v. SIMON DE LA NELONDE AND HERMAN THE SUMMONER

London. The sheriff was ordered to attach master Simon de la Nelonde and Herman the summoner in order that they be here on this day to answer both the lord king and Adam Payne as to why, whereas there was a plea pending in the king's court here as to why they sued a plea in Court Christian concerning chattels and debts that are not testamentary or matrimonial, contrary to the king's prohibition etc., master Simon continued to hear and Herman to sue that plea in Court Christian until master Simon, having promulgated a sentence against Adam at Herman's suit, excommunicated him and caused him publicly to be excommunicated throughout the entire archdeaconry of London. And thereafter they delivered the king's writ to the sheriffs so that Adam might be arrested as an excommunicate in contempt of the keys of the church, to the manifest wrong to the king's crown and dignity and in contempt of the king's court, and to the not insignificant damage and grievance to Adam, as the king learns from Adam's grave complaint. And similarly the sheriffs were ordered that, if it is apparent to them that Adam was excommunicated on the aforesaid occasion and no other, then they should desist entirely from arresting Adam in accordance with any writ obtained from the king or to be obtained by master Simon and Herman and in the interim to allow Adam to have peace etc. And the sheriffs have done nothing in this regard but have answered that master Simon and Herman are clerks and have no lay fee. And it is attested that they have sufficient property at Bassishaw ward in the parish of St Michael's. Therefore as previously the sheriffs are ordered to attach them that they may be here on the octave of Hilary etc. And the sheriffs etc. And it is attested etc.

1.18c

THE KING AND ADAM PAYN v. SIMON DE LA NEYLONDE AND HERMAN THE SUMMONER

Middlesex. Master Simon de la Neylonde and Herman the summoner were attached to answer both the king and Adam Payn concerning a plea as to why, whereas Simon was attached in this court to answer to Adam concerning a plea as to why he heard a plea in Court Christian concerning a debt of one mark which is not testamentary or matrimonial

attachiatus esset ad respondendum prefato Ade de placito quare tenuit placitum in curia christianitatis de quodam debito unius marce quam predictus Hermannus coram eodem magistro Simone a prefato Adam exigebat que non est de testamento vel matrimonio contra prohibitionem etc., idem magister Simon pendente predicto placito inter eos in curia hic die sabbati proxima post octabas sancti Johannis Baptiste anno regis nunc vicesimo apud Lond' in ecclesia sancte Marie de Aldermanbury tenuit ulterius predictum placitum etc. et idem Hermannus predictum placitum ibidem coram eo secutus fuit etc., ita quod idem magister Simon ipsum Adam excommunicavit, in lesionem corone regis et predicti Ade dispendium etc. viginti librarum etc.

Et magister Simon et Hermannus veniunt et bene defendunt quod predictus magister nuncquam pendente predicto placito prohibitionis etc. in curia hic tenuit placitum in predicta curia christianitatis de predicto debito unius marce etc. nec idem Hermannus placitum illud secutus fuit etc. sicut eis inponitur. Et de hoc ponunt se super patriam. Et Adam similiter. Ideo preceptum est vicecomitibus Lond' quod venire faciant hic a die sancte Trinitatis in xv dies xij etc. per quos etc. Quia tam etc. Et predictus Simon [i]<et Hermannus>[i] invenerunt manucaptores essendi hic ad prefatum terminum audituri inquisitionem etc., scilicet Willelmus de Claveryng, Petrus Child, Johannes de Jakesle, et Hubertus de Colcestre de comitatu Essex etc.

Postea a die sancte Trinitatis in xv dies anno regis nunc xxiij veniunt predicti Simon et Hermannus et Adam pro se et domino rege pro quo sequitur. Et juratores de consensu partium electi, qui dicunt super sacramentum suum [quod][1] predictus magister Simon nuncquam aliquod placitum de debito predicte marce tenuit nec predictus Hermannus idem placitum secutus fuit, set dicunt quod, quia idem Adam convictus fuit super quadam fornicatione commissa, predictus magister Simon voluit induxisse eidem Ade penam corporalem tantum. Et juratores, quesiti si predictus magister Simon aliquam pecuniam numeratam a predicto Adam exigebat pro predicta pena [i]<corporali>[i] inflicta redimenda, dicunt simpliciter quod non. Ideo consideratum est quod predicti magister Simon et Hermannus inde sine die. Et predictus Adam nichil capiat per breve suum set in misericordia pro falso clamore etc.

1.19

CP 40/105, m. 24
Common Pleas, Trinity term 1294

Lond'. Magister Simon de Wymundham, Willelmus le Somenur, et Matheus le Someter attachiati fuerunt ad respondendum domino regi et Willelmo Faure et Alicie uxori eius de placito quare, cum placita de transgressionibus contra pacem regis factis in regno regis ad dominum regem et coronam et dignitatem suam et non ad alium pertineant in eodem regno ac iidem magister Simon, Willelmus, et Matheus secuti fuissent placitum in curia

[1] MS. reads quod quod

that Herman exacted from Adam before master Simon, contrary to prohibition etc., master Simon, while the plea in this court was pending between them, on the first Saturday after the octave of John the Baptist in the twentieth year of this king's reign,[1] at London in the church of St Mary Aldermanbury, continued to hear the plea in Court Christian etc. and Herman continued to sue it before him etc., so that master Simon excommunicated Adam, to the wrong to the king's crown and damage to Adam etc. of 20 pounds etc.

And master Simon and Herman appear and deny that the master ever heard the plea in Court Christian concerning the debt of one mark etc. while the prohibition plea was pending in this court or that Herman sued that plea as is alleged against them. And concerning this they put themselves upon the country. And Adam likewise. Therefore the sheriff of London is ordered to produce here on the quindene of Trinity 12 etc. through whom etc. because both parties etc. And Simon and Herman find mainpernors that they will be here on that term to hear the inquisition etc., namely William of Clavering, Peter Child, John de Jakesle, and Hubert de Colchester of Essex etc.

Later on the quindene of Trinity in the twenty-third year of this king's reign[2] Simon and Herman appear and also Adam on his own behalf and for the king on whose behalf he sues. And likewise the jurors chosen with consent of the parties, who say on their oath that master Simon never heard any plea concerning the alleged debt of one mark, nor did Herman sue that plea. They say instead that, because Adam was convicted of having committed a certain act of fornication, Simon wished to bring Adam to corporal penance only. And the jurors, asked if master Simon exacted any specific sum of money from Adam in order to redeem the corporal penance inflicted upon him, simply say no. Therefore it is adjudged that master Simon and Herman are without day. And Adam is to take nothing by his writ but is in mercy for the false claim etc.

1.19

THE KING AND WILLIAM AND ALICE FAURE v. SIMON OF WYMONDHAM AND OTHERS

London. Master Simon of Wymondham,[3] William the Summoner and Matthew the Sumpter were attached to answer the lord king and William Faure and his wife Alice concerning a plea as to why, since pleas of trespass against the king's peace in the king's realm belong

[1] 1 July 1292.
[2] 13 June 1295.
[3] A person of this name also appears in Case no. 1.13.

christianitatis super huiusmodi transgressionibus in lesionem corone et dignitatis regis et contra prohibitionem regis eisdem magistro Simoni, Willelmo, et Matheo directam ne predictum placitum ulterius in curia christianitatis sequerentur, iidem Willelmus et Alicia ad sectam ipsorum magistri Simonis, Willelmi, et Mathei sentencia excommunicationis in ipsos fulminata ab ingressu ecclesie suspensi fuerunt et postmodum breve regis de capiendo ipsos Willelmum Faure et Aliciam tanquam claves ecclesie contempnentes maliciose inpetraverunt ut sic eos inpediant quominus predictum placitum in prefata curia regis coram justiciariis inde motum prosequi non possunt secundum legem et consuetudinem regni regis, in ipsorum Willelmi et Alicie dampnum non modicum et domini regis contemptum manifestum. Et unde iidem Willelmus Faure et Alicia queruntur quod, cum ipsi Willelmus et Alicia die lune proxima ante festum annunciationis beate Marie anno regni regis nunc vicesimo secundo in ecclesia beate Marie que vocatur Aldermaneschirche in Cordewanestrete prohibitionem domini regis predictam in presencia Ade Paynel et Reginaldi le Taliur [et][1] Bidau de Cos et Roberti de Munpellers eisdem magistro Simoni, Willelmo, et Matheo liberassent, iidem magister Simon, Willelmus, et Matheus secuti sunt predictum placitum in curia christianitatis quousque iidem Willelmus et Alicia ad sectam ipsorum magistri Simonis, Willelmi, et Mathei sentencia excommunicationis in ipsis fulminata ab ingressu ecclesie suspensi fuerunt et postmodum breve regis de capiendo ipsos tanquam claves ecclesie contempnentes maliciose inpetraverunt ut sic eos inpedirent quominus predictum placitum in prefata curia regis coram justiciariis domini regis motum prosequi non potuerunt etc., in domini regis contemptum manifestum. Et unde dicunt quod deteriorati sunt et dampnum habent ad valenciam centum marcarum. Et inde producunt sectam etc.

Et magister Simon, Willelmus, et Matheus per attornatum suum veniunt et defendunt vim et injuriam quando etc. Et bene defendunt quod ipsi nullum placitum de transgressionibus in curia christianitatis versus eos secuti fuerunt et quod predicti Willelmus et Alicia nullam prohibitionem domini regis eis liberaverunt secundum quod eis inponunt. Et de hoc ponunt se super patriam. Et Willelmus de Welleby qui sequitur pro rege et predicti Willelmus et Alicia similiter. Ideo preceptum est vicecomitibus quod venire faciant hic a die sancti Michaelis in xv dies xij etc. per quos etc. Et qui nec etc. ad recognoscendum etc. Quia tam etc.

Postea a die Pasche in unum mensem anno regni regis nunc xxiii venerunt predicti [i]<Willelmus Faure et Alicia et similiter magister Simon>[i] et similiter juratores, qui dicunt super sacramentum suum quod predicti Willelmus et Alicia liberaverunt predicto Simoni prohibitionem domini regis, set dicunt precise quod predictus magister Simon post predictam prohibitionem ei liberatam nuncquam aliquod placitum de transgressione que ad coronam et dignitatem domini regis pertinet tenuit etc. Et quesiti de cuiusmodi transgressione etc. dicunt quod de adulterio. [i]<Et quesiti si aliquam pecuniam numeratam ab eis petiit dicunt precise quod non etc.>[i] Et ideo consideratum est quod predictus magister Simon eat sine die et predicti Willelmus et Alicia sint in misericordia pro falso clamore etc.

[1] MS. omits.

to the lord king and his crown and dignity and to no one else in the realm, and master Simon, William, and Matthew sued a plea in Court Christian concerning trespasses of this kind, to the wrong of the king's crown and dignity and contrary to the king's prohibition directed to master Simon, William, and Matthew that they should not sue that plea further in Court Christian, William and Alice at the suit of master Simon, William and Matthew had sentence of excommunication proclaimed against them and they were suspended from entry to the church; and soon afterwards master Simon, William and Matthew maliciously sued out a royal writ of caption against William Faure and Alice for contempt of the church's keys so that they might be impeded and disabled from prosecuting a plea in the king's court before his justices according to the law and custom of the king's realm, to the great damage of William Faure and Alice and in manifest contempt of the lord king. And in this regard William Faure and Alice complain that, whereas, on the Monday immediately before the feast of the Annunciation in the twenty-second year of this king's reign[1] in St Mary's church, which is called Aldermary and is located in Cordwainer Street,[2] they delivered the king's prohibition to master Simon, William and Matthew in the presence of Adam Paynel, Reginald le Taliur, Bidau de Cos and Robert de Munpellers, master Simon, William and Matthew sued the plea in Court Christian until William and Alice, at the suit of master Simon, William and Matthew, had sentence of excommunication proclaimed against them and were suspended from entry to the church; and soon afterwards master Simon, William and Matthew maliciously sued out the king's writ of caption against them for contempt of the church's keys so that they might be impeded and disabled from prosecuting their plea in the king's court before the lord king's justices etc., in manifest contempt of the lord king. They say they are thereby harmed and damaged to the value of 100 marks. And they produce suit etc.

And master Simon, William and Matthew by their attorney appear and deny force and wrong whenever etc. And they deny that they ever sued any plea concerning trespasses in Court Christian against William and Alice or that they ever delivered the lord king's prohibition to them as is alleged against them. And concerning this they put themselves on the country. And William de Welleby who sues for the king and for William and Alice likewise. Therefore the sheriff is ordered to cause to appear here on the quindene of Michaelmas 12 etc. through whom etc. and who are not etc. to give their verdict etc. Because both parties etc.

Later, one month after Easter in the twenty-third year of this king's reign[3], William Faure and Alice appear and likewise master Simon and the jurors, who say on their oath that William and Alice delivered the lord king's prohibition to Simon, but they say simply that master Simon never held any plea of trespass that pertains to the crown and dignity of the lord king etc. after the prohibition was delivered to him. And asked what sort of trespass it was, they say that it concerned adultery. And asked whether he sought any specific sum of money from them, they simply say no. Therefore it is adjudged that master Simon go without day and that William and Alice are in mercy for the false claim etc.

[1] 22 March 1294.

[2] Cordwainer Street is now called Bow Lane. St Mary Aldermary is to be found at the junction of Bow Lane and Watling Street.

[3] 2 May 1295.

1.20

CP 40/109, m. 27
Common Pleas, Trinity term 1295

Suff', Linc'. Frater Willelmus prior de Belvero et Robertus persona ecclesie de Athelyngton de comitatu Linc' et Galfridus de Wileby clericus de comitatu Suff' alias, scilicet in octabis sancti Michaelis proximo preteritis, attachiati fuerunt ad respondendum domino regi de placito quare, cum Galfridus le Waleys capellanus teneat ecclesiam de Wylyngham de advocatione domini regis, iidem prior et Robertus simul cum fratre Willelmo de Holt tenuerunt placitum in curia christianitatis de advocatione quarte partis ecclesie de Wylyngham contra prohibitionem etc. et de placito quare predictus Galfridus de Wileby secutus est idem placitum in eadem curia christianitatis contra prohibitionem etc. Et unde Nicholaus de Warrewyk qui sequitur pro domino rege questus fuit quod, cum idem Galfridus de Wileby traxisset predictum Galfridum le Waleys capellanum in placitum in curia christianitatis coram predictis prior et aliis de advocatione quarte partis ecclesie predicte ac idem Galfridus le Waleys die jovis proxima post festum nativitatis beate Marie anno regni regis nunc decimonono in ecclesia de Graham in presencia Willelmi de Horlyng, Phillipi filii Thome, Thome Skarlet, Radulfi de Barneby, Henrici servientis comitis Warenn, Galfridi Andreu, et aliorum detulisset eisdem priori et aliis regiam prohibitionem ne placitum illud in eadem curia christianitatis tenerent nec idem Galfridus de Wileby idem placitum sequeretur etc., iidem prior et Robertus simul cum predicto Willelmo nichilominus spreta regia prohibitione predictum placitum in predicta curia christianitatis ulterius tenuerunt et similiter idem Galfridus de Wileby idem placitum ulterius ibidem secutus est quousque predictus Galfridus le Waleys ab ingressu ecclesie suspensus fuit et postea excommunicatus in contemptum domini regis mille librarum. Et hoc paratus fuit verificare pro domino rege etc.

Et prior, Robertus, et Galfridus de Wileby per attornatum suum tunc venerunt et defendunt vim et injuriam quando etc. Et bene defendunt quod ipsi prior et Robertus nunquam tenuerunt placitum in curia christianitatis de advocatione quarte partis predicte ecclesie nec predictus Galfridus de Wileby idem placitum ibidem secutus fuit. Et hoc petierunt quod inquireretur etc.

Et predictus Nicholaus dixit quod predicti prior et alii ad huiusmodi verificationem admitti non debuerunt quia dixit quod predicta responsio sua quam pretenderunt verificare multiplex fuit et plures causas veritatis habere potuit, videlicet quod predictus prior et Robertus nullum placitum ibidem inde tenuerunt nec predictus Galfridus de Wileby idem placitum secutus fuit vel quod idem prior et alii idem placitum tenuerunt ibidem et secuti fuerunt set non attingens ad quartem partem advocationis predicte ecclesie vel quod ipsi tenuerunt idem placitum et secuti fuerunt ibidem ante prohibitionem eis porrectam set non post. Unde petiit pro domino rege quod certam dent inde responsionem.

Et prior et Robertus bene cognoscunt quod ipsi tenuerunt placitum de quibusdam decimis in predicta curia christianitatis, videlicet de quibusdam decimis provenientibus de quatuor acris terre in campo qui vocatur Cumyng et etiam de decimis provenientibus de medietate triginta et unius acris terre in campis de Elegh per loca jacentia, set dixerunt

1.20

THE KING AND THE PARSON OF WILLINGHAM v. THE PRIOR OF BELVOIR AND OTHERS

Suffolk, Lincolnshire. Brother William, prior of Belvoir, and Robert, parson of the church of Allington in Lincolnshire, and Geoffrey de Wileby, clerk, of Suffolk, were previously attached, namely on the octave of Michaelmas just past,[1] to answer the lord king concerning a plea as to why, whereas Geoffrey le Waleys chaplain held the church of Willingham of the lord king's advowson, the prior and Robert together with brother William de Holt held a plea in Court Christian concerning the advowson of a quarter part of the church of Willingham, contrary to prohibition etc., and also to answer concerning a plea as to why Geoffrey de Wileby sued the same plea in Court Christian, contrary to prohibition etc. And in this regard Nicholas de Warrewyk[2] who sues for the lord king complained that, whereas Geoffrey de Wileby drew Geoffrey le Waleys chaplain into a plea in Court Christian before the prior and others concerning the advowson of a quarter part of the aforesaid church and, on the first Thursday after the feast of the Nativity of the Virgin in the nineteenth year of this king's reign[3] in the church of Grantham in the presence of William de Horlyng, Phillip, son of Thomas, Thomas Skarlet, Ralph de Barneby, Henry, servant of the earl Warenne, Geoffrey Andreu, and others, Geoffrey le Waleys delivered to the prior and others a royal prohibition that they should not sue the same plea etc., scorning the royal prohibition the prior and Robert together with William nevertheless continued to hear the plea in Court Christian and likewise Geoffrey de Wileby continued to sue the plea, until Geoffrey le Waleys was suspended from entry to the church and afterwards excommunicated, in contempt of the lord king 1,000 marks. And he was prepared to verify this for the lord king etc.

And the prior, Robert, and Geoffrey de Wileby by their attorney then appeared and denied force and wrong whenever etc. And they denied that the prior and Robert ever heard a plea in Court Christian concerning the advowson of a quarter part of the aforesaid church and that Geoffrey sued that plea. And this they prayed be inquired of etc.

And Nicholas said that the prior and others should not be admitted to this form of proof because the response that they offered to prove had several meanings and could be true for several reasons, namely that the prior and Robert heard no plea and Geoffrey de Wileby did not sue a plea or that the prior and others heard the plea and sued it but it did not amount to a quarter part of the advowson of the church or that they heard the plea and sued it before a prohibition was presented to them but not after. And concerning this he prayed on the lord king's behalf that they give a definite response.

And the prior and Robert acknowledge that they heard a plea concerning certain tithes in Court Christian, namely tithes issuing from four acres of land in the field called Cumyng and also from half of 31 acres in fields of Elegh lying nearby, but they said that those tithes did not amount to a quarter part of the advowson of the church. And likewise Geoffrey

[1] The record is found at CP 40/106, m. 16d (1294).
[2] King's serjeant.
[3] 13 September 1291.

quod decime ille non attingebant ad quartam partem advocationis predicte ecclesie. Et similiter predictus Galfridus de Wileby sectam illam ibidem per ipsum factam cognoscit. Et tam predicti prior et Robertus quam predictus Galfridus de Wileby dixerunt quod post prohibitionem eis porrectam, optenta inde consultatione a G. de Thornton consultatore quam protulerunt hic in curia, in eodem placito in eadem curia christianitatis tenendo et sequendo processerunt. Unde tam predictus Galfridus de Wileby quam predicti prior et Robertus dixerunt ut prius quod predicte decime non attingebant ad quartam partem advocationis etc. Et hoc petunt quod inquiratur. Set quia videbatur curie quod ad istam verificationem ad tunc inde non fuerunt admittendi, datus fuit eis dies de audiendo judicio etc. hic in octabis sancti Hillarii proximo sequentibus etc. si verificationem illam habere debeant etc. Ad quem diem predictus Galfridus de Wileby fuit essoniatus et predicti prior, Robertus, et Galfridus le Waleys comparuerunt. Et habuerunt diem per essoniatorem ipsius Galfridi de Wileby hic ad hunc diem.

Et tam predicti prior et alii per attornatum suum quam predictus Nicholaus qui sequitur pro rege modo veniunt. Et Nicholaus dicit quod dominus rex nunc et predecessores sui a tempore quo non extat memoria extiterunt in seisina de advocatione predicte ecclesie integre in qua predicte decime de predictis tenementis provenientes continentur et etiam omnes clerici eorumdem regum persone eiusdem ecclesie etc. easdem decimas tanquam pertinentes ad eandem ecclesiam hucusque perceperunt. Unde desicut predictis priori et aliis per statutum tantum et non aliter quoad verificationem in hac parte attingendam, si ad verificationem etc. esset subveniendum quod quidem statutum personam ipsius domini regis non ligat, petit judicium si ad aliquam verificationem versus ipsum dominum regem in hac parte debeant admitti. Dicit etiam quod si predicti prior et alii ad predictam verificationem attinxissent, predicta advocatio per huiusmodi placita et alia in curia christianitatis inde agitanda in ipsius domini regis dispendium et exheredationem manifestam tractu temporis de facili maximam [i]<sui>[i] pateretur minorationem. Unde petit pro ipso domino rege quod super hiis rationibus et similibus curia prospecte se circumspiciat in hac parte etc.

Dies datus est eis de audiendo judicio suo hic si ad verificationem etc. in crastino Animarum etc.

1.21

CP 40/110, m. 231
Common Pleas, Michaelmas term, 1295

Ebor'. Thomas vicarius ecclesie sancti Laurentii de suburbio Ebor' attachiatus fuit ad respondendum domino regi de placito quare, cum placita de catallis et debitis in regno regis que non sunt de testamento vel matrimonio ad dominum regem et coronam et dignitatem regis et non ad alium pertineant in eodem regno, predictus Thomas sicut ex relatu plurium accepit dominus rex secutus est placitum in curia christianitatis de catallis et debitis Roberti le Graunt capellani magistri hospitalis sancti Nicholai Ebor', in lesionem

de Wileby ackowledges that he brought that suit there. And both the prior and Robert and also Geoffrey de Wileby said that after the prohibition was shown to them, having obtained a consultation from G. de Thornton[1] as official adviser, which they produce here in court, they proceeded with hearing and prosecuting the plea in Court Christian. And both Geoffrey de Wileby and the prior and Robert said, as previously, that the tithes did not amount to a quarter part of the advowson etc. And this they asked be inquired of. But because it then appeared to the court that they should not be admitted to this form of proof, day was given them to hear judgment as to whether they ought to have that form of proof here on the next octave of Hilary. On which day Geoffrey de Wileby was essoined and the prior, Robert, and Geoffrey le Waleys appeared. And they were given day by the essoiner of Geoffrey de Wileby here on this day.

And both the prior and others by their attorney and Nicholas who sues for the king now appear. And Nicholas says that the lord king and his predecessors since time out of mind have been in seisin of the advowson of the aforesaid church in its entirety, in which the tithes issuing from the aforesaid tenements are contained, and also that all clerks of those kings who have been parsons of that church until now have received those tithes as belonging to that church. Accordingly, whereas the claim of the prior and others to proof by a jury is based on the statute[2] only and not otherwise, and if they are admitted to proof etc. it should be recalled that that statute does not bind the lord king's person, he prays judgment whether they ought to be admitted to any proof against the lord king in this regard. He says also that if the prior and others should be awarded proof, by this sort of plea and others to be prosecuted in Court Christian the advowson will suffer great loss of value by the passage of time, to the wrong and manifest disinheritance of the lord king. And so he prays on behalf of the lord king that for these and similar reasons the court should proceed deliberately and cautiously in this matter etc.

Day is given to them to hear the judgment here whether to proof etc. on the morrow of All Souls' etc.

1.21

THE KING AND THE MASTER OF ST NICHOLAS'S HOSPITAL v. VICAR OF ST LAWRENCE'S, YORK

Yorkshire. Thomas, vicar of St Lawrence's church in the suburb of York, was attached to answer the lord king on a plea as to why, since pleas of chattels and debts in the realm of this king that are not testamentary or matrimonial belong to the lord king and to his

[1] Appointed justice of King's Bench in 1290 and soon thereafter elevated to chief justice, a position he held until his death in 1295.

[2] Apparently a reference to Circumspecte Agatis.

corone et dignitatis regis et contra prohibitionem etc. Et unde Willelmo de Estthorp qui sequitur pro domino rege queritur quod, cum idem Thomas traxisset predictum Robertum in placitum in curia christianitatis coram decano et capitulo ecclesie sancti Petri Ebor' in eadem ecclesia exigendo ab ipso [i]<Roberto>[i] lanam pretii viginti solidorum, viginti solidos, et quatuor marcas qui non sunt de testamento vel matrimonio ac quidem Ricardus le Mareschal die lune proxima ante festum Purificationis beate Marie anno regni regis nunc vicesimo tercio in ecclesia predicta in presencia Walteri de Spofford, Johannis de Kexeby, Johannis le Barbour, Nicholai de Hundesleye, et Thome de Burton et aliorum porrexisset eidem Thome regiam prohibitionem ne placitum illud in curia illa ulterius sequeretur, idem Thomas spreta predicta prohibitione placitum illud nichilominus secutus fuit quousque idem Robertus suspensus fuit ab ingressu ecclesie, in contemptum domini regis mille librarum. Et hoc paratus est verificare etc.

Et Thomas venit et defendit vim et injuriam quando etc. Et dicit quod predictus magister, fratres, et sorores hospitalis predicti tempore predicto habuerunt centum oves in parochia sua de quibus noluerunt solvere decimam ac ipse fecit predictum magistrum convenire coram predictis decano et capitulo ordinariis loci et petiit ab eis inde decimam ad estimationem viginti solidorum tantum prout decuit, pro quo predictus Ricardus porrexit ei regiam prohibitionem et ipse adivit Gilbertum de Thornton tunc justiciarium domini regis monstrando ei libellum inde editum sub sigillo judicis, qui quidem Gilbertus fecit consultationem eisdem judicibus quod ipsi cognoscerent in foro ecclesiastico de decimis tam majoribus quam minoribus dum tamen decime petite non extenderent ad quartam partem valoris totius ecclesie regia prohibitione non obstante. Unde idem Thomas traxit in placitum in curia christianitatis predictos magistrum, fratres, et sorores etc., quam [consultationem][1] profert sub sigillo ipsius Gilberti. Unde dicit quod nullum placitum sequebatur nisi [i]<in>[i] forma predicta. Et de hoc ponit se super patriam. Et Willelmus qui sequitur pro domino rege similiter. Ideo preceptum est vicecomiti quod venire faciat hic a die sancti Hillarii in xv dies xij etc. per quos etc. Et qui nec etc. ad recognoscendum etc. Quia tam etc.

1.22

KB 27/150, m. 24
King's Bench, Hilary term 1297

Norf'. Henricus Fouch de Staunfeld, Willelmus filius Simonis le Fevre, [i]<Phillipus de ecclesia de Godewyk >[i], Johannes filius Roberti Haghne attachiati fuerunt ad respondendum Radulfo de Semere persone ecclesie de Staunfeld de placito conspiracionis et transgressionis secundum ordinationem regis nuper inde provisam sicut rationabiliter

[1] MS. omits.

crown and dignity and to no one else in this realm, Thomas, as the lord king has learned from many people, sued a plea in Court Christian concerning the chattels of Robert le Graunt, chaplain, master of the hospital of St Nicholas, York,[1] to the wrong of the king's crown and dignity and contrary to prohibition etc. And in this regard William de Estthorp who sues for the lord king complains that, whereas Thomas drew Robert into a plea in Court Christian before the dean and chapter of St Peter's church, York,[2] demanding in that church from Robert wool worth 20 shillings and 20 shillings and four marks that were not testamentary or matrimonial and, on Monday immediately preceding the feast of the Purification of Mary in the twenty-third year of this king's reign,[3] in that church, in the presence of Walter de Spofford, John de Kexeby, John le Barbour, Nicholas de Hundesleye, and Thomas de Burton and others, a certain Richard le Mareschal delivered to Thomas a royal prohibition that he should not sue that plea further in that court, scorning the prohibition Thomas nonetheless continued to sue the plea until Robert was suspended from entry to the church, in the contempt of the lord king 1000 pounds. And this he is prepared to prove etc.

And Thomas appears and denies force and wrong whenever etc. And he says that the master, brethren and sisters of the hospital at that time had 100 sheep in his parish from which they did not wish to pay tithes and he caused the master to appear before the dean and chapter, local ordinaries, and sought from them tithes estimated at 20 shillings only, as was fitting for him to do, on account of which Richard delivered to him a royal prohibition. And he went to Gilbert de Thornton,[4] then justice of the lord king, showing him the libel thus declared under the seal of the judges, who issued a consultation to the same judges that they might have cognizance in the ecclesiastical forum of tithes both greater and lesser as long as the tithes demanded did not extend to a quarter part of the value of the whole church, royal prohibition notwithstanding. Accordingly Thomas impleaded the master, brethren and sisters in Court Christian, which consultation he proffers under Gilbert's seal, and says that he sued no plea other than in that form. And concerning this he puts himself upon the country. And William who sues for the lord king likewise. Therefore the sheriff is ordered to cause to appear here on the quindene of Hilary 12 etc. through whom etc. and who are not etc. to give their verdict etc. Because both parties etc.

1.22

PARSON OF STANFIELD v. HENRY FOUCH AND OTHERS

Norfolk. Henry Fouch of Stanfield, William son of Simon le Fevre, Phillip of Godwick church, and John son of Robert Haghne were attached to answer Ralph de Semere, parson

[1] Robert le Graunt was appointed master of the hospital in 1281 but was removed from office three years later, retaining the chaplaincy: *VCH York*, 3:336–352. [2] York Minster. [3] 31 January 1295.

[4] Appointed justice of King's Bench in 1290 and soon thereafter elevated to chief justice, a position he held until his death in 1295.

monstrare poterit quod ei inde etc. Et unde queritur quod idem Henricus et alii [per][1] conspiracionem et confederacionem suam falso et maliciose presentaverunt coram vicecomite comitatus predicti ad magnum turnum suum quod tenuit apud Magnam Dunham in festo apostolorum Petri et Pauli anno regni regis nunc vicesimo quarto quod idem Radulfus de Semere inplacitasse debuit quendam Henricum [Fouch][2] in curia christianitatis contra prohibitionem et defensionem domini regis et ubi idem Radulfus consultationem habuit de curia regis sibi concessam quod judices ecclesiastici procedere possent in loquela que fuit coram eis inter ipsum Radulfum de Semere et predictum Henricum Fouch. Per quod idem Radulfus coram vicecomite predicto amerciatus fuit ad quadraginta solidos quos postmodum pacavit. Unde dicit quod deterioratus est et dampnum habet ad valenciam centum solidorum. Et inde producit sectam etc.

Et predicti Henricus et alii veniunt et defendunt vim et injuriam quando etc. Et dicunt quod ipsi fuerunt de duodena jurata coram vicecomite predicto ad turnum suum predictum qui vicecomes liberavit eis quosdam articulos in [scriptos][3] ad quod respondere debuerunt et inter articulos illos fuit ille articulus, quod ipsi inquirerent si aliquis esset in patria qui aliquem in curia christianitatis inplacitavit contra prohibitionem seu defensonem domini regis. Et quia vicecomes predictus articulum illum eis liberavit et idem Radulfus prefatum Henricum in curia christianitatis inplacitavit [i]<prout intellexerint>[i] hoc idem coram vicecomite predicto presentaverunt et non per maliciam seu aliquam conspirationem suam. Et de hoc ponunt se super patriam etc. Et Radulfus similiter. Ideo veniat inde jurata coram rege a die Pasche in tres septimanas ubicumque etc.

1.23a

CP 40/118, m. 68d
Common Pleas, Easter term 1297

Midd'. Rogerus de Arderne, Robertus filius Thome le Lyndraper, Alicia et Juliana sorores eiusdem Roberti attachiati fuerunt ad respondendum Radulfo de Hunylane et Emme de Hunylane de placito quare secuti sunt placitum in curia christianitatis de catallis et debitis que non sunt de testamento vel matrimonio contra prohibitionem regis etc. et de placito quare pendente placito in curia hic inter eos idem Rogerus et alii nichilominus in eadem curia christianitatis secuti sunt versus eos predictum placitum in eadem curia christianitatis quousque predicti Radulfus et Emma ad prosecutionem eorum fuerunt excommunicati etc. Et unde iidem Radulfus et Emma per attornatum suum queruntur quod, cum predicti Rogerus et alii traxissent ipsos in curia christianitatis coram [i]<archiepiscopo Cantuar'>[i] et magistro Henry de Nassington de triginta marcis que non sunt de testamento vel matrimonio ac iidem Radulfus et Emma die mercurii proxima ante Pascha Floridum

[1] MS. reads pro
[2] MS. reads Fulch
[3] MS. reads scriptis

of Stanfield church, concerning a plea of conspiracy and trespass according to the king's recent ordinance,[1] as he was able reasonably to show that etc. And in this regard Ralph complains that Henry and the others through their conspiracy and confederacy falsely and maliciously presented him before the sheriff of Norfolk's great tourn held at Great Dunham on the feast of the apostles Peter and Paul in the twenty-fourth year of this king's reign,[2] alleging that he impleaded a certain Henry Fouch in Court Christian contrary to the lord king's prohibition and protection, whereas Ralph had a consultation from the king's court granted to him stating that the ecclesiastical judges might proceed in the case before them between Ralph de Semere and Henry Fouch. As a result of this Ralph was fined 40 shillings before the sheriff, which he thereafter paid. He says he is thereby harmed and damaged to the value of 100 shillings. And he produces suit etc.

And Henry and the others appear and deny force and wrong whenever etc. And they say that they were among twelve jurors before the sheriff at his tourn and the sheriff presented them with certain written articles to which they were supposed to answer, and among those articles was this article, that they should inquire into whether there was anyone in the locality who had impleaded anyone in Court Christian contrary to the prohibition and injunction of the lord king. And because the sheriff delivered this article to them and Ralph, as they understood it, had impleaded Henry in Court Christian, they presented this to the sheriff, and not out of any malice or conspiracy. And concerning this they put themselves on the country etc. And Ralph likewise. Therefore let the jury come before the king three weeks after Easter wheresoever etc.

1.23a

RALPH AND EMMA DE HUNYLANE v. ROGER DE ARDERNE AND OTHERS

Middlesex. Roger de Arderne, Robert, son of Thomas le Lyndraper, and Alice and Juliana, sisters of Robert, were attached to answer Ralph de Hunylane and Emma de Hunylane concerning a plea as to why they sued a plea in Court Christian concerning chattels and debts that are not testamentary or matrimonial, contrary to the king's prohibition etc., and concerning a plea as to why, while the plea was pending in this court between them, Roger and the others nevertheless in the same Court Christian continued to sue the plea against them until Ralph and Emma at their suit were excommunicated etc. And in this regard Ralph and Emma by their attorney complain that, whereas Roger and the others drew them into Court Christian[3] before the archbishop of Canterbury[4] and master Henry

[1] The so-called Statute Concerning Conspirators of 1293, printed at *SR*, 1:216, provided a new writ for use by those complaining of conspiracies designed to interfere with legitimate legal process in the king's courts.

[2] 29 June 1296.

[3] The reference is to a lengthy set of proceedings in church court. A number of documents are printed in Canterbury Cases 633–689. The church court records include no reference to a writ of prohibition.

[4] Robert Winchelsey was consecrated archbishop of Canterbury in 1294 and served until his death in 1313.

anno regis nunc vicesimo quarto in ecclesia beate Marie de Arcubus Lond' in presencia Ricardi de Hecham et Stephani de Heref' porrexissent eis regiam prohibitionem ne placitum predictum ulterius sequerentur etc., iidem Rogerus et alii nichilominus placitum illud secuti fuerunt in eadem curia quousque iidem Radulfus et Emma fuerunt excommunicati ad prosecutionem predictorum Rogeri et aliorum etc. Et postea pendente predicto placito prohibitionis hic inde inter eos nichilominus secuti sunt predictum placitum [i]<per quod excommunicati fuerunt>[i] et breve regis de corporibus ipsorum Radulfi et Emme [capiendis][1] impetraverunt, in lesionem corone et dignitatis regis etc. Unde dicunt quod deteriorati sunt et dampnum habent ad valenciam quadraginta librarum. Et inde producunt sectam etc.

Et Rogerus, Robertus per custodem ipsius Roberti, Alicia et Juliana veniunt et defendunt vim et injuriam quando etc. Et Rogerus bene defendit quod ipse nuncquam secutus fuit predictum placitum in prefata curia christianitatis predictis die et anno sicut ei inponitur. Et hoc paratus est defendere contra [ipsos][2] et sectam suam sicut curia etc. Ideo consideratum est quod vadiat eis legem se duodecima manu etc. Et idem Rogerus incontinenti fecit inde legem suam etc. Ideo predictus Rogerus inde sine die. Et Radulfus et Emma in misericordia pro falso clamore etc.[3]

Et Robertus, Alicia, et Juliana qui infra etatem sunt etc. dicunt quod predictus Thomas le Lyndraper pater ipsorum Roberti, Alicie, et Juliane in ultima voluntate sua legavit ipsis Roberto, Alicie, et Juliane triginta marcas etc. Et iidem Robertus, Alicia, et Juliana coram prefato decano de Arcubus prefatos Radulfum et Emmam executores testamenti predicti Thome traxerunt in placitum occasione illius legati ipsis Roberto, Alicie, et Juliane post mortem predicti testatoris non soluti quousque predicti executores regiam prohibitionem eis inde porrexerunt ne ipsi placitum de catallis et debitis que non sunt de testamento vel matrimonio sequerentur in curia christianitatis etc., occasione cuius brevis iidem Robertus, Alicia, et Juliana a prosequendo supersederunt quousque per consultationem inde habitam per R Brabazun licitum fuit eis predictum placitum de legato suo predicto consequendo ulterius prosequi in curia christianitatis etc. Et bene defendunt quod ipsi nuncquam aliquod aliud placitum in curia christianitatis secuti sunt versus predictos executores nisi tantum de predictis triginta marcis sibi ut predictum est legatis etc. Et de hoc ponunt se super patriam. Et Radulfus et Emma similiter. Et quia predicti Radulfus et Emma dicunt quod placitum fuit secutum in Arcubus Lond' etc. preceptum est vicecomitibus Lond' quod venire faciant hic a die sancti Michaelis in tres septimanas xij etc. de visnetu de Arcubus Lond' per quos etc. Et qui nec etc. Quia tam etc.

Postea in crastino Purificationis beate Marie anno regis nunc vicesimo sexto veniunt partes. Et similiter juratores de consensu partium electi, qui dicunt super sacramentum suum quod predictus Thomas pater predictorum Roberti, Alicie, et Juliane aliquo tempore condidit quoddam testamentum in quo testamento legavit prefatis Roberto, Alicie, et Juliane viginti libras qui quidem Thomas postea convaluit et prefatis Roberto, Alicie, et Juliana [i]<quemdam>[i] redditum loco legati predicti contulit et cuilibet eorum custodem assignavit per quam assignationem et predicti redditus collationem prefatum testamentum

[1] MS. reads capiendo
[2] MS. reads ipsum
[3] In the margin at this point are written 12 dots and misericordia (stricken through).

de Nassington[1] concerning 30 marks that are not testamentary or matrimonial and, on the Wednesday before Palm Sunday in the twenty-fourth year of this king's reign[2] in the church of St Mary-le-Bow, London, in the presence of Richard de Hecham and Stephen de Hereford, Ralph and Emma delivered to them a royal prohibition that they should not sue the plea further etc., Roger and the others nevertheless sued that plea in the same court until Ralph and Emma were excommunicated at their suit etc. And later, while the prohibition plea was pending here between them, they nevertheless continued to sue the plea, whereby Ralph and Emma were excommunicated, and they obtained the king's writ for arresting the bodies of Ralph and Emma, to the wrong of the king's crown and dignity etc. They say they are thereby harmed and damaged to the value of 40 pounds. And they produce suit etc.

And Roger, Robert (by his guardian), Alice and Juliana appear and deny force and wrong whenever etc. And Roger denies that he ever sued the plea in Court Christian on the day and year as is alleged against him. And this he is prepared to deny against them and their suit as the court should adjudge etc. Therefore it is adjudged that he is to wage his law twelve-handed etc. And Roger immediately makes his law etc. Therefore Roger is without day. And Ralph and Emma are in mercy for the false claim etc.

And Robert, Alice, and Juliana who are underage etc. say that their father Thomas le Lyndraper in his last will left to Robert, Alice and Juliana 30 marks etc. And Robert, Alice and Juliana drew Ralph and Emma as executors of Thomas's testament into a plea before the dean of the court of Arches by reason of that legacy, which was not paid to them after the testator's death, until the executors delivered a royal prohibition to them that they should not sue a plea concerning chattels and debts not testamentary or matrimonial in Court Christian etc. And on account of that writ Robert, Alice and Juliana ceased prosecution until they were allowed by a consultation, obtained from Roger Brabazon,[3] to resume prosecution in Court Christian of their plea concerning their legacy etc. And they deny that they ever sued any other plea in Court Christian against the executors other than concerning the 30 marks left to them by will etc. And concerning this they put themselves on the country. And Ralph and Emma likewise. And because Ralph and Emma say that the plea was sued in the court of Arches, London etc., the sheriffs of London are ordered to cause to appear here three weeks after Michaelmas 12 etc. from the vicinity of St Mary-le-Bow, London, through whom etc. and who do not etc. Because both parties etc.

Later on the morrow of the Purification of Mary in the twenty-sixth year of this king's reign[4] the parties appear. And likewise the jurors chosen by consent of the parties, who say on their oath that Thomas, father of Robert, Alice and Juliana, at one time made a will in which he left a legacy to Robert, Alice and Juliana of 20 pounds and Thomas later recovered and granted to Robert, Alice and Juliana a certain rent in place of the former legacy and assigned a guardian to each of them, by which assignment and grant of rent he completely revoked the earlier will and legacy. And they say further that Thomas, later

[1] Henry de Nassington was appointed dean of the Court of Arches in May 1295. Previously he had served as official of Lincoln from as early as 1286 until at least 1293. Canterbury Cases 634 n. 3.

[2] 14 March 1296.

[3] Appointed justice of King's Bench in 1290 and elevated to chief justice of that court in 1295, where he served until 1316.

[4] 3 February 1298.

et prius legatum penitus revocavit. Et dicunt ulterius quod idem Thomas postea quadam infirmitate detentus condidit quoddam testamentum in quo legavit prefatis Roberto, Alicie, et Juliane cuilibet eorum viginti solidos de quibus eis satisfactum est in quo testamento prefatos Radulfum et Emmam constituit executores. Et dicunt ulterius quod prefati Robertus, Alicia, et Juliana secuti fuerunt predictum placitum tanquam testamentum per virtutem primi legati et non tanquam debitum. Quesiti se prefati Robertus, Alicia, et Juliana sequebantur placitum predictum post prohibitionem eis liberatam dicunt quod sic, quia dicunt quod prefati Radulfus et Emma liberaverunt eis prohibitionem regiam in ecclesia beate Marie de Arcubus die mercurii proxima ante festum palmarum anno regis nunc vicesimo quarto post cuius admissionem secuti fuerunt versus eos per sentenciam excommunicationis a tempore illo usque festum sancti Johannis Baptiste proximo sequens, infra quod tempus mandatum fuit ad curiam domini regis pro brevi de captione impetranda. Et dicunt ulterius quod ad Pascha anno regis nunc vicesimo quinto adierunt dominum Rogerum Brabazoun pro consultatione habenda, ob quam consultationem secuti sunt placitum predictum asserentes illam consultationem tacita veritate primi processus in foro ecclesiastico prodesse.[1] Quesiti si ad sectam predictorum Roberti, Alicie, et Juliana prefati Radulfus et Emma capti fuerunt et imprisonati, dicunt quod non. Dies datus est eis de audiendo judicio suo hic in crastino sancti Johannis Baptiste eo quod judicium nondum etc.

1.23b

CP 40/118, m. 51d
Common Pleas, Easter term 1297

Midd'. Magister Henricus de Nassington attachiatus fuit ad respondendum Radulfo de Honylane et Emme de Honylane de placito quare ipse simul cum Roberto archiepiscopo Cantuar' tenuit placitum in curia christianitatis de catallis et debitis que non sunt de testamento vel matrimonio contra prohibitionem etc. Et unde iidem Radulfus et Emma per attornatum suum queruntur quod cum Rogerus de Arderne, Robertus filius Thomae Lyndraper, Alicia et Juliana sorores eiusdem Roberti traxissent ipsos Radulfum et Emmam in placitum in curia christianitatis coram prefatis archiepiscopo et magistro Henrico de triginta marcis que non sunt de testamento vel matrimonio etc. et ipsi die mercurii proxima ante Pascha Floridum anno regni domini regis nunc vicesimo quarto in ecclesia beate Marie de Arcubus London' in presencia Ricardi de Hocham et Stephani de Hereford porrexissent eidem magistro Henrico regiam prohibitionem ne predictum placitum tenetur in curia christianitatis etc. idem magister Henricus similiter etc. spreta prohibitione illa nichilominus tenuit placitum illud in eadem curia et fecit ipsos suspendi ab ingressu ecclesie et postea excommunicari in contemptum domini regis etc. Unde [dicunt][2] quod

[1] In the margin is written ad judicium
[2] MS. reads dicit

weakened by an infirmity, made a will in which he named Ralph and Emma his executors and left legacies of 20 shillings each to Robert, Alice and Juliana, which have been satisfied. And they say further that Robert, Alice and Juliana sued the plea in Court Christian by virtue of the first testamentary legacy and not on account of a debt. Asked if Robert, Alice and Juliana sued that plea after a prohibition had been delivered to them, they say yes, because Ralph and Emma delivered a royal prohibition to them in the church of St Mary-le-Bow on the Wednesday before Palm Sunday in the twenty-fourth year of this king's reign,[1] after the receipt of which they continued their suit against them seeking a sentence of excommunication from that time until the feast of St John the Baptist next following,[2] during which time the lord king's court was written to asking for a writ of caption. And they say further that at Easter in the twenty-fifth year of this king's reign[3] they went to lord Roger Brabazoun for a consultation, on account of which they sued the aforesaid plea relying on the consultation but keeping silent regarding the first proceeding in the ecclesiastical forum. Asked if Ralph and Emma were arrested and imprisoned at the suit of Robert, Alice and Juliana, they say no. Day is given them to hear their judgment here on the morrow of St John the Baptist because judgment has not yet etc.

1.23b

RALPH AND EMMA DE HONYLANE v. HENRY DE NASSINGTON

Middlesex. Master Henry de Nassington was attached to answer Ralph de Honylane and Emma de Honylane concerning a plea as to why he together with Robert, archbishop of Canterbury, held a plea in Court Christian concerning chattels and debts that are not testamentary or matrimonial, contrary to prohibition etc. And in this regard Ralph and Emma by their attorney complain that when Roger de Arderne, Robert, son of Thomas Lyndraper, Alice and Juliana, sisters of Robert, drew Ralph and Emma into a plea in Court Christian before the archbishop and master Henry concerning 30 marks that are not testamentary or matrimonial etc. and, on the Wednesday before Palm Sunday in the twenty-fourth year of this king's reign[4] in the church of St Mary-le-Bow, London, in the presence of Richard de Hocham and Stephen de Hereford, they presented a royal prohibition to master Henry that he should not hold the plea in Court Christian etc., scorning that prohibition master Henry nevertheless held that plea in that court and caused them to be suspended from the church

[1] 14 March 1296.
[2] 24 June 1296.
[3] 14 April 1297.
[4] 14 March 1296.

deteriorati sunt et dampnum habent ad valenciam mille marcarum. Et unde [producunt][1] sectam etc.

Et magister Henricus venit et defendit vim et injuriam quando etc. et quicquid etc. Et bene defendit quod ipse non tenuit aliquod placitum in curia christianitatis de laicis catallis predictorum Radulfi et Emme contra prohibitionem etc. Et hoc paratus est defendere contra ipsos et sectam suam sicut curia consideraverit. Ideo consideratum est quod vadiat eis legem suam se duodecima manu. Plegii de lege Henricus de Sutton’ et Ricardus de Assheby. Et idem magister Henricus instanter fecit eis legem suam. Ideo consideratum est quod predictus magister Henricus inde sine die. Et quod predicti Radulfus et Emma nichil capiant etc. set sint in misericordia pro falso clamore etc.[2]

1.23c

CP 40/119, m. 98d
Common Pleas, Trinity term 1297

Lond’. Magister Henricus de Nassington attachiatus fuit ad respondendum domino regi de placito quare cum idem magister Henricus nuper in curia hic attachiatus esset ad respondendum Radulfo de Hunylane et Emme de Hunylane de placito quare tenuit placitum in curia christianitatis de catallis predictorum Radulfi et Emme que non sunt de testamento vel matrimonio contra prohibitionem regis etc. idem magister Henricus pendente inter eos in curia hic predicto placito nichilominus placitum illud ulterius tenuit in curia christianitatis quousque sentencia excommunicationis in ipsos Radulfum et Emmam promulgata ipsos excommunicare fecit in corone et dignitatis domini regis lesionem et curie regis hic contemptum etc. Et unde Nicholaus [i]<de Warr’>[i] qui sequitur pro rege etc. dicit quod predictus magister Henricus pendente predicto placito in curia hic de eo quare idem magister Henricus tenuit predictum placitum de predictis catallis etc. in curia christianitatis contra prohibitionem etc. nichilominus placitum illud ulterius tenuit in eadem curia christianitatis quousque etc. in corone et dignitatis regis lesionem etc. et in contemptum ipsius regis centum librarum etc.

Et magister Henricus venit et defendit vim et injuriam etc. Et dicit quod ipse alias in curia hic ad sectam predictorum Radulfi et Emme venit et vadiavit eisdem Raldulfo et Emme legem suam quod ipse nuncquam tenuit predictum placitum de predictis catallis etc. in curia christianitatis etc. quam legem idem Henricus postea fecit in curia hic per quod consideratum fuit quod idem Henricus iret sine die. Et ex quo predictum placitum ad quod ipse modo attachiatus est ad respondendum domino regi in hac parte etc. sumit originem suum de predicto placito de predictis catallis ipsorum Radulfi et Emme quod quidem placitum de predictis catallis est principale etc. petit judicium si de placito isto ad sectam regis etc. quod est accessorium etc. respondere debeat.

[1] MS. reads producit
[2] In the margin are written lex (stricken through) and 12 dots and misericordia (also stricken through).

and later excommunicated in contempt of the lord king etc. They say they are thereby harmed and damaged to the value of 1000 marks. And they produce suit etc.

And master Henry appears and denies force and wrong whenever etc. and whatever etc. He completely denies that he ever held any plea in Court Christian concerning the lay chattels of Ralph and Emma contrary to prohibition etc. And this he is prepared to deny against them and their suit as the court may adjudge. Therefore it is adjudged that he is to wage his law twelve-handed. Pledges for his law Henry of Sutton and Richard of Ashby. And master Henry makes his law immediately. Therefore it is adjudged that master Henry be without day and that Ralph and Emma take nothing etc. but are in mercy for their false claim etc.

1.23c

THE KING AND RALPH AND EMMA DE HUNYLANE v. HENRY DE NASSINGTON

London. Master Henry de Nassington was attached to answer the lord king concerning a plea as to why, since master Henry recently was attached to answer Ralph de Hunylane and Emma de Hunylane in this court concerning a plea as to why he held a plea in Court Christian concerning the chattels of Ralph and Emma that were not testamentary or matrimonial, contrary to the king's prohibition etc., master Henry, while that plea was pending between them here in this court, nevertheless continued to hear the plea in Court Christian until sentence of excommunication was promulgated against Ralph and Emma, to the wrong of the lord king's crown and dignity and in contempt of the king's court here etc. And in this regard Nicholas de Warr'[1] who sues for the king etc. says that master Henry, while the plea was pending in this court concerning why master Henry held the plea concerning the chattels etc. in Court Christian contrary to prohibition etc., nevertheless continued to hold that plea in Court Christian until etc., to the wrong of the king's crown and dignity and in contempt of the king 100 pounds etc.

And master Henry appears and denies force and wrong etc. And he says that at another time he was sued in this court by Ralph and Emma and appeared and waged his law against them, to the effect that he never held the plea concerning their chattels etc. in Court Christian etc., which law he later made in this court, as a result of which it was adjudged that Henry go without day.[2] And since the plea on account of which he now is attached to answer to the lord king etc. has its origin in the plea concerning the chattels of Ralph and Emma, which plea concerning those chattels is the principal action etc., he prays judgment whether he ought to have to answer concerning this plea at the king's suit, which is accessory etc.

And Nicholas de Warwick who sues etc. says that, while the prohibition plea was pending in this court between these parties, master Henry was forbidden by the king's writ

[1] Nicholas de Warrewyk was a King's serjeant.

[2] Case no. 123b.

Et Nicholaus de Warr' qui sequitur etc. dicit quod pendente predicto placito prohibitionis etc. in curia hic inter partes predictas inhibitum fuit predicto magistro Henrico per breve regis de judicio etc. ne idem magister Henricus predictum placitum de catallis etc. in curia christianitatis teneret etc., qui quidem Henricus in contemptum domini regis prefatos Radulfum et Emmam postmodum excommunicavit etc. in corone et dignitatis lesionem etc. Et hoc paratus est verificare per patriam pro domino rege etc. unde cum predictus magister Henricus se excusare non potest quin predictum breve de judicio recepit et post receptionem eiusdem brevis predictos Radulfum et Emmam excommunicavit ut predictum est, petit judicium etc. Dies datus est eis hic a die sancti Michaelis in tres septimas de audiendo [judicio][1] suo etc. salvis utrique parti rationibus suis alias proponendis etc.

Postea ad diem illum datus est eis dies de audiendo judicio suo hic in crastino Purificationis Beate Marie etc.

Postea ad diem illum datus est eis dies de audiendo judicio hic in crastino sancti Johannis Baptiste etc. Ad quem diem loquela predicta remansit sine die per absenciam justiciariorum etc.

Postea predicta loquela resummonita etc. in crastino Purificationis beate Marie anno regis nunc xxix apud Ebor' venit predictus Nicholaus qui sequitur pro rege et similiter predictus magister Henricus per attornatum suum. Et datus est eis dies de audiendo judicio suo hic a die Pasche in tres septimanas etc.

Postea ad diem illum venit predictus Nicholaus qui sequitur etc. et similiter predictus magister Henricus per attornatum suum. Et dies datus est eis dies de audiendo judicio suo hic a die sancte Trinitatis in xv dies etc. Ad quem diem datus est eis dies de audiendo judicio suo hic a die sancti Michaelis in xv dies etc.

1.23d

CP 40/121, m. 263d
Common Pleas, Michaelmas term, 1297

Midd'. Robertus filius Thome le Lyndraper, Alicia et Juliana sorores eiusdem Roberti attachiati fuerunt per breve de judicio ad respondendum domino regi de eo quare, cum Robertus archiepiscopus Cantuar', Rogerus de Ardern, et predicti Robertus, Alicia, et Juliana nuper hic attachiati essent ad respondendum Radulfo de Honilane et Emme de Honilane de placito quare predictus archiepiscopus simul cum magistro Henrico de Nassington tenuit placitum in curia christianitatis de catallis et debitis ipsorum Radulfi et Emme que non sunt de testamento vel matrimonio et de placito quare predicti Rogerus de Arderne, Robertus, Alicia, et Juliana secuti fuerunt idem placitum in eadem curia christianitatis contra prohibitiones regis eis inde prius porrectas, idem archiepiscopus simul cum prefato magistro Henrico pendente in curia regis hic predicto placito inter eos nichilominus ulterius tenuit predictum placitum de predictis debitis et catallis et similiter idem

[1] MS. omits.

of judgment etc. that he should not hold the plea concerning the chattels etc. in Court Christian etc., but Henry in contempt of the lord king thereafter excommunicated Ralph and Emma, to the wrong of the king's crown and dignity etc. And this he is prepared to prove by the country for the lord king etc. And in this regard, since master Henry cannot excuse himself on the ground that he did not receive the writ of judgment and after receipt of that writ excommunicated Ralph and Emma, he prays judgment etc. Day is given them here three weeks after Michaelmas for the hearing of their judgment etc., saving to both parties their reasons to be propounded at another time etc.

Later, on that day,[1] day is given them for hearing their judgment here on the morrow of the Purification of Mary etc.

Later, on that day,[2] day is given them for hearing their judgment here on the morrow of St John the Baptist etc. On which day,[3] the case remains without day on account of the justices' absence etc.

Later, the case having been resumed etc. on the morrow of the Purification of Mary in the thirtieth year of this king's reign[4] at York, Nicholas who sues for the king and likewise master Henry by his attorney appear. And day is given them for hearing their judgment here three weeks after Easter etc.

Later on that day,[5] Nicholas who sues etc. and likewise master Henry by his attorney appear. And day is given them for hearing their judgment here on the quindene of Trinity etc. On which day,[6] day is given them for hearing their judgment here on the quindene of Michaelmas etc.

1.23d

THE KING AND RALPH AND EMMA DE HONILANE v. ROBERT LE LYNDRAPER AND OTHERS

Middlesex. Robert, son of Thomas le Lyndraper, and Alice and Juliana, Robert's sisters, were attached by writ of judgment to answer the lord king as to why, whereas Robert, archbishop of Canterbury, Roger de Ardern, and Robert, Alic, and Juliana were recently attached to answer here to Ralph de Honilane and Emma de Honilane concerning a plea as to why the archbishop together with master Henry de Nassington held a plea in Court Christian concerning Ralph's and Emma's chattels and debts that were not testamentary or matrimonial and concerning a plea as to why Roger de Ardern, Robert, Alice and Juliana sued that plea in the same Court Christian contrary to the king's prohibitions previously delivered to them in that regard, the archbishop together with master Henry, while the plea against them was pending here in the king's court, nevertheless continued to hold the

[1] 21 October 1297. [2] 3 February 1298. [3] 25 June 1299. [4] 3 February 1302.
[5] 14 May 1302. [6] 2 July 1302.

Rogerus, Robertus, Alicia, et Juliana secuti fuerunt idem placitum in prefata curia christianitatis quousque idem archiepiscopus simul cum magistro Henrico predictos Radulfum et Emmam ad sectam ipsorum Rogeri, Roberti, Alicie, et Juliane excommunicari fecit et postea breve regis de capiendo predictos Radulfum et Emmam tanquam claves ecclesie contempnentes vicecomiti porrexit in corone et dignitatis regis lesionem et curie regis contemptum et ipsorum Radulfi et Emme dispendium non modicum etc. Et unde Willelmus de Claveryng qui sequitur pro domino rege dicit quod, cum predicti Radulphus et Emma hic inplacitassent predictos Rogerum, Robertum, Aliciam, et Julianam quare ipsi secuti fuissent placitum in curia christianitatis de catallis et debitis que non sunt de testamento vel matrimonio ac iidem Robertus, Alicia, et Juliana pendente predicto placito hic inter eos traxissent ipsos Radulfum et Emmam in placitum in curia christianitatis coram predictis archiepiscopo et magistro Henrico in ecclesia de Arcubus London exigendo ab eis triginta marcas que non sunt de testamento vel matrimonio ac idem Radulphus die mercurii proxima ante Pascha Floridum anno regni regis nunc vicesimo quarto ad pontem de Flete in presencia Ricardi de Hecham, Stephani de Hereford, et aliorum tradidisset eis regiam prohibitionem ne placitum illud ulterius sequerentur, iidem Robertus et alii simul cum predicto Rogero pendente predicto placito hic inter eos spreta regia prohibitione placitum illud ulterius secuti fuerunt quousque iidem Radulfus et Emma excommunicati fuerunt ad sectam ipsorum Roberti et aliorum, in contemptum huius curie et domini regis mille marcarum et hoc paratus est verificare etc.

Et Robertus filius Thome, Alicia, et Juliana per custodem suum veniunt et defendunt vim et injuriam quando etc. Et dicunt quod ipsi nuncquam [pendente][1] predicto placito secuti fuerunt placitum de predicto debito in curia christianitatis sicut eis inponit. Et de hoc ponunt se super patriam. Et Willelmus qui sequitur similiter. Ideo preceptum est vicecomitibus Lond' quod venire faciant hic in crastino Purificationis beate Marie xij de [i]<visneto>[i] [parochie][2] de Arcubus Lond' per quos etc. Et qui etc. ad recognoscendum etc. Quia etc.

Postea in crastino Purificationis beate Marie anno regis nunc vicesimo sexto veniunt partes. Et similiter juratores de consensu partium electi, qui dicunt super sacramentum suum quod predicti Roberti, Alicia, et Juliana secuti fuerunt predictum placitum in prefata curia christianitatis pendente inde inter eos in prefata curia hic predicto placito. Dies datus est eis de audiendo judicio suo hic in crastino sancti Johannis Baptiste etc. eo quod judicium nondum etc.[3]

1.23e

CP 40/136, m. 72d
Common Pleas, Hilary term 1301

Midd'. Rogerus de Arderne in misericordia pro pluribus defaltis.

[1] MS. reads pendende [2] MS. reads parochia [3] In the margin is written ad judicium

plea in Court Christian and likewise Roger, Robert, Alice and Juliana continued to sue that plea until the archbishop together with master Henry caused Ralph and Emma to be excommunicated at the suit of Roger, Robert, Alice and Juliana and later delivered a writ to the sheriff for the arrest of Ralph and Emma as contemnors of the keys of the church, to the wrong of the king's crown and dignity and in contempt of the king's court and not insignificant harm to Ralph and Emma etc. And in this regard William de Claveryng who sues for the lord king says that, whereas Ralph and Emma impleaded Roger, Robert, Alice and Juliana in this court concerning why they sued a plea in Court Christian concerning chattels and debts that are not testamentary or matrimonial and Robert, Alice and Juliana, while that the plea was pending in this court, drew Ralph and Emma into a plea in Court Christian before the archbishop and master Henry in the church of St Mary-le-Bow, London, demanding of them 30 marks that are not testamentary or matrimonial, and Ralph, on the Wednesday before Palm Sunday in the twenty-fourth year of this king's reign[1] at the Fleet Bridge[2] in the presence of Richard de Hecham, Stephen de Hereford and others delivered to them a royal prohibition that they should not sue that plea further, Robert and others together with Roger, while the plea was pending here between them, scorned the royal prohibition and continued to sue that plea until Ralph and Emma were excommunicated at the suit of Robert and the others, in contempt of this court and of the lord king 1000 marks. And this he is prepared to prove etc.

And Robert son of Thomas, Alice and Juliana by their guardian appear and deny force and wrong whenever etc. And they say that they never sued a plea concerning this debt in Court Christian while the plea against them was pending here, as is alleged against them. And concerning this they put themselves upon the country. And William who sues for the king likewise. Therefore the sheriffs of London are ordered to cause to appear here on the morrow of the Purification of Mary 12 of the parish of St Mary-le-Bow, London, through whom etc. and who are not etc. in order to give their verdict etc. Because etc.

Later on the morrow of the Purification of Mary in the twenty-sixth year of this king's reign[3] the parties appear. And likewise the jurors chosen by consent of the parties, who say on their oath that Robert, Alice and Juliana sued the plea in Court Christian while the plea between them was pending here in this court. Day is given them for hearing their judgment here on the morrow of St John the Baptist etc. because judgment is not yet etc.

1.23e

RALPH DE HONYLANE v. ROGER DE ARDERNE

Middlesex. Roger de Arderne is in mercy for many defaults.

[1] 14 March 1296.
[2] A bridge over the Fleet River between Fleet Street and Ludgate Hill.
[3] 3 February 1298.

Idem Rogerus attachiatus fuit ad respondendum Radulfo de Honylane de placito quare ipse simul cum Roberto filio Thome le Lyndraper, Juliana et Alicia sororibus eiusdem Roberti secutus est placitum in curia christianitatis de catallis et debitis que non sunt de testamento vel matrimonio contra prohibitionem regis etc. Et unde idem Radulfus per attornatum suum queritur quod cum predictus Rogerus simul etc. traxisset ipsum in placitum in ecclesia beate Marie de Arcubus London' coram decano de Arcubus etc. exigendo ab ipso viginti libras que non sunt de testamento vel matrimonio etc. ac idem Radulfus die sancti Mathie apostoli anno regni regis nunc vicesimo octavo in prefata ecclesia porrexisset eidem Rogero et aliis prohibitionem regiam in presencia Ricardi de Watford, Johannis Hamund, Thome le Calicer, Radulfi le Coteler, Johannis Bogeys et Rogeri le Fever ne ulterius sequerentur idem placitum in eadem curia christianitatis etc., idem Rogerus simul etc. nichilominus secutus fuit idem placitum in prefata curia christianitatis contra prohibitionem etc. Unde dicit quod deterioratus est et dampnum habet ad valenciam quadraginta librarum. Et inde producit sectam etc.

Et Rogerus per attornatum suum venit et defendit vim et injuriam quando etc. Et bene defendit quod ipse nunquam secutus fuit predictum placitum in prefata curia christianitatis contra prohibitionem regis etc. Et hoc paratus est verificare contra ipsum et sectam suam sicut curia consideraverit etc. Ideo consideratum est quod vadiat ei inde legem etc. se duodecima manu etc. Et veniat in propria persona sua cum lege sua hic a die Pasche in tres septimanas etc. per P.M. Plegii de lege Ricardus de Essheby de comitatu Leyc' et Radulfus Peny de comitatu Midd' etc.

Postea a die sancte Trinitatis in xv dies anno regni regis nunc vicesimo nono veniunt partes etc. Et predictus Rogerus fecit legem suam etc. Ideo idem Rogerus inde sine die. Et predictus Radulfus nichil capiat per breve suum set sit in misericordia pro falso clamore etc.[1]

1.24

CP 40/125, m. 153
Common Pleas, Michaelmas term 1298

Kanc' Preceptum fuit vicecomiti quod, cum Sabina de Grove traxisset Hugonem le Blak in placitum in curia christianitatis coram magistro Willelmo de Gloucester et magistro Willelmo de Chadeleshunte de catallis et debitis que non sunt de testamento vel matrimonio et idem Hugo litteras regis de prohibitione prefatis Willelmo et Willelmo porrexisset ne placitum illud ulterius tenerent in eadem curia qui quidem Willelmus et Willelmus nichilominus idem placitum tenuerunt in curia predicta per quod rex ipsos Willelmum et Willelmum postea per breve suum ad prosecutionem predicti Hugonis vicecomiti directum prout moris est in regno regis attachiare precepisset quod essent coram justiciariis regis apud Westm' a die Pasche in xv dies proximo preteritos ostensuri quare tenuerunt

[1] In the margin are written lex and 12 dots and misericordia (stricken through).

Roger was attached to answer Ralph de Honylane concerning a plea as to why he together with Robert, son of Thomas the Lyndraper, and Juliana and Alice, Robert's sisters, sued a plea in Court Christian concerning chattels and debts that are not testamentary or matrimonial, contrary to the king's prohibition etc. And in this regard Ralph by his attorney complains that, whereas Roger together with etc. drew him into a plea in the church of St Mary-le-Bow, London, before the dean of the court of Arches etc., demanding of him 20 pounds that are not testamentary or matrimonial etc., and Ralph on the day of St Matthew the Apostle in the twenty-eighth year of this king's reign[1] in that church delivered to Roger and the others a royal prohibition in the presence of Richard de Watford, John Hamund, Thomas le Calicer, Ralph le Coteler, John Bogeys and Roger le Fever that they should not sue the plea further in Court Christian etc., Roger together with etc. nevertheless sued that plea in Court Christian contrary to prohibition etc. And he says he is thereby harmed and damaged to the value of 40 pounds. And he produces suit etc.

And Roger by his attorney appears and denies force and wrong whenever etc. And he denies that he ever sued the plea in Court Christian contrary to the king's prohibition etc. And this he is prepared to prove against him and his suit as the court shall adjudge etc. Therefore it is adjudged that he is to wage his law etc. twelve-handed etc. And let him appear here in person with his law three weeks after Easter etc. as authorised by Peter Mallore.[2] Pledges for his law Richard of Ashby of Leicestershire and Ralph Peny of Middlesex etc.

Later on the quindene of Trinity in the twenty-ninth year of this king's reign[3] the parties appear etc. And Roger makes his law etc. Therefore Roger is without day in this matter. And Ralph is to take nothing by his writ but shall be in mercy for the false claim etc.

1.24

HUGH LE BLAK v. SABINA DE GROVE

Kent. Whereas Sabina de Grove drew Hugh le Blak into a plea in Court Christian before master William de Gloucester and master William de Chadeleshunte concerning chattels and debts that are not testamentary or matrimonial, and Hugh delivered the king's letters of prohibition to William and William that they should not hear that plea further in that court, and William and William nevertheless heard the plea in that court, on account of which the king at Hugh's prosecution by royal writ to the sheriff as is customary in the king's realm ordered him to attach William and William to be before the king's justices at Westminster on the most recent quindene of Easter to show why they heard the plea in Court Christian

[1] 24 February 1300. [2] Meaning that the special return day in the adjournment has been authorised by Mallore, one of the justices of the court. [3] 12 June 1301.

predictum placitum in curia christianitatis contra prohibitionem regis ac iidem Willelmus et Willelmus occasione predicti brevis regis de attachiamento predicto coram prefatis justiciariis regis apud Westm' ad prefatam quindenam Pasche retornati prefatum Hugonem tanquam excommunicatum et claves ecclesie contempnentem per breve regis ad denunciationem venerabilis patris archiepiscopi Cantuar' super hoc impetratum per vicecomitem capi et in prisona regis de Maydenstan detineri maliciose procurassent ut sic eum inpedire possent quo minus placitum attachiamenti predicti coram prefatis justiciariis regis secundum legem et consuetudinem regni regis prosequi, in ipsius Hugonis dispendium non modicum et regis contemptum manifestum etc. Et vicecomiti iterato preceptum fuisset quod ipsum Hugonem si ea occasione et non alia detentus fuisset in prisona predicta sine dilatione deliberari faceret quousque placitum attachiamenti predicti inter eos terminatum fuisset secundum legem et consuetudinem regni regis. Et qualiter illud preceptum fuisset executus scire faceret justiciariis hic a die sancte Trinitatis in xv dies proximo preteritos etc. Idem vicecomes in executione precepti regis quod sibi inde venit necgligenter se gerens justiciariis hic ad diem illum mandavit quod predictus Hugo detentus fuit in prisona predicta pro offensa commissa in causa matrimoniali eo quod noluit uxorem suam matrimoniali affectione pertractare. Et quia ex parte ipsius Hugonis conquerendo graviter regi ostensum fuit quod idem Hugo captus et inprisonatus fuit pro eo quod prosecutus fuit placitum attachiamenti predicti et non ob aliquam aliam causam per quod preceptum fuit vicecomiti sicut prius quod ipsum Hugonem si ea occasione et non alia detentus fuisset etc. sine dilatione deliberari faceret quousque placitum attachiamenti predicti inde inter eos terminaretur secundum legem etc. Et qualiter etc. scire faceret hic ad hunc diem etc. Et vicecomes modo mandat quod preceperat ballivis libertatis archiepiscopi Cantuar' qui sibi respondent quod predictus Hugo detinetur in prisona pro offensa commissa in causa matrimoniali eo quod [noluit][1] uxorem suam matrimoniali affectione pertractare et non propter aliquam aliam causam etc. Et quia testatum est hic et pupplicum esse dicitur et notorium quod predicti Willelmus et Willelmus sunt clerici familiares predicti archiepiscopi et commissarii sui in causarum cognitionibus et aliis negotiis exequendis vices ipsius archiepiscopi gerentes et ea occasione predicta responsio ballivorum libertatis predicti archiepiscopi prefatis Willelmo et Willelmo faventium est suspecta ac huiusmodi placitum prohibitionis etc. coronam et dignitatem regiam specialiter tangit per quod curia regis prefato Hugoni conquerenti ad predictam maliciam si perpetrata fuerit convincendam potius debet assistere quatenus absque offenso juris et libertatis ecclesiastice lesione fuerit faciendum. Et tam iuri quam equitati esset inconsonum quod querela predicti inprisonati occasione predicti inprisonamenti expiraret absque remedio eidem inde faciendo ne quod absit contra tenorem Magne Carte de libertatibus Anglie ei de recto seu iusticia facienda deficiat curia regis et presertim in hoc casu cum ad denunciationem predicti archiepiscopi prefatus Hugo captus sit et in prisona infra libertatem archiepiscopi detentus etc. Et forsan predictus archiepiscopus causam suam curie regis scribendi de prefato Hugone capiendo sumpsit de facto processu seu suggestione predictorum Willelmi et Willelmi qui sunt prefato Hugoni pars adversa, preceptum est vicecomiti quod sub salvo et securo conductu etc. habeat prefatum Hugonem hic in octabis sancti Hillarii etc. querelam suam prosecuturus etc. Et de predictis Willelmo et Willelmo mandatum fuit archiepiscopo

[1] MS. reads non

contrary to the king's prohibition, and William and William on account of the king's writ of attachment maliciously procured at the denunciation of the venerable father Robert, archbishop of Canterbury,[1] to have the sheriff arrest Hugh by the king's writ as excommunicate and contemnor of the key's of the church and detain him in the prison of Maidstone so that they might be able to impede him from prosecuting his plea of attachment on the prohibition before the king's justices according to the law and custom of the king's realm, to Hugh's not insignificant harm and in manifest contempt of the king etc., the sheriff was ordered that, if Hugh was detained in prison on this account and no other he should without delay cause him to be delivered until the plea of attachment between them should be concluded according to the law and custom of the king's realm; and he was to inform the justices here as to how that order was executed on the most recent quindene of Trinity etc. And the sheriff in execution of the king's order in this matter, conducting himself negligently, on that day informed the justices here that Hugh was detained in prison for a matrimonial offence in that he would not treat his wife with marital affection. And because by grave complaints on Hugh's behalf it was shown to the king that Hugh was arrested and imprisoned because he prosecuted the plea of attachment, and not for any other cause, the sheriff was ordered as before that if for this reason and no other he had been detained etc. without delay he should cause him to be delivered until the plea of attachment between them might be concluded according to law etc.; and how etc. he should inform the justices here on this day etc. And the sheriff now states that he so ordered the bailiffs of the liberty of the archbishop of Canterbury who answered him that Hugh is detained in prison for an offence committed in a matrimonial cause, in that he does not treat his wife with marital affection, and for no other cause etc. And because it is attested here and is said to be public and notorious knowledge that William and William are clerks of the archbishop's household and his commissaries acting in the archbishop's place in the hearing of causes and execution of other matters, and for that reason the answer of the bailiffs of the archbishop's liberty is suspected of favour to William and William, and because a plea of prohibition of this kind etc. especially touches the royal dignity, it is appropriate that the king's court assist Hugh the complainant in demonstrating this malice, if it was perpetrated, insofar as is possible without causing offence to right and also wrong to ecclesiastical liberty.[2] And it would be inconsonant both with right and with equity that the prisoner's complaint should expire without remedy on account of this imprisonment, and it would be contrary to the tenor of the Great Charter of the liberties of England if the king's court should be deficient in doing right or justice to him, and especially in this case in which Hugh was arrested by the archbishop's denunciation and is detained in prison within the archbishop's liberty etc. And perhaps the archbishop followed his own interests in writing to the king's court to arrest Hugh concerning the action, process or suggestion of William and William, who are adverse parties to Hugh. Therefore, the sheriff is ordered to have Hugh here under

[1] Robert Winchelsey was consecrated archbishop of Canterbury in 1294 and served until his death in 1313.

[2] The record of the sheriff's earlier response referred to here notes that the bailiffs' response was also challenged on the ground that the asserted matrimonial offence was punishable by excommunication but was not a ground for imprisonment: 'predicta responsio quam predicti ballivi fecerunt etc. minus sufficiens est in hoc quod respondent predictus Hugo detinetur in prisona pro offensa commissa in causa matrimoniali etc. cum huiusmodi offensa sit causa sentencie excommunicationis late etc. et non causa inprisonamenti etc.' This record is found at CP 40/124, m. 22d (1298).

Cantuar' quod venire faceret eos hic ad hunc diem. Et archiepiscopus nichil inde fecit. Ideo preceptum est vicecomiti quod attachiat predictum archiepiscopum quod sit hic ad prefatum terminum. Et hic habeat predictos Willelmum et Willelmum clericos suos ad respondendum predicto Hugoni de predicto placito etc.[1]

1.25a

CP 40/146, m. 136
Common Pleas, Hilary term 1303

Norff' Magister Rogerus de Felethorp' et Henricus de Wramplingham persona ecclesie Omnium Sanctorum de Suthpikenham attachiati fuerunt ad respondendum Henrico Child de Houton' de placito quare predictus Rogerus tenuit placitum in curia christianitatis de catallis et debitis que non sunt de testamento vel matrimonio contra prohibitionem regis etc. et de placito quare predictus Henricus de Wramplingham secutus est idem placitum in eadem curia contra prohibitionem regis etc. Et unde idem Henricus Child per attornatum suum queritur quod cum predictus Henricus de Wramplingham traxisset ipsum in placitum in curia christianitatis coram predicto magistro Rogero exigendo ab ipso unum quarterium frumenti, duo quarteria ordei, duo quarteria avene etc. que non sunt de testamento vel matrimonio etc. ac idem Henricus Child die martis proxima ante festum sancti Michaelis anno regni regis nunc vicesimonono in ecclesia parochiali de Gothereston' in presencia Galfridi le Loverd, Willelmi Tercel de Cleye, Johannis Brun, et Johannis de la Rode de Bradenham liberasset predicto magistro Rogero regiam prohibitionem ne predictum placitum ulterius teneret in curia christianitatis etc. et similiter predictis die et anno in prefata ecclesia de Gothereston' in presencia predicti Galfridi et aliorum liberasset prefato Henrico de Wramplingham regiam prohibitionem ne placitum illud ulterius sequeretur in eadem curia christianitatis etc. predictus magister Rogerus nichilominus tenuit predictum placitum in eadem curia christianitatis etc. quousque excommunicatus fuit etc. contra prohibitionem etc. Unde dicit quod deterioratus est et dampnum habet ad valenciam quadraginta librarum. Et inde producit sectam etc.

Et magister Rogerus et Henricus de Wramplingham per attornatum suum veniunt. Et defendunt vim et injuriam quando etc. Et predictus magister Rogerus bene defendit quod ipse numquam tenuit placitum in prefata curia christianitatis contra prohibitionem regis etc. Et predictus Henricus de Wramplingham bene defendit quod ipse nunquam secutus fuit idem placitum in prefata curia christianitatis contra prohibitionem regis etc. Et hoc

[1] In the margin is written Nichil de defalta ista ad presens eo quod non dum constat curie quod querens habeat attornatum in placito isto

safe and secure conduct on the octave of Hilary etc. so that he may prosecute his complaint etc. And concerning William and William the archbishop of Canterbury was ordered to cause them to appear here on this day. And the archbishop did nothing in this regard. Therefore the sheriff is ordered to attach the archbishop to be here at the said term. And he should have here William and William, his clerks, to answer Hugh concerning his plea of attachment etc.

Nothing has been done concerning this default at present, because it is not yet clear to the court that the complainant has an attorney in this plea.

1.25a

HENRY CHILD v. ROGER DE FELTHORP AND THE PARSON OF SOUTH PICKENHAM

Norfolk. Master Roger de Felthorp and Henry de Wramplingham, parson of the church of All Saints of South Pickenham, were attached to answer Henry Child of Houghton concerning a plea as to why Roger held a plea in Court Christian concerning debts and chattels that are not testamentary or matrimonial, contrary to the king's prohibition etc., and concerning a plea as to why Henry de Wramplingham sued that plea in Court Christian contrary to the king's prohibition etc. And in this regard Henry Child by his attorney complains that, whereas Henry de Wramplingham drew him into a plea in Court Christian before master Roger, demanding from him one quarter of wheat, two quarters of barley and two quarters of oats etc. that are not testamentary or matrimonial etc., and Henry Child on the Tuesday before Michaelmas in the twenty-ninth year of this king's reign,[1] in the parish church of Gooderstone in the presence of Geoffrey de Loverd, William Tercel de Cleye, John Brun and John de la Rode of Brandenham delivered a royal prohibition to master Roger that he should not hold further the plea in Court Christian etc., and likewise on that day and year in the same church of Gooderstone in the presence of Geoffrey and the others delivered to Henry de Wramplingham a royal prohibition that he should not sue the plea in Court Christian further, master Roger nevertheless held the plea in Court Christian etc. until Henry Child was excommunicated etc. contrary to the prohibition etc. And he says he is thereby harmed and damaged to the value of 40 pounds. And he produces suit etc.

And master Roger and Henry de Wramplingham appear by their attorney and deny force and wrong whenever etc. And Roger completely denies that he ever held the plea in Court Christian contrary to royal prohibition etc. And Henry Wramplingham completely denies that he ever sued that plea in Court Christian contrary to royal prohibition etc. And this they are prepared to deny against him and his suit as the court should adjudge etc. Therefore it is adjudged that each of them is to wage his law twelve-handed etc. And let them come with their law here on the quindene of Trinity in their own persons etc. Pledges

[1] 26 September 1301.

parati sunt defendere contra ipsum et sectam suam sicut curia consideraverit etc. Ideo consideratum est quod quilibet eorum vadiat ei inde legem suam se duodecima manu etc. Et veniant cum legibus suis hic a die sancte Trinitatis in xv dies in propriis personis etc. Plegii de lege predicti magistri Rogeri Ranulphus de Trowes de comitatu Norff' et Willelmus de Lassefede de eodem comitatu etc. Plegii Henrici de Wramplingham de lege etc. Johannes de Morle de comitatu Norff' et Thomas de Rollesby de eodem comitatu etc.

Postea in crastino sancti Martini anno regni regis nunc [tricesimo primo][1] predictus Henricus Child per attornatum suum et magister Rogerus et Henricus veniunt. Et iidem magister Rogerus et Henricus fecerunt leges suas. Ideo consideratum [i]<est>[i] quod predicti magister Rogerus et Henricus eant inde sine die et Henricus Child de Houton' in misericordia.[2]

1.25b

CP 40/145, m. 279
Common Pleas, Michaelmas term 1303

Norff' Preceptum fuit vicecomiti quod, cum magister Rogerus de Felethorp et Henricus de Wramplingham persona ecclesie omnium sanctorum de Suthpikenham in curia hic in crastino sancti Martini anno regni regis nunc vicesimo nono essent attachiati ad respondendum Henry Child de Houton' de placito quare predictus magister Rogerus tenuit placitum in curia christianitatis de catallis et debitis ipsius Henrici Child scilicet de uno quarterio frumenti, duobus quarteriis ordei et duobus quarteriis avene que non sunt de testamento vel matrimonio contra prohibitionem regis et de placito quare predictus Henricus de Wramplingham secutus fuit idem placitum in eadem curia christianitatis contra prohibitionem regis etc. ac iidem magister Rogerus et Henricus de Wramplingham postea a die sancti Hillarii in xv dies proximo preteritos venissent in curia hic et vadiassent ei inde leges suas et habuerunt diem hic in crastino sancti Martini proximo futuro ad prefatas leges faciendas [et][3] predictus magister Rogerus pendente inde inter eos in curia hic predicto placito nichilominus tenuit idem placitum in prefata curia christianitatis de eisdem catallis et debitis et prefatus Henricus de Wramplingham in prefata curia christianitatis secutus est idem placitum in eadem curia christianitatis in ipsius Henrici Child prejudicium et regis contemptum manifestum et lesionem corone et dignitatem regis etc., <>[4] attachiaret predictos magistrum Rogerum et Henricum de Wramplingham quod essent hic etc. ad respondendum tam domino regi quam predicto Henrico Child de predictis transgressione et contemptu etc. Et modo [venunt][5] predictus Henricus de Wramplingham et Henricus Child etc. Et predictus Henricus Child queritur quod predictus Henricus de Wramplingham pendente placito predicto in curia hic post predictam legem suam inde vadiatam etc. nichilominus secutus fuit placitum de eisdem catallis coram predicto magistro Rogero ita quod

[1] MS. reads vicesimo primo [2] In the margin are written leges and 12 dots and misericordia (stricken through).
[3] MS. omits. [4] MS. includes quod [5] MS. reads venit

for master Roger's law are Ralph de Trowes and William de Lassefede of Norfolk etc. Pledges for Henry de Wramplingham's law are John de Morle and Thomas de Rollesby of Norfolk etc.

Later, on the morrow of Martinmas in the thirty-first year of this king's reign,[1] Henry Child appears by his attorney and master Roger and Henry also appear. And master Roger and Henry make their law. Therefore it is adjudged that master Roger and Henry are without day and Henry Child de Houton' is in mercy.

1.25b

HENRY CHILD v. ROGER DE FELETHORP AND THE PARSON OF SOUTH PICKENHAM

Norfolk. Whereas master Roger de Felethorp and Henry de Wramplingham, parson of the church of All Saints, South Pickenham, were attached on the morrow of St Martin in the twenty-ninth year of this king's reign to answer Henry Child of Houghton in this court concerning a plea as to why master Roger heard a plea in Court Christian concerning Henry Child's chattels and debts that are not testamentary or matrimonial, namely one quarter of wheat, two quarters of barley, and two quarters of oats, contrary to the king's prohibition and concerning a plea as to why Henry de Wramplingham sued that plea in the same Court Christian contrary to the king's prohibition etc. and master Roger and Henry de Wramplingham later on the quindene of Hilary just past[2] appeared in this court and waged their laws and were given day here on the forthcoming morrow of Martinmas to make their laws[3] and master Roger, while the prohibition plea was pending in this court, nevertheless continued to hear the plea in Court Christian concerning the chattels and debts and Henry de Wramplingham continued to sue that plea in Court Christian, to the prejudice of Henry Child and manifest contempt of the king and wrong to the king's crown and dignity etc., the sheriff was ordered to attach the aforeaid master Roger and Henry de Wramplingham to be here etc. to answer both the lord king and the said Henry Child concerning the aforesaid trespass and contempt etc. And now Henry de Wramplingham and Henry Child appear etc.[4] and Henry Child complains that Henry de Wramplingham sued the plea concerning Henry Child's chattels before master Roger while the prohibition plea

[1] 12 November 1303. The record incorrectly refers to the king's twenty-first year; presumably the thirty-first year is intended.

[2] 27 January 1303.

[3] Their appearances are noted in Case no. 1.25a, where the actual order was to return to make their law on the quindene of Trinity.

[4] For the contempt case against Roger de Felethorp, see CP 40/152, m. 88d (1304). No verdict is recorded in that case.

predictus magister Rogerus ad sectam ipsius Henrici de Wramplingham die dominica proxima post carniprivium anno regni regis nunc tricesimo primo fecit ipsum Henricum Child excommunicatum denunciari in ecclesiis de Suthpikenham et Houton et postea fecit ipsum summoneri essendi coram ipso Rogero in ecclesia de Bodeney die martis proxima post festum sancti Mathei apostoli anno supradicto et similiter fecit ipsum Henricum Child summoneri essendi coram eodem Rogero apud Shropham die jovis proxima sequente et eciam fecit ipsum Henricum Child citari essendi coram ipso Rogero apud Mundeford die sabbati proxima sequente etc. in lesionem corone et dignitatis domini regis [et][1] in ipsius domini regis contemptum mille marcarum etc. Et unde idem Henricus Child dicit quod deterioratus est et dampnum habet ad valenciam centum librarum etc.

Et Henricus de Wramplingham defendit vim et injuriam quando etc. Et bene defendit quod ipse nunquam post predictam legem suam in curia hic vadiatam etc. secutus fuit placitum aliquod in curia christianitatis de predictis catallis sicut predictus Henricus Child queritur. Et de hoc ponit se super patriam. Et Henricus Child similiter. Ideo preceptum est vicecomiti quod venire faciat hic a die sancti Hillarii in xv dies xij etc. per quos etc. et qui nec etc. ad recognoscendum etc. Quia tam etc.

Postea continuato processu usque in crastino sancti Martini anno regni domini regis nunc xxxij W. Howard coram quo etc. misit hic veredictum predicte jurate in hec verba:

Postea die martis in festo sancti Michaelis anno regni regis nunc xxxij apud Lenn coram W. Howard associato sibi Johanne le Bretoun milite venerunt partes per attornatos suos et similiter juratores etc. Qui dicunt super sacramentum suum quod predictus Henricus de Wramplingham nunquam traxit ipsum Henricum Child in aliqua curia christianitatis de aliquo blado. Dicunt tamen quod predictus Henricus de Wramplingham petiit apportum ad ecclesiam suam pertinens de quodam Roberto Brok de Houton' pro quodam mesuagio quod idem Robertus tenuit in parochia predicti Henrici de Wramplingham per quod idem Henricus de Wramplingham fecit ipsum Robertum citari coram officiali inde responsurum etc. Ad quem diem predictus Robertus non comperuit, ita quod propter contumaciam suam fuit fustigatus circa ecclesiam per tres dies solempnes in camisia sua et tamen postea compertum fuit quod idem Robertus nullum apportum debuit de iure ecclesie predicte de Suthpykenham. Postea ad visum francii plegii tentum apud Stondelee in hundredo de Suthgrenehowe predictus Henricus de Wramplingham indictatus fuit per Henricum Chyld et alios pro eo quod prius traxit predictum Robertum Brok in curia christianitatis ob quam causam idem Henricum de Wramplingham amerciatus fuit in eodem hundredo ad dimidiam marcam. Et quia sic fuit amerciatus predictus Henricus Chyld citatus fuit coram officialis archideaconi Norffolk coram quo idem Henricus Chyld petiit articulum etc. qui quidem officiali aliquem articulum sibi tradendo omnino recusavit set ipsum excommunicatum incontinenti denunciavit. Et dicunt ulterius quod postea convenuit inter predictum Henricum Chyld et Henricum de Wramplingham quod predictus Henricus Chyld aquietaret predictum Henricum de Wramplingham de predicta dimidia marca in hundredo predicto et predictus Henricus de Wramplingham ipsum aquietaret in curia christianitatis et quod procuraret absolutionem suam a dicto officiali qui quidem officialis ipsum absolvere recusavit per quod idem Henricus Chyld adivit dominum Norwici episcopum qui quidem episcopus ipsum pro una libra cere ad ecclesiam de Suthpykenham eroganda absoluit.

[1] MS. omits.

was pending in this court, after the parties' wager of law, so that master Roger at Henry de Wramplingham's suit on the Sunday after Carniprivium in the thirty-first year of this king's reign[1] first caused Henry Child to be denounced as excommunicate in the churches of South Pickenham and Houghton and later caused him to be summoned to appear before Roger in the church of Bodney on the first Tuesday after the feast of St Matthew in the same year,[2] and likewise caused Henry Child to be summoned to appear before Roger at Shropham on the following Thursday,[3] and also caused him to be cited to appear before Roger at Mundford on the following Saturday[4] etc., to the wrong of the lord king's crown and dignity and in contempt of the lord king 1000 marks etc. Henry Child says that he has been thereby harmed and damaged in the amount of 100 pounds etc.

And Henry de Wramplingham denies force and wrong whenever etc. And he denies that he ever sued any plea in Court Christian after his wager of law in this court etc. concerning the aforesaid chattels as Henry Child complains. And concerning this he puts himself upon the country. And Henry Child likewise. Therefore the sheriff is ordered to cause to appear here on the quindene of Hilary 12 men etc. through whom etc. and who do not etc. to give their verdict etc. Because both parties etc.

Later, process being continued to the morrow of Martinmas in the thirty-second year of this king's reign,[5] William Howard,[6] before whom etc., sent here the jury's verdict in these words:

'Later, on Tuesday Michaelmas in the thirty-second year of this king's[7] reign at Lynn before W. Howard and his associate John le Bretoun knight the parties appeared by their attorneys and likewise the jury etc. And the jurors say on their oath that Henry de Wramplingham never drew Henry Child into any Court Christian concerning any grain. They say however that Henry de Wramplingham brought a suit for revenue belonging to his church from one Robert Brok of Houghton for a certain messuage that Robert held in Henry de Wramplingham's parish, on account of which Henry de Wramplingham caused Robert to be cited to appear before the official to answer in this matter etc. On which day Robert did not appear. Therefore, because of his contumacy, he was solemnly beaten around the church for three days in his smock. However, later it became clear that Robert by right owed no revenue to the church of South Pickenham. Later, at the view of frankpledge held at Stondelee in the hundred of South Greenhoe, Henry de Wramplingham was accused by Henry Child and others because he had earlier drawn Robert Brok into Court Christian, and for this reason Henry de Wramplingham was amerced in the same hundred one half mark. And because he was thus amerced, Henry Child was cited to appear before the official of the archdeacon of Norfolk before whom Henry Child prayed the article etc., and the official refused entirely to hand over any article to him but instead immediately denounced him as excommunicate. And they say further that later there was an agreement between Henry Child and Henry de Wramplingham that Henry Child would acquit Henry de Wramplingham of the half mark imposed in the hundred and Henry de Wramplingham would acquit him in Court Christian and would procure his absolution from the official. The official then refused to absolve him, so Henry Child went to the lord bishop of Norwich and the bishop absolved him for one pound of wax to be donated to

[1] 24 February 1303. [2] 26 February 1303. [3] 28 February 1303. [4] 2 March 1303.
[5] 12 November 1304. [6] Justice of Common Pleas from 1297 to 1308. [7] 29 September 1304.

Quesiti si ad procurationem predicte persone, dicunt quod non. Et dicunt tamen quod predictus Henricus Chyld semper fuit paratus ipsum aquietare de predicta dimidia marca in hundredo predicto. Et dicunt similiter quod ad procurationem predicte persone pro causa predicta predictus Henricus Chyld postea summonitus fuit essendi in curia christianiatis coram predicto Rogero tunc officiali. Et quia idem Henricus Chyld sic fuit fatigatus per predictam personam, impetravit prohibitionem domini regis predictis magistro Rogero et Henrico de Wramplingham etc. Et dicunt quod non obstante prohibitione illa idem Henricus de Wramplingham ante legem et post semper hucusque tam coram [episcipo][1] quam officiali predicti archideaconi ipsum vexari procuravit coram quibus excommunicatus fuit et adhuc est. Et fuit excommunicatus per tres annos continue ad dampnum ipsius Henrici viginti marcarum etc.[2]

1.26a

CP 40/145, m. 135d
Common Pleas, Michaelmas term 1303

Wilt' Magister Petrus de Pyriton et Nicholaus Poynz persona ecclesie de Bradeford attachiati fuerunt ad respondendum Willelmo filio Willelmi Peres de Wroxhale de placito quare predictus magister Petrus simul cum magistro Johanne de Tarente tenuit placitum in curia christianitatis de catallis et debitis que non sunt de testamento vel matrimonio contra prohibitionem etc. et de placito quare predictus Nicholaus secutus est idem placitum in eadem curia christianitatis contra prohibitionem etc. Et unde idem Willelmus per attornatum suum queritur quod cum predictus magister Petrus simul etc. tenuisset placitum in curia christianitatis de quodam bove ipsius Willelmi qui non est de testamento vel matrimonio ad sectam predicti Nicholai ac idem Willelmus die veneris proxima post festum sancti Gregorii anno regni domini regis nunc tricesimo in ecclesia Sarum' in presencia magistri Reginaldi de Rosteshale, Willelmi de Rosteshale et Thome de la Pile et aliorum porrexisset eidem magistro Petro regiam prohibitionem ne placitum illud ulterius teneret in prefata curia christianitatis et etiam eidem Nicholao ne placitum illud ulterius sequeretur, idem magister Petrus nicholominus placitum illud in eadem curia christianitatis tenuit et idem Nicholaus placitum illud ulterius secutus est quousque sentencia in ipsum Willelmum promulgata, idem Willelmus ab ingressu ecclesie tanquam claves ecclesie contempnens suspensus fuit et postea excommunicatus in contemptum domini regis etc. Unde dicit quod deterioratus est et dampnum habet ad valenciam centum librarum. Et inde producit sectam etc.

Et magister Petrus et Nicholaus per attornatum suum veniunt. Et defendunt vim et injuriam etc. et omnem contemptum etc. Et bene defendunt quod idem magister Petrus nullum placitum tenuit nec idem Nicholaus aliquod placitum secutus fuit in curia christianitatis de laicis catallis predicti Willelmi filii Willelmi contra prohibitionem domini regis. Set revera dicunt quod idem Nicholaus traxit ipsum Willelmum in placitum coram prefato magistro Petro in curia christianitatis pro quodam mortuario ipsi Nicholao debito de bonis que

[1] MS. reads archiepiscopo
[2] The entry immediately following records the appearance of Henry Child against Roger de Felethorp on the same matter.

the church of South Pickenham. Asked if it was at the instigation of the parson, they say no. They say that Henry Child was always willing to acquit him of the half mark in the hundred. And they say likewise that at the instigation of the parson for the aforesaid cause Henry Child later was summoned to appear in Court Christian before Roger, then the official. And because Henry Child was thus tormented by the parson, he obtained the lord king's prohibition to master Roger and Henry de Wramplingham etc. And they say that the prohibition notwithstanding Henry de Wramplingham both before and after his wager of law and continuously until now caused him to be vexed both before the bishop and also before the archdeacon's official by whom he was excommunicated and still is. And he has been excommunicate for three years continuously, to the damage of Henry 20 marks etc.'

1.26a

WILLIAM PERES v. PETER DE PYRITON AND THE PARSON OF BRADFORD

Wiltshire. Master Peter de Pyriton and Nicholas Poynz, parson of the church of Bradford, were attached to answer William, son of William Peres, of Wraxhall concerning a plea as to why master Peter together with master John de Tarente heard a plea in Court Christian concerning chattels and debts that are not testamentary or matrimonial, contrary to prohibition etc., and concerning a plea as to why Nicholas sued the same plea in the same Court Christian contrary to prohibition etc. And in this regard William by his attorney complains that, whereas Peter together with etc. heard a plea in Court Christian concerning a certain ox of William that is not testamentary or matrimonial, at Nicholas's suit, and William on the first Friday after the feast of St Gregory in the thirtieth year of this king's reign[1] in Salisbury cathedral, in the presence of master Reginald de Rosteshale, William de Rosteshale and Thomas de la Pile and others delivered to master Peter a royal prohibition that he should not hear that plea further in Court Christian and also to Nicholas that he should not sue that plea further, master Peter nevertheless sued until sentence against William was promulgated and William was suspended from entry to the church as a contemnor of the keys of the church and later was excommunicated, in contempt of the lord king etc. He says he is thereby harmed and damaged to the value of 100 pounds. And he produces suit etc.

And master Peter and Nicholas by their attorney appear. And they deny force and wrong etc. and all contempt etc. And they deny that master Peter heard any plea or that Nicholas sued any plea in Court Christian concerning the lay chattels of William son of William contrary to the king's prohibition. They say instead that in truth Nicholas drew William into a plea before master Peter in Court Christian for a certain mortuary owed to Nicholas from the goods of William Peres, his deceased parishioner, at the time of his death, William Peres being the father of William, son of William, who is his father's executor, demanding

[1] 16 March 1302.

fuerunt predicti Willelmi Peres parochiani sui defuncti patris predicti Willelmi filii Willelmi cuius executor ipse est tempore mortis eiusdem exigendo secundum melius animal ipsius defuncti nomine mortuarii secundum consuetudinem patrie ab antiquo usitatam. Ita quod predictus Willelmus filius Willelmi porrexit eis regias prohibitiones, videlicet ipsi Petro ne placitum illud teneret in curia christianitatis et ipsi Nicholo ne placitum illud ulterius sequeretur in eadem curia, per quod ipsi in placito illo supersederunt etc. quousque habita consultatione Rogeri Brabazun justiciarii ad placita domini Regis pretextu consultationis eiusdem in eodem placito processerunt etc. Et profert quemdam libellum qui testatur quod predictus Nicholaus in curia christianitatis coram prefato Petro asserens secundum melius animal in bonis defuncti tempore mortis eiusdem existens nomine mortuarii ad ipsum rectorem ecclesie sue predicte nomine pertinere debet petiit predictum Willelmum ad restitutionem cuiusdam bovis precii quindecim solidorum qui secundum melius animal inter alia animalia predicti defuncti tempore mortis eiusdem reputabatur vel estimationem eiusdem bovis supradictam condempnari etc., qui quidem libellus consultatione predicta indorsatur et que testatur quod procedendum est ad cognitionem huiusmodi mortuarii Deo et ecclesie ab antiquo et ex consuetudine loci debitorum maxime ubi defunctus percepit sacramenta ecclesiastica et apud quam sepelitur prohibitione regia de catallis etc. non obstante. Unde dicunt quod ipse Petrus nullum aliud placitum tenuit nec idem Nicholaus aliud placitum secutus fuit in curia predicta etc.

Et Willelmus filius Willelmi bene concedit predictum libellum et consultationem predictam et quod non fuit aliud placitum in prefata curia nisi per eundem libellum. Set dicit quod cum in eodem libello contineatur quod predictus Nicholaus coram prefato Petro exigebat certum animal scilicet predictum bovem vel eius certum precium qui quidem bos fuit in possessione ipsius Willelmi filii Willelmi manifeste liquet quod predictus Nicholaus petiit bovem illum extra seisinam eiusdem Willelmi tanquam laicum catallum etc. Dicit etiam quod predicti Petrus et Nicholaus per predictam consultationem se excusare non possunt in hac parte quin predictum placitum fuit de laico catallo ipsius Willelmi quia dicit quod cum consultatio illa testatur quod procedendum est ad cognitionem mortuarii etc. ab antiquo et ex consuetudine debiti etc. ac ipse paratus sit verificare quod nuncquam aliquod mortuarium post mortem alicuius antecessoris suorum tenentis tenementa que ipse modo tenet in predicta villa et de quibus predictus Willelmus pater suus obiit seisitus nec etiam post mortem alicuius alterius libere tenentis in eadem villa dari consuevit. Et ex quo predictus Petrus ad sectam ipsius Nicholai tenuit placitum in curia christianitatis de predicto bove petendo illum tanquam mortuarium ubi nullum mortuarius debetur etc. manifeste sequitur quod placitum illud fuit de laico catallo ipsius Willelmi. Unde petit judicium etc.

Et predicti Petrus et Nicholaus dicunt quod cum predictus Willelmus cognoscat predictum libellum etc. et quod non fuit aliud placitum in curia christianitatis etc. nisi per eundem libellum per quem compertum est quod placitum illud fuit de quodam mortuario exacto de bonis que fuerunt predicti defuncti tempore mortis eiusdem, ac idem Willelmus in narrando asserit predictum placitum fuisse de quodam bove ipsius Willelmi [i]<filii Willelmi>[i] et sic sequitur quod idem Willelmus per cognitionem suam contrariatur sue narrationi, [petunt][1] judicium de brevi etc.

Dies datus est eis de audiendo judicio suo hic a die sancti Hillarii in xv dies parte querente etc.

1 MS. reads petit

the deceased's second best beast as a mortuary according to the custom of the country observed of old. Because William, son of William, delivered royal prohibitions to them, namely to Peter that he should not hear that plea in Court Christian and to Nicholas that he should not sue that plea further in the same court, they suspended that case until they had obtained a consultation from Roger Brabazun,[1] justice for the lord king's pleas, and on the basis of that consultation they then proceeded with the plea. And they proffer a certain libel attesting that Nicholas claimed before Peter in Court Christian that the second best beast from among the goods of the deceased at the time of his death ought to belong to Nicholas in the name of his church as mortuary, and prayed that William be condemned to make restitution either of a certain ox worth 15 shillings that was reputed to be the second best beast among the animals of the deceased at the time of his death, or of the value of the same ox, which libel was endorsed with the consultation attesting that it is appropriate to proceed to cognizance of this kind of mortuary owed to God and to the church of old and by local custom, especially to the church where the deceased received the holy sacraments and was buried, the royal prohibition concerning chattels etc. notwithstanding. And in this regard they say that Peter heard no other plea and Nicholas sued no other plea in the Court Christian etc.

And William, son of William, acknowledges the libel and consultation and that there was no other plea in the Court Christian except by that libel. But he says that, whereas in the libel it is said that Nicholas demanded before Peter a certain animal, namely the ox or its certain price, which ox was in the possession of William, son of William, it manifestly appears that Nicholas claimed that ox from the seisin of William as a lay chattel etc. He says also that Peter and Nicholas may not excuse themselves by the consultation in this matter on the ground that the plea did not concern the lay chattel of William because, while the consultation attests that it is appropriate to proceed to cognizance of a mortuary etc. owed of old and by local custom etc., he was prepared to prove that no mortuary was ever accustomed to be given after the death of any of his ancestors holding tenements that he now holds in this vill, and of which William his father died seised, nor after the death of any other free tenant in that vill. And because Peter heard the plea in Court Christian at the suit of Nicholas concerning the ox, claiming it as mortuary when no mortuary was owed etc, it manifestly follows that that plea concerned William's lay chattel. Whence he prays judgment etc.

And Peter and Nicholas say that, since William confesses the libel etc. and that there was no other plea in Court Christian etc. except by this libel, that clearly indicates that that plea concerned a certain mortuary demanded of the goods that belonged to the deceased at the time of his death, and William counts that the plea in Court Christian concerned a certain ox of William, son of William, and thus it follows that William by his confession contradicts his count, they pray judgment concerning the writ etc.

Day is given them for hearing their judgment here on the quindene of Hilary to the party complaining etc.

[1] Appointed justice of King's Bench in 1290 and elevated to chief justice of that court in 1295, where he served until 1316.

1.26b

CP 40/152, m. 61d
Common Pleas, Trinity term 1304

Wilts' Magister Petrus de Piriton' et Nicholaus Poynz persona ecclesie de Bradeford attachiati fuerunt ad respondendum [i]<domino regi et>[i] Willelmo filio Willelmi Peres de Wroxhale de placito [i]<quare>[i] idem magister Petrus simul cum Johanne de Tarente tenuit placitum in curia christianitatis de catallis et debitis que non sunt de testamento vel matrimonio et de placito quare idem Nicholaus secutus est idem placitum in eadem curia christianitatis contra prohibitiones regis etc. Ac iidem magister Petrus et Nicholaus simul cum predicto Johanne postmodum habuissent diem hic in octabis sancti Hilarii anno regni regis nunc tricesimo primo versus predictum Willelmum de predicto placito et iidem magister Petrus et Nicholaus simul cum predicto Johanne ad diem illum in eadem curia hic fecissent defaltam per quod vicecomiti preceptum fuisset quod attachiaret Simonem episcopum Sarum ita quod haberet hic in octabis sancte Trinitatis proximo sequentibus predictum magistrum Petrum clericum suum et similiter mandatum fuisset custodi spiritualitatis episcopatus Wygorn' quod venire faceret hic ad prefatum terminum predictum Nicholaum clericum suum ad respondendum predicto Willelmo de predicto placito, idem magister Petrus simul cum predicto Johanne pendente inde inter eos in prefata curia hic predicto placito predictum placitum in prefata curia christianitatis nichilominus ad sectam predicti Nicholai ulterius tenuit quousque sentencia in ipsum Willelmum ea occasione promulgata ipsum excommunicare fecit et postea breve regis de ipso Willelmo sic excommunicato tanquam claves ecclesie contempnente capiendo iam vicecomiti porrexit ut per sic ipsum Willelmum a prosecutione placiti sui predicti impediret, in corone et dignitatis regis lesionem, curie sue predicte contemptum manifestum, et ipsius Willelmi dispendium etc. Et unde idem Willelmus per attornatum suum queritur quod pendente placito inde inter eos in curia hic prefatus Nicholaus a die Pasche in xv dies anno regni domini regis nunc tricesimo traxit ipsum Willelmum in placitum de catallis et debitis que non sunt de testamento etc. coram predicto magistro Petro in maiori ecclesia beate Marie Sarum et ipsum Willelmum postea ad sectam ipsius Nicholai excommunicavit et similiter breve regis de ipso Willelmo sic excommunicato tanquam claves ecclesie contempnente capiendo vicecomiti comitatus predicti porrexit per quod idem vicecomes prefatum Willelmum cepit et in prisona regis castri Sarum imprisonavit et diu imprisonatum detinuit in corone et dignitatis regis lesionem etc. et ipsius Willelmi dispendium etc., in contemptum domini regis mille librarum etc. Unde dicit quod deterioratus est et dampnum habet ad valenciam quadraginta librarum. Et inde producit sectam etc.

Et Petrus et Nicholaus per attornatum suum veniunt. Et defendunt vim et injuriam quando etc. et omnem contemptum etc. Et [i]<idem Petrus>[i] bene defendit quod ipse nuncquam pendente placito in curia hic tenuit placitum in curia christianitatis de laicis catallis ipsius Willelmi nec idem Nicholaus placitum illud coram prefato magistro Petro secutus est sicut queritur. Et de hoc ponunt se super patriam. Ideo preceptum est vicecomiti quod venire faciat hic a die sancti Michaelis in xv dies xij etc. per quos etc. et qui nec etc. ad

1.26b

WILLIAM PERES v. PETER DE PIRITON AND THE PARSON OF BRADFORD

Wiltshire. Master Peter de Piriton and Nicholas Poynz, parson of the church of Bradford, were attached to answer the lord king and William, son of William Peres, of Wraxhall concerning a plea as to why master Peter together with John de Tarente heard a plea in Court Christian concerning chattels and debts that are not testamentary or matrimonial and concerning a plea as to why Nicholas sued that plea in Court Christian contrary to the king's prohibitions etc. And master Peter and Nicholas together with John after they were given day here in the octave of Hilary in the thirty-first year of this king's reign[1] against William concerning the plea in Court Christian and master Peter and Nicholas together with John on that day defaulted in this court, on account of which the sheriff was ordered to attach Simon, bishop of Salisbury,[2] so that he should have here master Peter his clerk in the octave of Trinity next following, and likewise the guardian of the spiritualities of the bishopric of Worcester[3] was ordered to cause Nicholas his clerk to appear here at that term to answer William concerning that plea.[4] Master Peter together with John, while the prohibition plea was pending against them in this court, nevertheless continued to hear the plea in Court Christian at Nicholas's suit until on that account sentence having been promulgated against William he excommunicated him and then delivered the king's writ to the sheriff to arrest William thus excommunicated as contemnor of the keys of the church in order thus to impede him from the prosecution of his prohibition plea, to the damage of the king's crown and dignity, manifest contempt of this court, and wrong to William etc. And in this regard William by his attorney complains that, while the plea was pending between them in this court, on the quindene of Easter in the thirtieth year of this king's reign[5] Nicholas drew William into a plea concerning chattels and debts that are not testamentary etc. before master Peter in the greater church of St Mary, Salisbury,[6] and then excommunicated William at Nicholas's suit and likewise delivered to the sheriff of Wiltshire the king's writ for William's arrest thus excommunicated as contemnor of the keys of the church, on account of which the sheriff arrested William and detained him in the king's prison at Salisbury castle and for a long time held him there, to the damage of the king's crown and dignity etc. and wrong of William etc. and in contempt of the lord king 1,000 pounds etc. And William says he is thereby harmed and damaged to the value of 40 pounds. And he produces suit etc.

And Peter and Nicholas by their attorney appear. And they deny force and wrong whenever etc. all contempt etc. And Peter denies that he ever heard a plea in Court Christian concerning the lay chattels of William while a plea was pending in this court or that

[1] Case no. 1.26a, which refers to the quindene of Hilary.

[2] Simon of Ghent was consecrated bishop of Salisbury in 1297 and served until his death in 1315.

[3] William Gainsborough was consecrated bishop of Worcester on 28 October 1302 but restitution of temporalities did not occur until 4 February 1303.

[4] The record noting the parties' defaults and the orders of attachment to the sheriff appears at CP 40/146 m. 21 (1303).

[5] 7 May 1302.

[6] Salisbury cathedral.

recognoscendum etc. quia tam etc. Et idem Nicholaus ponit loco suo Johannem Percehay vel Johannem Soleney etc.

Postea a die Pasche in tres septimanas anno regni regis nunc tricesimo tercio venerunt partes et similiter juratores de consensu partium electi qui dicunt super sacramentum suum quod predictus magister Petrus non tenuit placitum in curia christianitatis de laicis catallis ipsius Willelmi nec alicuius alii pendente placito in curia regis apud Ebor' etc. nec idem Nicholaus placitum illud coram prefato magistro Petro secutus fuit etc. Set dicunt quod pendente placito [i]<predicto etc.>[i] in curia regis apud Ebor' etc. idem Willelmus ad sectam ipsius Nicholai in predicta curia christianitatis fuit excommunicatus tancquam claves ecclesie contempnens [i]<etc.>[i] et postea ipsum Willelmum per breve domini regis ceperunt et inprisonaverant etc. Datus est dies partibus de audiendo judicio super veredicto predicto in octabis sancti Johannis Baptiste etc. Et quia non constat curie de dampnis etc. preceptum est vicecomiti quod venire faciat hic predictos juratores ad prefatum terminum nisi P. Malorre prius etc.

1.27

KB 27/177, m. 61d
King's Bench, Trinity term 1304

Kanc' Robertus Archiepiscopus Cantuar' attachiatus fuit ad respondendum regi et Willelmo de Cotes de placito quare cum per breve regis Henrico de Cobeham vicecomiti regis [comitatus][1] predicti precepit rex quod omnem vim laicam seu etiam armatam que se tenuit in ecclesiis sancti Pauli extra muros Cantuar', Chistelet, Menstre, Wevelesbergh, Kenynton, Parve Menigham, Estlangedon, Stonore, Swalclyve, Kyngesdoune, Frythingdene, Stone in Oxene, Borewardesmersh, Demecherche, Broclonde, omnium sanctorum Cantuar', sancte Marie Magdalene Cantuar', sancte Marie de castro Cantuar', sancti Andree Cantuar', sancti Johannis Cantuar', et sancte Mildrede Cantuar' in lesionem pacis regis quam inviolabiliter tenemur observare sine dilatione amoveri faceret ab eisdem et predictus Willelmus tunc subvicecomes comitatus predicti dictum preceptum regis de mandato predicti vicecomitis executus fuisset predictus archiepiscopus ea de causa secutus est placitum versus ipsum Willelmum in curia christianitatis et sentenciam excommunicationis in eundem Willelmum ea occasione fulminavit in regis prejudicium et dicti Willelmi dispendium non modicum ac status sui scandalum manifestum et contra prohibitionem regis. Et unde idem Willelmus queritur quod cum ipse tunc extiterat subvicomes [comitatus][1] predicti [i]<et>[i] dictum preceptum regis de mandato predicti vicecomitis executus fuisset predictus archiepicopus ea de causa secutus est placitum versus ipsum Willelmum in curia christianitatis et sentenciam excommunicationis in eundem Willelmum ea occasione fulminavit per

[1] MS. reads comitatis

Nicholas sued that plea before master Peter as is alleged. And concerning this they put themselves upon the country. Therefore the sheriff is ordered to cause to appear here on the quindene of Michaelmas 12 etc. through whom etc. and who are not etc. in order to hear their verdict etc. because both parties etc. And Nicholas puts in his place John Percehay or John Soleney etc.

Later three weeks after Easter in the thirty-third year of this king's reign[1] the parties appear and likewise the jurors chosen by consent of the parties, who say on their oath that master Peter did not hear a plea in Court Christian concerning the lay chattels of William or of anyone else while a plea was pending in the king's court at York etc. nor did Nicholas sue that plea before master Peter. But they say that while the plea was pending in the king's court at York etc. William was excommunicated at the suit of Nicholas in the Court Christian as contemnor of the keys of the church etc. and later they arrested and imprisoned William by the king's writ etc. Day is given the parties for hearing judgment on the verdict on the octave of St John the Baptist etc. And because it is not clear to the court concerning the damages etc. the sheriff is ordered to cause the same jurors to appear here at that term unless Peter Mallore[2] should first etc.

1.27

THE KING AND WILLIAM DE COTES v. ARCHBISHOP OF CANTERBURY

Kent. Robert, archbishop of Canterbury,[3] was attached to answer the king and William de Cotes concerning a plea as to why, since by royal writ the king ordered Henry de Cobeham, sheriff of Kent, that he cause to be removed without delay all lay and armed force holding itself in the churches of St Paul, Canterbury, Chistlet, Minster, Willesborough, Kennington, Little Mongeham, East Langdon, Shorne, Swalecliffe, Kingston, Frittenden, Stone in Oxney, Burmarsh, Dymchurch, Brookland, All Saints, Canterbury, St Mary Magdalene, Canterbury, St Mary de Castro, Canterbury, St Andrew, Canterbury, St John, Canterbury, and St Mildred, Canterbury, in breach of the king's peace, which we are held to observe inviolably, and William, then under-sheriff of Kent, executed the king's order according to the sheriff's mandate, on account of this the archbishop sued a plea against William in Court Christian and fulminated a sentence of excommunication against him for that reason, to the prejudice of the king and substantial wrong of William and manifest scandal of his estate and contrary to the king's prohibition. And in this regard William complains that, whereas he was under-sheriff of Kent and executed the order of the lord king according to the sheriff's mandate, on account of this the archbishop sued a plea against William in Court Christian and fulminated a sentence of excommunication against him for that

[1] 10 May 1305.
[2] Justice of Common Pleas from 1291 to 1305.
[3] Robert Winchelsey was consecrated archbishop of Canterbury in 1294 and served until his death in 1313.

quod idem Willelmus die martis proxima post festum sancti Barnabe apostoli anno regni regis nunc tricesimo primo in presencia Johannis de Helles, Willelmi de Falewesle, magistri Jacobi de Cobeham, magistri Willelmi de Chadeleshunte, et aliorum [i]<apud prioratum de Legh' in comitatu Essex>[i] predicto archiepiscopo prohibitionem domini regis liberavit de supersedendo de placito predicto idem archiepiscopus non obstante prohibitione regis predicta predictum placitum versus prefatum Willelmum in curia christianitatis secutus est et sentenciam in eundem Willelmum ea occasione fulminavit. In contemptum domini regis mille librarum et dampnum dicti Willelmi centum librarum. Et hoc petit verificare pro rege etc.

Et predictus Robertus archiepiscopus venit et defendit totum et quicquid etc. Et dicit quod nichil in contemptum domini regis fecit. Dicit enim quod postquam predictus Henricus de Cobeham tunc vicecomes etc. virtute predicti brevis regii sibi directi ad ecclesias predictas iuxta officii sui debitum accesserat. Et officium suum secundum tenorem brevis illius prout decebat plene excercuerat. Idem Willelmus tunc vicecomes etc. sub colore officii predicti temeritate sua propria et absque waranto vel precepto vicecomitis etc. accepta secum multitudine magna hominum abbatis sancti Augustini Cantuar' de missione ipsius abbatis eo quod idem Willelmus tunc feodum cepit de eodem abbate accessit ad ecclesias predictas et in ecclesia de Demechirche invenit quendam Willelmum capellanum eadem hora divina celebrantem ibidem cum clerico suo solummodo et in ecclesia sancti Andree Cantuar' invenit quendam Robertum capellanum cum clerico suo et predictum Willelmum capellanum vestimentis sacris indutum in altari spoliavit et in ipsum Willelmum ibidem et etiam in predictum Robertum capellanum in dicta ecclesia sancte Andree existentes ad divina in eisdem celebranda manus violentas iniecit et ipsos ab ecclesiis illis extraxit, imprisonavit, et male tractavit et vim laicam in eisdem induxit sacrilegium continuando per quod idem archiepisopus ad querelam ipsorum capellanorum et clericorum ministrorum suorum predictum Willelmum citari fecit super huiusmodi violencia et sacrilegio responsurum et pro inobediencia et contumacia ipsius Willelmi super hiis commissis legitime processu excommunicationis sentencias in ipsum fulminavit etc. Unde dicit quod ipse ratione huiusmodi criminum et delictorum etc. secutus fuit versus eundem Willelmum prout ad ipsum pertinuit iuris ordine inde in curia sua observato, absque hoc quod aliquid ei in contemptum domini regis fecit vel ratione alicuius officii vi vel virtute brevis regii sibi commissi prout idem Willelmus superius asserit pro ipso rege excercendi etc. Et de hoc ponit se super patriam etc.

Et predictus Willelmus dicit quod ipse preceptum domini regis predictum de mandato predicti vicecomitis virtute brevis regis predicti ratione officii sui executus fuit et quod predictus archiepiscopus ea de causa secutus fuit placitum versus eum in curia christianitatis etc. et sentenciam excommunicationis ea occasione in ipsum fulminavit prout superius queritur, absque hoc idem Willelmus aliquam violenciam seu sacrilegium in ecclesiis predictis commisit aut aliquam vim laicam in eisdem induxit vel aliquod delictum seu aliquam transgressionem predictis capellanis aut clericis fecit prout prefatus archiepiscopus ei imponit etc. Et hoc petit quod inquiratur etc. Et archiepiscopus similiter. Ideo veniat inde jurata coram rege a die sancti Michaelis in tres septimanas ubicumque etc. Et qui nec etc. Quia tam etc.

Postea in crastino animarum apud Westm' anno regni regis nunc tricesimo quarto predictus Willelmus venit et predictus archiepicopus non venit. Ideo capiatur jurata versus

reason, on account of which, on the first Tuesday after the feast of St Barnabas the Apostle in the thirty-first year of this king's reign[1] in the presence of John de Helles, William de Falewesle, master James de Cobeham, master William de Chadeleshunte, and others at Leighs priory in the county of Essex, William delivered the lord king's prohibition to the archbishop that he refrain from that plea, notwithstanding the king's prohibition the archbishop sued the plea against William in Court Christian and fulminated the sentence against William for that reason, in contempt of the lord king 1,000 pounds and damage to William 100 pounds. And he asks to prove this for the king etc.

And archbishop Robert appears and denies all and whatever etc. And he says that he has done nothing in contempt of the lord king. He says indeed that, after Henry de Cobeham, then sheriff etc., by virtue of the royal writ directed to him went to the churches according to the obligation of his office and fully performed his office according to the tenor of the writ, as was fitting, William, then under-sheriff etc., under colour of his office, by his own temerity and without warrant or precept of the sheriff etc., taking with him a great multitude of men of the abbot of St Augustine, Canterbury, sent by him because William then received a fee from the abbot, went to the churches and in the church of Dymchurch found one William, a chaplain, alone with his clerk at that hour celebrating divine services and in the church of St Andrew, Canterbury, he found one Robert, a chaplain, with his clerk, and he despoiled chaplain William, dressed in sacred vestments, at the altar and laid violent hands on him at that time and also on chaplain Robert in the church of St Andrew, both celebrating divine services in those churches, and removed them from the churches, imprisoned them, maltreated them, and applied lay force upon them to continue the sacrilege, on account of which and upon the complaint of these chaplains and his clerks and ministers, the archbishop caused William to be cited to answer for this violence and sacrilege, and for the disobedience and contumacy regarding these acts fulminated sentences of excommunication against him by legitimate process etc. Whence he says that by reason of these kinds of crimes and delicts etc. he brought suit against William as belongs to him, the order of law having been observed in his court, but without this that he did anything to him in contempt of the lord king or by reason or force of any office or by virtue of the king's writ sent to him to be executed for the king, as William asserts above etc. And concerning this he puts himself upon the country etc.

And William says that by reason of his office he executed the lord king's order according to the sheriff's mandate by virtue of the king's writ and that the archbishop for that cause sued a plea against him in Court Christian etc. and for that reason fulminated a sentence of excommunication against him, as is complained of above, but without this that he committed any violence or sacrilege in these churches or applied any lay force there or committed any delict or other trespass to the chaplains or clerks as the archbishop alleges against him etc. And this he prays be inquired etc. And the archbishop likewise. Therefore let jurors appear before the king three weeks after Michaelmas wherever etc. and who are not etc. because both parties etc.

Later on the morrow of All Souls at Westminster in the thirty-fourth year of this king's reign[2] William appears and the archbishop does not. Therefore let the jury's verdict be

[1] 18 June 1303.
[2] 2 November 1306.

eum per defaltam. Et juratores similiter venerunt qui dicunt super sacramentum suum quod predictus Willelmus nullum sacrilegium seu violenciam aliquam fecit in predictis ecclesiis de Denechirche et sancti Andree Cantuar' nec aliquos capellanos vel clericos ab eisdem extraxit, spoliavit, vel imprisonavit sicut predictus archiepiscopus ei inposuit. Immo quod idem archiepiscopus pro eo quod predictus Willelmus breve domini regis predictum predicto vicecomiti directum loco ipsius vicecomitis executus fuit prout ad ipsum ratione officii sui pertinuit secutus fuit placitum versus ipsum [i]<Willelmum>[i] in curia christianitatis et sentenciam excommunicationis in ipsum ea occasione fulminavit contra prohibitionem domini regis predictam, ad dampnum ipsius Willelmi quadraginta librarum.

Ideo consideratum est quod predictus Willelmus de Cotes recuperet damna sua quadraginta librarum versus predictum archiepiscopum. Et idem archiepiscopus capiatur.[1]

Dampna xl libre

1.28

CP 40/155, m. 159
Common Pleas, Easter term 1305

Hertf' Magister Radulfus de Baldok et magister Ricardus [i]<de>[i] Graveshende persona ecclesie de Aldebury attachiati fuerunt ad respondendum Phillipo de Patemere de placito quare predictus magister Radulfus tenuit placitum in curia christianitatis de catallis et debitis que non sunt de testamento vel matrimonio contra prohibitionem etc. et de placito quare predictus magister Ricardus secutus est idem placitum in eadem curia contra prohibitionem etc. Et unde idem Phillipus per attornatum suum queritur quod cum predictus Ricardus traxisset prefatum Phillipum in placitum in curia christianitatis coram predicto magistro Radulfo de catallis scilicet de frumento et avena et aliis bladis que non sunt de testamento etc. et idem Phillipus die lune proxima post festum omnium sanctorum anno regis nunc tricesimo primo in presencia magistri Ade de Lindeseye, Anselmi Wynberd, Walrami Reynberd, Roberti de Sancto Edmundo, et aliorum in ecclesia beati Pauli London' predicto magistri Radulfo liberasset regiam prohibitionem ne placitum illud ulterius teneret [i]<etc.>[i] et similiter eisdem die et anno et loco predicto Ricardo aliam prohibitionem liberasset ne placitum illud ulterius sequeretur etc., predictus magister Radulfus non obstante prohibitione etc. nichilominus tenuit idem placitum in eadem curia christianitatis ad sectam predicti Ricardi etc. quousque fuit excommunicatus etc. Unde dicit quod deterioratus est et dampnum habet ad valenciam quadraginta librarum. Et inde producit sectam etc.

Et magister Radulfus et magister Ricardus per attornatum suum veniunt et defendunt vim et injuriam quando etc. Et dicunt quod idem magister Ricardus est persona ecclesie de Aldebury annexe thesaurarie sancti Pauli London' et quod parochiani predicte ecclesie ex antiqua consuetudine decimare debent decimas bladorum suorum per shockos et non per garbas etc. et quia predictus Phillipus parochianus eiusdem ecclesie blada sua

[1] In the margin at this point is written capiatur

taken by default. And the jurors appear and say on their oath that William did not commit sacrilege or violence in the churches of Dymchurch and St Andrew, Canterbury, nor did he drag out, despoil, or imprison any chaplains or clerks as the archbishop alleges. On the contrary, because William, acting in place of the sheriff as belongs to him according to his office, executed the lord king's writ directed to the sheriff, the archbishop sued a plea against William in Court Christian and fulminated a sentence of excommunication against him for that reason, contrary to the prohibition of the lord king, and to the damage of William 40 pounds.

Therefore it is adjudged that William de Cotes recover his damages in the amount of 40 pounds against the archbishop. And let the archbishop be arrested.

Damages 40 pounds.

1.28

PHILLIP DE PATEMERE v. RALPH DE BALDOCK AND THE PARSON OF ALDBURY

Hertfordshire. Master Ralph de Baldock and master Richard de Gravesend, parson of the church of Aldbury, were attached to answer Phillip de Patemere concerning a plea as to why master Ralph heard a plea in Court Christian concerning chattels and debts that are not testamentary or matrimonial, contrary to prohibition etc., and concerning a plea as to why Richard sued that plea in Court Christian contrary to prohibition etc. And in this regard Phillip by his attorney complains that, whereas Richard drew Phillip into a plea in Court Christian before master Ralph concerning wheat, oats and other grain that are not testamentary etc., and Phillip on the first Monday after All Saints' day in the thirty-first year of this king's reign,[1] in the presence of master Adam de Lindeseye, Anselm Wynberd, Walramus Reynberd, Robert de Sancto Edmundo and others in the church of St Paul, London, delivered to master Ralph a royal prohibition that he should not hear that plea further etc., and likewise on the same day and year and at the same place delivered another prohibition to Richard that he should not sue that plea further, notwithstanding the prohibition etc. master Ralph nevertheless heard the plea in Court Christian at the suit of Richard etc. until he was excommunicated etc. He says he is thereby harmed and damaged to the value of 40 pounds. And he produces suit etc.

And master Ralph and master Richard by their attorney appear and deny force and wrong whenever etc. And they say that master Richard is parson of the church of Aldbury, which is annexed to the treasury of St Paul's, London, and that the parishioners of that church by ancient custom are supposed to pay their tithes of grain by shocks and not by garbs etc. and because Phillip, a parishioner of the church, did not wish to tithe his grain by shocks but rather by garbs, contrary to the custom observed since time out of mind,

[1] 4 November 1303.

noluit decimare per shockos immo per garbas contra consuetudinem predictam a tempore cuius non extat memoria usitatam, idem Ricardus traxit predictum Phillipum in placitum occasione predicta coram ipso Radulfo decano sancti Pauli London' ad quem spectabat cognitio in hac parte etc. qui quidem Phillipus postea breve domini regis de prohibitione [i]<eis liberavit etc.>[i] ratione cuius brevis idem magister Radulfus supersedit quousque per consultationem sibi factam per curiam domini regis mandatum fuit eidem quod sicut de decimis cognitio spectat ad forum ecclesiasticum et sic idem de modo decimandi quam quidem consultationem idem magister Radulfus profert etc. Et dicit quod ipse postmodum tenuit predictum placitum de modo decimandi etc. sicut ei bene licuit etc. ad sectam ipsius magistri Ricardi etc.

Et Phillipus dicit quod consuetudo decimandi hucusque usitata in parochia predicta talis est quod parochiani ecclesie predicte decimare debent blada sua ibidem decimanda per garbas et non per shockos etc. Et hoc petit quod inquiratur per patriam. Et magister Radulfus et magister Ricardus similiter. Ideo preceptum est vicecomiti quod venire faciat hic a die sancti Michaelis in xv dies xii etc. per quos etc. et qui nec etc. ad recognoscendum etc. quia tam etc.

Postea continuato processu usque in crastino sancti Martini anno regis nunc tricesimo quarto veniunt partes etc. Et quia inspecto processu etc. videtur curie quod placitum istud in forma qua partes posuerunt se in juratam etc. debitum exitum sortiri non potest etc. scilicet inquirendi de predicta consuetudine decimandi etc. cuius placiti cognitionem predictus magister Radulfus Baldok advocat ratione consultationis predicte etc., dictum est predicto Phillipo quod dicat aliud sibi viderit expedire etc. Et idem Phillipus dicit quod predictus magister Radulfus tenuit placitum in curia christianitatis de laicis catallis ipsius Phillipi [i]<et idem Ricardus secutus est idem placitum>[i] sicut queritur etc. et non de modo decimandi sicut idem magister Radulfus [i]<et Ricardus>[i] asserunt. Et hoc paratus est verificare etc.

Et predictus magister Ricardus hic presens in curia bene defendit quod ipse non fuit secutus predictum placitum in eadem curia christianitatis etc. Et hoc paratus est defendere contra ipsum et sectam suam sicut curia consideraverit etc. Ideo consideratum est quod vadiat ei inde legem suam se .xij.^{ma} manu etc. Et idem Ricardus instanter in curia hic fecit legem suam etc. Ideo consideratum est quod predicti magister Ricardus et magister Radulfus inde sine die. Et predictus Phillipus nichil capiat per breve suum set sit in misericordia pro falso clamore etc.[1]

1.29

CP 40/164, m. 315
Common Pleas, Trinity term 1307

Ebor' Magister Johannes Fraunceys attachiatus fuit ad respondendum domino regi de placito quare cum placita de catallis et debitis in regno regis que non sunt de testamento

[1] In the margin are written four dots and misericordia (stricken through).

Richard drew Phillip into a plea on that account before Ralph, dean of St Paul's, London, to whom cognizance pertains in this regard etc. And Phillip later delivered to them the king's writ of prohibition, by reason of which writ master Ralph refrained until, by consultation provided to him by the lord king's court, it was ordained that jurisdiction concerning tithes pertains to the ecclesiatical forum and likewise concerning the manner of tithing, which consultation master Ralph proffers etc. And he says that he thereafter heard the plea concerning the manner of tithing etc. as he well might etc. at the suit of master Richard etc.

And Phillip says that the custom of tithing until now observed in that parish is such that parishioners of the church are supposed to tithe their grain in that place by garbs and not by shocks etc. And this he asks be inquired of by the country. And master Ralph and master Richard likewise. Therefore the sheriff is ordered to cause to appear here on the quindene of Michaelmas 12 etc. by whom etc. and who do not etc. in order to give their verdict etc. Because both parties etc.

Later, process having been continued until the morrow of Martinmas in the thirty-fourth year of this king's reign,[1] the parties appear etc. And because, having inspected the process etc., it seems to the court that this plea in the form in which the parties have put it to the jury etc. cannot yield an appropriate issue, namely inquiring concerning the custom of tithing etc., the hearing of which plea master Ralph Baldok avows by reason of the consultation etc., Phillip is told that he should say something else if it seems expedient to him to do so etc. And Phillip says that master Ralph heard a plea in Court Christian concerning Phillip's lay chattels and Richard sued the same plea as he complains etc. and not a plea concerning the manner of tithing as master Ralph and Richard assert. And this he is ready to prove etc.

And master Richard present here in court denies that he sued that plea in Court Christian etc. And this he is prepared to deny against Phillip and his suit as the court should adjudge etc. Therefore it is adjudged that he is to wage his law twelve-handed etc. And Richard immediately makes his law here in court etc. Therefore it is adjudged that master Richard and master Ralph are without day in this matter. And Phillip shall take nothing by his writ but shall be in mercy for a false claim etc.

1.29

THE KING AND THE ABBOT OF SAWLEY v. JOHN FRAUNCEYS

Yorkshire. Master John Fraunceys was attached to answer the lord king concerning a plea as to why, since pleas concerning chattels and debts in the king's realm that are not

[1] 12 November 1306.

vel matrimonio ad coronam et dignitatem regis et non ad alium pertineant in eodem regno idem Johannes sicut ex relatu plurium accepit rex tenuit placitum in curia christianitatis de catallis et debitis abbatis de Salleye que non sunt de testamento vel matrimonio in lesionem corone et dignitatis regis et contra prohibitionem etc. Et unde Nicholaus Tempest qui sequitur pro rege dicit quod cum predictus magister Johannes tenuisset placitum in curia christianitatis in ecclesia beati Petri Ebor' de catallis predicti abbatis, scilicet de frumento, ordeo, avena, fabis et aliis bladis ad valenciam viginti librarum ac postea die lune proxima post festum sancti Barnabe apostoli anno regis nunc tricesimo tercio in presencia magistri Rogeri de Haslarton, magistri Elie de Wandesford, Petri de Chyrche, et aliorum etc. prohibitio regia in eadem ecclesia ei porrecta fuisset ne placitum illud ulterius teneret etc. idem magister Johannes non obstante prohibitione illa placitum illud nichilominus in eadem curia christianitatis tenuit quousque predictus abbas excommunicatus fuit etc. in contemptum domini regis mille librarum. Et hoc paratus est verificare pro rege etc.

Et magister Johannes venit et defendit vim et injuriam quando etc. Et bene defendit quod ipse tenuit aliquod placitum de laicis catallis ipsius abbatis sicut ei imponitur etc. Dicit revera quod quidam Adam [i]<de Osegodby>[i] persona ecclesie de Gayrgrave traxit predictum abbatem et conventum suum in placitum coram eo in predicta curia christianitatis super quibusdam decimis eisdem persone subtractis per ipsum abbatem infra limites predicte ecclesie prout continetur in quodam libello ipsius persone quem profert etc. et quod quidem placitum post prohibitionem domini regis ei liberatam etc. tenuit ulterius per consultacionem a curia domini regis sibi directam etc. eo quod cognitio decimarum spiritualium etc. spectat ad curiam christianitatis dum tamen decime ille non excedant quartam partem valoris ecclesie etc. Unde dicit quod ipse nullum placitum tenuit de laicis catallis etc. Et hoc paratus est verificare etc.

Et Nicholaus qui sequitur etc. dicit quod predictus magister Johannes tenuit placitum in curia christianitatis de laicis catallis ipsius abbatis contra prohibitionem etc. et non de decimis predictis etc. Et hoc paratus est verificare etc. Et magister Johannes similiter. Ideo preceptum est vicecomiti quod venire faciat hic a die sancti Michaelis in tres septimanas xii etc. per quos etc. et qui predictum magistrum Johannem nulla affinitate etc. ad recognoscendum etc. Quia tam etc.

testamentary or matrimonial pertain to the the king's crown and dignity and to no other, as the king learns from the relation of many, John held a plea in Court Christian concerning the chattels and debts of the abbot of Sawley that are not testamentary or matrimonial, to the wrong of the king's crown and dignity and contrary to prohibition etc. And in this regard Nicholas Tempest who sues for the king says that, whereas master John heard a plea in Court Christian in the church of St Peter, York,[1] concerning the abbot's chattels, namely wheat, barley, oats, beans and other grain worth 40 pounds, and later on the first Monday after the feast of St Barnabas the Apostle in the thirty-third year of this king's reign,[2] in the presence of master Roger de Haslarton, master Elias de Wandesford, Peter de Chyrche and others etc. a royal prohibition was delivered to him that he should not hear that plea further etc., notwithstanding that prohibition master John nevertheless continued to hear that plea in Court Christian until the abbot was excommunicated etc. In contempt of the lord king 1,000 pounds. And this he is prepared to prove for the king etc.

And master John comes and denies force and wrong whenever etc. And he denies that he heard any plea concerning the abbot's lay chattels as is alleged against him etc. He says that in truth a certain Adam of Osgodby, parson of the church of Gargrave,[3] sued the abbot and his convent before him in Court Christian concerning certain tithes taken from the parson by the abbot within the bounds of the parish, as is contained in a certain libel of the parson that he proffers etc. and that he continued to hear the plea after the lord king's prohibition was delivered to him etc. because of a consultation directed to him by the lord king's court etc. to the effect that jurisdiction over spiritual tithes pertains to Court Christian as long as the tithes do not exceed a quarter part of the value of the church etc. Whence he says that he heard no plea concerning lay chattels etc. And this he is prepared to prove etc.

And Nicholas who sues etc. says that master John heard a plea in Court Christian concerning the abbot's lay chattels contrary to prohibition etc. and not concerning these tithes etc. And this he is prepared to prove etc. And master John likewise. Therefore the sheriff is ordered to cause to appear her three weeks after Michaelmas 12 etc. through whom etc. and who have no affinity to master John etc. in order to give their verdict etc. because both parties etc.

[1] York Minster.

[2] 14 June 1305.

[3] The same Adam was party to another dispute over tithes involving the abbot and convent of Furness. See Case no. 2.16. He was a senior clerk in chancery.

OTHER ECCLESIASTICAL CASES AT COMMON LAW

2.1

KB 27/49, m. 13
King's Bench, Michaelmas term 1279

Cant'. Willelmus Joye de Kyngeston' queritur de Guydone de Mortuo Mari rectore ecclesie de Kyngeston' et Thome le Clerk de Harengton' de hoc quod iidem Guydo et Thomas die sabbati proxima post festum Nativitatis Beate [Marie][1] anno regni regis nunc septimo venerunt simul cum Willelmo de Knolley de comitatu Kanc' et Willelmo de Cotes de comitatu Leyc' in quemdam campum extra Kyngeston' et obviaverunt predicto Willelmo Joye sedenti in quadam carecta et dictus Guydo interrogavit eum si vendere voluerit equum [i]<suum>[i] de carecta sua et prospexerint dentes dicti equi et predicti et alii jusserunt predictum Willelmum descendere de carecta et quod levaret pedem equi sui et cum predictus Willelmus descendisset predicti Thomas simul cum aliis ex precepto predicti Guydonis ipsum Willelmum insultaverunt, verberaverunt, et maletractaverunt, ita quod de vita ipsius desperabatur et dictus Guydo manu sua propria et knypulo suo labium ipsius Willelmi superius abscidit. Unde dicit quod deterioratus est et dampnum habet ad valenciam centum librarum et inde producit sectam.

Et predicti Guydo et Thomas veniunt. Et dicunt quod clerici sunt et non debent hic respondere. Et sepius quesiti si velint respondere semper dicunt quod clerici sunt et sine ordinariis suis nolunt respondere. Et quia querela ista non tangit vitam et membrum set est de quadam transgressione personali nec ipsi volunt in curia domini regis respondere ad querelam illam, consideratum est quod predicti Guydo et Thomas de predicta transgressione convincantur et satisfaciant predicto Willelmo Joye de dampnis scilicet quilibet eorum de centum libris et domino regi de misericordia. Et commitantur gaole pro transgressione etc.

Postea predictus Willelmus et predicti Guido et Thomas le Clerk concordati sunt per licenciam. Et est concordia talis quod predictus Guido dabit predicto Willelmo Joye triginta marcas unde reddet ei incontinenti decem marcas et [d]<decem marcas>[d] ad festum nativitatis sancti Johannis Baptiste proximo venturum decem marcas et ad festum Omnium Sanctorum proximo sequens decem marcas. Et super hoc venit Willelmus de Mortuo Mari de Kingeston' et manucepit pro predictis denariis solituris ad predictos terminos et concedit quod nisi predictus Guido solverit etc. quod ipse soluet et nisi fecerit concedit quod vicecomes fieri faciat de terris etc. Et preterea predictus Willelmus de Mortuo Mari concedit et dabit predicto Willelmo Joye quolibet anno ad [i]<festum>[i] Natalis Domini quamdiu vixerit unam robam precii unius marce vel unam marcam et preterea idem Willelmus de Mortuo Mari concessit eidem Willelmo Joye unum mesuagium et octo acras terre cum

[1] MS. omits.

OTHER ECCLESIASTICAL CASES AT COMMON LAW

2.1

WILLIAM JOYE v. RECTOR OF KINGSTON AND THOMAS LE CLERK

Benefit of clergy for trespass

Cambridgeshire. William Joye of Kingston complains of Guy de Mortimer, rector of the church of Kingston, and Thomas le Clerk of Harrington, that Guy and Thomas on the first Saturday after the feast of the Nativity of Mary in the seventh year of this king's reign,[1] together with William de Knolley of Kent and William de Cotes of Leicestershire, came to a certain field outside Kingston and met William Joye sitting in a cart, and Guy asked him if he wished to sell his horse from the cart, and inspected the horse's teeth, and they and others ordered William to get down from the cart and lift up the horse's hoof, and when William had descended Thomas with the others, at Guy's command, assaulted, beat, and mistreated William so that he despaired of his life, and Guy with his own hand and knife tore off his upper lip. He says he is thereby harmed and damaged to the value of 100 pounds. And he produces suit.

And Guy and Thomas appear and say they are clerks and ought not answer here. And, asked several times if they would answer, they say repeatedly that they are clerks and will not answer without their ordinaries. And because this complaint does not touch life and limb but instead concerns a personal trespass, and they are unwilling to answer this complaint in the lord king's court, it is adjudged that Guy and Thomas be convicted of the trespass and satisfy William Joye for his damages, namely each of them 100 pounds, and the lord king for his mercy. And let them be committed to gaol for the trespass etc.

Later William and Guy and Thomas le Clerk reach a concord with leave. And the concord is such that Guy will give William Joye 30 marks, of which he will pay him 10 immediately, and 10 more at the next feast of the Nativity of St John the Baptist, and the remaining 10 at the next feast of All Saints. And likewise William de Mortimer of Kingston appears and mainperns for the money to be paid on these dates and agrees that, if Guy does not pay etc., he will pay, and if he does not he agrees that the sheriff may cause to be levied of his lands etc. And moreover William de Mortimer agrees that he will pay to William Joye annually on the feast of the Lord's Nativity for as long as he shall live either a robe worth one mark or one mark, and moreover William de Mortimer grants to William Joye one messuage and eight acres of land with appurtenances in Kingston in Cambridgeshire to be held by William Joye and the heirs of his body legitimately borne for one penny at Easter in place of all services saving any services of the lord king. And if William Joye should die without an heir conceived of his body, the tenements shall remain to Geoffrey of Soham, brother of William Joye, to be held by Geoffrey and his

[1] 9 September 1279.

pertinenciis in Kingeston in comitatu Canteb' tenendum eidem Willelmo Joye et heredis suis de corpore suo legitime procreatis pro uno denario ad Pascham pro omni servicio salvo servicio domini regis. Et si Willelmus Joye obierit sine herede de corpore suo procreato predictus Willelmus de Mortuo Mari concedit pro se et heredibus suis quod predicta tenementa remaneant Galfrido de Saham fratri predicti Willelmi Joye tenenda eidem Galfrido et heredibus suis inperpetuum per predicta servitia de predicto Willelmo de Mortuo Mari et heredibus suis. Et pro transgressione domino regi facta Hugo filius Otonis senescallus regis recordatur quod tradidit predictos clericos Galfrido de Mortuo Mari archidiacono London' ad habendum eos coram rege quandocumque voluerit de etc. Ideo deliberentur etc.[1]

2.2

CP 40/32, m. 67d
Common Pleas, Hilary term 1280

Linc'. Symon de Wymblethorp', Matilda que fuit uxor Jordani Selyman, et Johannes Feyrweder executores testamenti Jordani Selyman attachiati fuerunt ad respondendum Nicholao de Weston' de placito quod reddant ei centum solidos quos ei injuste detinent etc.

Et Symon et alii veniunt et petunt si quid habet de predicto debito. Et predictus Nicholaus dicit quod predictus Jordanus Selyman legavit ei predictam pecuniam in testamento suo. Et quia huiusmodi placitum spectat ad forum ecclesiasticum, dictum est ei quod sequatur in foro ecclesiastico si voluerit. Et predicti Symon et alii coexecutores sui inde sine die etc.

2.3a

JUST 1/1147, m. 25
Special Commission Session, Montgomery, 1279

Isabella de Mortuomari optulit se ad petendum versus Anianum episcopum Assavensis advocationem ecclesie de Thlannymennach que ad ipsam pertinet ratione dotis sue sibi assignate de advocationibus ecclesiarum que fuerunt Johannis filii Alani quondam viri sui etc. Et ipse non venit. Et somonicio etc. Et alias fecit defaltam scilicet in crastino clausi Pasche. Et somonicio etc. judicium resummoneatur quod sit coram domino rege

[1] In the margin is written de predictis Guydone de Mortuo Mari et Thome le Clerk de fine i<xx marce>i et sciendum quod sunt in extractis et liberent per se scaccario

heirs in perpetuity for the aforesaid services of William de Mortimer and his heirs. And for the trespass done to the lord king, Hugh, son of Otto, the king's steward, records that he handed over these clerks to Geoffrey de Mortimer, archdeacon of London, so that he may have them before the lord king wherever he may wish etc. Therefore let them go free etc.

2.2

NICHOLAS DE WESTON v. SIMON DE WYMBLETHORP AND OTHERS
Debt

Lincolnshire. Simon de Wymblethorp, Matilda widow of Jordan Selyman, and John Feyrweder, executors of the testament of Jordan Selyman, were attached to answer Nicholas de Weston concerning a plea that they render to him 100 shillings that they unjustly detain etc.

And Simon and the others appear and ask what they have concerning this debt. And Nicholas says that John Selyman bequeathed the money to him in his testament. And because this sort of plea belongs to the ecclesiastical forum, it is said to him that he may sue in the ecclesiastical forum if he wishes. And Simon and the other coexecutors are without day etc.

2.3a

ISABEL DE MORTIMER v. BISHOP OF ST ASAPH
Advowson

Isabel de Mortimer appeared against Anian, bishop of St Asaph,[1] to claim the advowson of the church of Llanymynech that belongs to her by reason of the dower assigned to her from the advowsons of churches held by her deceased husband, John fitz Alan. And he did not appear. And he was summoned etc. And he defaulted at another time, namely on the morrow of the close of Easter. And he was summoned etc. to be before the king wherever etc. three weeks after Michaelmas to hear his judgment etc., on which day the bishop was

[1] Anian II was bishop of St Asaph from 1249 to 1293.

ubicumque etc. a die sancti Michaelis in tres septimanas etc. ad audiendum judicium suum etc. ad quem diem idem A. episcopus somonitus non venit etc. Et datus fuit dies eidem Isabelle de audiendo inde judicio suo apud Mongomery in octabis sancti Michaelis anno regni regis E. predicto incipiente viij^{o}. Ad quem diem idem A. episcopus hinc somonitus ad audiendum judicium suum etc. non venit etc. Ipsa Isabella per attornatum suum cum instancia petenti judicium super pluribus defaltis ipsius episcopi etc. Consideratum est quod dicta Isabella recuperet seysinam de dicta advocationem ecclesie de Thlannymenach versus dictum episcopum per defaltam ipsius etc. Et dictus episcopus in misericordia.[1]

2.3b

CP 40/42, m. 88d
Common Pleas, Michaelmas term 1281

Salop'. Ananus Assavensis episcopus in misericordia pro pluribus defaltis. Idem episcopus summonitus fuit ad respondendum Isabelle que fuit uxor Johannis filii Alani de placito quare, cum predicta Isabella in curia domini regis coram dilecto et fideli suo Waltero de Hopton et sociis suis justiciariis ad placita in partibus Marchie et Wallie audienda et terminanda assignatis recuperasset [versus][2] prefatum Anianum presentationem suam ad ecclesiam de Thlenymenagh per considerationem eiusdem curie regis et dominus rex mandasset eidem episcopo quod ad presentationem ipsius Isabelle idoneam personam ad predictam ecclesiam admitteret, idem episcopus idoneam personam ad ecclesiam predictam ad presentationem ipsius Isabelle non admisit etc. Et unde queritur quod, cum ipsa coram predicto Waltero et sociis suis predictis apud Mongomery a die sancti Michaelis in tres septimas anno Regis nunc septimo recuperasset presentationem suam ad predictam ecclesiam versus predictum episcopum per defaltam ipsius episcopi et detulisset ei breve domini regis de judicio die martis proxima post Clausum Pasche apud Wrokwardyn anno regis predicti octavo quod ad presentationem ipsius Isabelle ad predictam ecclesiam idoneam personam admitteret prefatus episcopus presentatum ipsius Isabelle ad predictam ecclesiam admittere recusavit, in contemptum mandati domini regis predicti. Unde dicit quod deteriorata est et dampnum habet ad valenciam quingentarum librarum. Et inde producit sectam etc.

Et episcopus venit et dicit quod advocatio ecclesie est quoddam mere spirituale cuius cognitio pure spectat in partibus Wallie ad ordinarios loci. Unde dicit quod non wlt nec debet hic de advocatione predicte ecclesie nec alterius cuiuscumque in curia regis respondere.

Et Isabella dicit quod predictus episcopus debet de huiusmodi placitis hic respondere et petit judicium de ipso tanquam de indefenso nisi aliud ostendere possit quare hic placitare non debeat. Et quia compertum est et testificatum quod consimilia placita placitata fuerunt

[1] In the margin is written misericordia (stricken through).
[2] MS. omits.

summoned and did not appear etc. And day was given to Isabel for hearing her judgment at Montgomery on the octave of Michaelmas in the eighth year of King Edward's reign. On which day the bishop summoned from here to hear his judgment etc. does not appear. Isabel by her attorney vehemently prays judgment on the bishop's many defaults etc. It is adjudged that Isabel recover seisin of the advowson of Llanymynech church against the bishop by his default etc. And the bishop is in mercy.

2.3b

ISABEL FITZ ALAN v. BISHOP OF ST ASAPH
Advowson

Shropshire. Anian, bishop of St Asaph, in mercy for many defaults. The bishop was summoned to answer Isabel, who was the wife of John fitz Alan, concerning a plea as to why, since Isabel, in a case heard in the lord king's court before his beloved and faithful Walter of Hopton[1] and his associates assigned to hear and determine pleas in the Marches and in Wales, recovered against Anian the presentation to the church of Llanymynech by judgment of the king's court,[2] and the lord king ordered the bishop to admit a suitable parson at Isabel's presentation, the bishop did not admit a suitable parson to the church at Isabel's presentation etc. And in this regard she complains that, whereas she recovered her presentation to the church before Walter and his associates at Mongomery three weeks after Michaelmas in the seventh year of this king's reign[3] by the bishop's default, and she delivered to him a writ of judgment of the lord king on the first Tuesday after the close of Easter at Wrockwardine in the eighth year of this king's reign[4] that he should admit a suitable parson at Isabel's presentation to the church, the bishop refused to admit the parson presented by her to this church, in contempt of the lord king's mandate. She says she is thereby injured and damaged to the value of 500 pounds. And she produces suit.

And the bishop appears and says that the advowson of a church is something purely spiritual, the jurisdiction over which in Wales belongs wholly to the local ordinaries. Whence he says he does not wish to and should not answer here in the king's court concerning the advowson of this church or any other.

And Isabel says that the bishop ought to answer here concerning pleas of this sort and prays judgment against him as undefended unless he can show some other reason why he should not plead here. And because it is known and attested that similar cases were pleaded in the king's court here by similar writs, and the bishop shows nothing as to why he should not plead here but instead withdraws contumaciously in contempt of the court,

[1] Served as justice on several eyres and was a justice of King's Bench from 1274 to 1278.
[2] Case no. 2.3a.
[3] 20 October 1279.
[4] 30 April 1280.

in curia regis hic per consimilia brevia nec idem episcopus aliquid ostendit cur hic placitare non debet immo in contemptum curie contumaciter recessit, consideratum est quod predictus episcopus distringatur quod ad presentationem ipsius Isabelle ad predictam ecclesiam idoneam personam admittat. Et preceptum est vicecomiti quod distringat eum quod ad presentationem predicte Isabelle ad predictam ecclesiam idoneam personam etc. Et episcopus in misericordia. Et inquirat de dampnis etc.

2.4

JUST 1/578, m. 38
Norfolk Eyre, 1286

Galfridus le Marescal, Radulfus Semod, Henricus Codling', Willelmus Bese, et Willelmus Smyth attachiati fuerunt ad respondendum Hugoni persone ecclesie de Magna Fransham de placito quare ipsi bona et catalla ipsius Hugonis apud Magnam Fransham inventa ad valenciam decem librarum vi et armis ceperunt et asportaverunt et alia enormia ei intulerunt ad grave dampnum ipsius Hugonis et contra pacem etc. Et unde queritur quod predicti Galfridus et alii die sabbati proxima ante festum exaltationis Sancte Crucis anno regno regis nunc decimo et similiter anno undecimo et similiter die lune proxima post festum nativitatis beate Marie anno regno eiusdem regis terciodecimo ceperunt [i]<et asportaverunt>[i] ordeum, avenam, et pisas ipsius Hugonis et similiter alia blada ad valenciam decem librarum et homines suos ibidem inventos verberaverunt. Unde dicit quod deterioratus est et dampnum habet ad valenciam decem librarum. Et inde producit sectam etc.

Et Galfridus et alii venunt et defendunt vim et injuriam etc. Et bene defendunt quod nuncquam predicta blada asportaverunt nec homines suos verberaverunt [i]<contra pacem>[i] sicut eis inponit. Et de hoc ponunt se super patriam. Et Hugo similiter. Ideo fiat inde jurata.

Juratores de consensu partium electi dicunt super sacramentum suum quod locus ubi predictum bladum captum fuit et asportatum fuit quedam placia assertata et de novo redacta in culturam[1] et dicunt quod postquam predictus Galfridus le Marescall cuius predicta placia fuit asportasset bladum suum predictus Hugo persona cepit decimam predicti bladi de primo anno post predictam terram assertatam tanquam pertinentem ad ecclesiam suam predictam. Dicunt etiam quod idem Hugo persona habuit decimam de predicta terra secundo anno modo quo prius. Et dicunt quod predicti Galfridus et alii postea in annis sequentibus ceperunt decimam provenientem de predicta terra in autumpno nomine rectoris ecclesie de Bestone et decimam illam asportaverunt ad opus eiusdem rectoris de Beston'. Et juratores [i]<requisiti>[i] in cuius parochia predicta placia consistit dicunt quod in parochia de Fransham. Et quia placitum istud totaliter est de decimis ideo ad judicium. Postea dictum est ei quod sequatur placitum istud coram ordinario eo quod totaliter est de decimis etc.[2]

[1] In the margin at this point is written die sabbati post Trinitatem (stricken through).
[2] In the margin is written ad judicium (stricken through).

it is adjudged that the bishop be distrained to admit a suitable parson at Isabel's presentation to the church. And the sheriff is ordered to distrain him to admit a suitable parson at Isabel's presentation to that church. And the bishop is in mercy. And let there be an inquiry as to damages etc.

2.4

PARSON OF GREAT FRANSHAM v. GEOFFREY LE MARESCAL AND OTHERS

Trespass to tithes

Geoffrey le Marescal, Ralph Semod, Henry Codling, William Bese and William Smyth were attached to answer Hugh, parson of the church of Great Fransham, concerning a plea as to why with force and arms they seized and carried off Hugh's goods and chattels found at Great Fransham to the value of 10 pounds and inflicted other enormities on him to Hugh's great damage and against the peace etc. And in this regard he complains that on the Saturday before the feast of the exaltation of the Holy Cross in the tenth year of this king's reign[1] and again in his eleventh year, and likewise on the first Monday after the Nativity of Mary in the thirteenth year of this king's reign,[2] Geoffrey and the others seized and carried off Hugh's barley, oats and peas and also other grain to the value of 10 pounds and also beat his men found there. He says he is thereby injured and damaged to the value of 10 pounds. And he produces suit etc.

And Geoffrey and the others appear and deny force and wrong etc. And they well deny that they ever carried off this grain or beat Hugh's men against the peace as is alleged against them. And concerning this they put themselves upon the country. And Hugh likewise. Therefore let a jury be made.

The jurors chosen with the consent of the parties say on their oath that the place from where the grain was taken and carried off was a certain place assarted and newly brought under cultivation, and they say that after Geoffrey le Marescall, whose place it was, carried off his grain, Hugh the parson took tithes of corn in the first year after the land was assarted as belonging to his church. They say also that Hugh the parson had tithes from that land in the second year in the same manner as previously. And they say that Geoffrey and the others in the years following took tithes issuing from that land in the autumn in the name of the rector of the church of Beeston and carried those tithes off to the use of the the rector of Beeston. And asked in which parish this place is the jurors say that it is in the parish of Fransham. And because this plea is entirely about tithes, it is adjourned for judgment. Later, Hugh was told to sue this plea before the ordinary because it is entirely about tithes etc.

[1] 12 September 1282.
[2] 10 September 1285.

2.5

CP 40/68, m. 9
Common Pleas, Trinity term 1287

Hunt'. Prior de Huntingdon summonitus fuit ad respondendum priori sancti Andree Norht' de placito quod reddat ei viginti et quinque libras, tresdecim solidos, et quatuor denarios qui ei aretro sunt de annuo redditu triginta et sex solidorum et octo denariorum quem ei debet etc. Et unde idem prior Norht' per attornatum suum dicit quod [ ][1] quidam Rogerus quondam prior de Huntingdon predecessor predicti prioris de Huntingdon ad festum sancti Michaelis anno regis nunc primo obligasset se et successores suos et ecclesiam suam de Huntingdon cuidam Radulfo quondam priori de Norht' predecessori ipsius prioris in predicto annuo redditu percipiendo per manus ipsius Rogeri quondam prioris de Hunt' et successorum suorum ipsi Radulfo quondam priori de Norht' et successoribus suis ad duos anni terminos, scilicet medietatem ad festum sancti Petri Advincula et aliam medietatem ad Natale Domini. Et dicit quod omnes predecessores sui a tempore predicto fuerunt seisiti de predicto annuo redditu per manus predecessorum predicti prioris de Huntingdon ut de feodo et jure ecclesie sue sancti Andrei Norht' quousque iam quatuordecim annis elapsis quod predictus prior de Huntingdon predictum annuum redditum ei detinuit et reddere contradicit. Unde dicit quod deterioratus est et dampnum habet ad valenciam viginti librarum. Et inde producit sectam etc. Et profert quoddam scriptum quondam confectum inter ipsos priores quod hoc testatur in quadam clausula in eodem scripto ibi, scilicet quod prior et monachi de Norht' concesserunt priori et canonicis de Hunt' omnes decimas que eis de jure competebant in Stivecle, tam eas scilicet quas uterque possidebant quam omnes decimas de assartis tunc factis et postea faciendis in eadem villa, tenendas eisdem imperpetuum pro triginta et sex solidis et sex denariis sibi reddendis annuatim ad terminos subscriptos etc.

Et prior de Hunt' venit et defendit vim et injuriam quando etc. Et dicit quod non debet ei inde ad istud breve respondere nec curia ista habet cognoscere inter ipsos in placito isto cum illud scriptum inter predecessores suos confectum per quod idem prior de Norht' vult predictum annuum redditum et arreragia eiusdem redditus recuperare versus eum testatur quod origo et causa principalis predicti redditus sint decime. Unde cum placitum de decimis sive de hiis que decimis sint accessoria non habet terminari in curia ista, unde petit judicium etc. Dicit etiam quod post compositionem inde inter eos factam mota fuit questio in curia christianitatis coram judicibus delegatis et postea per appellationes devoluta fuit ad curiam Romanam et ibi per sentenciam diffinitivam recessit ipse quietus et quod ipse et successores sui et ecclesia sua extunc essent deonerati de predicta pensione imperpetuum non obstante predicta compositione, cum compositio illa potius debet dici coruptela quam compositio. Unde petit judicium si debeat ei inde in curia ista respondere etc.

Et prior de Norht' dicit quod curia ista habet cognoscere in omnibus placitis exceptis placitis de testamento, matrimonio, et de decimis, unde cum per compositionem predictam actio de decimis fuit adnichilata et actio de arreragiis annui redditus que habet placitari in curia ista per eandem compositionem ei competit, petit judicium etc.

[1] MS. reads cum

2.5

PRIOR OF ST ANDREW'S, NORTHAMPTON v. PRIOR OF HUNTINGDON
Annual rent

Huntingdonshire. The prior of Huntingdon was summoned to answer the prior of St Andrew's, Northampton, concerning a plea that he render to him 25 pounds, 13 shillings, and four pence of arrears of an annual rent of 36 shillings and eight pence which he owes to him etc. And in this regard the prior of Northampton by his attorney says that a certain Roger, formerly prior of Huntingdon, predecessor of the present prior, on Michaelmas in the first year of this king's reign[1] bound himself and his successors and his church of Huntingdon to a certain Ralph, formerly prior of Northampton, predecessor of the present prior, in the annual rent to be paid by the hand of Roger, formerly prior of Huntingdon, and his successors, to Ralph, formerly prior of Northampton, and his successors, in two instalments annually, namely half on the feast of St Peter's Chains and the other half on the Lord's Nativity. And he says that all his predecessors since that time were seised of the annual rent by the hand of the predecessors of the prior of Huntingdon as of fee and right of his church of St Andrew's, Northampton, until 14 years ago when the present prior of Huntingdon withheld the annual rent and has refused to render it to him. He says he is thereby harmed and damaged in the amount of 20 pounds. And he produces suit etc. And he proffers a certain writing made between the same priors which, in a certain clause in the same writing, witnesses that the prior and monks of Northampton have granted to the prior and canons of Huntingdon all the tithes in Stukeley that belong to them as of right, both those that each possesses as well as all tithes of assarts made and later to be made in the same vill, to be held by them in perpetuity for 36 shillings and six pence to be rendered annually on the abovewritten dates etc.

And the prior of Huntingdon appears and denies force and wrong whenever etc. And he says that he is not bound to answer this writ nor does this court have jurisdiction between them in this plea because the writing made between their predecessors by which the prior of Northampton wishes to recover this annual rent and the arrears against him attests that the origin and principal cause of the rent are tithes. And since a plea concerning tithes, or those matters that are accessory to tithes, is not to be determined in this court, he prays judgment in this regard etc. He says also that after the agreement made between them a question was moved in Court Christian before judges delegate and later by appeals it devolved to the Roman court, and there by definitive sentence he was acquitted so that he and his successors and his church were thenceforth disburdened of this pension in perpetuity, notwithstanding the agreement, since that agreement ought better to be called a corruption than a composition. Whence he prays judgment whether he ought to answer him in this matter in this court etc.

And the prior of Northampton says that this court has jurisdiction in all pleas except pleas concerning testament, marriage, and tithes, wherefore since by this agreement an action concerning tithes was annulled and he should rather have an action concerning

[1] 29 September 1273.

Et quia predictus prior Huntingdon non dedicit predictum scriptum in quo continetur quod debet predicto priori Norht' predictum annuum redditum triginta et sex solidorum et sex denariorum nec quin debeat ei predicta arreragia, consideratum est quod predictus prior Norht' recuperet inde predictum annuum redditum versus predictum priorem Hunt' et similiter predicta arreragia et etiam dampna sua que taxantur per justiciarios ad quadraginta solidos. Et prior Hunt' in misericordia etc. Et predictus Prior Norht' dat clericis quadraginta solidos [i]<de arreragiis>[i]. Et similiter dampna etc.

2.6

CP 40/69, m. 129d
Common Pleas, Michaelmas term 1287

Suff'. Robertus de Valeyns summonitus fuit ad respondendum coram Salomone de Roff' et sociis suis justiciariis itinerantibus in comitatu Suff' Thome de Hykeling de placito quod reddat ei quadraginta marcas quas ei debet et injuste detinet etc. Et unde queritur quod, cum quidam Willelmo de Kirketot aliquo tempore concessisset cuidam Thome filio Briani de Hykeling pro contractu matrimoniali inito inter ipsum Thomam et quandam Amiciam filiam ipsius Willelmi quaterviginti marcas sterlingorum ei reddendas, scilicet in quindena sancti Michaelis anno regni regis Henrici patris domini regis nunc quadragesimo sexto viginti marcas et infra vicesimam diem Natalis Domini proximam sequentis viginti marcas et infra quindenam Pashe proximam sequentem viginti marcas et infra quindenam nativitatis beate Marie proximam sequentem viginti marcas et ad predictam solutionem faciendam predictus Robertus principalem debitorem se obligasset, predictus Robertus predictas quadraginta marcas de predicto debito ei non reddidit set adhuc ei reddere contradicit. Unde dicit quod deterioratus est et dampnum habet ad valenciam viginti librarum. Et inde producit sectam etc.

Et Robertus per attornatum suum venit et defendit vim et injuriam quando etc. Et peciit sibi ostendi per quod ei tenetur in predicto debito. Et predictus Thomas profert quoddam scriptum sub nomine cuiusdam Willelmi de Criketot quod testatur quod predictus Willelmus cognovit se teneri predicto Thome in predicto debito pro contractu matrimoniali inito inter ipsum et Amiciam filiam ipsius Willelmi et ad predictam solutionem faciendam in quindena sancti Michaelis anno regni regis Henrici patris domini regis nunc quadragesimo sexto istos invenit fidejussores, videlicet Willelmum le Blund, predictum Robertum de Valeynes, Robertum de Crek, Martinum Hovel, quorum singuli per se et in solidum in predicta pecunia se obligarunt et principales eiusdem pecunie se constituerunt debitores.

Et Robertus dicit quod placita de catallis et debitis matrimonium [tangentibus][1] ad forum spectant ecclesiasticum et non ad curiam istam. Et desicut in predicto scripto continetur quod predictum debitum concessum fuit pro contractu matrimoniali petit judicium

[1] MS. reads tangentia

arrears of the annual rent, which he has by the composition, to be pleaded in this court, he prays judgment etc.

And because the prior of Huntingdon does not deny the writing stating that he owes the prior of Northampton the annual rent of 36 shillings and six pence, nor that he owes him the arrears, it is adjudged that the prior of Northampton recover the annual rent against the prior of Huntingdon and likewise the arrears and also his damages, which are assessed by the justices at 40 shillings. And the prior of Huntingdon is in mercy etc. And the prior of Northampton gives the clerks 40 shillings from the arrears. And likewise the damages etc.

2.6

THOMAS DE HYKELING v. ROBERT DE VALEYNS
Debt

Suffolk. Robert de Valeyns was summoned before Solomon of Rochester[1] and his associates, justices itinerant in the county of Suffolk, to answer Thomas de Hykeling concerning a plea that he render to him 40 marks that he owes to him and unjustly detains etc.[2] And in this regard he complains that, whereas a certain William de Kirketot at another time granted to a certain Thomas, son of Brian de Hykeling, 80 marks sterling for a matrimonial contract entered into between Thomas and William's daughter Amice, 20 marks to be paid to him on the quindene of Michaelmas in the forty-sixth year of the reign of King Henry father of the present king[3] and 20 marks within the twentieth day after the day of the Lord's Nativity next following[4] and 20 marks within the quindene of Easter next following[5] and 20 marks within the quindene of the Nativity of the Virgin next following[6] and Robert bound himself as principal debtor to make these payments, Robert has not rendered and until now refuses to render 40 marks of this debt to him. He says he is thereby harmed and damaged to the value of 20 pounds. And he produces suit etc.

And Robert by his attorney appears and denies force and wrong whenever etc. And he prays that he may be shown by what he is bound in this debt. And Thomas proffers a certain writing under the name of William de Criketot which witnesses that William acknowledged himself to be bound to Thomas in this debt for a matrimonial contract entered into between him and William's daughter Amice, and for making the payment on the quindene of Michaelmas in the forty-sixth year of the reign of King Henry, father of the present king, he finds these pledges, namely William le Blund, Robert de Valeynes, Robert de

[1] Served as a justice on several eyres from 1274 until his disgrace in 1290 as a result of complaints arising out of his conduct of the Norfolk eyre of 1286.

[2] The record of the proceeding before the justices itinerant is found at JUST 1/832, m. 23 (Suffolk, 1286). That record is enrolled verbatim in the instant Common Pleas record, except that the earlier record includes an adjournment to Westminster.

[3] 14 October 1262.

[4] 14 January 1263.

[5] 16 April 1263.

[6] 23 September 1263.

si debeat inde respondere. Dicit etiam quod si idem Thomas peteret versus eum predictum debitum in curia christianitatis idem Robertus non posset placitum per prohibitionem domini regis impedire eo quod dominus rex in omni brevi suo de prohibitione de catallis et debitis excipit debita testamentum vel matrimonium tangentia. Dicit etiam quod si idem Thomas modo predictum debitum per breve istud versus eum recuperaret et alias illud idem debitum in curia christianitatis versus eum peteret idem Robertus non posset eum in prefata curia christianitatis ab actione sua repellere per recordum istud et sic bis recuperaret unicum debitum. Unde sicut prius petit judicium si debeat ei in curia illa respondere. Et datus fuit eis dies hic ad hunc diem. Et Thomas et Robertus modo veniunt. Et dictum est predicto Thome quod sequatur in curia christianitatis si voluerit etc. Ideo predictus Robertus inde sine die etc.

2.7

KB 27/107, m. 2d
King's Bench, Michaelmas term 1287

Buk'. Fulco Neyrnuyt persona ecclesie de Pychelesthorn, Nicholaus frater ejus et Fulco filius Willelmi de Pychelesthorn in misericordia pro pluribus defaltis.

Iidem Fulco et alii attachiati fuerunt ad respondendum priori de Burncestre de placito quare bona et catalla ipsius prioris ad valenciam decem marcarum apud Pycheleston inventa vi et armis ceperunt et asportaverunt et alia enormia etc. ad grave dampnum etc. et contra pacem etc. Et unde queritur quod in crastino assumptionis beate Marie anno regno regis nunc xiiij bona [i]<et catalla>[i] ipsius prioris, scilicet frumentum, siliginem, ordeum, avenam, et pisas, et alia bona et catalla ad valenciam centum solidorum ceperunt et asportaverunt. Unde dicit quod deterioratus est et dampnum habet ad valenciam decem marcarum. Et inde producit sectam etc.

Et predicti Fulco et alii veniunt et defendunt vim et injuriam quando etc. Et Fulco persona respondit pro se et aliis et dicit quod ipse est persona ecclesie predicte et quod blada unde prior queritur fuerunt decime pertinentes ad ecclesiam suam predictam et ipse postquam decime ille segregate fuerunt per parochianos suos blada adunare fecit et domi cariavit sicut in anno precedenti fecerat et non blada ipsius prioris. Et hoc petit quod inquiratur per patriam.

Et predictus prior dicit quod predicta blada fuerunt blada ipsius prioris adunata et in seisina sua posita quousque predicti Fulco et alii blada illa vi et armis ceperunt et asportaverunt. Et quod ita sit petit quod inquiratur per patriam. Ideo veniat jurata a die sancti Hilarii in xv dies ubicumque etc.

Postea a die Pasche in tres septimanas anno regno regis nunc sextodecimo veniunt juratores, qui dicunt super sacramentum suum quod predecessores predicti prioris

Crek and Martin Hovel, each of whom individually and as a group binds himself as to this money and constitutes himself principal debtor as to it.

And Robert says that pleas concerning chattels and debts related to marriage belong to the ecclesiastical forum and not to this court. And since the writing states that the debt was granted for a matrimonial contract, he prays judgment whether he ought to answer. He says also that if Thomas were to claim this debt against him in Court Christian Robert could not impede that plea by the lord king's prohibition because the lord king in every writ of prohibition concerning chattels and debts makes exception of debts relating to testament or marriage. He says also that if Thomas now recovers this debt against him by this writ, and at another time should seek to recover that same debt against him in Court Christian, Robert could not bar him from his action in Court Christian by this record, and thus Thomas would recover a single debt twice. Therefore, as previously, he prays judgment whether he ought to answer him in this court. And day was given to the parties here to this day. And Thomas and Robert now appear. And it is said to Thomas that he should sue in Court Christian if he wishes etc. Therefore Robert is without day therein etc.

2.7

PRIOR OF BICESTER v. PARSON OF PITSTONE AND OTHERS
Trespass to tithes

Buckinghamshire. Fulk Neyrnuyt, parson of the church of Pitstone, Nicholas his brother, and Fulk, son of William de Pitstone, are in mercy for many defaults.

The same Fulk and others were attached to answer the prior of Bicester concerning a plea as to why with force and arms they seized and carried off the prior's goods and chattels found at Pitstone, valued at 10 marks, and other enormities etc., to the grave damage etc. and contrary to the king's peace etc. And in this regard he complains that on the morrow of the Assumption of the Virgin in the fourteenth year of this king's reign[1] they seized and carried off the prior's goods and chattels, namely wheat, rye, barley, oats and peas, and other goods and chattels valued at 100 shillings. He says he is thereby harmed and damaged to the value of 10 marks. And he produces suit etc.

And Fulk and the others appear and deny force and wrong whenever etc. And Fulk the parson answers for himself and the others and says that he is parson of Pitstone church and that the grain of which the prior complains was tithe belonging to his church and that after those tithes were segregated by his parishioners he caused that grain, and not the same prior's grain, to be gathered together and carried to his house as he had done in the previous year. And this he prays be inquired of by the country.

And the prior says that the grain was the prior's grain gathered and placed in his seisin until Fulk and the others with force and arms seized that grain and carried it away. And that this is so he prays may be inquired of by the country. Therefore let the jurors appear on the quindene of Hilary wheresoever etc.

[1] 16 August 1286.

aliquo tempore capere solebant quandam portionem decimarum in predicta parochia de Pychelesthorn qui dimiserunt illam portionem predecessoribus ipsius Fulconis pro quadam summa pecunie de qua summa plenarie fuerunt perpacati usque adventum istius Fulconis, set cum idem Fulco presentatus esset ad ecclesiam predictam predictus prior colligere fecit quasdam garbas decime predicte in solo ubi decimate fuerunt et idem Fulco eas domi cariare fecit tanquam decimas suas. Et requisiti si blada illa adunata fuerunt in aliqua grangia vel alio certo loco extra campum dicunt quod non set statim cum idem prior vellet colligere decimas illas idem Fulco per suos eas domi cariare fecit. Et quia placitum istud de decimis non potest hic terminari, consideratum est quod predictus Fulco eat inde sine die. Et predictus prior nichil capiat per breve suum set sit in misericordia pro falso clamore. Postea venit predictus prior et finem fecit pro dimidia marca.

2.8

CP 40/80, m. 71d
Common Pleas, Michaelmas term 1289

Suff'. Johannes de Cokefeld persona ecclesie de Whatfeld in misericordia pro pluribus defaltis.

Idem Johannes attachiatus fuit ad respondendum Aveline que fuit uxor Ricardi de Whatefeld de placito quare quemdam equum ipsius Aveline apud Whatefeld precii centum solidorum vi et armis cepit et abduxit et alia enormia ei intulit ad grave dampnum ipsius Aveline et contra pacem etc. Et unde queritur quod predictus Johannes die veneris proxima post festum sancti Johannis ante Portam Latinam anno regni regis nunc quintodecimo in regia strata aput Whatefeld cum gladiis, arcubus, et sagittis quemdam equum ipsius Aveline precii centum solidorum cepit et abduxit et alia enormia ei intulit contra pacem etc. Unde dicit quod [deteriorata][1] est et dampnum habet ad valenciam decem librarum. Et inde producit sectam etc.

Et Johannes venit et defendit vim et injuriam quando etc. Et dicit quod predictus Ricardus quondam vir ipsius Aveline [in][2] lecto suo mortali legavit corpus suum sepeliendum in cimiterio de Whatefeld et similiter predictum equum predicto Johanni persone predicte ecclesie tamquam principale mortuarium. Dicit [i]<etiam>[i] quod quidam Radulfus filius Radulfi duxit ante corpus predicti Ricardi predictum equum usque ad scalarium predicte ecclesie de Whatefeld. Et ibidem predictus Johannes cepit predictum equum ex liberatione ipsius Radulphi tamquam principale mortuarium.

Et Avelina dicit quod predictus Ricardus quondam vir suus legavit predicto Johanni persone etc. quemdam bovem tamquam principale mortuarium de quo bove ipse fuit in seisina per legatum predictum. Unde dicit quod predictus Johannes persona predictis die

[1] MS. reads deterioratus
[2] MS. omits.

Later three weeks after Easter in the sixteenth year of this king's reign[1] the jurors appear. And they say on their oath that the prior's predecessors were heretofore accustomed to take a certain portion of the tithes in the parish of Pitstone and they relinquished that portion to Fulk's predecessors for a certain sum of money, which sum of money was fully paid until Fulk's arrival, but when Fulk was presented to the church the prior caused certain garbs of these tithes to be gathered together in the field where they were tithed and Fulk caused them to be carried to his house as his tithes. And asked if that grain was gathered together in any grange or other certain place outside the field, they say no, but immediately when the prior wished to collect those tithes Fulk, by his men, caused them to be carried to his house. And because this plea concerning tithes cannot be decided here, it is adjudged that Fulk go without day. And let the prior take nothing by his writ but be in mercy for a false claim. Later the prior comes and makes fine for half a mark.

2.8

AVELINA OF WHATFIELD v. PARSON OF WHATFIELD
Trespass and mortuary

Suffolk. John de Cockfield, parson of the church of Whatfield, is in mercy for many defaults.

The same John was attached to answer Avelina, who was the wife of Richard of Whatfield, concerning a plea as to why with force and arms he seized and abducted a certain horse of Avelina's at Whatfield, worth 100 shillings, and inflicted other enormities upon her, to the grave damage of Avelina and against the king's peace etc. And in this regard she complains that on the first Friday after the feast of St John ante Portam Latinam in the fifteenth year of this king's reign,[2] in the royal street at Whatfield, with swords, bows and arrows John seized and abducted a certain horse of Avelina worth 100 shillings and inflicted other enormities upon her, against the king's peace etc. She says she is thereby harmed and damaged to the amount of 10 pounds. And she produces suit etc.

And John appears and denies force and wrong whenever etc. And he says that Richard, formerly Avelina's husband, on his deathbed bequeathed his body to be buried in Whatfield churchyard and likewise bequeathed the horse to John, parson of that church, as principal mortuary. He says also that one Ralph, son of Ralph, led the horse before the body of Richard to the steps of the church of Whatfield; and there John took the horse by delivery from Ralph as principal mortuary.

And Avelina says that Richard, formerly her husband, bequeathed a cow to John the parson etc. as principal mortuary, of which cow he was seised according to this legacy. And she says that John the parson, on the said day and year, seized the horse with force and arms and against the king's peace as she complains. And concerning this she puts herself upon the country. And John likewise. Therefore the sheriff is ordered to cause 12 etc. to

[1] 19 April 1288.
[2] 9 May 1287.

et anno vi et armis contra pacem cepit predictum equum sicut ipsa queritur. Et de hoc ponit se super patriam. Et Johannes similiter. Ideo preceptum est vicecomiti quod venire faciat hic in crastino [Purificacionis][1] beate Marie nisi justiciarii ad assisas capiendas assignatis prius etc. xij etc. per quos etc. Et qui nec etc. ad recognoscendum in forma predicta. Quia tam etc.

Postea die lune proxima ante gulam augusti anno decimo octavo regni regis nunc coram justiciariis assignatis apud Catteshill venerunt partes in propriis personis et similiter juratores qui dicunt super sacramentum suum quod predictus Johannes vi et armis cepit quendam equum ipsius Aveline precii unius marce in regia strata contra pacem etc. Et quod idem equus non erat ei legatus pro principali mortuario immo fuit quedam vacca pro qua vacca predicta Avelina fecit ei liberari quendam bovem de quo predictus Johannes adhuc est seisitus etc. Requisiti que dampna predicta Avelina habuit occasione predicte trangressionis dicunt quod ad valenciam viginti solidorum. Et predictus Johannes ibi liberatus fuit manucaptoribus subscriptis habendum hic ad hunc diem videlicet in crastino sancti Martini anno predicto videlicet Edmundo de Whelfacl< >[2], < >[2] de Gedding', Simoni de Cokefeld, Johanni de Wygenhal', Ricardo de Saxham, Georgio de Bradeford, et Willelmo de Stanham. Et predicta Avelina modo venit et quia predicti manucaptores non habent hinc ad hunc diem predictum Johannem ideo ipsi in misericordia. Et consideratum est quod predicta Avelina recuperet predicta dampna sua versus < >[2] et Johannes in misericordia et capiatur.[3]

2.9

CP 40/86, m. 194d
Common Pleas, Michaelmas term 1290

Linc'. Ricardus abbas de Croiland et Reginaldus le Ferur attachiati fuerunt ad respondendum Bartholomeo de Castello de placito quare ipsi simul cum Johanne de Colingham, Henrico de Bercham, Alano filio Willelmi, et Roberto Dole bona et catalla ipsius Bartholomei ad valenciam quadraginta marcarum apud Holebeck inventa [ ][4] vi et armis ceperunt et asportaverunt et homines suos ibidem existentes verberaverunt, wlneraverunt, et maletractaverunt et alia enormia ei intulerunt ad grave dampnum ipsius Bartholomei et contra pacem etc. Et unde queritur quod predicti abbas et Reginaldus simul cum predictis Johanne et aliis venerunt [i]<vi et armis>[i] die lune proxima post Gulam Augusti anno regni regis nunc duodecimo in villa de Holebeck et bona et catalla sua scilicet frumentum, siliginem, ordeum, avenam, fabas, et pisas ad valenciam quadraginta marcarum ibidem inventa ceperunt et asportaverunt et homines suos ibidem existentes verberaverunt, wlneraverunt, et maletractaverunt [i]<et>[i] alia enormia ei intulerunt. Unde dicit

[1] MS. omits.
[2] MS. damaged.
[3] In the margin is written misericordia (stricken through).
[4] MS. reads ad

appear here on the morrow of the Purification, unless first the justices assigned to take assizes etc., by whom etc. and who do not etc. in order to give their verdict in the aforesaid form, because both parties etc.

Later on the last Monday before Lammas day in the eighteenth year of this king's reign,[1] before the justices assigned at Cattishall, the parties appear in person, and likewise the jurors, who say on their oath that John with force and arms seized a horse belonging to Avelina worth one mark in the royal street contrary to the king's peace etc. And that the horse was not bequeathed to him as principal mortuary but rather a cow, in place of which Avelina caused to be delivered to him an ox of which John has been seised until now etc. Asked what damages Avelina has on account of this trespass they assess her damages at 20 shillings. And John then was handed over to the below-named mainpernors to be present here on this day, the morrow of Martinmas in the aforesaid year,[2] namely Edmund de Whelfacl. . ., . . . de Gedding, Simon de Cockfield, John de Wiggenhall, Richard de Saxham, George de Bradford, and William de Stonham. And Avelina now appears and because the manucaptors do not have John here on this day they are in mercy. And it is adjudged that Avelina recover her damages against . . . and John is in mercy; and let him be arrested.

2.9

PARSON OF HOLBEACH v. ABBOT OF CROYLAND AND REGINALD LE FERUR

Trespass to tithes

Lincolnshire. Richard, abbot of Croyland, and Reginald le Ferur were attached to answer Batholomew de Castello [parson of Holbeach] concerning a plea as to why they, together with John de Colingham, Henry de Bercham, Alan son of William, and Robert Dole, with force and arms seized and carried off Bartholomew's goods and chattels found at Holbeach, valued at 40 marks, and beat, wounded and mistreated his men there, to Bartholomew's grave damage and against the peace etc. And in this regard he complains that the abbot and Reginald together with John and the others came with force and arms on the first Monday after Lammas day in the twelfth year of this king's reign[3] in the vill of Holbeach and seized and carried off his goods and chattels found there, namely wheat, rye, barley, oats, beans and peas valued at 40 marks, and beat, wounded and mistreated his men there and inflicted other enormities. He says he is thereby harmed and damaged to the value of 20 pounds. And he produces suit etc.

[1] 31 July 1290.
[2] 13 November 1290.
[3] 7 August 1284.

quod deterioratus est et dampnum habet ad valenciam viginti librarum. Et inde producit sectam etc.

Et abbas et Reginaldus per attornatum suum veniunt. Et defendunt vim et injuriam quando etc. Et dicunt quod ipsi non ceperunt nec asportaverunt aliqua bona et catalla predicti Bartholomei predictis die et anno nisi tantum suas proprias decimas que ad ecclesiam ipsius Abbatis de jure pertinent et prout ipse et predecessores sui a tempore quo non extat memoria facere [i]<et capere>[i] consueverunt nec homines ipsius Bartholomei verberaverunt nec wlneraverunt nec aliquam transgressionem eis fecerunt sicut eis imponit. Et de hoc [ponunt][1] se super patriam. Et Bartholomeus similiter. Ideo preceptum est vicecomiti quod venire faciat hic a die Pasche in unum mensem xij etc. per quos etc. et qui nec etc. ad recognoscendum in forma predicta. Quia tam etc.

Postea in crastino Purificationis beate Marie anno xxij veniunt partes et similiter juratores qui dicunt super sacramentum quod a tempore cuius non extat memoria persone ecclesie de Quappelade habere et percipere solebant decimas garbas totius bladi crescentis in villa de Quappelade et persone de Holebech similiter decimas garbas totius bladi crescentis in villa de Holebech usque ad tempus cuiusdam Johannis quondam persone de Holebech predecessoris predicti Bartholomei et cuiusdam Radulfi abbatis de Croylaund predecessoris abbatis nunc, qui quidem Radulfus abbas et Johannes persona mutuo consensu fecerunt quamdam compositionem pro se et successoribus suis sub hac forma quod omnes decime garbarum provenientes de terris cultis in Quappelade per homines et carucas cubantes et levantes in Holebech remanerent persone de Holebech et successoribus suis absque contradictione persone de Quappelade et successorum suorum et quod omnes decime garbarum provenientes de terris cultis in Holebech per homines et carucas cubantes et levantes in Quappelade remanerent persone de Quappelade et successoribus suis absque contradictione persone de Holebech vel successorum suorum. Et dicunt quod predictus Radulfus abbas qui aliquo tempore fuit patronus predicte ecclesie de Quappelade tempore constitutionis huiusmodi compositionis fuit persona de Quappelade eo quod ecclesiam illam perquisierat in proprios usus sibi et conventui suo tenendam. Et dicunt quod abbas nunc quamdam culturam que continet circiter sexaginta acras in villa de Holebech que aliquo tempore tenebantur de ipso abbate in villenagium propriis carucis ipsius abbatis de Quappelade excolere fecit. Et dicunt quod cum blada in predicta cultura crescencia in autumpno adunerentur in garbis homines predicti Bartholomei venerunt et decimas garbas predicte culture percepisse et asportasse voluerunt et abbas nunc hoc audiens et percipiens misit ibi homines suos qui omnes garbas de eadem cultura provenientes perceperunt et ad opus ipsius abbatis usque Quappelade cariaverunt. Quesiti si assensus patronorum et loci diocesani unquam ad istam compositionem exigebantur dicunt quod nec consensus loci diocesani nec patroni de Holebech nunquam ad hoc exigebantur. Quesiti si Johannes persona de Holebech et omnes persone post eum ibi preter predictum Bartholomeum predictam compositionem ratam habuerunt dicunt quod sic. Et dicunt quod predictus Bartholomeus toto tempore suo predictam compositionem ratam habuit usque nunc quod decimas garbas de predicta cultura percepisse voluit. Dicunt enim quod idem Bartholomeus de omnibus terris preter quam de ista cultura tantum in villa de Quappelade cultis per homines et carucas cubantes et levantes in Holebech decimas garbas percipit et

[1] MS. reads ponit

And the abbot and Reginald appear by their attorney. And they deny force and wrong whenever etc. And they say they did not seize or carry off any of Bartholomew's goods and chattels on the aforesaid day and year except only their own tithes belonging to the abbot's church by right, and in the same manner as he and his predecessors have been accustomed to do and to take time out of mind, nor did they beat or wound Bartholomew's men or do any trespass against them as he accuses them. And concerning this they put themselves upon the country. And Bartholomew likewise. Therefore the sheriff is ordered to cause to appear here one month from Easter 12 men etc. by whom etc. and who are not etc. to give their verdict on the aforesaid matter, because both parties etc.

Later on the morrow of the Purification of the Virgin of the twenty-second year[1] the parties appeared, and likewise the jurors, who say on their oath that since time immemorial the parsons of the church of Whaplode have been accustomed to have and to gather tithes of sheaves of all grain growing in the vill of Holbeach, until the time of one John, formerly parson of Holbeach, predecessor of Bartholomew, and of one Ralph, abbot of Croyland, predecessor of the present abbot, who by mutual consent made a settlement for themselves and for their successors upon the terms that all tithes of sheaves issuing from lands in Whaplode cultivated by the men and plough-teams couchant and levant in Holbeach should remain with the parson of Holbeach and his successors without objection from the parson of Whaplode or his successors, and that all tithes of sheaves issuing from lands in Holbeach cultivated by the men and plough-teams couchant and levant in Whaplode should remain with the parson of Whaplode and his successors without objection from the parson of Holbeach or his successors. And they say that abbot Ralph, who was formerly patron of the church of Whaplode, at the time of the making of this settlement was parson of Whaplode because he acquired that church to be held to the use of himself and his abbey. And they say that the present abbot caused to be cultivated by the abbot's own ploughs a certain field containing approximately 60 acres in the vill of Holebeach that previously were held of the abbot in villeinage. And they say that, whereas the grain growing in the field in the autumn was gathered into sheaves, Bartholomew's men came and would have seized and carried off the tithes of sheaves of that field, and the present abbot on hearing and understanding this sent his men there, who gathered all the sheaves issuing from that field and carted them to Whaplode to the abbot's use. Asked if the assent of the patron and of the local diocesan was ever obtained to this settlement, the jurors say that neither the assent of the local diocesan nor of the patron of Holbeach was ever obtained as to this. Asked if John, parson of Holbeach, and all parsons after him there except Bartholomew, have at all times regarded the settlement as valid, the jurors say yes. And they say that Bartholomew during his time has regarded the settlement as valid until now, insofar as he would have gathered the tithes of sheaves from the field. They say also that Bartholomew receives tithes of sheaves from all lands in the vill of Whaplode cultivated by the men and plough-teams couchant and levant in Holbeach, excepting only those from this field, and of these he is now in seisin without contradiction or impediment of anyone. Asked if the tithes of sheaves issuing from the field were ever separated by anyone from the nine parts, in such a way that Bartholomew or his men might know which part they should carry off as tithe, the jurors say no. Asked if the abbot or his men

[1] 3 February 1294.

de eisdem modo est in seisina absque contradictione seu impedimento alicuius. Quesiti si decime garbe de predicta cultura provenientes unquam per aliquem separate fuerunt a novem partibus per quod predictus Bartholomeus seu homines sui scire potuissent qualem partem tanquam decimam deberent asportare dicunt quod non. Quesiti si predictus abbas seu homines sui homines predicti Bartholomei verberaverunt, wlneraverunt, etc. dicunt quod non. Et ideo consideratum est quod predictus abbas et omnes alij inde sine die. Et predictus Bartholomeus in misericordia pro falso clamore.[1]

2.10

CP 40/89, m. 45
Common Pleas, Easter term 1291

Ebor'. Abbas de Seleby per attornatum suum petit versus Johannem de Lovetot advocationem decimarum quarte partis ecclesie de Sneyth ut jus ecclesie sue Sancti Germani de Seleby. Et unde dicit quod quidam Hugo quondam abbas de Seleby predecessor suus fuit in seisina de advocatione predictarum decimarum ut de feodo et jure ecclesie sue predicte tempore pacis tempore domini Henrici regis patris domini regis nunc et eodem tempore fuit idem Hugo quondam abbas etc. persona impersonata de eisdem decimis de advocatione sua propria capiendo inde explecia ut de minutis decimis, oblationibus, majoribus decimis, et aliis obventionibus etc. ad valenciam etc. Et quod tale sit jus ecclesie sue sancti Germani de Seleby predicte offert etc.

Et Johannes venit. Et defendit jus suum quando etc. Et dicit quod in hujusmodi brevibus de recto ubi petuntur advocationes ecclesiarum sive decimarum secundum legem et consuetudinem regni etc. petens narrare debet de aliqua persona ad presentationem petentis vel antecessoris sue predecessoris sui ad ecclesiam seu decimas illas admissa et instituta qui obventiones inde percepisset. Et desicut abbas in narratione sua aliquam personam ad presentationem predecessoris sui ad predictas decimas non dicit admissam fuisse nec institutam etc. petit judicium si ad talem narrationem ad breve [de recto][2] debeat responderi.

Postea a die sancti Hillarii in quindecim dies anno regis nunc vicesimo primo veniunt partes etc. Et abbas dicit quod cum istud breve sit de mero jure et ipse super hoc [ ][3] offert disrationare etc. ad quod predictus Johannes nichil respondit etc. petit judicium de ipso tamquam de indefenso etc.

Et Johannes dicit eandem exceptionem quam prius etc. Et petit judicium etc. Dicit etiam quod si predictus abbas peteret versus eum advocationem predicte ecclesie integraliter necesse haberet dicere in narratione sua quod aliquis predecessor suus presentasset ad eandem etc. et quod persona presentata fuisset instituta etc. Et desicut idem abbas petendo quartam partem advocationis etc. aliam prerogativam placitandi habere non debet quam

[1] In the margin is written misericordia (stricken through).
[2] MS. reads de recto de recto
[3] MS. reads ipse

beat, wounded, etc. Bartholomew's men, the jurors say no. And therefore it is adjudged that the abbot and all the others are without day. And Bartholomew is in mercy for a false claim.

2.10

ABBOT OF SELBY v. JOHN DE LOVETOT
Writ of right of advowson

Yorkshire. The abbot of Selby by his attorney claims against John de Lovetot the advowson of a quarter part of the tithes of the church of Snaith as the right of his church of St Germain of Selby. And he says that one Hugh, formerly abbot of Selby, his precedecessor, was in seisin of the advowson of these tithes as of fee and right of his church in the time of the lord king Henry, father of the present king, and at that time Hugh, formerly abbot, was parson imparsonate of the same tithes, of his own advowson, taking therefrom the esplees, that is, small tithes, oblations, great tithes, and other obventions etc., to the value etc. And he offers to prove that such is the right of his church of St Germain of Selby etc.

And John appears. And he denies his right whenever etc. And he says that in these writs of right where advowsons of churches or tithes are claimed, according to the law and custom of the realm etc. the demandant ought to count of some parson who was admitted and instituted to the church or to those tithes by presentation of the claimant, or of his ancestor or predecessor, and who had received obventions therefrom. And whereas the abbot in his count did not say that some parson at the presentation of his predecessor was admitted or instituted to these tithes, he prays judgment whether to such a count he ought to be answered in a writ of right.

Later on the quindene of Hilary in the twenty-first year of this king[1] the parties appeared etc. And the abbot says that, since this writ is purely of right and thereupon he offers to prove etc., which John in no way answers etc., he prays judgment against him as undefended etc.

And John states the same exception as previously etc. and prays judgment etc. He says also that if the abbot claimed against him the advowson of the church entirely he would need to have said in his count that some predecessor of his presented to the same etc. and that the parson presented was instituted etc. And, whereas the abbot by claiming a quarter part of the advowson etc. should not have another prerogative of pleading than by claiming the whole church entirely, he prays judgment etc. He says also that this writ for a fourth

[1] 28 January 1293.

petendo advocationem totius ecclesie integraliter etc. petit judicium etc. Dicit etiam quod istud breve de quarta parte decimarum etc. primo locum habere cepit a tempore statuti regis nunc apud Westmonasterium [i]<inde>[i] editi etc. Et dicit quod hoc breve per statutum etc. tantum competit patrono etc. in casu quando persona alicuius ecclesie repulsus fuerit ad agendo super decimis petitis in curia christianitatis per breve indicavit etc. Et ex quo predictus abbas ferendo predictum breve non est in casu statuti etc. petit judicium etc.

Et abbas dicit quod ipse petit advocationem predictarum decimarum de advocatione sua propria etc. Et decimas illas clamat ut jus ecclesie sue et tamquam persona in proprios usus etc. Et dicit quod statutum satis operatur pro ipso in hoc casu ex quo ipse est patronus et persona etc. Dicit etiam quod si breve suum in hoc casu esset cassatum necesse esset ei recursum habere ad curiam christianitatis ubi ipse [i]<per>[i] regiam prohibitionem ab agendo repelleretur etc. Et cum ipse tunc aliud non haberet recuperare neque in una curia neque in alia etc. et sic curia regis eidem in exhibitione justicie deficeret et per consequens melioris conditionis foret huiusmodi decimarum occupator nichil juris habens in eisdem nisi de injuria sua propria quam petens jus habens in eisdem quod esset racioni inconsonum etc. petit judicium etc.

Et [i]<abbas>[i] dicit ut prius quod ex quo ipse offert disrationare etc. nec predictus Johannes aliquid aliud dicit etc. petit judicium de ipso tamquam de indefenso etc. Et super hoc dictum est predicto Johanni per justiciarios quod ex quo istud breve est super mero jure etc. quod habito respectu ad hoc et ad rationes predicti abbatis etc. quod sub periculo in huiusmodi brevibus de recto etc. dicat pro responso quod sibi melius viderit expedire etc.

Et Johannes dicit quod predicte exceptiones quas ipse pretendit sunt pro brevi cassando etc. Et si visum fuerit curie quod hoc non sufficiat dicet aliud etc.

Dies datus est eis hic de audiendo [judicio][1] suo a die sancti Trinitatis in xv dies etc.

[d]<Dies datus est eis de audiendo judicio suo hic a die sancti Michaelis in xv dies etc.>[d2]

2.11

CP 40/98, m. 94
Common Pleas, Hilary term 1293

Norht'. Simon Basset de Ryston' et Johannes de Peco attachiati fuerunt ad respondendum abbati de Cyrencestr' de placito quare ipsi simul cum Roberto Basset, Ricardo le Messer, Ricardo Bollok, Johanne filio Henrici de Aylenton', Willelmo de Houtot, Roberto de Asseleye, Petro de Asseleye, Johanne Brideshalesman, Johanne Brun, Rogero le Personespenser, et Alano le Flecher vi et armis bona et catalla ipsius abbatis ad valenciam centum solidorum apud Rowell in Ryston' inventa ceperunt et asportaverunt et alia enormia ei intulerunt ad grave dampnum ipsius abbatis et contra pacem etc. Et unde queritur quod predicti Simon et alij die mercurii proxima ante festum sancte Marie Magdalene

[1] MS. omits.
[2] In the margin is written ad judicium

part of the tithes etc. first began to be available from the time of the statute of the present king proclaimed at Westminster etc.[1] And he says that this writ according to the statute etc. lies only for the patron etc. in a case where the parson of some church has been prevented by the writ *Indicavit* from bringing an action in Court Christian to recover tithes etc. And since the abbot in bringing the aforesaid writ is not within the case covered by the statute etc., he prays judgment etc.

And the abbot says that he claims the advowson of the tithes of his own advowson etc. And he claims those tithes as the right of his church and as parson to his own use etc. And he says that the statute sufficiently applies to him in this case because he is patron and parson etc. He says also that if his writ in this case should be quashed he would need to have recourse to Court Christian, where he would be prevented from bring an action by royal prohibition etc.; and since in that case he would have no recovery in either court etc., and the king's court would be deficient in doing justice to him, and as a result an occupier of tithes of this sort, having no right to them except through his own wrongdoing, would be in a better condition than one claiming to have right in the same, which would be inconsistent with reason, he prays judgment etc.

And the abbot says, as previously, that since he offers to prove etc. and John has not said anything else he prays judgment against him as undefended etc. And as to this it is said to John by the justices that, since this writ is purely of right etc., and having regard to that and to the abbot's arguments, at the peril in writs of right of this kind he should say in answer whatever seems to him most expedient etc.

And John says that the exceptions that he is putting forward are to quash the writ etc. And if it seems to the court that this is insufficient he will say something else etc.

Day is given to them here on the quindene of Trinity Sunday for hearing judgment etc.

2.11

ABBOT OF CIRENCESTER v. PARSON OF RUSHTON AND JOHN DE PECO

Trespass to tithes

Northampton. Simon Basset of Rushton and John de Peco were attached to answer the abbot of Cirencester concerning a plea as to why they together with Robert Basset, Richard le Messer, Richard Bollok, John fitz Henry de Aylenton, William de Houtot, Robert de Asseleye, Peter de Asseleye, John Brideshalesman, John Brun, Roger le Personespenser and Alan le Flecher with force and arms seized and carried off the abbot's goods and chattels found at Rothwell in Rushton to the value of 100 shillings and committed other wrongs against him, to the abbot's grave damage and against the peace etc. And in this regard he complains that on the Wednesday before the feast of St Mary Magdalene in the twentieth

[1] St West. II c. 5, printed in SR 1:75–76.

anno regis nunc vicesimo apud Rowell fenum ipsius abbatis in quodam prato quod vocatur Canunmede in Ryston' et similiter die lune proxima ante festum sancti Laurentii anno supradicto blada ipsius abbatis scilicet frumentum et ordeum apud Rowell in Ryston' inventa ad valenciam etc. ceperunt et asportaverunt et alia enormia etc. Unde dicit quod deterioratus est et dampnum habet ad valenciam centum solidorum. Et inde producit sectam etc.

Et Simon Basset et Johannes de Peco per attornatum suum veniunt. Et defendunt vim et injuriam quando etc. Et bene defendunt quod ipsi nuncquam predictis die et anno aliqua catalla ceperunt etc. nec asportaverunt etc. Set dicunt quod ipsi predicta fenum et blada ceperunt et asportaverunt ut decimam ecclesie ipsius Simonis de Ryston' que quidem blada et fenum fuerunt decimata etc. set non vi et armis nec contra pacem etc.

Et abbas dicit quod predicta blada et fenum fuerunt propria catalla ipsius abbatis et in locis ubi idem Simon nullas decimas habere consuevit unita et inventa etc. Et de hoc ponit se super patriam. Et Simon et Johannes similiter. Ideo preceptum est vicecomiti quod venire faciat hic in crastino sancti Johannis Baptisti xij etc. per quos etc. et qui nec etc. ad recognoscendum etc. Quia tam etc.

Postea a die Pasche in unum mensem anno regni regis nunc vicesimo secundo venerunt partes et similiter juratores de consensu partium electi. Qui dicunt super sacramentum suum quod predictus Johannes non venit predictis die et anno vi et armis etc. nec aliquam transgressionem eidem abbati fecit. Et pro predicto Simone dicunt quod quidam Robertus quondam persona ecclesie de Riston predecessor predicti Simonis recuperavit in curia christianitatis versus ipsum abbatem decimas suas de istis eisdem tenementis de quibus idem abbas modo queritur predicta fena et blada modo fore asportata et inde fuit in seisina tanquam pertinens ad ecclesiam suam de Riston. Et dicunt quo ad predicta blada asportata quod predictus abbas injuste se queritur etc. Quia dicunt quod predicta tenementa de quibus predicta blada provenerunt non sunt nec fuerunt ipsius abbatis set sunt libere tenencium suorum. Unde dicunt precise quod predicta blada non fuerunt ipsius abbatis. Et quo ad fenum dicunt quod pratum unde fenum illud provenit est ipsius abbatis. Et dicunt quo ad illud quod predictus Simon sine vi et armis venit ad predictum pratum per visum virorum fidedignorum et in loco quo decimas suas percipere debuit pratum illud admensurari fecit et decimas suas rationabiles et non ultra per visum eorumdem virorum cepit sicut predictus Robertus predecessor etc. fecit. Et juratores quesiti qualiter rectores ecclesie de Riston' decimas suas in pratis et fenis percipere debeant, dicunt quod predictus Robertus predecessor etc. anno quo decimas suas recuperavit in curia christianitatis per consideracionem eiusdem curie eo quod predictus abbas decimas suas dare nolebat licet judicialiter in hoc condempnatus set illas sicut prius consuevit [i]<voluit totaliter asportasse>[i] venit [i]<idem Robertus>[i] per visum legalium hominum ad prata postquam falcata fuerunt et per visum ad prata postquam falcata fuerint et per visum eorumdem prata illa admensurari fecit et decimas debitas et rationabiles a novem partibus separavit et eiecit et inde pro voluntate sua disposuit. Et dicunt quod predictus Simon venit in hunc modum et non contra pacem et decimas suas inde percepit. Quesiti etiam si predicte placee terre et prati sint in parochia de Riston' vel Rowell unde predictus abbas est persona dicunt precise quod sunt in parochia de Riston'.

Postea quia quedam restant examinanda per juratores inquisitionis predicte maxime cum ipsi nichil dixerint qualiter sit consuetudo [i]<illius patrie>[i] fenum decimandi et

year of this king,[1] at Rothwell, Simon and the others seized and carried off the abbot's hay in a certain meadow called Canunmede in Rushton, and similarly on the Monday before the feast of St Lawrence in the same year[2] seized and carried off the abbot's grain, namely wheat and barley, found at Rothwell in Rushton, and committed other wrongs etc. He says he is thereby harmed and damaged to the value of 100 shillings. And he produces suit etc.

And Simon Basset and John de Peco appear by their attorney. And they deny force and wrong whenever etc. And they deny that they ever on the said day and year seized or carried off any chattels etc. But they say that they seized and carried off the hay and grain as tithes of Simon's church of Rushton, which hay and grain were tithed etc., but not with force and arms nor against the peace etc.

And the abbot says that the hay and grain were his own chattels and were made and found in places where Simon was accustomed to have no tithes etc. And concerning this he puts himself upon the country. And Simon and John likewise. Therefore the sheriff is ordered to cause to appear here on the morrow of St John the Baptist 12 men etc. by whom etc. and who are not etc. to give their verdict on the aforesaid matter, because both parties etc.

Later, one month after Easter in the twenty-second year of this king's reign,[3] the parties came; and likewise the jurors chosen by consent of the parties. They say on their oath that John did not come on the said day and year with force and arms etc., nor did he commit any trespass against the abbot. And as for Simon they say that one Robert, formerly parson of the church of Rushton, Simon's predecessor, recovered his tithes against the abbot in Court Christian from these same tenements from which the abbot now complains the hay and grain were taken, and was in seisin thereof as belonging to his church of Rushton. And they say that, as to the grain carried off, the abbot complains unjustly etc., because they say that the tenements from which the grain issued are not and were not the abbot's but belong to his free tenants. Wherefore they say precisely that the grain is not the abbot's. And as for the hay they say that the meadow whence that hay issued is the abbot's. And as to that they say that Simon came without force and arms to the meadow, and by the view of trustworthy men, and in the place where he should receive his tithes, he had the meadow measured and took his reasonable tithes and not more, according to their view, just as Robert his predecessor did. And the jurors, asked how rectors of the church of Rushton are accustomed to take their tithes in meadows and hay fields, say that Robert the predecessor etc. in the year when he recovered his tithes in Court Christian by judgment of that court, because the abbot did not wish to pay his tithes, though judicially ordered to do so, and would instead have carried off all the hay, as he was previously accustomed, Robert, according to the view of lawful men, came to the meadow after it had been mowed and according to their view had the meadow measured and separated his due and reasonable tithes from the nine parts and removed them and disposed of them at his will. And they say that Simon came in this manner and not contrary to the peace and thence took his tithes. Asked also whether these places and meadows are in the parish of Rushton or Rothwell where the abbot is parson they say precisely that they are in the parish of Rushton.

[1] 16 July 1292.
[2] 4 August 1292.
[3] 17 May 1294.

etiam de cuius advocatione vel dono predicta terre et pratum sint, preceptum est vicecomiti quod habeat corpora predictorum juratorum hic a die sancti Johannis Baptiste in xv dies etc.[1]

2.12

CP 40/106, m. 243
Common Pleas, Michaelmas term 1293

Norff'. Radulfus le Bret persona ecclesie de Acolt summonitus fuit ad respondendum magistro Hugoni Sampson de placito quod reddat ei triginta et octo libras que ei aretro sunt de annuo redditu quadraginta solidorum quem ei debet etc. Et unde idem magister Hugo per attornatum suum dicit quod, cum contentio mota esset inter ipsum magistrum Hugonem ex una parte et predictum Radulfum ex altera coram [i]<Rogero nuper>[i] episcopo Norwycensis de ecclesia de Acolt cum capella de Benyngham Norwycensis diocesis tandem pax conquievit inter eos sub hac forma: quod iidem Hugo et Radulfus se ordinationi Godefredi de Norton officialis consistorii Norwycensis episcopi super predicta ecclesia die sancti Jacobi anno regni domini regis nunc primo submiserunt ac idem Godefridus eodem die ex consensu eiusdem episcopi ordinasset quod predictus Hugo perciperet de predictis ecclesia et capella per manus predicti Radulfi singulis annis tota vita ipsius Hugonis quadraginta solidos ad duos anni terminos, videlicet medietatem ad sinodum proximum post Pascha apud Gyppewycum et alteram medietatem ad sinodum proximum post festum sancti Michaelis, solvendos eidem Hugoni nomine personatus et quam quidem ordinationem idem episcopus postea die sanctorum septem dormientium eodem anno confirmavit, idem Radulfus predictum annuum redditum semper hucusque detinuit et arreragia predicta ei reddere contradixit. Unde dicit quod deterioratus est et dampnum habet ad valenciam quadraginta librarum. Et inde producit sectam etc.

Et Radulfus per attornatum suum venit et dicit quod non debet ei hic inde respondere, quia dicit quod, cum predictus magister Hugo exigat predictum annuum redditum versus eum nomine personatus prout patet per narrationem ipsius Hugonis, videtur ei quod placitum istud spectat ad forum ecclesiasticum cum sit mere spirituale. Unde petit judicium si curia ista de huiusmodi causa que est mere spirituale cognoscere debeat etc., cum idem Hugo per cessum vel decessum ipsius Radulfi personatum predicte ecclesie ratione predicti annui redditus si in causa ista optineret consequi posset etc. Dicit etiam quod idem Hugo alias coram Salamone de Roff' et sociis suis justiciariis ultimo intinerantibus in comitatu predicto implacitavit ipsum [Radulfum][2] de isto eodem annuo redditu coram quibus ipse alegavit quod placitum istud mere fuit spirituale et quod mere pertinuit ad curiam christianitatis inde cognoscere, per quod idem Radulfus per considerationem eiusdem curie recessit inde quietus et dictum fuit ipsi Hugoni quod adiret curiam christianitatis

[1] In the margin is written ad judicium
[2] MS. reads Robertum

Later because certain matters remain to be examined by the jurors of this inquisition, especially since they have said nothing of the custom of how hay should be tithed in this locality and also of whose advowson or gift these lands and meadow are, the sheriff is ordered to have the bodies of the jurors here on the quindene of St John the Baptist etc.

2.12

HUGH SAMPSON v. PARSON OF ACLE

Annual rent

Norfolk. Ralph le Bret, parson of the church of Acle, was summoned to answer master Hugh Sampson concerning a plea that he pay him 38 pounds that are the arrears of an annual rent of 40 shillings owed to him etc. And in this regard master Hugh by his attorney says that, whereas there was a controversy between master Hugh and Ralph before Roger, lately bishop of Norwich,[1] concerning the church of Acle with the chapel of Banningham in the diocese of Norwich, and a peace was finally made between them in this form, that Hugh and Ralph should submit themselves to the order of Geoffrey de Norton, official of the consistory court of the bishop of Norwich, on the feast of St James in the first year of the lord king,[2] and Geoffrey on that day with the consent of the bishop ordered that Hugh should receive from the church and chapel at the hand of Ralph each year for the rest of Hugh's life 40 shillings to be paid twice annually, namely half at the first synod after Easter at Ipswich and the other half at the first synod after Michaelmas, to be paid to Hugh in the name of the parsonage, and the bishop later, on the feast of the Seven Sleepers in the same year,[3] confirmed that order, Ralph has never paid the annual rent to this day and refuses to pay the arrears to him. He says he is thereby harmed and damaged to the value of 40 pounds. And he produces suit etc.

And Ralph by his attorney appears and says that he ought not answer him here, because he says that, whereas master Hugh demanded this annual rent against him in the name of his parsonage, as appears in Hugh's count, it seems to him that that plea belongs to the ecclesiastical forum since it is purely spiritual. In this regard he prays judgment whether this court ought to hear this kind of claim which is purely spiritual etc., since Hugh through the retirement or the death of Ralph would still be able to sue the parson of the church for this annual rent if he should prevail in this case etc. He says also that Hugh previously sued Ralph before Solomon of Rochester[4] and his associates, the latest justices itinerant in this county, concerning the same annual rent, and that Ralph argued that that plea was purely spiritual and that it belonged only to Court Christian for decision, and by judgment of that court Ralph was acquitted and Hugh was told that he should proceed in Court Christian

[1] Roger Skerning served from 1266 until his death in 1278.
[2] 25 July 1273.
[3] 27 July 1273.
[4] Served as a justice on several eyres from 1274 until his disgrace in 1290 as a result of complaints arising out of his conduct of the Norfolk eyre of 1286.

[i]<etc.>[i] si sibi vidisset expedire. Et de hoc ponit se super recordum rotulorum predicte itineris. Unde cum ipse alias per judicium curie regis recessit quietus de predicto annuo redditu quod quidem judicium [i]<ad huc>[i] stat in suo robore, petit judicium etc.

Et Hugo dicit quod postquam placitum fuerat inde inter ipsum Hugonem et predictum Radulfum in curia [i]<regis>[i] coram prefatis justiciariis itinerantibus traxit ipse ipsum Radulfum in placitum in curia christianitatis coram magistro Johanne de Peneston comissario domini pape super predicto annuo redditu. Et dicit quod idem Radulfus postea regiam prohibitionem porrexit ipsi magistro Johanni ne placitum illud ulterius teneret in curia christianitatis, occasione cuius brevis idem magister Johannes de placito illo ulterius tenendo in eadem curia omnino supersedit etc. Et hoc paratus verificare etc. Unde, cum per predictam prohibitionem predicto magistro Johanni per predictum Radulfum porrectam jurisdictio ipsius judicis in causa predicta cognoscendi ablata fuit et adnullata nec esset juri consonum quod ipse in utraque curia in casu proposito recederet sine remedio etc., petit judicium si predictus Radulfus ei hic inde respondere non debeat etc. Et idem Radulfus quesitus si porrexit inde predictam regiam prohibitionem prefato comissario et hoc postquam placitum inde fuerat coram prefatis justiciaribus itinerantibus vel ante, dicit quod ad hoc non habet necesse respondere. Dicit enim quod licet prohibitionem illam ipsi comissario porrexisset non tamen propter hoc attribuitur curie hic auctoritas quod de huiusmodi causa que est mere spirituale cognoscere possit etc.

Dies datus est eis hic in crastino Purificationis beate Marie etc.[1]

2.13

JUST 1/375, m. 91
Kent Eyre, 1293

Magister hospitalis sancti Bartholomei de Hethe per attornatum suum queritur de Willelmo le Archer persona ecclesie de Saltwode de hoc quod idem Willelmus die lune proxima ante festum assumptionis beate Marie anno domini regis nunc septimo in villa de Hethe blada ipsius magistri in garbis de frumento, ordeo, et pisarum nonam partem vesture octo acrarum terre ad valenciam decem solidorum vi et armis cepit et asportavit etc. Et similiter quod idem Willelmus die martis proxima post festum sancti Laurencii anno regis predicti [i]<octavo>[i] nonam partem vesture predictarum octo acrarum de predictis generibus bladi ad valenciam sex solidorum et octo denariorum vi et armis cepit et asportavit etc. Et similiter quod idem Willelmus de anno in annum semper tempore messionis usque nunc blada ipsius magistri in garbis, videlicet nonam partem vesturarum octo acrarum terre, cepit et asportavit contra voluntatem ipsius magistri, ad dampnum suum viginti librarum et contra pacem etc.

Et predictus Willelmus venit et bene cognoscit quod asportavit predicta blada, videlicet nonam partem vesture cuiuslibet generis bladi octo acrarum terre predictarum, sicut

[1] In the margin is written ad judicium

if it seemed expedient for him to do so.[1] And concerning this Ralph puts himself upon the records of the aforesaid eyre. In this regard, since he was acquitted at another time by judgment of the king's court concerning this annual rent, which judgment still remains in force, he prays judgment etc.

And Hugh says that after the plea between him and Ralph in the king's court before the justices itinerant he sued Ralph in Court Christian before master John de Peneston, commissary of the lord pope, concerning the same annual rent. And he says that Ralph then presented a royal prohibition to master John forbidding the further hearing of that plea in Court Christian, as a result of which writ master John altogether ceased the further hearing of that plea in his court etc. And this he is prepared to prove etc.

In this regard, since by the royal prohibition directed by Ralph to master John his jurisdiction in that case was taken away and annulled, and since it is not consonant with right that he should depart from either court in the case presented without remedy etc., he prays judgment whether Ralph should answer him here in this regard etc. And Ralph, asked whether he presented the royal prohibition to the commissary, and whether he did so before or after the plea before the justices itinerant, says that he need not answer. He says further that, even if he presented that prohibition to the commissary, no authority is conferred on this court on that account to decide cases like this that are purely spiritual etc.

Day is given to them here on the morrow of the Purification of the Virgin etc.

2.13

MASTER OF HYTHE HOSPITAL v. PARSON OF SALTWOOD

Trespass to tithes

The master of St Bartholomew's Hospital, Hythe, by his attorney complains of William le Archer, parson of the church of Saltwood, that on the Monday immediately before the feast of the Assumption of the Virgin in the seventh year of this king's reign,[2] in the vill of Hythe, William seized and carried off with force and arms the master's sheaves of grain of wheat, barley and peas from the ninth part of the crop from eight acres of land to the value of 10 shillings etc. And likewise that William, on the Tuesday immediately after the feast of St Laurence in the eighth year of this king's reign,[3] seized and carried off with force and arms the ninth part of the crop of the same kinds of grain from the said eight acres to the value of six shillings and eight pence etc. And likewise that William, from year to year until now at harvest time has seized and carried off the master's sheaves of grain, namely the ninth part of the crops of those eight acres of land, against his will to his damage of 20 pounds and against the peace etc.

[1] No record of this case has been found.
[2] 14 August 1279.
[3] 13 August 1280.

ei bene licuit, quia dicit quod predictus magister est parochianus suus et quod predicte [i]<octo>[i] acre terre sunt infra procinctum parochie sue et dicit quod singulis annis predictis quando predictus magister decimavit bladum suum de predictis octo acris terre ipse Willelmus decimas illas cepit et asportavit tanquam pertinentes ad ecclesiam suam predictam de Saltwode etc. Et petit judicium [i]<si>[i] de decimis suis debeat hic respondere etc.

Et predictus magister dicit quod predicta blada que predictus Willelmus asportavit non fuerunt decime ipsius Willelmi nec blada decimata nec pertinencia ad ecclesiam suam predictam, set dicit quod idem Willelmus singulis annis predictis blada illa non decimata contra voluntatem ipsius magistri cepit et asportavit et contra pacem etc. Dicit etiam pro rege quod quam cito predictus Willelmus percepit quod idem magister questus fuit de eo coram justiciariis hic de die in diem ipsum magistrum excommunicavit et sentenciam illam promulgavit et insuper eidem magistro gravi morbo languenti et jura ecclesie petenti expresse negavit donec idem magister tactis sacrosanctis jurasset quod amplius in curia domini regis hic querelam suam versus eundem Willelmum de transgressione predicta non prosequeretur, in contemptum domini regis mille librarum et lesionem corone sue et dampnum ipsius magistri centum librarum etc.

Et predictus Willelmus dicit quod ipse asportavit predicta decimata ut decimas pertinentes ad ecclesiam suam de Saltwode predictam et quod predictum magistrum occasione predicte querele non excommunicavit nec jura sancte ecclesie negavit in forma predicta sicut predictus magister queritur. Et [i]<de>[i] hoc ponit se super patriam. Et predictus magister similiter. Ideo fiat inde jurata etc.

Juratores dicunt super sacramentum suum quod predictus Willelmus die lune proxima ante Assumpcionem beate Marie anno domini regis predicti septimo et singulis annis tempore messionis usque nunc, videlicet per quindecim annos continuos, vi et armis blada ipsius magistri de predictis octo acris [i]<terre>[i] asportavit, videlicet quolibet anno nonam partem vesture illarum octo acrarum, et dicunt quod quando contingebat predictum magistrum cariasse partem predicti bladi in grangiam suam prout moris est predictus Willelmus per suos vi et armis grangiam illam intravit et garbas illas ibidem [i]<sic>[i] cariatas numerare fecit et postea in campis de bladis ipsius magistri usque ad summam garbarum none partis vesture predictarum octo acrarum terre cepit et asportavit in forma predicta etc., ad dampnum ipsius magistri decem librarum et contra pacem etc. Dicunt eciam quod postquam predictus magister questus fuit coram justiciariis hic de transgressione ista, idem Willelmus eundem magistrum de die in diem excommunicavit et postea jura sancte ecclesie eidem magistro negavit ut predictum est, in contemptum domini regis et dampnum ipsius magistri etc. Ideo consideratum est quod predictus magister recuperet dampna sua decem librarum versus predictum Willelmum le Archer. Et idem Willelmus quia asportavit predicta blada vi et armis et excommunicavit predictum magistrum occasione predicta commitatur prisone. Postea venit predictus Willelmus le Archer et finem fecit per centum marcas per plegios Stephani atte Doune, magistri Johannis de Dovoria, Alani atte Doune, Alani de Eastwell, Johannis atte Stone, Thome de Brochill’, Nicholai de Rode, Hugonis de Ladewode, et Willelmi le Pyke.

And William appears and fully confesses that he took the grain, namely a ninth part of the crop of each kind of grain from those eight acres, as was fully permitted to him, because the master is his parishioner and the eight acres are within the boundaries of his parish, and in each of those years when the master tithed his grain from those eight acres William took and carried off those tithes as pertaining to his church of Saltwood etc. And he prays judgment whether he ought to answer here concerning his tithes etc.

And the master says that the grain that William took was not his tithes and that the grain was not tithed and did not belong to his church. He says that in each of these years William seized and carried off the untithed grain against the master's will and against the peace etc. He says also on behalf of the king that, as soon as William learned that the master had complained of him here before these justices, William excommunicated him from day to day and pronounced that sentence against him, and moreover, when the master was weak with a grave disease and requested last rites he expressly refused until the master, touching halidoms, swore that he would not prosecute further this complaint of trespass against William in the king's court, in contempt of the lord king 1,000 pounds and wrong to his crown and damage to the master 100 pounds etc.

And William says that he carried off the tithed grain as tithes belonging to his church of Saltwood and that he did not excommunicate the master or refuse him last rites as alleged on account of the complaint as the master now alleges. And concerning this he puts himself upon the country. And the master likewise. Therefore let a jury be made etc.

The jurors say on their oath that William, on the Monday immediately before the feast of the Assumption of the Virgin in the lord king's seventh year,[1] and every year at harvest time until now, for 15 consecutive years, carried off with force and arms the master's grain from those eight acres, namely a ninth part of the crop of those eight acres each year. And they say that when it was time for the master to cart part of the grain to his grange, as is customary, William, by his men, entered that grange with force and arms and caused the sheaves carted there to be counted and after that in the fields he seized and carried off from the master's grain sheaves amounting to the ninth part of the crop from the eight acres in the manner aforesaid etc., to the master's damage 10 pounds and against the peace etc. They say also that, after the master complained before the justices here of that trespass, William excommunicated the master from day to day and after that refused him last rites, as has been said, in contempt of the lord king and damage to the master etc.

Therefore judgment is given that the master recover his damages of 10 pounds against William le Archer. And William, because he carried off the grain with force and arms and excommunicated the master for that reason, is committed to prison.

Later William le Archer comes and makes a fine of 100 marks, according to pledges Stephen atte Doune, master John de Dover, Alan atte Doune, Alan de Eastwell, John atte Stone, Thomas de Brochill, Nicholas de Rode, Hugh de Ladewode, and William le Pyke.

[1] 4 August 1279.

2.14

CP 40/136, m. 69
Common Pleas, Hilary term 1301

Wygorn'. Magister Johannes de Ebroitis persona ecclesie de Tredyinton' summonitus fuit ad respondendum magistro Radulfo de Leycestre et Thome de Sutham de placito quare cepit averia et catalla ipsorum magistri Radulfi et Thome et ea injuste detinuit contra vadium etc. Et unde iidem magister Radulfus et Thomas per attornatum ipsius Radulfi queruntur quod predictus magister Johannes die dominica proxima post festum sancti Marce ewangeliste anno regni domini regis nunc vicesimo octavo apud Tredyinton' in quadam via que ducit de Blakele usque Tredynton' cepit quadraginta et duos agnos ipsorum magistri Radulfi et Thome et illos imparcavit et imparcatos detinuit ed adhuc detinet contra vadium etc. Et eisdem die et anno idem magister Johannes apud Neubaud cepit decem et octo quarteria et unum bussellum et dimidium fabarum et pisarum, duo tassa frumenti precii viginti librarum, duo tassa ordei precii viginti librarum, et unum tassum pisarum ipsorum magistri Radulfi et Thome etc. et catalla illa injuste detinuit et abduxit et adhuc detinet etc. Unde [dicunt][1] quod [deteriorati sunt][2] et dampnum [habent][3] ad valenciam sexaginta librarum. Et inde [producunt][4] sectam etc.

Et magister Johannes per attornatum suum venit. Et defendit vim et injuriam quando etc. Et dicit quod ipse non cepit predicta averia neque catalla etc. set dicit revera quod ipse dimisit predictis magistro Radulfo et Thome ecclesiam suam de Tredynton' predictam a festo Pentecostes anno supradicto usque ad idem festum proximo sequens etc. pro centum libris solvendis ad tres anni terminos de quibus iidem magister Radulfus et Thomas detinuerunt ei sexaginta marcas ob quod idem magister Johannes secutus fuit versus eos coram domino episcopo Wygorn' in curia christianitatis ita quod bona illa sequestrata fuerunt per preceptum eiusdem episcopi ad sectam suam etc. Et hoc paratus est verificare etc.

Et magister Radulfus et Thomas dicunt quod idem magister Johannes cepit predicta averia, bona, et catalla de facto suo proprio sicut queruntur etc. Et de hoc ponunt se super patriam. Et magister Johannes similiter etc. Ideo preceptum est vicecomiti venire faciat hic a die Pasche in tres septimanas xij etc. per quod etc. et qui nec etc. quia tam etc. Et super hoc veniunt ballivi predicti episcopi de Osewaldeslowe et petunt inde curiam suam per cartam Henrici regis patris regis nunc etc. Ideo etc.

Postea continuato processu usque nunc scilicet a die sancti Michaelis in xv die anno regni regis nunc vicesimo nono Willelmus de Beref' coram quo etc misit hic recordum suum in hec verba: Postea apud pontem de Stycheford die lune proxima post festum sancti Michaelis coram W. de Beref'assoc' sibi Johanne de Clynton' de Maxstok' venerunt partes et similiter juratores de consensu partium electi. Qui dicunt super sacramentum suum

[1] MS. reads dicit
[2] MS. reads deterioratus est
[3] MS. reads habet
[4] MS. reads producit

2.14

RALPH DE LEYCESTRE AND THOMAS DE SUTHAM v. PARSON OF TREDINGTON

Replevin

Worcester. Master John de Ebroitis, parson of the church of Tredington, was summoned to answer master Ralph de Leycestre and Thomas de Sutham on a plea as to why he seized animals and chattels of master Ralph and Thomas and detained them unjustly despite an offer of gage etc. And in this regard master Ralph and Thomas by Ralph's attorney complain that, on the Sunday immediately after the feast of St Mark in the twenty-eighth year of the present king,[1] at Tredington in a certain road that runs from Blockley to Tredington, master John took 52 lambs belonging to master Ralph and Thomas and impounded and detained them and still detains them despite an offer of gage etc. And on the same day and year at Newbold master John took 18 quarters and one and a half bushels of master Ralph's and Thomas's beans and peas, two stacks of wheat worth 20 pounds, two stacks of barley worth 20 pounds, and one stack of peas, and unjustly carried off and detained those chattels and still detains them etc. He says he is thereby harmed and damaged to the value of 60 pounds. And he produces suit etc.

And master John appears by his attorney. And he denies force and wrong whenever etc. And he says that he did not take the animals or chattels etc. but says that in truth he demised Tredington church to master Ralph and Thomas for a term running from Pentecost in the said year[2] to the same feast day in the following year for 100 pounds to be paid on three dates of that year, and that master Ralph and Thomas withheld 60 marks of that sum, on account of which master John sued them in Court Christian before the bishop of Worcester so that those goods were sequestered by order of the bishop at his suit etc. And this he is prepared to prove etc.

And Ralph and Thomas say that master John took the animals, goods and chattels of his own act as they have alleged etc. And concerning this they put themselves upon the country. And master John likewise etc. Therefore the sheriff is ordered to cause to appear here three weeks after Easter 12 men etc. by whom etc. and who are not etc. And concerning this the bishop's bailiffs from Oswaldstow[3] come and claim his court according to a charter of King Henry, father of the present king etc. Therefore etc.

Later, process having continued until now, namely the quindene of Michaelmas in the twenty-ninth year of the present king's reign,[4] William de Bereford,[5] before whom etc., sends this record here in these words:

'Later at Stechford Bridge on the first Monday after Michaelmas,[6] before William de Bereford and his associate John de Clynton of Maxstoke, the parties appear, and likewise

[1] 1 May 1300.
[2] 29 May 1300.
[3] A hundred held by the bishop of Worcester according to local custom. VCH Worcester, 1:287.
[4] 13 October 1301.
[5] Justice of Common Pleas from 1294 until his elevation to the chief justiceship in 1308.
[6] 2 October 1301.

quod predictus magister Johannes predictis die et anno cepit predictos quinquaginta duos agnos ipsorum Radulfi et Thome et ipsos inparcavit et adhuc detinet prout iidem Radulfus et Thomas queruntur. Et quo ad predicta blada dicunt quod predictus magister Johannes est archidiacanus episcopi Wygorn' eiusdem archidiaconatus et quod ipse auctoritate sua propria predicta blada per ipsos Radulfum et Thomam apud Neubald adunata sequestrare et sub arto sequestro ea custodiri fecit per quod iidem Radulfus et Thomas commodum suum inde facere non potuerunt et preterea maxima pars ejusdem bladi triturati et non triturati deperiit ratione illius sequestri ad dampnum etc. sex marcarum etc. Et ideo consideratum est quod predictum [Radulfus][1] et Thomas recuperent dampna sua que taxantur per juratores ad sex marcas. Et magister Johannes in misericordia etc.[2]

2.15

CP 40/135, m. 107
Common Pleas, Michaelmas term 1301

Staff'. Stephanus persona ecclesie de Swynnerton' summonitus fuit ad respondendum priori de Stanes de placito quod reddat ei viginti et tres solidos et quatuor denarios qui ei aretro sunt de annuo redditu duarum marcarum quem ei debet etc. Et unde idem prior per attornatum suum dicit quod cum quidam finis levasset in curia domini Henrici regis patris domini regis nunc apud Westmonasterium die dominica proxima ante Ascencionem Domini anno regni sui secundo coram Martino de Pateshill' et sociis suis justiciariis etc. inter Robertum de Swynnerton' petentem et Willelmum priorem de Kenilworth' deforciatorem de advocatione ecclesie de Swynnerton' unde assisa ultime presentationis etc. scilicet quod predictus prior cognovit advocationem predicte ecclesie esse ius ipsius Roberti et illam remisit et quietumclamavit de se et successoribus suis predicto Roberto et heredibus suis imperpetuum et predictus Robertus concessit pro se et heredibus suis de assensu et voluntate Willelmi tunc Coventr' episcopi ecclesie de Stanes et canonicis ibidem Deo servientibus duas marcas argenti percipiendas annuatim ipsis canonicis ad ecclesiam suam de Stanes per manum persone ecclesie predicte de Swynnerton' quicumque fuerit etc. ad duos terminos scilicet ad Pascha unam marcam et ad festum sancti Michaelis unam marcam. Et de quo quidem annuo redditu quidam Reginaldus quondam prior de Stanes predecessor ipsius prioris fuit seisitus per manus cuiusdam Willelmi de Tebesey prime persone ecclesie de Swynnerton' post confectionem predicti finis. Et similiter omnes priores predecessores sui postmodum successive seisiti fuerunt de annuo redditu illo per manus personarum eiusdem ecclesie. Et etiam idem prior seisitus fuit per manus predicti Stephani nunc persone etc. de eadem annuitate, idem Stephanus predictos viginiti et tres solidos et quatuor denarios ante diem impetrationis predicti brevis reddere contradixit et ad huc contradicit unde dicit quod deterioratus est et dampnum habet ad valenciam centum solidorum. Et inde

[1] MS. reads Ricardus
[2] In the margin is written misericordia (stricken through) and dampna xj marce

the jurors chosen with the parties' consent. The jurors say on their oath that on the said day and year master John took the said 52 lambs of Ralph and Thomas and impounded them and still detains them as Ralph and Thomas have alleged. And as for the grain they say that master John is the bishop of Worcester's archdeacon and that, by his own authority, he caused the grain that Ralph and Thomas had gathered together at Newbold to be sequestered and caused it to be kept under close sequestration, as a result of which Ralph and Thomas were unable to have use of it, and moreover that the greater part of the grain both threshed and unthreshed was ruined on account of that sequestration, to their damage etc. six marks etc.' Therefore it is adjudged that Ralph and Thomas recover their damages, which are assessed by the jury at six marks. And master John is in mercy etc.

2.15

PARSON OF SWYNNERTON v. PRIOR OF STONE

Annual rent

Staffordshire. Stephen, parson of the church of Swynnerton, was summoned to answer the prior of Stone concerning a plea that he pay him 23 shillings and four pence that are in arrears of an annual rent of two marks that he owes him etc. And in this regard the prior says through his attorney that a certain fine was levied in the court of the lord king Henry, father of the present king, at Westminster on the first Sunday before Ascension Day in the second year of his reign,[1] before Martin de Pattishall[2] and his associate justices, between Robert de Swynnerton, demandant, and William, prior of Kenilworth, deforciant, concerning the advowson of the church of Swynnerton, whereof an assize of darrein presentment etc., namely the prior acknowledged the advowson of the church to be the right of Robert and remitted and quitclaimed it from himself and his successors to Robert and his heirs in perpetuity, and Robert granted for himself and his heirs, with the assent of William, then bishop of Coventry,[3] two marks of silver to be paid to the church of Stone[4] and its canons there serving God by the hand of the parson of the church of Swynnerton, whoever he might be, in two annual instalments, one mark at Easter and another on Michaelmas. And one Reginald, formerly prior of Stone, predecessor of the present prior, was seised of this annual rent by the hand of one William de Tebesey, the first parson of Swynnerton after the making of the fine. And likewise all the prior's predecessors were thereafter seised successively of this annual rent by the hands of the church's parsons. And also this prior was seised of the same annuity by the hand of Stephen, the present parson. And Stephen refused to pay the 23 shillings and four pence owed before the initiation of this suit and still refuses. The prior says he is thereby harmed and damaged to the

1 17 June 1218.
2 An ordained clerk, he served as one of the king's justices on eyre from 1218 until his retirement from the bench in 1228 to become dean of St Paul's.
3 William Cornhill, consecrated in 1215, resigned 1223.
4 I.e., Stone Priory.

producit sectam etc. Et profert quandam partem predicti finis que predictam grantem nomine elemosine et non nomine pensionis ex assensu predicti episcopi factam etc. testatur etc.

Et Stephanus per attornatum suum venit. Et dicit quod non debet ei hic inde respondere quia dicit quod cum predictus prior exigat predictum annuum redditum asserendo eum de predicta ecclesia provenire videtur ei quod placitum istud ad forum spectat ecclesiasticum cum sit mere spirituale petit judicium si curia ista de huiusmodi causa que spiritualis est cognoscere debeat etc. Postea dictum est ei quod respondeat si etc. Et idem Stephanus defendit vim et injuriam quando etc. Et dicit quod ipse per predictum finem ad predictam annuitatem solvendam onerari non debet in hac parte quia dicit quod cum quis per huiusmodi finem in tali casu de annuitate aliqua debeat obligari necessario oporteret in levationem eiusdem finis assensum trium personarum intervenire videlicet assensum patronis concedentis loci diocesani grantem illam ratificantis et persone se per grantem et ratificationem illas de annuitate illa solvenda onerantis etc. Unde per predictum finem manifeste liquet quod tempore confectionis eiusdem fuit ecclesia illa vacans ex quo levavit super assisa ultime presentationis et sic sequitur quod nullus clericus eo tempore per illum finem de predicta annuitate oneravit aut fini illi assensum prebuit petit judicium etc.

Et prior dicit quod cum predictus Stephanus non dedicit quin predictus finis inter predictos Robertum de Swynnerton' et Willelmum quondam priorem predecessorem de assensu loci diocesani etc. levavit in forma predicta pretextu cuius finis predictus Willelmus de Tebesey qui post levationem eiusdem finis fuit persona predicte ecclesie inmediata acceptendo finem illum predictum annuum redditum predicto Willelmo quondam priori etc. se inde onerando soluit et etiam omnes clerici persone ecclesie predicte tempore subsequenti tam predictus Stephanus quam alii annuum redditum illum predicto priori et predecessoribus suis eundem finem acceptantes et ratificantes reddiderunt prout [paratus est][1] verificare etc. [petit][2] judicium si predictus Stephanus se de annuitate predicta devolvere possit cum hoc esset ad predictum finem in omni sui effectu enervandum et evacuandum etc.[3]

Postea continuato hinc inde processu usque in octabis sancti Johannis Baptiste venerunt partes. Et datus est eis dies hic in a die sancti Michaelis in xv dies de audiendo judicio etc. Postea a die sancti Hillarii in xv dies anno regni domini regis nunc tricesimo primo veniunt tam predictus prior per attornatum suum quam predictus Stephanus per Robertum de Lichefeld attornatum suum. Et idem Stephanus quesitus per justiciarios si quid aliud velit dicere petit licenciam inde loquendi qua optenta idem Stephanus postmodum solempniter vocatus non venit immo recessit in contemptum curie. Et super hoc predictus prior petit judicium secundum prius allegata. Et quia predictus Stephanus dedicere non potest quin predictus finis levavit in forma predicta et pax inde in tam solempni [forma][4] admissa fuit et acceptata nec necesse erat quod assensus persone etc. in levatione eiusdem finis interveniret cum finis ille levavit super assisa ultime presentationis per quam supponebatur quod ecclesia illa tunc fuit vacans etc. videtur curie quod finis ille rite fuit levatus et quod patronus eiusdem ecclesie de assensu loci diocesani ipsam ecclesiam tunc temporis vacantem etc. de predicto annuo redditu in casu isto bene potuit onerare etc. Et ideo consideratum est quod quod predictus prior recuperet predictum annuum redditum versus predictum Stephanum. Et similiter predictos viginti et tres solidos et quatuor denarios de

[1] MS. reads parati sunt.
[2] MS. reads petunt.
[3] In the margin at this point is written ad judicium.
[4] MS. reads curia.

value of 100 shillings. And he produces suit etc. And he proffers a part of the fine, which attests that this grant done with the bishop's assent was made in the name of alms not as a pension etc.

And Stephen appears by his attorney. And he says that he ought not answer him here because, since the prior demands the annual rent asserting that it issues from his church, it seems to him that this plea pertains to the ecclesiastical forum because it is purely spiritual. He prays judgment whether this court ought to decide a spiritual case like this etc. Later he is told that he should answer if etc. And Stephen denies force and wrong whenever etc. And he says that he should not be burdened to pay this annuity by the fine because for anyone to be burdened by a fine like this in this sort of annuity case it is necessary in the levying of the fine to have the assent of three people, namely the patron granting the annuity, the local diocesan ratifying the grant, and the parson who by the grant and ratification is to be burdened with paying the annuity etc. And, since by the fine it is manifestly clear that at the time of its making the church was vacant, since it was levied on an assize of darrein presentment, and thus it follows that no clerk at that time was burdened by the fine as to the annuity, or assented to the fine, he prays judgment etc.

And the prior says that, since Stephen does not deny that the fine between Robert de Swynnerton and William, the former prior, with the assent of the local diocesan etc., was levied in this form, and that by virtue of the fine William de Tebesey, first parson of the church after the fine was made, paid the annual rent to William, the former prior, thus accepting the fine and burdening himself, and that also all subsequent parsons of the church, Stephen as well as the others, paid the annual rent to the prior and his predecessors, accepting and ratifying the fine, as he is prepared to prove etc., he prays judgment whether Stephen is able to deprive him of the annuity since this would have the effect of weakening and avoiding the fine etc.

Later, process having been continued to the octave of St John the Baptist,[1] the parties appear. And day is given to them here on the quindene of Michaelmas to hear judgment etc. Later on the quindene of Hilary in the thirty-first year of the lord king's reign[2] the prior through his attorney, and Stephen through his attorney Robert de Lichefeld, appear. And Stephen, questioned by the justices whether he wishes to say anything else, prays leave to imparl therein, which having been obtained Stephen afterwards, having been solemnly called, does not appear but instead withdraws in contempt of the court. Thereupon the prior prays judgment according to what he has said earlier. And because Stephen cannot deny that the fine was levied in this form, or that the peace was accepted and admitted in such solemn form, or that the parson's assent was unnecessary in levying the fine (since the fine was levied on an assize of darrein presentment, whereby it can be supposed that the church was vacant), it seems to the court that the fine was properly levied and that the patron of the church, with the assent of the local diocesan in this case, the church then being vacant, was able to burden the church with the annual rent etc. And therefore it is adjudged that the prior recover the annual rent against Stephen; and likewise the 23 shillings and four pence of arrears up to the initiation of this suit and also seven marks of

[1] 2 July 1302.
[2] 28 January 1303.

arreragiis etc. ante impetrationem brevis etc. Et etiam septem marcas de arreragiis post impetrationem etc. Et dampna sua que taxantur per justiciarios ad quadraginta solidos. Et Stephanus in misericordia etc.

Dampna xl solidi unde medietas clericis.

2.16

CP 40/149, m. 340d
Michaelmas term, 1304

Ebor'. Memorandum quod cum dominus Adam de Osgoteby rector ecclesie de Gairegrave Eboraci diocesis petierit in curia christianitatis coram officiale archiepiscopi Eboraci versus abbatem et conventum de Furneys decimas provenientes de terris et culturis ipsorum abbatis et conventus in eorum grangia de Wynterbourn' infra parochiam et loca decimabilia dicte ecclesie constitutis et sentenciam de eisdem decimis ad ipsum rectorem et successores suos nec non et ad ecclesiam illam de jure spectantibus contra dictos abbatem et conventum non obstantibus privilegiis, exceptionibus, et aliis quibuscumque coram eodem officiale propositis et exhibitis per eosdem fuerit assecutus, iidemque abbas et conventus post pronunciationem illius sentencie ac mandatum executionis ejusdem quoddam breve regium quod dicitur indicavit in cancellaria regis ficta suggestione impetraverint dicto officiali directum asserentes se tenere quartam partem illius ecclesie de advocatione sua propria cum non sint advocati dictus officialis executioni predicte faciende supersedit, cumque dictus dominus Adam ex inde sentiens se gravatum cum instancia petierit coram toto consilio domini regis apud Eboracum consultationem sibi fieri in hoc casu tandem coram eodem consilio ibidem presentibus W. Coventr' et Lich' episcopo thesaurario, magistro W. de Grenefeld cancellario domini regis, Rogero le Brabazon, Radulfo de Hengham, Phillipo de Wylghby, Willelmo de Bereford, Gilberto de Roubury, Petro Malorre, Willelmo de Carleton', Rogero de Hegham, Johanne de Insula, magistro Ricardo de Abyndon', Lamberto de Thrikyngham, Johanne de Kyrkeby, Nicholao de Warwyk, et aliis ordinatum fuit et concordatum quod dictus dominus Adam prefato officiali de conservando ipsum erga dominum regem inde indempnem cautionem idoneam inveniret et quod dictus officialis in executione illius sentencie in forma debita procederet et secure et illud idem eidem officiali ipso ibidem tunc presente dictum fuit per totum consilium et injunctum. Ista acta fuerunt coram consilio regis apud Eboracum nono die Julij anno etc. xxxij.

arrears since then etc., and his damages, which are assessed by the justices at 40 shillings. And Stephen is in mercy.

Damages 40 shillings—of which half to the clerks.

2.16

RECTOR OF GARGRAVE v. ABBOT AND CONVENT OF FURNESS

Tithes, indicavit and consultation

Yorkshire. Let it be remembered that, whereas lord Adam of Osgodby, rector of the church of Gargrave, in the diocese of York,[1] sued the abbot and convent of Furness in Court Christian before the official of the archbishop of York, seeking to recover tithes issuing from cultivated lands of the abbot and convent in their grange of Winterburn, located within the parish and titheable places of the rector's church; and whereas, notwithstanding the privileges, exceptions and whatsoever else was propounded and exhibited before the official, lord Adam obtained a sentence against the abbot and convent concerning these tithes as belonging of right to him and to his successors and also to his church; and whereas the abbot and convent, after pronouncement of that sentence and the mandate for its execution, obtained by means of a fictitious allegation a royal writ called *Indicavit* from the king's chancery directed to the official asserting that they hold one-fourth of that church of their own advowson, whereas they were not patrons, the official refrained from causing execution. And whereas lord Adam, feeling himself aggrieved by this, urgently requested a consultation in this case before the entire king's council at York, finally before the council, in the presence of Walter Langton, bishop of Coventry and Lichfield, treasurer,[2] master William de Greenfeld, the king's chancellor,[3] Roger le Brabazon,[4] Ralph de Hengham,[5] Phillip de Wylghby,[6] William de Bereford,[7] Gilbert de Rothbury,[8] Peter Mallore,[9] William de Carlton, Roger de Higham,[10] John de Lisle,[11] master Richard de Abingdon, Lambert de Threckingham,[12] Nicholas de Warwyk,[13] and others, it was ordered and agreed that lord Adam find suitable security for preserving the official's immunity against the lord king and that the official proceed with the execution of that sentence in due form and correctly. And the same was said and enjoined by the full council to the official who was then present. Enacted before the king's council at York on the ninth day of July in the king's thirty-second year.[14]

[1] See Case no. 1.27 for a dispute over tithes between the same Adam and a different religious house. He was a senior clerk in chancery. [2] Treasurer from 1295 to 1307. [3] Chancellor from 1302 to 1305 and archbishop of York from 1306 until his death in 1315. [4] Chief Justice of King's Bench from 1295 until his retirement in 1316. [5] Chief Justice of Common Pleas from 1301 until 1309. [6] Lieutenant of the treasurer late in Edward's reign. [7] Justice of Common Pleas from 1294 until his elevation to the chief justiceship in 1308. [8] Justice of King's Bench from 1295 to 1316. [9] Justice of Common Pleas from 1292 to 1308. [10] Appointed a baron of the Exchequer in 1301. [11] Appointed a baron of the Exchequer in 1295. [12] Justice of Common Pleas from 1300 to 1316. [13] Served as king's serjeant from 1294 to 1306. [14] 1304.

2.17

CP 40/149, m. 389
Common Pleas, Michaelmas term 1304

Notyngh'. Paulinus de Pavely appellat Willelmum fratrem Stephani de Pavely de morte Ricardi de Pavely patris sui, videlicet de vi et auxilio cuiusdam Stephani de Pavely qui de facto convictus est, quod cum predictus Ricardus pater etc. fuisset in pace dei et domini regis nunc etc. die martis in festo sancti Gregorii pape anno regis nunc tricesimo primo hora meridiana in villa de Rotyngton' in domo eiusdem Stephani in eadem villa in medio domus a parte boriali quindecim pedes et a parte australi xv pedes et a parte occidentali quindecim pedes et a parte orientali quindecim pedes ibi venit predictus Willelmus de Pavely felonice et insultu premeditato et eisdem die et anno et hora in medio placee predicte tenuit predictum Ricardum de Pavely utraque manu sua per sinistram scapulam quousque predictus Stephanus fecit ei unam plagam in medio capitis unde statim obiit etc. Et post predictam feloniam predictus Paulinus statim levavit hutesium et clamorem et sequebatur. Et hoc offert etc.

Et Willelmus venit et dicit quod clericus est et non debet in curia hic respondere. Et super hoc venit quidam Johannes decanus christianitatis Eboraci gerens vices decani et capituli ecclesie beati Petri Eboraci sede eiusdem vacante per litteras ipsorum patentes quas profert in hec verba: 'W. decanus et capitulum ecclesie sancti Petri Eboraci sede eiusdem vacante dilectis nobis in Christo filiis dominis Johanni decano nostro christianitatis Eboraci ac Johanni sancti Dionisii et Thome sancti Edwardi ecclesiarum rectoribus in eadem salutem in omnium salvatore. De vestra fida et circumspecta industria plenius confidentes ad petendum et recipiendum clericos quoscumque tam religiosos quam alios super quibuscumque criminibus irrettatos coram domino nostro rege vel ipsius locum tenentibus ac justiciariis suis quibuscumque necnon et aliis assignatis vel assignandis datis vel dandis ac carcerem liberandis vobis conjunctim et divisim cum potestate cohercionis canonice committimus vices nostras, proviso quod clericos tam religiosos quam alios quos receperitis sub salva servari custodia faciatis quousque quid de illis agendum fuerit consultius ordinetur. In cuius rei testimomium sigillum nostrum presentibus est appensum. Datus Eboracum xvi kalendarum Decembris anno domini mcccquarto'. Et idem Johannes virtute commissionis predicte petit ipsum Willelmum tanquam clericum. Et ut sciatur pro quali ei liberari debeat, inquiratur rei veritatis per patriam. Et preceptum est vicecomiti quod venire faciat apud Westmonasterium a die sancti Hillarii in xv dies xij etc. per quos etc. ad recognoscendum etc. Et interim predictus Willelmus liberatur vicecomiti Eboraci custodiendus et ducendus apud Westmonasterium ad prefatum terminum etc.

Postea ad diem illum idem vicecomes produxit [apud][1] Westmonasterium predictum Willelmum. Et idem Willelmus liberatur custodi de Flete custodiendus etc. Postea ad diem illum veniunt predicti Paulinus et Willelmus. Et jurata inter eos ponitur in respectum usque a die Pasche in tres septimanas pro defecto juratorum quia nullus venit. Ideo vicecomes habeat corpora etc. Et predictus Willelmus interim liberatur Johanni de Lincoln uni vicecomitum London' custodiendus etc. Postea in octabis sancte Trinitatis anno regni regis

[1] MS. reads apud apud

2.17

PAUL DE PAVELY v. WILLIAM DE PAVELY
Benefit of clergy in an appeal of felony

Nottinghamshire. Paul de Pavely appeals William, brother of Stephen de Pavely, for the death of Richard de Pavely, his father, namely for using force and aiding Stephen de Pavely, who was convicted of the deed, for that, whereas Richard, his father etc., was in the peace of God and of the present lord king etc. on Tuesday, the feast of Saint Gregory Pope, in the thirty-first year of this king's reign[1] at noon, in the vill of Ruddington, in Stephen's house in the same vill, in the middle of the house, 15 feet from the northern part, 15 feet from the southern part, 15 feet from the western part, and 15 feet from the eastern part, William de Pavely came there and feloniously and in premeditated assault on that day and year and hour in the middle of that place held Richard de Pavely with both hands by his left shoulder until Stephen wounded him in the middle of the head, from which he immediately died etc. And after this felony Paul immediately raised the hue and cry and pursued. And this he offers etc.

And William appears and says that he is a clerk and ought not answer in this court. And concerning this one John, dean of the Court Christian of York, acting in place of the dean and chapter of St Peter's, York, the see being now vacant, comes by their letters patent which he presents in these words: 'W., dean and the chapter of St Peter's, York, the see being now vacant, to our beloved sons in Christ, lords John, our dean of the Court Christian of York, John, rector of St Dionysius's church, and Thomas, rector of St Edward' s church, greetings in the saviour of all. Fully confident of your trustworthy and circumspect industry, we commit to you jointly and separately with power of canonical coercion our office for requesting and receiving all clerks, religious as well as others, accused of any crime before our lord king or those holding his place, or any of his justices, and also others assigned or given authority, and those assigned to deliver gaols, provided that you cause to be placed under safe custody any religious as well as other clerks whom you receive until we may order more deliberately what should be done with them. Done at York on the sixteenth kalends of December in the year of our Lord 1304'.[2] And John, by virtue of this commission, claims William as a clerk. And so that it may be known how he ought to be delivered, let the truth of the matter be inquired of the country. And the sheriff is ordered to cause to appear at Westminster on the quindene of Hilary 12 men etc. by whom etc. to give their verdict in the aforesaid matter etc. And meanwhile William is to be delivered to the sheriff of Yorkshire to be held and brought to Westminster at the said term etc.

Later, on that date,[3] the sheriff produced William at Westminster. And William was delivered to the warden of the Fleet to be kept in custody etc. Later on that day Paul and William appear. And their jury is postponed until three weeks after Easter for lack of jurors because none appears. Therefore let the sheriff have their bodies etc. And meanwhile William is delivered to John de Lincoln, one of the sheriffs of London, to be kept in

[1] 12 March 1303.
[2] 17 January 1304.
[3] 27 January 1304.

nunc xxxiij venit predictus Willelmus et similiter jurata et predictus Paulinus solempniter vocatus non venit. Et fuit querens. Ideo plegii sui de prosequendo in misericordia. Et predictus Paulinus capiatur etc. Et juratores dicunt super sacramentum suum quod predictus Willelmus in nullo est culpabilis de morte predicta etc. Ideo predictus Willelmus inde quietus etc.[1]

2.18

KB 27/179, m. 6
King's Bench, Hilary term 1305

London'. Magister Walterus de Thorp [i]<decanus consistorii de Arcubus London' et magister Gilbertus de Middelton' attachiati fuerunt ad respondendum domino regi de placito quare>[i] cum dominus rex in curia regis coram eo per considerationem ejusdem curie recuperaverit versus Robertum archiepiscopum Cantuarensis, episcopum Wygornie, priorem de Wygornia, et Johannem de Middelton' clericum presentationem domini regis ad ecclesiam de Doderhill Wygornie diocesis et per breve domini regis de judicio idem dominus rex mandaverit predicto episcopo loci diocesano quod non obstante reclamatione predictorum archiepiscopi, prioris, Johannis, et sua idoneam personam ad ecclesiam predictam ad presentationem domini regis admitteret ac dominus rex pro eo quod iidem archiepiscopus et Johannes admissionem clerici regis ad dictam ecclesiam per ipsum regem presentati et ad eam iuxta vim et effectum judicii predicti admissi et in eadem instituti nitebantur et adhuc ut dicitur nituntur impugnare et judicium predictum enervare. Eidem archiepiscopo et suis commissariis necnon et predicto Johanni dominus rex per litteras suas prohibuerit ne quicquam in hac parte quod in juris domini regis regii derogationem aut executionis dicti judicii retardationem vel enervationem cedere valeret atemptarent seu quoquomodo presumerent atemptare, magister Gilbertus de Midelton' ut dominus rex ex testimonio didicit fidedingno ad statum honoris regii nullum habens respectum litteras regis predictas in pleno consistorio de Arcubus London' porrectas violenter cepit illasque ad parietes contemptibiliter projecit eas ibidem legi vel videri minime permittendo et contemptum contemptui addendo dignitatemque domini regis regiam deridendo coram omnibus ibidem assistentibus palam dixit se non magis pro domino rege quam pro filia ipsius regis facere in hac parte dominumque regem et ministros suos in curia sua dictum archiepiscopum super negotio dictam ecclesiam de Dodirhill tangente non deducere sicut archiepiscopum Eborbaci de capella sancti sepulcri Eboraci dominus rex deduxit. Idemque Gilbertus coram omnibus in dicto consistorio tunc existentibus vovit seu votum emisit quod dicto episcopo Wygornie pro eo quod mandato domini regis predicto paruit in hac parte contemptus grandes et enormes juste vel injuste inferret et inferre pro viribus non desistet. Insuper dictus Gilbertus et etiam magister Walterus de Thorp' decanus consistorii predicti ipsius Gilberti complex et fautor judicialiter considerari fecerunt quod procurator dicti episcopi pro eo quod a quadam sentencia dictum negotium tangente ad curiam

[1] In the margin are written misericordia and a large Q

custody etc. Later on the octave of Trinity in this king's thirty-third year[1] William appears as does the jury and Paul solemnly called does not appear. And he was the complainant. Therefore his pledges for prosecution are in mercy. And let Paul be taken etc. And the jurors on their oath say that William was in no way guilty of the aforesaid death etc. Therefore William is to go quit etc.

2.18

R. v. THE DEAN OF ARCHES AND GILBERT DE MIDDLETON
Contempt

London. Master Walter de Thorp, dean of the consistory court of Arches, London, and master Gilbert de Middelton were attached to answer the lord king concerning a plea as to why, whereas the lord king in his court in his presence recovered by judgment of that court[2] from Robert, archbishop of Canterbury,[3] the bishop of Worcester,[4] the prior of Worcester,[5] and John de Middelton, clerk, the lord king's presentation to the church of Dodderhill in the diocese of Worcester, and by royal writ of judgment the king ordered the bishop, the local diocesan, that notwithstanding any claim of the archbishop, the prior, John, and their people, he admit a suitable parson to that church at the king's presentation; and the lord king, because the archbishop and John have striven and, as it is said, are striving to resist the admission of the king's clerk presented to the church by the king, and admitted to it and instituted in it according to the force and effect of the judgment, and to impair that judgment, by his letters prohibited the archbishop and his commissaries and also John from attempting or in any way presuming to attempt anything in this regard that would have the effect of causing a derogation from the lord king's right or delay or impairment of execution of the judgment: Master Gilbert de Midelton, as the lord king learns from trustworthy testimony, having no respect for the king's honourable status, violently seized the king's letters presented in the full consistory court of Arches, London and contemptuously threw them against the wall, not permitting them to be read or seen at all, and adding contempt to contempt and mocking the king's royal dignity before all those present publicly declared that he would do no more for the lord king in this regard than for his daughter, and that the lord king and his ministers in his court would not treat the archbishop of York on the matter touching Dodderhill church as the lord king treated the archbishop of York concerning St Sepulchre's Chapel, York;[6] and Gilbert, before all present in the consistory court, vowed

[1] 21 June 1305. [2] KB 27/175, m. 19 (1304), printed in King's Bench Cases 3:125–27. [3] Robert Winchelsey was archbishop of Canterbury from 1294 to 1313. [4] William Gainsborough was bishop of Worcester from 1302 to 1307. [5] Worcester Cathedral was a Benedictine priory. [6] The reference appears to be to the king's dispute with the archbishop regarding the king's appointment of a clerk, John Bouhs, to the prebend of Stillington at St Peter's, York. The archbishop had refused to admit Bouhs to the prebend on the ground that the pope had already appointed to that vacancy but was ordered to admit Bouhs anyway. See King's Bench Cases 3:136–137. Bouhs was also appointed sacrist of the collegiate chapel of St Mary and the Holy Angels, often referred to as St Sepulchre's Chapel, in 1300 and may have received the prebendary in connection with that appointment. For the appointment of Bouhs to the sacristy, see CPR 1292–1301 512. Bouhs was apparently also the king's initial choice for appointment to Dodderhill. Denton, Winchelsey 215.

romanam appellavit et in appellatione sua sentenciam illam in regis contemptum et corone [et][1] dignitatis domini regis regie prejudicium latam fuisse inseruit nisi idem procurator verba illa contemptum et prejudicium domini regis in dicta appellatione designancia amoveret vel amoveri faceret a curia consistorii predicti imperpetuum banniretur. Et alia enormia domino regi ibidem perpetrarunt in regis contemptum jurisque domini regis regii prejudicium ac status [i]<ipsius>[i] domini regis scandalum manifestum. Et unde Johannes de Cestr' qui sequitur pro domino rege dicit quod predicti magister Walterus de Thorp' et magister Gilbertus de Middelton' proximo die juridico post festum [i]<Sancte Fidis virginis>[i] [d]<apostolorum Simonis et Jude>[d] ultimo preterito huiusmodi contemptus, violencias, et transgressiones supradictas domino regi perpetrarunt. Unde dicit quod dominus rex deterioratus est et dampnum habet ad valenciam mille librarum. Et inde producit sectam etc.

Et predicti magister Walterus de Thorp' et magister Gilbertus de Middelton' veniunt et defendunt quicquid est in contemptum domini regis seu status sui regii. Et dicunt quod in nullo sunt culpabiles de contemptibus, violenciis, seu transgressionibus supradictis. Et de hoc ponunt se super patriam. Ideo veniat inde jurata coram rege in octabis Purificationis beate Marie ubicumque etc. ad recognoscendum etc. Et super hoc magister Walterus de Thorp' [i]<invenit>[i] magistrum Thomam de Eadburbyry et magistrum Thomam de Bray manucaptores suos auditurus recognitionem predicte inquisitionis. Et predictus magister Gilbertus de Middelton' invenit Reginaldum de Cobham de comitatu Kanc' et Gilbertum de Touthebi de comitatu Linc', Johannem de Illeye de comitatu Suff', et Thomam Alewy de comitatu Berks' manucaptores suos auditurus etc.

Ad quem diem predictus Johannes de Cestr' qui sequitur pro rege et predicti magister Walterus et magister Gilbertus coram toto consilio domini regis apud Westmonasterium veniunt et etiam juratores similiter ibidem veniunt. Qui dicunt super sacramentum suum quod predicti magister Walterus et magister Gilbertus in nullo sunt culpabiles de contemptibus, violenciis, seu aliquibus transgressionibus eis superius impositis etc. Ideo inde quieti etc.

2.19

KB 27/184, m. 45d
King's Bench, Easter term 1306

Bedef' Magister Radulfus persona de Wrastlyngworth attachiatus fuit ad respondum magistro Johanni de Sodyngton persone ecclesie de Potton de placito quare cum idem magister Johannes in curia domini regis coram eo per breve suum implacitet predictum magistrum Radulfum et alios in brevi domini regis contentos de quadam transgressione eidem

[1] MS. omits.

that justly or unjustly he would inflict weighty and great contempt upon the bishop of Worcester because he obeyed the lord king's mandate and would not desist from doing so with all his might; moreover Gilbert and master Walter de Thorp, dean of the consistory court, Gilbert's accomplice and supporter, caused it to be adjudged that the bishop's proctor, because he appealed from a certain sentence touching this matter to the Roman Curia and inserted in his appeal that that sentence had been issued in contempt of the king and of his crown and prejudice to his royal dignity, would be banned for ever from the consistory court unless he removed or caused to be removed the words 'contempt and prejudice of the lord king' included in the appeal; and they perpetrated other enormities against the lord king, in contempt of the king and prejudice of the royal right of the lord king and the manifest slander of the lord king's estate. And John of Chester, who sues for the lord king, says that master Walter de Thorp and master Gilbert de Middelton perpetrated these contempts, violences and trespasses to the lord king on the first juridical day after the most recent feast of St Faith.[1] He says that the lord king is thereby injured and damaged to the extent of 1,000 pounds. And he produces suit etc.

And master Walter de Thorp and master Gilbert de Middelton appear and deny anything that is in contempt of the lord king or of his royal estate. And they say they are in no way guilty of these contempts, violences or trespasses. And concerning this they put themselves upon the country. Therefore let the jurors appear before the king on the octave of the Purification of the Virgin wherever etc. to give their verdict etc. And on this master Walter de Thorp finds master Thomas of Adderbury and master Thomas de Bray as his mainpernors to hear the verdict of the inquisition. And master Gilbert de Middelton finds Reginald de Cobham of Kent, Gilbert de Toutheby of Lincolnshire,[3] John de Illeye of Suffolk and Thomas Alewy of Berkshire as his mainpernors to hear etc.

On which day[2] John of Chester, who sues for the king, and masters Walter and Gilbert appear before the king's full council at Westminster and the jurors likewise appear. And they say on their oath that masters Walter and Gilbert are in no way guilty of the contempts, violences, or other trespasses alleged against them above etc. Therefore let them go quit etc.

2.19

PARSON OF POTTON v. PARSON OF WRESTLINGWORTH
Contempt

Bedfordshire. Master Ralph, parson of Wrestlingworth, was attached to answer master John de Sodington, parson of the church of Potton, concerning a plea as to why, whereas master John by royal writ sued master Ralph and others named in the writ in the court of

[1] 6 October 1304. [2] 9 February 1305. [3] A counter of the Bench since *c.* 1293: Baker, *Serjeants at Law*, 146.

magistro Johanni per prefatum magistrum Radulfum et alios illata ut dicitur prefatus magister Radulfus predictum magistrum Johannem occasione prosecutionis placiti sui predicti in curia regis predicta trahit in placitum in curia christianitatis in regis contemptum et predicti Johannis dampnum non modicum et gravamen. Et unde queritur quod prefatus magister Radulfus predictum magistrum Johannem occasione prosecutionis placiti sui predicti in curia regis predicta [traxit][1] in placitum in curia christianitatis, videlicet die dominica proxima post festum Purificationis beate Marie anno regni regis nunc tricesimo quarto coram archiepiscopo Cantuar' de diversis transgressionibus contra pacem regis factis occasione prosecutionis placiti predicti. In regis contemptum mille librarum. Et dampnum predicti magistri Johannis centum librarum. Et inde producit sectam etc.

Et predictus magister Radulfus venit et [defendit vim et][2] iniuriam et quicquid est in regis contemptum etc. Et bene defendit quod in nullo est cupabilis de transgressione predicta. Et de hoc ponit se super patriam etc. Et magister Johannes similiter. Ideo veniat inde jurata coram rege a die sancte Trinitatis in xv dies ubicumque etc. Et qui nec etc. Ad recognoscendum etc.

Postea apud Schefford die sabbati proxima post festum sancti Jacobi apostoli anno regni regis nunc xxxiiij coram G. de Roubyry veniunt partes predicte et similiter juratores. Qui dicunt super sacramentum suum quod occasione placiti quod predictus magister Johannes de Sudington prosequebatur versus predictum magistrum Radulfum in curia domini regis idem magister Radulfus traxit prefatum magistrum Johannem in placitum in curia christianitatis coram archiepiscopo Cantuar' [i]<in contemptum domini regis et>[i] dampnum ipsius magistri Johannis sexaginta solidorum etc. Ideo consideratum est quod predictus Johannes recuperet dampna sua sexaginta solidorum. Et predictus Radulfus presens committitur gaole.

Dampna lx solidi unde Roberto de Wolsthorp xx solidi.[3]

[1] MS. reads traxhit
[2] MS. omits.
[3] In the margin is written Gaola

the King's Bench concerning a certain trespass done against master John, as alleged, master Ralph sued master John in Court Christian on account of his prosecution of his plea in the king's court, in contempt of the king and not insubstantial damage and wrong to John. And in this regard he complains that master Ralph sued master John in Court Christian on account of his prosecution of his plea in the king's court concerning various trespasses against the king's peace, namely on the first Sunday after the feast of the Purification of Mary in the thirty-fourth year of this king's reign[1] before the archbishop of Canterbury[2] on account of the prosecution of the plea in the king's court, in contempt of the king 1,000 pounds and to the damage of master John 100 pounds. And he produces suit etc.

And master Ralph appears and denies force and wrong and whatever is in contempt of the king etc. And he says that he is in no way guilty of the trespass. And concerning this he puts himself upon the country etc. And master John likewise. Therefore let the jurors appear before the king on the quindene of Trinity wheresoever etc. and who do not etc. to give their verdict etc.

Later at Shefford on the first Saturday after the feast of St James in the thirty-fourth year of this king's reign,[3] before Gilbert de Rothbury,[4] the parties appear and likewise the jurors, who say on their oath that on account of the plea that John de Sodington prosecuted against master Ralph in the court of the lord king master Ralph sued master John in Court Christian before the archbishop of Canterbury, in contempt of the lord king and to the damage of the same master John 60 shillings etc. Therefore it is adjudged that John recover his damages of 60 shillings. And Ralph who is present is committed to gaol.

Damages 60 shillings, of which 20 shillings to Robert de Wolsthorp.

[1] 6 February 1306.
[2] Robert Winchelsey was archbishop of Canterbury from 1294 to 1313.
[3] 30 July 1306.
[4] Justice of King's Bench from 1295 to 1316.

CASES FROM THE NORFOLK EYRE OF 1286

3.1

JUST 1/575, m. 101

Juratores presentant quod iidem[1] capiunt de portantibus aucas, gallinas, et alia volatilia vendenda in civitate predicta per dies festivos ad estimationem x solidos.

Et predicti magister Henricus et Johannes dicunt [quod][2] ipsi [nuncquam][3] aliquid ceperunt nec capere fecerunt de huiusmodi portantibus vel vendentibus aucas, gallinas, vel aliqua alia [volatilia][4] ut predictum est. Et de hoc ponunt se super patriam.

Et juratores [i]<ad>[i] hoc electi dicunt super sacramentum suum quod predictus Johannes subdecanus ipsius magistri Henrici summonere fecit coram eo omnes pollitarios civitatis qui aliqua volatilia emerint vel [vendiderint][5] per dies festivos et eos amerciare facit coram eo, quosdam ad ij solidos per annum et quosdam ad plus et ad minus. Sed bene dicunt quod de forinsecis volatilia vendendibus nihil sciunt. Et dicunt quod numquam aliqui coacti fuerunt ad huiusmodi theoloneum prestandum infra civitatem istam nisi per predictos magistrum Henricum et Johannem subdecanum suum. Ideo loquendum cum domino rege etc.

Postea per dominum regem et per eius consilium provisum est et ordinatum quod, quia huiusmodi consuetudines injuriose sunt et ad nocumentum totius populi et detrimentum, [ ][6] decetero aliquod huiusmodi theoloneum ut predictum est [ ][7]decetero non capiatur nec aliquis cogitur ad huiusmodi teoloneum vel consuetudinem prestandum. Et preceptum est vicecomiti quod proclamare faciat per totum episcopatum Norwic' quod nullus decetero huiusmodi teoloneum vel consuetudinem capiat etc.

3.2

JUST 1/575, m. 101

Walterus de Daleby et Cassandra [uxor][8] eius quereutur de predicto Johanne [de Berstrete][9] subdecano de hoc quod idem Johannes maliciose summonere fecit ipsos coram eo et ipsos traxit in placitum in curia christianitatis de catallis et debitis que non fuerunt de testamento vel matrimonio et de [eis][10] levare fecit iiii solidos ad opus Willelmi de Wells et quos iidem Walterus et Cassandra alias coram eo probaverunt eidem Willelmo soluisse et

[1] Identified in previous entry as Henricus Sampson decanus Norwic' et Johannes de Berstrete subdecanus suus [2] MS. omits. [3] MS. reads nucquam [4] MS. reads volotilia [5] MS. reads vendenderint [6] MS. reads quod [7] MS. reads decetero [8] MS. omits. [9] Identified in a previous entry. [10] MS. reads eiis

CASES FROM THE NORFOLK EYRE OF 1286

3.1

IN RE THE DEAN AND SUBDEAN OF NORWICH

The jury presents that the same [Henry Sampson, dean of Norwich, and John de Berstrete, his subdean,] took 10 shillings from those bringing geese, hens and other fowls on feast days to be sold in that city on feast days.

And master Henry and John say that they never took nor caused to be taken anything of this sort from those bringing or selling geese, hens or any other fowls as has been said. And concerning this they put themselves upon the country.

And the jurors chosen for this say on their oath that John, master Henry's subdean, caused to be summoned before him all poulterers of the city who bought or sold any fowls on feast days and caused them to be amerced before him, some at two shillings annually and others more or less. But they well say that as to non-resident poulterers they know nothing. And they say that no one was ever compelled to pay this kind of toll within this city except by master Henry and John his subdean. Therefore the lord king is to be consulted etc.

Later, it is provided and ordained by the lord king and his council that, because customs of this kind are injurious and to the harm and detriment of all the people, henceforth any toll of this kind is not to be taken nor is anyone to be compelled to pay this kind of toll or custom. And the sheriff is ordered to cause to be proclaimed throughout the entire diocese of Norwich that no one henceforth is to collect this kind of toll or custom etc.[1]

3.2

WALTER AND CASSANDRA DE DALEBY v. SUBDEAN OF NORWICH

Walter de Daleby and Cassandra his wife complain of John de Berstrete, subdean, that John maliciously caused them to be summoned before him and drew them into a plea in Court Christian concerning chattels and debts that were not testamentary or matrimonial

[1] The two entries immediately preceding this one also involve jury presentments declaring that Henry Sampson and John de Berstrete collected tolls unjustly. The first presentment concerned 'haliday tol', said to have been levied on men, horses, boats, and carts bringing merchandise into the city on feast days. The second involved a toll levied on brewers, butchers, and fishmongers who engaged in commerce on feast days. Each case was adjourned and the entry concludes with a statement that judgment appears below (Judicium patet inferius), presumably a reference to the provision declared in Case no. 3.1.

ipsos excommunicavit de die in diem quousque iterato soluisset predictos iiii solidos et quousque finem cum ipso Johanne fecissent per v solidos quos cepit ab [eis][1] [pro][2] sentencia illa remittenda. Unde dicunt quod deteriorati sunt et dampnum habent ad valenciam xx solidorum.

Et Johannes bene cognoscit quod ipse convenire fecit eos coram eo et pro fidei datione cepit predictos v solidos et quod tenuit placitum inter eos ut predictum est. Et ideo consideratum est quod predictus Johannes [satisfaciet][3] predictis Waltero et Cassandre de predictis v solidis et de dampnis suis que taxantur ad iiii solidos. Et idem Johannes custodiatur.

3.3

JUST 1/575, m. 101

Convictum est per juratam in quam Gilbertus Hakun querens et predictus Johannes [de Berstrete][4] subdecanus se posuerunt quod predictus Johannes summonere fecit ipsum et duos filios suos coram [eo][5] vendiderunt victualia messoribus et aliis operariis in autumpno per diem festivum et ipsos vexavit de capitulo ad capitulum quousque finem cum eo fecissent per v solidos quos cepit ab [eis][6] injuste et contra voluntatem suam. Et ideo consideratum est quod Johannes satisfaciet eis de predictis v solidis et de dampnis suis que taxantur ad v solidos et idem Johannes custodiatur.

3.4

JUST 1/575, m. 101

Convictum est per juratam in quam Willelmus de Pangeford querens et predictus Johannes [de Berstrete][7] subdecanus se posuerunt quod predictus Johannes summoneri fecit ipsum coram eo ad capitulum suum eo quod concubuisse debuit cum uxore sua antequam ipsam disponsasset postquam ipsam disponsaverat et vexavit ipsum de capitulo ad capitulum quousque finem cum eo fecisset per dimidiam marcam quam ab eo cepit injuste. Et ideo consideratum est quod predictus Willelmus recuperet predictam dimidiam marcam versus eundem Johannem et dampna sua que taxantur ad xl solidos. Et Johannes custodiatur.

[1] MS. reads eiis
[2] MS. reads per
[3] MS. reads satisfecit
[4] Identified in a previous entry.
[5] MS. omits.
[6] MS. reads eiis
[7] Identified in a previous entry.

and caused four shillings to be levied from them to the use of William de Wells, which Walter and Cassandra had previously proved before him that they had paid to William, and excommunicated them from day to day until they again paid those four shillings and made a fine with John for five shillings that he took from them for remission of the sentence. They say they are thereby harmed and damaged to the value of 20 shillings.

And John fully confesses that he caused them to appear before him and exacted five shillings from them for their pledge of faith and that he held a plea involving them as has been said. Therefore it is adjudged that John satisfy Walter and Cassandra of these five shillings and of their damages assessed at four shillings. And let John be taken into custody.

3.3

GILBERT HAKUM v. SUBDEAN OF NORWICH

The jury on which Gilbert Hakum, plaintiff, and John de Berstrete, subdean, put themselves found that John caused Gilbert and his two sons to be summoned before him because they sold victuals to reapers and other workers during harvest on a feast day, and harassed them from chapter to chapter until they made a fine with him for five shillings, which he took from them unjustly and against their will. Therefore it is adjudged that John satisfy them of these five shillings and of their damages assessed at five shillings. And let John be taken into custody.

3.4

WILLIAM DE PANGEFORD v. SUBDEAN OF NORWICH

The jury on which William de Pangeford, plaintiff, and John de Berstrete, subdean, put themselves found that John caused William to be summoned before him to his chapter, after he had married his wife, because he was reputed to have slept with her before he had married her, and harassed him from chapter to chapter until he made a fine with him for half a mark, which he took from him unjustly. Therefore it is adjudged that William recover that half mark from John and his damages assessed at 40 shillings. And let John be taken into custody.

3.5

JUST 1/575, m. 101

Convictum est per juratam in quam Gilbertus filius Warini querens et predictus Johannes [de Berstrete][1] subdecanus se posuerunt quod predictus Johannes maliciose inposuit ei commisisse adulterium cum in nullo deliquisse et summoneri fecit ipsum de capitulo ad capitulum quousque finem cum eo fecisset per xij denarios quos ab eo cepit injuste. Et ideo consideratum [est] quod predictus Gilbertus recuperet predictos xij denarios et dampna sua que taxantur ad xij denarios. Et Johannes custodiatur.

3.6

JUST 1/575, m. 101d

Convictum est per juratam in quam Matilda uxor Henrici le Gaunter querens et Benedictus de Brakne se posuerunt quod cum idem Benedictus mutuasset predicte Matilde sex quarteria ordei pretii xxiiij solidorum et cum terminus predicti debiti advenisset idem Benedictus exigebat a predicta Matilda xl solidos pro blado predicto et quia eadem Matilda termino predicto predictos xl solidos solvere non potuit, ipse postmodum in anno sequente exigebat ab ea vj marcas et coegit eam ad faciendam ei tallias et scripta de vj marcis et postmodum ipsam citare fecit coram ordinario et vexavit eam in curia christianitatis quousque soluisset ei iiij libras predictas, ad dampnum ipsius Matilde xx solidorum. Et ideo consideratum est quod predicta Matilda recuperet predictum debitum exceptis xxiiij solidis de principale debito ei allocatis et predicta dampna sua, unde summa totius est lxxvj solidi. Et Benedictus committatur gayole. Postea venit predictus Benedictus et finem fecit per plegium Gervasii le Gaunt et Ade le Clerc de Norwic'.

3.7

JUST 1/575, m. 102

Convictum est per juratam in quam Clemens Spynk querens et Ricardus de Erpyngham se posuerunt quod idem Ricardus traxit in predictum placitum Clementem coram archiepiscopo et commissariis suis in ultima visitatione sua in comitatu isto exigendo ab eodem quadraginta solidos de quodam debito quod non fuit de testamento vel matrimonio et

[1] Identified in a previous entry.

3.5

GILBERT FITZ WARIN v. SUBDEAN OF NORWICH

The jury on which Gilbert fitz Warin, plaintiff, and John de Berstrete, subdean, put themselves found that John maliciously accused Gilbert of having committed adultery although he was in no way delinquent, and caused him to be summoned from chapter to chapter until he made a fine with him for 12 pence, which he took from him unjustly. Therefore it is adjudged that Gilbert recover those 12 pence and his damages assessed at 12 pence. And let John be taken into custody.

3.6

MATILDA LE GAUNTER v. BENET DE BRAKNE

The jury on which Matilda, wife of Henry le Gaunter, plaintiff, and Benet de Brakne put themselves found that, whereas Benet advanced six quarters of barley priced 24 shillings to Matilda and when the term of that debt arrived Benet demanded 40 shillings from Matilda for the grain, and because she was unable to pay 40 shillings on that date he later, in the next year, demanded six marks from her and coerced her into making tallies and writings concerning those six marks, and later caused her to be cited before the ordinary and harassed her in Court Christian until she paid him four pounds, to her damage of 20 shillings. Therefore it is adjudged that Matilda recover the debt, except for 24 shillings of the principal debt allocated to her, and her damages, such that the total sum is 76 shillings. And let Benet be committed to gaol. Later Benet comes and makes a fine by pledge of Gervase le Gaunt and Adam le Clerc of Norwich.

3.7

CLEMENT SPYNK v. RICHARD DE ERPINGHAM

The jury on which Clement Spynk, plaintiff, and Richard de Erpingham put themselves found that Richard drew Clement into a plea before the archbishop and his commissaries during his last visitation in this county claiming from him 40 shillings of a certain debt that was not testamentary or matrimonial and harassed him in that court until Clement delivered a royal prohibition to him; and whereas Richard dared not sue that plea further after the prohibition had been delivered to him he went to master Alan de

ipsum vexavit in eadem curia quousque idem Clemens detulisset ei regiam prohibitionem et quod cum predictus Ricardus non ausus fuisset ulterius sequi predictum placitum post prohibitionem predictam ei delatam adivit magistrum Alanum de Freston' tunc archidiaconum [Norf'][1] et dedit ei intelligi predictum Clementem esse infractorem fidei et falsum decimatorem et procuravit ipsum citari coram ipso magistro Alano et trahi inde in placitum et cum idem Clemens venisset coram [i]<predicto>[i] magistro Alano cum legitima purgatione sua ad ipsum de huiusmodi transgressione ei inposita purgandum predictus magister Alanus per procurationem ipsius Ricardi purgationem ipsius Clementis admittere recusavit et ipsum excommunicavit de die in diem. Ita quod absolvi non potuit antequam satisfecisset eidem Ricardo de debito predicto ad dampnum ipsium Clementis viginti solidorum. Et ideo consideratum est quod predictus Clemens recuperet predicta dampna sua xx solidorum. Et Ricardus custodiatur.

3.8

JUST 1/575, m. 102

Convictum est per juratam in quam Galfridus le Bret de [Holkham][2] querens et Ricardus de Berkyng' se posuerunt quod idem Ricardus traxit predictum Galfridum in placitum coram magistro Thoma de Oxon' per dominum papam [assignato][3] ad promissiones in subsidium terre sancte factas levandum et colligendum exigendo ab eodem Galfrido triginta et octo marcas que non fuerunt de testamento nec matrimonio quousque idem Galfridus detulit ei regiam prohibitionem et quod idem Ricardus post regiam prohibitionem ei delatam nichilominus secutus fuit placitum predictum non obstante regia prohibitione et ipsum [d]<excommunicavit>[d] [i]<vexavit>[i] et excommunicare fecit in contemptum domini regis ad dampnum ipsius Galfridi x marcarum. Et ideo consideratum est quod predictus Galfridus recuperet dampna sua x marcarum. Et Ricardus custodiatur. Postea venit predictus Ricardus de Berkyng' et finem fecit per dimidiam marcam.

3.9

JUST 1/575, m. 102d

Convictum est per juratam in quam Beatricia que fuit uxor Ricardi de Bradenham querens et magister Johannes de Feryby se posuerunt quod cum predictus Ricardus dum viveret finem fecisset cum predicto magistro Johanne per xl solidos pro transgressione adulterii quod commiserat et in vita sua predicto [Johanni][4] de denariis predictis non satisfecisset

[1] MS. reads Norwic'. [2] MS. reads Helkham. [3] MS. reads assignatum. [4] MS. reads Johanne.

Freston, archdeacon of Norfolk,[1] and gave him to understand that Clement was a breaker of faith and false tither and caused him to be cited before master Alan and to be drawn into a plea; and when Clement came before master Alan to clear himself with his lawful compurgation assigned to him for a trespass of this kind, at Richard's instigation master Alan refused to admit Clement to compurgation and excommunicated him from day to day so that he could not be absolved before having satisfied Richard concerning the aforesaid debt, to Clement's damage of 20 shillings. Therefore it is adjudged that Clement recover his damages in the amount of 20 shillings. And let Richard be taken into custody.

3.8

GEOFFREY LE BRET v. RICHARD DE BERKYNG

The jury on which Geoffrey le Bret of Holkham, plaintiff, and Richard de Berkyng put themselves found that Richard drew Geoffrey into a plea before master Thomas de Oxonia, assigned by the lord pope for levying and collecting offerings made in support of the Holy Land, exacting from Geoffrey 38 marks that were not testamentary or matrimonial until Geoffrey delivered a royal prohibition to him. And, after the royal prohibition had been delivered to him, Richard nevertheless sued that plea notwithstanding the royal prohibition and harrassed him and caused him to be excommunicated, in contempt of the lord king, to Geoffrey's damage of 10 marks. Therefore it is adjudged that Geoffrey recover his damages of 10 marks. And let Richard be taken into custody. Later Richard de Berkyng comes and makes a fine for half a mark.

3.9

BEATRICE DE BRANDENHAM v. JOHN DE FERYBY

The jury on which Beatrice, who was the wife of Richard de Brandenham, plaintiff, and master John de Feryby put themselves found that, whereas Richard made a fine while he was living with master John for 40 shilling for a trespass of adultery that he had committed, and did not satisfy John of that money in his lifetime, after Richard's death master

[1] Alan de Freston was archdeacon during the latter decades of the thirteenth century.

quod idem magister Johannes post mortem predicti Ricardi predictam Beatricem coram eo citare fecit exigendo ab ea predictos quadraginta solidos cum non esset executrix testamenti predicti Ricardi viri sui et eam vexavit coram eo in curia christianitatis injuste quousque soluisset denarios predictos ad dampnum ipsius [Beatricie][1] xx solidorum. Et ideo consideratum est quod predicta Beatricia recuperet predictos xl solidos et dampna sua xx solidorum versus predictum magistrum Johannem. Et magister Johannes in misericordia.

3.10

JUST 1/575, m. 102d

Convictum est per juratam in quam Robertus de Bechalle querens et magister Nicholaus de Capella se posuerunt quod predictus magister Nicholaus ipsum Robertum implacitavit in curia christianitatis ipsum citando per litteras apostolicas coram decano de Lenn ibidem et deinde citare fecit ipsum usque Eye in comitatu Suff' et postea apud Gipp' coram commissario predicti decani de Lenn inponendo ei quod injuste quasdam minutas decimas suas detinuit et quod noluit decimas bladi sui in campo de Weleby crescentis metere ad opus ipsius magistri Nicholai, cum minutas decimas suas bene et fideliter persoluisset et cum ad ipsum magistrum Nicholaum pertinere predictum bladum metere postquam decimatum fuerit et non ad ipsum Robertum et hoc secundum consuetudinem ipsius ville. Et similiter quod, cum predictus Robertus eidem magistro Nicholao detulisset regiam prohibitionem ne predictum placitum ulterius sequeretur in curia christianitatis, quod non obstante regia prohibitione predictum placitum ulterius secutus fuit ipsum citando et vexando de loco in locum ut prius, videlicet coram priore de [Haffedpeverel][2] in comitatu Essex et alibi, ad dampnum ipsius Roberti quinque marcarum. Et ideo consideratum est quod predictus Robertus recuperet predicta dampna sua v marcarum versus predictum magistrum. Et magister Nicholaus custodiatur.

3.11

JUST 1/575, m. 103

Petrus Lefstan de Dallyng queritur de magistro Gregorio de Pontefracto quod idem Gregorius per sectam priorisse de Blakeberwe tenuit placitum in curia christianitatis de quoddam annuo redditu ij solidorum [quod][3] placitum ad coronam domini regis pertinet et ipsum super hoc vexavit, ad dampnum ipsius Petri i marce. Et magister Gregorius venit et hoc non potest dedicere. Ideo consideratum est quod predictus Petrus recuperet predictam marcam versus predictum Gregorium. Et Gregorius custodiatur.

[1] MS. reads Beatrici. [2] MS. reads Hassedpeverel. [3] MS. reads et quid.

John caused Beatrice to be cited before him, demanding those 40 shillings from her, even though she was not the executor of her husband Richard's testament, and unjustly harassed her in Court Christian before himself until she paid that money, to Beatice's damage of 20 shillings. Therefore it is adjudged that Beatrice recover the 40 shillings and her damages of 20 shillings from master John. And master John is in mercy.

3.10

ROBERT DE BECHALLE v. NICHOLAS DE CAPELLA

The jury on which Robert de Bechalle, plaintiff, and master Nicholas de Capella put themselves found that master Nicholas impleaded Robert in Court Christian, citing him by apostolic letters before the dean of Lynn himself, and thereafter caused him to be cited at Eye in Suffolk and later at Ipswich before a commissary of the dean of Lynn, alleging against him that he unjustly withheld certain lesser tithes and would not reap his tithes of grain growing in the field of Welby to the use of master Nicholas, although Robert had well and faithfully paid his lesser tithes, and although according to the custom of the vill it belonged to master Nicholas to reap the grain after it had been tithed and not to Robert; and likewise that, whereas Robert delivered a royal prohibition to master Nicholas that he should not sue that plea further in Court Christian, he continued notwithstanding the royal prohibition to sue that plea, citing him and harassing him from place to place as before, namely before the prior of Hatfield Peverel in Essex and elsewhere, to Robert's damage of 50 marks. Therefore it is adjudged that Robert recover his damages of five marks against the master. And let master Nicholas be taken into custody.

3.11

PETER LEFSTAN v. GREGORY DE PONTEFRACTO

Peter Lefstan of Dalling complains of Gregory de Pontefracto that Gregory held a plea in Court Christian at the suit of the prioress of Blackborough concerning an annual rent of two shillings, which plea belongs to the lord king's crown and dignity, and harassed him about this, to Peter's damage of one mark. And master Gregory appears and cannot deny this. Therefore it is adjudged that Peter recover his one mark against Gregory. And let Gregory be taken into custody.

3.12

JUST 1/575, m. 103

Convictum est per juratam in quam Johannes Huberd de Upwelle et Willelmus filius Thome de eadem querentes et Simon Hulm de Dunham decanus de Fyncham se posuerunt quod cum idem Simon teneretur predictis Johanni et Willelmo in quadraginta solidis sterlingorum pro quoddam dolio vini ab eisdem empto et ipsi venissent ad predictum Simonem petendo ab eo debitum predictum [i]<et qui quidem quadraginta solidi eis [arretro][1] sunt>[i] idem Simon ea occasione ipsos citare fecit de loco in locum et ipsos maliciose vexavit ad dampnum ipsorum dimidie marce. Et ideo consideratum est quod predicti Johannes et Willelmus recuperent predictos xl solidos versus predictum Simonem et dampna sua predicta. Et Simon ideo in misericordia.

3.13

JUST 1/575, m. 103

Convictum est per juratam in quam Galfridus Blakeman querens et Willelmus de Redemeld' quondam subdecanus de Fyncham se posuerunt quod per quandam subgestionem quam quidam Simon de Welles capellanus eidem Willelmo [ ][2] de Redemeld' fecerat quod idem Galfridus manus violenter in ipsum [injecisse][3] debuit idem Willelmus subdecanus predictum Galfridum coram eo citare fecit et ipsum vexavit de die in diem in curia christianitatis quousque predictus Galfridus detulit ei regiam prohibitionem ne predictum placitum ulterius teneret et prohibitione regia ei obtenta statim adivit episcopum Norwic' et dedit ei intelligi predictum Galfridum fore excommunicatum per xl dies et amplius per quod idem episcopus scripsit domino regi prout moris est ita quod idem Galfridus per preceptum domini regis captus fuit et in prisona detentus quousque finem fecisset cum predicto Willelmo per x solidos antequam liberari potuit a prisona predicto. Ideo custodiatur.

3.14

JUST 1/575, m. 103

Convictum est per juratam in quam Adam de Bosco querens et Johannes filius Reginaldi de Pokedich se posuerunt quod, cum quidam Johannes de Bosco pater predicti Ade qui

[1] MS. reads aretro. [2] MS. reads fecerat. [3] MS. reads eiecisse

3.12

JOHN HUBERD AND WILLIAM OF UPWELL v. DEAN OF FINCHAM

The jury on which John Huberd of Upwell and William son of Thomas of the same place, plaintiffs, and Simon Hulm of Dunham, dean of Fincham, put themselves found that when Simon was bound to John and William in the amount of 40 shillings sterling for a tun of wine he had bought from them, and they came to Simon seeking payment of this debt, which is in arrears, on that account Simon caused them to be cited from place to place and maliciously harassed them, to their damage of half a mark. And therefore it is adjudged that John and William recover their 40 shillings against Simon and also their aforesaid damages. And Simon is therefore in mercy.

3.13

GEOFFREY BLAKEMAN *v.* WILLIAM DE REDEMELD

The jury on which Geoffrey Blakeman, plaintiff, and William de Redemeld, formerly subdean of Fincham, put themselves found that, on the suggestion that Simon de Welles made to William de Redemeld that Geoffrey was reputed to have laid violent hands on him, William as subdean caused Geoffrey to be cited before him and harassed him from day to day in Court Christian until Geoffrey delivered a royal prohibition to him that he should not hold that plea further, and having received that prohibition William immediately went to the bishop of Norwich and gave him to understand that Geoffrey had been excommunicated for 40 days and more, so that the bishop wrote to the lord king as is customary with the result that Geoffrey was arrested and detained in prison by the lord king's order until he made a fine with William for 10 shillings before he could be delivered from prison. Therefore let him be taken into custody.

3.14

ADAM DE BOSCO v. JOHN DE POKEDICH

The jury on which Adam de Bosco, plaintiff, and John, son of Reginald de Pokedich, put themselves found that, whereas one John de Bosco Adam's father (now dead) was bound during his lifetime to John in the amount of 36 shillings and agreed with him to pay him 24 measures of barley in place of the 36 shillings, and did not satisfy that obligation during

obiit [i]<dum viveret>[i] teneretur predicto Johanni in xxxvj solidis et pepigisset cum eo ad solvendum ei xxiiij cumbas ordei pro predictis xxxvj solidis de quo debito eidem Johanni in vita sua non satisfecit, predictus Johannes filius Reginaldi post mortem ipsius Johannis de Bosco ipsum Adam inplacitavit in curia christianitatis de debito predicto tanquam heredem ipsius Johannis de Bosco exigendo ab eodem lxxij solidos pro predictis xxxvj solidis et ipsum vexavit quousque cepisset ab eo predictos lxxij solidos. Et ideo consideratum est quod predictus Adam recuperet predictos lxxij solidos versus predictum Johannem filium Reginaldi et dampna sua que taxantur ad xx solidos per juratam. Et Johannes filius Reginaldi custodiatur.

3.15

JUST 1/575, m. 103d

Convictum est per juratam in quam Johannes Lamberd querens et Alanus Colyn se posuerunt quod cum idem Johannes tenebatur predicto Alano in quatuor libris, x solidis et duobus bobus precii xxiiij solidorum, idem Alanus dedit magistro Hugoni de Pagrave filio suo debitum predictum ea occasione [i]<ut>[i] idem magister Hugo ipsum Johannem inde traheret in curia christianitatis pro debito predicto et qui quidem Hugo per abettum predicti Alani ipsum Johannem vexavit in curia christianitatis apud Suthmallyng' in comitatu Kant' coram decano eiusdem exigendo de eo debitum predictum cum non esset de testamento nec matrimonio ad dampnum ipsius Johannem decem solidorum. Et ideo consideratum est quod predictus Johannes recuperet predictos decem solidos versus predictum Alanum. Et Alanus in misericordia.

3.16

JUST 1/575, m. 103d

Convictum est per juratam in quam Henricus Boterel de Est Walton' querens et Ricardus vicarius ecclesie sancti Andree de Est Walton' se posuerunt quod idem Ricardus traxit in placitum in curia christianitatis predictum Henricum primo coram magistro Johanne Feryby eo quod predictus [i]<Henricus>[i] Boterel deliberare fecit bestiam suam per ballivum de Frethebrigg'quam predictus Ricardus imparcaverat et quam deliberare noluerat per vadium et plegios et ipsum vexavit coram predicto magistro Johanne quousque ei regia prohibitio delata fuit. Et postmodum quia ipse se vindicare non potuit citare fecit predictum Henricum et Emmam uxorem suam coram decano de Lenn' pro debito unius quadrate et ipsum vexavit in curia christianitatis pro eodem quousque iterato detulisset ei regiam prohibitionem et postmodum tercio [i]<maliciose>[i] ipsum citare fecit coram magistro Godefrido commissario consistorii Norwyc' et ipsum ibidem coram eo vexavit de debitis et catallis que non fuerunt de testamento nec matrimonio quousque tercio detulit ei

his lifetime, after John de Bosco's death John son of Reginald impleaded Adam in Court Christian concerning that debt as John de Bosco's heir, demanding of him 72 shillings for the aforesaid 36 shillings, and harassed him until he took from him those 72 shillings. Therefore it is adjudged that Adam recover 72 shillings against John son of Reginald and his damages assessed at 20 shillings by the jury. And let John son of Reginald be taken into custody.

3.15

JOHN LAMBERD v. ALAN COLYN

The jury on which John Lamberd, plaintiff, and Alan Colyn put themselves found that, whereas John was bound to Alan for four pounds, 10 shillings, and two oxen worth 24 shillings, Alan gave that debt to master Hugh de Pagrave, his son, on account of which master Hugh drew John into Court Christian for that debt, and Hugh assisted by Alan harassed John in Court Christian at South Malling in Kent before the dean, demanding that debt of him although it was not testamentary or matrimonial, to John's damage of 10 shillings. Therefore it is adjudged that John recover 10 shillings against Alan. And Alan is in mercy.

3.16

HENRY BOTEREL v. VICAR OF EAST WALTON

The jury on which Henry Boterel of East Walton, plaintiff, and Richard, vicar of the church of St Andrew of East Walton, put themselves found that Richard drew Henry into a plea in Court Christian first before master John Feryby because Henry Boterel caused his beast to be delivered by the bailiff of Frethebridge [hundred], which beast Richard had impounded and was unwilling to have delivered by gage and pledge, and harassed him before master John until a royal prohibition was delivered to him; and later, because he was unable to prevail, he caused Henry and his wife Emma to be cited before the dean of Lynn for a debt of one farthing and harassed him in Court Christian for that debt until he again delivered a royal prohibition; and later, for the third time, he maliciously caused him to be cited before master Godfrey, commissary of the consistory court of Norwich, and likewise caused him to be harassed before him concerning debts and chattels that were not testamentary or matrimonial until for the third time he delivered to him a royal prohibition; and nevertheless

regiam prohibitionem. Et nichilominus post prohibitionem ei delatam secutus fuit placitum predictum contra prohibitionem predictam, in contemptum domini regis ad dampnum ipsius Henrici Boterel xx solidorum. Et ideo consideratum est quod predictus Henricus recuperet predictos xx solidos versus eundem Ricardum vicarium de Est Walton' et Ricardus custodiatur.

3.17

JUST 1/575, m. 103d

Bartholomeus de Burle queritur de magistro Henrico Sampson de hoc quod idem magister Henricus in ultima visitatione archiepiscopi Cantuar' [i]<in comitatu isto>[i] scilicet anno regno regis nunc septimo ipsum coram archiepiscopo et commissariis suis citare fecit videlicet primo die apud Kenynghal' secondo die apud Lopham tercio die apud Mortelak' quarto die apud Lamheth' quinto die apud Merlawe exigendo ab eodem centum et triginta marcas de debitis et catallis que non fuerunt de testamento nec matrimonio et postmodum cum ipse detulisset ei regiam prohibitionem videlicet die jovis proxima ante festum Assencionis domini anno predicto idem magister Henricus nichilominus dictum placitum secutus fuit coram ordinariis predictis et ipsum excommunicare fecit contra prohibitionem predictam in contemptum domini regis et dampnum ipsius Bartholomei viginti librarum. Et inde producit sectam etc.

Et magister Henricus venit et defendit vim et injuriam quando etc. et dicit quod revera ipse vendidit [i]<cuidam>[i] Willelmo de Colneye fructus unius anni ecclesie sue de Walsham pro centum et triginta marcis de quo debito idem Bartholomeus exstitit plegius et principalis debitor ob quod in visitatione predicti archiepiscopi ipsum Bartholmeum citare fecit coram predicto archiepiscopo et commissariis suis eo quod non satisfactum fuit ei de debito predicto set revera dicit quod postquam regia prohibitio ei delata fuit nunquam ulterius placitum predictum secutus fuit. Et quod ita sit petit quod inquiratur. Et Bartholomeus similiter. Ideo fiat inde jurata.

Juratores dicunt super sacramentum suum quod predictus magister Henricus postquam regia prohibitio ei delata fuit ut predictum est nichilominus infra quindenam proximam sequentem iterato ipsum summonire fecit coram commissariis ipsius archiepiscopi per duas vices unde dicunt quod post prohibitionem predictam idem magister Henricus secutus fuit placitum predictum. Et quia predictus magister Henricus cognoscit quod secutus fuit placitum predictum in curia christianitatis cum non fuit de testamento vel matrimonio et etiam quia convictum est [i]<per juratam predictam>[i] quod secutus fuit placitum predictum post prohibitionem [i]<regiam>[i] ei delatam, consideratum est quod predictus Bartholomeus recuperet dampna sua que taxantur per juratam ad sex marcas et magister Henricus custodiatur.

he sued that plea after the prohibition delivered to him, contrary to the prohibition, in contempt of the lord king and to Henry Boterel's damage of 20 shillings. Therefore it is adjudged that Henry recover 20 shillings against Richard, vicar of East Walton; and let Richard be taken into custody.

3.17

BARTHOLOMEW DE BURLE *v.* HENRY SAMPSON

Bartholomew de Burle complains of master Henry Sampson that during the most recent visitation of the archbishop of Canterbury in this county, namely in the seventh year of this king's reign, Henry caused him to be cited before the archbishop and his commissaries, namely on the first day at Kenninghall, on the second day at Lopham, on the third day at Mortlake, on the fourth day at Lambeth, and on the fifth day at Marlow, demanding of him 130 marks of debts and chattels that were not testamentary or matrimonial; and later, when he had delivered a royal prohibition, namely on the Thursday preceding the feast of the Ascension in that year,[1] master Henry nevertheless sued that plea before the ordinaries and caused him to be excommunicated, contrary to the prohibition and in contempt of the lord king, and to Bartholomew's damage of 20 pounds. And he produces suit etc.

And master Henry appears and denies force and wrong whenever etc. and says that in truth he sold to one William de Colneye the fruits of one year of his church of Walsham for 130 marks, concerning which debt Bartholomew was a pledge and principal debtor, on account of which he caused him to be cited before the archbishop and his commissaries during the archbishop's visitation because the debt owed to him had not been satisfied. And he says that in truth he never sued further after the royal prohibition delivered to him. And that it was thus he prays may be inquired. And Bartholomew likewise. Therefore let a jury be made therein.

The jurors say on their oath that after the royal prohibition had been delivered to him as alleged, within the next quindene master Henry again caused Bartholomew to be summoned before the archbishop's commissaries in two places. Hence the jurors say master Henry sued the plea after the prohibition. And because master Henry acknowledges that he sued the plea in Court Christian although it was not testamentary or matrimonial, and also because it is found by the jury that he sued the plea after the royal prohibition had been delivered to him, it is adjudged that Bartholomew recover his damages assessed by the jury at six marks; and let master Henry be taken into custody.

[1] 4 May 1279.

3.18

JUST 1/575, m. 105

Convictum est per juratam in quam Johannes Lamberd querens et magister Gregorius de Pontefracto se posuerunt quod, cum idem Johannes distrinxisset quemdam Eborardum tenentem suum pro quodam annuo redditu in quo ei tenebatur et ipse districtionem illam deliberare noluisset antequam satisfactum fuisset ei de predicto redditu, predictus magister Gregorius ad querimoniam ipsius Eborardi traxit ipsum Johannem in placitum in curia christianitatis et maliciose vexavit eum coram eo et quod cum regia prohibitio ei delata fuisset ipse prohibitionem predictam projecit contra parietem et nichilominus ulterius tenuit placitum predictum in contemptum domini regis, ad dampnum predicti Johannis xl solidorum. Et ideo consideratum est quod predictus Johannes recuperet dampna sua predicta versus eundem magistrum Gregorium. Et Gregorius custodiatur.

3.19

JUST 1/575, m. 105

Convictum est per juratam in quam Walterus le Mareschal et Katerina uxor eius de Tyrington' [i]<querentes>[i] et Henricus de Hampton subdecanus de Lenn' se posuerunt quod idem Henricus citare fecit Katerinam uxorem predicti Walteri coram eo inponendo ei quod fuit usuraria cum non esset per aliquam inquisitionem coram eo indictata nec [i]<ipsa>[i] usuaria sit et eam vexavit maliciose viro suo predicto existente in partibus remotis quousque cepisset ab ea x solidos per extorsionem. Et ideo consideratum est quod predicti Walterus et Katerina recuperent predictos x solidos versus predictum Henricum et dampna sua que taxantur ad iij solidos. Et Henricus custodiatur.

3.20

JUST 1/575, m. 105

Rogerus de Well' in misericordia pro falso clamore versus magistrum Gregorium de Pontefracto eo quod injuste questus fuit ab eo de hoc quod ipsum implacitavit in curia christianitatis de sex marcis cum per propriam confessionem predicti Rogeri compertum sit [i]<quod>[i] predicte sex marce fuerint de arreragio decimarum ecclesie Wynebodesham et quod quidem placitum spectat ad curiam christianitatis.

3.18

JOHN LAMBERD v. GREGORY DE PONTEFRACTO[1]
JUST 1/575, m. 105

The jury on which John Lamberd, plaintiff, and master Gregory de Pontefracto put themselves found that, whereas John distrained one Eborard his tenant for an annual rent to which he was obliged and did not wish to deliver that distraint before satisfaction of the rent, on Eborard's complaint master Gregory drew John into a plea in Court Christian and maliciously harassed him there and when a royal prohibition was delivered to him he threw it against a wall and nevertheless continued to hold the plea in contempt of the lord kind, to John's damage of 40 shillings. Therefore it is adjudged that John recover his damages against master Gregory. And let Gregory be taken into custody.

3.19

WALTER AND KATHERINE LE MARESCHAL v. SUBDEAN OF LYNN

The jury on which Walter le Mareschal and his wife Katherine of Terrington, plaintiffs, and Henry de Hampton, subdean of Lynn, put themselves found that Henry caused Katherine Walter's wife to be cited before him, alleging that she was a usurer, although she was not accused by any inquisition taken before him and was not a usurer, and harassed her maliciously while her husband was far away until he took from her 10 shillings by extortion. Therefore it is adjudged that Walter and Katherine recover 10 shillings against Henry and their damages assessed at three shillings; and let Henry be taken into custody.

3.20

ROGER DE WELL' v. GREGORY DE PONTEFRACT

Roger de Well' is in mercy for a false claim against master Gregory de Pontefract because he unjustly complained that Gregory impleaded him in Court Christian concerning six marks, when by Roger's own confession it is clear that the six marks were for arrears of tithes owed to the church of Wymondham and that plea belongs to Court Christian.

[1] The same parties appear in Case no. 3.22.

3.21

JUST 1/575, m. 105

Convictum est per juratam in quam Stephanus de Wygenhal cappellanus querens et magister Gregorius de Pontefracto se posuerunt quod, cum idem Stephanus et quidam Willelmus Helle inplacitati fuerunt in curia christianitatis coram ipso magistro Gregorio de quodam laico contractu et idem Willelmus Helle detulisset eidem Gregorio regiam prohibitionem per quod placitum predictum cessavit, idem magister Gregorius iterato traxit predictum Stephanum capellanum [i]<in placitum>[i] coram eo inponendo ei quod ipse impetravit prohibitionem predictam cum clericus esset et ipsum vexavit injuste quousque cepisset ab eo xx solidos et turbas ad valenciam dimidie marce, cum paratus esset se purgare quod regia prohibitio per [i]<ipsum>[i] impetrata non fuisset nec eidem Gregorio obtenta. Et similiter quod magister Gregorius postmodum procuravit magistrum Johannem de Feryby ipsum inplacitare pro predicto facto maliciose et ipsum vexavit quousque cepisset ab eo xx solidos. Et ideo consideratum est quod predictus Stephanus [i]<recuperet>[i] predictos xx solidos et dimidiam marcam et dampna sua que taxantur ad dimidiam marcam versus predictum magistrum Gregorium. Et Gregorius in misericordia.

3.22

JUST 1/575, m. 105d

Convictum est per juratam in quam Johannes Lamberd et magister Gregorius de Pontefracto se posuerunt quod, cum idem Johannes extitisset [executor][1] Mirielle uxoris sue et coram ordinario compotum suum reddisset [i]<de>[i] [executione][2] testamenti predicti, idem magister Gregorius iterato ipsum citare fecit coram eo ad compotum inde reddendum et cum ostendisset ei instrumenta sua compoti predicti idem Gregorius [eadem][3] instrumenta detinuit contra voluntatem ipsius Johannis ad dampna sua dimidie marce. Et ideo consideratum est quod predictus Johannes recuperet predictam dimidiam marcam. Et Gregorius in misericordia. Et Johannes Lamberd in misericordia eo quod iniuste questus fuit de predicto magistro Gregorio quod ipsum citare fecit pro debito vij marcarum cum convictum sit quod magister Thomas de Oxon' ipsum citare fecit pro debito predicto et non idem magister Gregorius.

[1] MS. reads exsecutor
[2] MS. reads exsecucione
[3] MS. reads ea

3.21

STEPHEN DE WIGGENHALL v. GREGORY DE PONTEFRACT

The jury on which Stephen de Wiggenhall, chaplain, plaintiff, and master Gregory de Pontefract put themselves found that, whereas Stephen and one William Helle were impleaded in Court Christian before master Gregory concerning a lay contract, and William Helle delivered a royal prohibition to Gregory whereby he ceased hearing that plea, master Gregory again drew chaplain Stephen into a plea before him, asserting that he obtained the prohibition although he is a clerk and harassed him unjustly until he took from him 20 shillings and turf worth a half mark, whereas Stephen was prepared to clear himself by compurgation that he did not obtain the royal prohibition or present it to Gregory. And likewise master Gregory later arranged for master John de Feryby to implead Stephen for the deed maliciously and to harass him until he took from him 20 shillings. Therefore it is adjudged that Stephen recover those 20 shillings and half mark and his damages assessed at a half mark against master Gregory. And Gregory is in mercy.

3.22

JOHN LAMBERD *v.* GREGORY DE PONTEFRACT[1]

The jury on which John Lamberd and master Gregory de Pontefract put themselves found that, whereas John was executor of the testament of Miriella his wife and rendered his account before the ordinary concerning execution of her testament, master Gregory again caused him to be cited before the ordinary to render his account, and when he showed him his documents of account Gregory detained those documents against John's will to his damage of a half mark. Therefore it is adjudged that John recover a half mark. And Gregory is in mercy. And John Lamberd is in mercy because he unjustly complained of master Gregory that he caused him to be cited for a debt of seven marks when it was found that master Thomas de Oxonia caused him to be cited for that debt and not master Gregory.

[1] The same parties appear in Case no. 3.18.

3.23

JUST 1/575, m. 105d

Convictum est per juratam in quam Rolandus Hose querens et magister Gregorius de Pontefracto se posuerunt quod idem magister Gregorius ipsum Rolandum citare fecit [i]<coram eo>[i] inponendo ei carnalem copulam cum quadam muliere habuisse et cum predictus Rolandus purgare se voluisset idem Gregorius purgationem suam noluit admittere sed ipsum vexavit de die in diem quousque cepisset ab eo x solidos per extorsionem. Et ideo consideratum est quod predictus Rolandus recuperet predictos x solidos et dampna sua que taxantur ad ij solidos. Et Gregorius custodiatur.

3.24

JUST 1/575, m. 105d

Convictum est per juratam in quam Ricardus Lomb querens et magister Gregorius de Pontefracto se posuerunt quod idem magister Gregorius ipsum Ricardum citare fecit coram priore de Eccleswell' in ecclesia prebendali de Suthwell' in comitatu Eboracii ad respondendum cuidam ignoto qui nunquam fuit in rerum natura et cum ibidem venisset neminem ibidem invenit ad aliquid ei obieciendum et quod ibidem et alibi ipsum Ricardum citare fecit et vexavit iniuste et maliciose ad dampnum suum xl solidorum. Et ideo consideratum est quod predictus Johannes recuperet predictos xl solidos. Et Gregorius custodiatur.

3.25

JUST 1/575, m. 106d

Convictum est per juratam in quam Benedictus prior de Suldham querens et Ricardus Maile se posuerunt quod idem Ricardus iniuste vexavit et inplacitavit predictum priorem in curia christianitatis coram archiepiscopo Cantuar' qui nunc est et secutus fuit coram eo quoddam placitum de mahemio et bateria quod quidem placitum non fuit de testamento nec matrimonio set ad coronam et dignitatem domini regis pertinebat ad dampnum predicti prioris quadraginta solidorum. Et ideo consideratum est quod predictus prior recuperet predicta dampna sua que taxantur ad xl solidos. Et Ricardus custodiatur.

Dampna xl solidorum: totum clericis

3.23

ROWLAND HOSE v. GREGORY DE PONTEFRACT

The jury on which Rowland Hose, plaintiff, and master Gregory de Pontefract put themselves found that master Gregory caused Rowland to be cited before him, alleging that he had carnal relations with a certain woman, and when Rowland sought to clear himself by compurgation Gregory would not accept his compurgation but instead harassed him from day to day until he took from him 10 shillings by extortion. Therefore it is adjudged that Rowland recover 10 shillings and his damages assessed at two shillings. And let Gregory be taken into custody.

3.24

RICHARD LOMB v. GREGORY DE PONTEFRACT

The jury on which Richard Lomb, plaintiff, and master Gregory de Pontefract put themselves found that master Gregory caused Richard to be cited before the prior of [?Ecclesfield] in the prebendal church of Southwell in Yorkshire to answer some unknown person, who never existed, and when he appeared he found no one charging anything against him, and that there and elswhere he caused Richard to be cited and harassed him unjustly and maliciously to his damage of 40 shillings. Therefore it is adjudged that John recover 40 shillings. And let Gregory be taken into custody.

3.25

PRIOR OF SHOULDHAM v. RICHARD MAILE

The jury on which Benet, prior of Shouldham, plaintiff, and Richard Maile put themselves found that Richard unjustly harassed and impleaded the prior in Court Christian before the present archbishop of Canterbury[1] and sued before him a plea of mayhem and battery that was not testamentary or matrimonial but belongs to the lord king's crown and dignity, to the prior's damage of 40 shillings. Therefore it is adjudged that the prior recover his damages assessed at 40 shillings. And let Richard be taken into custody.

Damages 40 shillings, all to the clerks.

[1] John Pecham was archbishop of Canterbury from 1279 to 1292.

TABLES AND INDEXES

TABLE OF STATUTES

Roman numerals refer to the Introduction by page number; arabic numerals refer to case numbers

TABLE OF ACTIONS AND WRITS

Roman numerals refer to the Introduction by page number; arabic numerals refer to case numbers

INDEX OF NAMES

Roman numerals refer to the Introduction by page number; arabic numerals refer to case numbers

INDEX OF SUBJECTS

Roman numerals refer to the Introduction by page number; arabic numerals refer to case numbers